BETWEEN THE
MIDDLE AGES AND
MODERNITY

BETWEEN THE MIDDLE AGES AND MODERNITY

Individual and Community in the Early Modern World

Edited by
Charles H. Parker and
Jerry H. Bentley

ROWMAN & LITTLEFIELD PUBLISHERS, INC.

Lanham • Boulder • New York • Toronto • Plymouth, UK

ROWMAN & LITTLEFIELD PUBLISHERS, INC.

Published in the United States of America
by Rowman & Littlefield Publishers, Inc.
A wholly owned subsidiary of The Rowman & Littlefield Publishing Group, Inc.
4501 Forbes Boulevard, Suite 200, Lanham, Maryland 20706
www.rowmanlittlefield.com

Estover Road, Plymouth PL6 7PY, United Kingdom

British Library Cataloguing in Publication Information Available

Library of Congress Cataloging-in-Publication Data

Between the Middle Ages and modernity : individual and community in the early
modern world / edited by Charles H. Parker and Jerry H. Bentley.
    p.   cm.
Includes bibliographical references and index.
ISBN-13: 978-0-7425-5309-5 (cloth : alk. paper)
ISBN-10: 0-7425-5309-4 (cloth : alk. paper)
ISBN-13: 978-0-7425-5310-1 (pbk. : alk. paper)
ISBN-10: 0-7425-5310-8 (pbk. : alk. paper)
    1. Civilization, Modern. 2. History, Modern. 3. Individualism—History.
4. Individuality—History. 5. Community life—History. 6. Social structure—History.
7. Intercultural communication—History. 8. Europe—Civilization—16th century.
9. Europe—Civilization—17th century. 10. Europe—Civilization—18th century.
I. Parker, Charles H., 1958– . II. Bentley, Jerry H., 1949– .
CB358.B47 2007
909—dc22
                                                                    2006014096

Printed in the United States of America

♾™ The paper used in this publication meets the minimum requirements of American
National Standard for Information Sciences—Permanence of Paper for Printed Library
Materials, ANSI/NISO Z39.48-1992.

This volume is dedicated to James Tracy.

James Tracy

Contents

Acknowledgments

MANY INDIVIDUALS AND INSTITUTIONS DESERVE special mention for the important roles they played in bringing this collection of essays to fruition. The Center for Early Modern History at the University of Minnesota, under the leadership of its director, William D. Phillips Jr., steadfastly supported the project from the beginning and provided judicious direction at several critical junctures. Marguerite Ragnow, formerly associate director of the Center and currently the curator of the James Ford Bell Library, proved enormously helpful in resolving numerous issues and in offering her perceptive comments on the first draft of the manuscript. Sue Tracy offered unwavering moral support, much needed in projects of this scope, and assisted in quite a few important, tangible matters. We are very thankful to Susan McEachern, editorial director of Rowman & Littlefield Publishers, for taking on the collection and for her steady guidance in shepherding it through the publication process. The authors in the volume brought remarkable intellectual creativity, rigor, and erudition to bear on issues relating to individuals and communities in the early modern world. We appreciate their work, patience, and good humor. Finally, we are most grateful to James D. Tracy, whose scholarship and life have meant so much to so many, for providing the purpose for this volume.

1

Introduction

Individual and Community in the Early Modern World

Charles H. Parker

THE SEARCH FOR THE BIRTH OF MODERNITY has cast a long shadow across historical scholarship. Owing largely to the influence of Jacob Burckhardt, the prevailing consensus since the early twentieth century has identified the origins of modernity with the Renaissance. The influence of Burckhardt's classic *Civilization of the Renaissance in Italy* (1860) made it commonplace for intellectuals across most of the twentieth century to associate the Renaissance with the emergence of a modern individualist spirit. Despite criticism from some medievalists who challenged the whole notion of a Renaissance, most scholars took for granted that humanism spawned an individualism that brought an end to the communal character of medieval society.[1] In addition to the acceptance of Renaissance individualism, an even older viewpoint traced modernity back to Martin Luther and the Protestant Reformation. By the time Burckhardt was writing *Civilization*, it had long been a staple among historical writers in Protestant countries and anticlericalists of all stripes that the Reformation brought an end to the papal tyranny of the Middle Ages and inaugurated the modern principle of liberty of conscience. Thus, for most of the twentieth century, a central premise underlying the historical understanding of Western civilization, particularly in American universities, was that Renaissance and Reformation rendered the corporate life of the medieval world obsolete and ushered in the individualism of the modern world.

Traditional "Renaissance-Reformation" understanding of modernity carried with it a decidedly Whiggish view of European global domination. The classic historical understanding of European expansion from exploration to colonization equated the European West with modernity and regarded non-Europeanized regions as impervious to the fundamental tenets of modernity: rationalism, capitalism, and individualism. Many scholars admitted that an unfortunate brutality accompanied European domination, though the benefits of modernity that Europeans brought to the world outweighed the damage to indigenous cultures, however regrettable. Thus, Renaissance and Reformation gave birth to a modern individualist spirit that was central to the triumph of Western civilization.

Important changes in the historical profession, beginning more than thirty years ago, gradually rendered the "Renaissance-Reformation" paradigm, along with its ramifications for individualism and modernity, problematic. As Jerry Bentley points out in this volume, changes in American history departments fueled interest in topics outside the conventional domains of the Renaissance and Reformation. The growth of the profession in the United States occurred at roughly the same time as new methods among European and American scholars were challenging basic assumptions about the discipline. Among others, *annalistes* and advocates for a new social history criticized the priority given to elites, the preoccupation with causative events, the reliance on narrative description, and the precedence of Eurocentric bias. New research focused on what Fernand Braudel called "the structures of everyday life" and on those Eric Wolf described as the "people without a history," as scholars attempted to uncover the lives of ordinary folk in Europe and to find new methods to analyze large-scale human interaction throughout the world.[2]

The attempt to understand preindustrial people on their own terms gave rise to the notion of an "early modern Europe" that eventually displaced "Renaissance-Reformation" as the moniker for the period from the end of the Middle Ages to the French Revolution. In light of this more integrated approach to historical study, topics pertaining to European expansion (especially long-distance trade and travel, missionary enterprise, and cross-cultural encounter) received greater attention, leading ultimately to broad comparative approaches and to attempts at placing Europe into a global framework. As a result of these historiographical trends, "early modern" is now emerging as a comprehensive way to understand world history from the advent of global travel to the emergence of industrial capitalism.

Just as early modern has recontextualized world history, the influence of social science and postmodern literary theory have thoroughly eroded Burckhardt's humanistic assumptions about individual consciousness. The Burckhardtian individual possessed a transparent nature, or, in the words of a recent scholar, "man *as he really is*."[3] In light of postmodernism and anthropological theory, this view now seems quite quaint. Yet to reduce individual autonomy to a mere cultural construct or artifact, as New Historicists often do, consigns the historical study of individuals to projections about power relations, which, in and of itself, is not very useful to most historians. A more promising strategy that incorporates New Historicist critiques without abandoning individual subjectivity takes into account the "layered quality" of the self. John Martin described this approach as recognizing that Renaissance writers distinguished between representation of the public self and valuation of the "interior self as the core of personal identity."[4] The powerful movements of the age—from the competing appeals of Catholic and Protestant preachers to the encounters with cultures around the world—afforded men and women occasion to reflect upon their own interior selves relative to their external actions. Individuals and the range of their activities, therefore, provide fertile ground for exploring the dynamic of this unique transitional period.

For most historians who work primarily outside the rarified heights of postmodern theory, the place of the individual is clearly within the corporate structures of early modern society. Research over the past twenty years has underscored the abiding influence of "medieval" forms of association, means of exchange, and ways of thought in Europe. For example, religious orders did not go into any general decline, as one would expect from a rising individualist mentality; rather the monastery became the model of discipline for society in Catholic countries. And even though factories (the separate premises for foreign merchants or factors) disappeared in Europe in the sixteenth century, they reappeared as a common way of dealing with European trade with Asia and Africa.[5] This volume in fact argues that individual identity in the early modern period drew from traditional forms of corporate association, so that the contrast between notions of modern individualism and medieval communalism has become an overdrawn dichotomy. Given the interest in individual subjectivity and modernity among scholars in a wide range of fields, the theme of individual and community forms an especially appropriate dynamic to reflect upon the concept of early modern and its ramifications for European and world history.

The fifteen essays in this volume address the complex relationships between individuals and their communities in the structures of society, in interactions around the world, and during the profound transitions of the period. This volume is offered in honor of James D. Tracy by friends, colleagues, and former students in recognition of his profound contribution to our understanding of early modern history. To a very large degree, Jim Tracy's fingerprints are all over the historiographical development described above, and his own growth as an historian reflects the expansion of early modern scholarship. This collection of essays thus provides an ideal opportunity to honor him, as he approaches the end of a long and productive tenure in the history department at the University of Minnesota.

A prolific scholar, Tracy to date has produced, by my count, six monographs, a textbook, two reference books, six edited volumes, and dozens of articles and essays. More importantly, the quality of Jim Tracy's scholarship has
embodied the important historiographical advances in early modern history
over the past forty years. Finally, Tracy has played a major role in shaping
scholarship by promoting early modern as a global historical epoch. During
his appointment as director of the Center for Early Modern History at Minnesota, he promoted early modern studies by organizing conferences, editing
collections of essays on global themes, developing a graduate program in
comparative history, and most recently by cofounding, with the late Heiko
Oberman, a journal for this purpose, the *Journal of Early Modern History*. His
scholarly breadth truly amazes; one scholar has stated, "The record of no other
living historian rivals that of Professor Tracy for breadth of scope and complexity of themes."[6] The fact that this volume contains fifteen essays also bears
witness to his international reputation, as well as his kind and generous spirit.

These fifteen authors demonstrate that historical theories of modernity,
which assume a linear development of individualism and individual subjectivity away from corporate life, can no longer be sustained. Taken as a whole,
these essays show that individual and community created and re-created one
another in the major structures, interactions, and transitions of early modern
times. Communities provided the necessary stability that allowed for individual agency and expression, even though communities also imposed new forms
of discipline that subjugated individuals to more rigid moral and social
norms. However, individuals established forms of association to meet basic
needs and constructed notions of communities to advance economic, social,
political, and religious agendas.

The first section of this volume contextualizes individual choice and action
in the currents of early modern history by stressing the import of corporate
structures in everyday life. Henk van Nierop directs attention to the pull of
communal values on individuals in explaining one of the critical turning
points in Dutch history, the Revolt against Spain in the towns of Holland in
the 1570s. The Revolt fractured civic solidarity as individuals had to choose
between confessional interests at odds with the tradition of urban corporatism in Holland. Though the Revolt created a crisis for civic unity, the resilience of urban corporatism enabled the cities ultimately to restore a sense
of solidarity with little lingering antagonism. Bridging Spain and the transatlantic Spanish world, Carla Rahn Phillips's essay also places individual agency
within a collective matrix, identifying kinship and affinity as among the most
basic components of community life in Spain throughout this entire period.
Kinship and affinity networks took on greater significance for Spaniards in the
Americas, for Phillips argues that family connections formed critical points of

contact across the Atlantic and made it possible for the Spanish to make their way in new environments. In this way, a traditional form of association in Spain became transferred to the Americas and fostered cultural cohesion in the transatlantic Spanish world.

It is from the archival trenches, according to Thomas Brady, that historians find ordinary individuals in the past and see them negotiate their own courses in the face of broad movements, such as those we call *Protestantism* and *capitalism*. Yet individuals tend to get lost in the narratives of the past, as historians necessarily focus on general patterns to account for historical change. Brady uses the debate between Peter Blickle and Tom Scott over communalism among peasants and burghers in Germany to make a compelling case that the sweeping narratives are well worth the effort, for they keep the historical profession energized and compel scholars to seek understanding about universal historical truths. Nevertheless, Brady reminds us that the grand explanations and collective movements bear little relation to the messy local realities in the lives of ordinary individuals. Jerry Bentley frames this section nicely by pointing out that the concept of early modern, with all its grand narratives, derived from basic changes in the community of historians interested in the relationship between the medieval and modern worlds. For Bentley, academic specialization and dissatisfying periodizations led American historians to identify an early modern transition in European history to bridge the chasm between medieval and modern. More importantly, the focus on historical processes rather than events cultivated an awareness of an early modern era in world history, as the development of maritime travel, biological exchange, and capitalist economies brought about unprecedented cultural interaction that fundamentally shaped the modern world.

The second group of essays takes as its point of departure the widespread migration of people across oceans and continents to spread religion, look for a better life, carry out business, and exploit resources. These authors exhibit two different approaches to the study of large-scale cultural interaction. Douglas Catterall and Michael Pearson explore the real-life actions and choices of individuals navigating their way around collective interests, while William Phillips and Sanjay Subrahmanyam take a more ethnographic tack, examining constructions of individuality and communality by European travelers, missionaries, and imperialists.

The circumstance of encountering different cultures produced a self-consciousness in response to the "other" that reveals the multifaceted ways in which explorers expressed subjectivity. Phillips surveys a variety of European travel accounts to Asia during the *Pax Mongolica* of the thirteenth and fourteenth centuries and he observes that narrators placed emphasis on their individuality, even though networks, contacts, and communities, lurking beneath

the narratives, actually had made travel possible. Writing for European consumption, chroniclers created descriptions of the heroic individual, suggesting
the import of manipulating imagery of the self, long before Renaissance self-
presentation became fashionable. Likewise, Subrahmanyam argues that Dutch
ethnographers in Asia accentuated their own individuality to conceal the violence of colonial culture and to present themselves as authoritative modern
witnesses of backward, uncivilized communities. In so doing, he casts doubt on
the precocious modernity of the Dutch, since regressive forms of violence per-
vaded relations between the Dutch East India Company (VOC) and many
Asian societies. Subrahmanyam, therefore, urges us to read these accounts of
Asia as merely Dutch claims to individuality and modernity.

Michael Pearson and Douglas Catterall turn the focus away from constructions of identity toward the ramifications of migration for individuals and
communities. Pearson suggests that itinerant missionaries and merchants
could foster a sense of commonality among very divergent peoples, while Catterall shows that communities were essential to the integration of migrants
into host societies. Pearson's essay offers examples of how very disparate littoral regions around the Indian Ocean came to acquire similar religious and
economic features, which provided a basis for community. Waves of itinerant
Muslim proselytizers converted elites along shorelines and later specialists
brought them into closer conformity to Islam. Pearson argues that religious
affinity greased the wheels for other types of exchange, notably trade, which
in turn reinforced a sense of shared needs and values. Religion and commerce
worked together to create community among peoples divided by geography,
culture, and ethnicity. Catterall, conversely, examines outsiders who attempted to forge their way into established societies in northwestern Europe.
He describes the choices facing individual migrants as they negotiated the
boundaries erected by host societies and the power relations within migrant
communities. Migrant networks, according to Catterall, provided new opportunities for newly arriving immigrants, but community leaders also wielded
considerable power that newcomers found oppressive. Nevertheless, the presence of dual communities, host and migrant, afforded individuals choices
they would not have otherwise been able to exercise.

While the entire volume lays stress on the transitional nature of the early
modern period, the essays in the third section take up the changing relationship between individual and community in particular forms of association,
such as convents, congregations, mercantile organizations, and legal institutions. Three major early modern movements—merchant capitalism, religious
reformation, and state formation—fundamentally altered long-established
organizations in ways that would ultimately give rise to forms and practices
we recognize as protomodern or modern. Change carried far-reaching conse-

quences for the birth of modernity, but for contemporaries, altered conditions compelled them to reorient themselves in their collective associations. Taking both James Tracy's historicist approach and his eye for long-term relevance, these essays connect the transformations in the lives of early modern people to the critical transitions in law, commerce, and religion for the modern age.

Marie Seong-Hak Kim and Hugo de Schepper analyze a fundamental shift from the reliance on customary law to the increasing power of royal law in France and the Low Countries and relate this change to the development of the early modern state. Kim outlines the route by which local legal customs in France became codified into a body of national law at the hands of professional jurists and at the instigation of the crown. After jurists went throughout France, investigating customs and recording practices, they eliminated obsolete codes and extended relevant laws for the entire realm. In this way, Kim demonstrates that local communal values, as expressed in legal custom, became homogenized in the codification process at a time when French kings were attempting to unify the realm. De Schepper traces a similar pattern in the core, urbanized provinces of the Netherlands (Brabant, Holland, Flanders, and Zeeland) in a study of lawsuits brought before customary and royal courts. Following the example of France, Netherlandish princes promoted the growth of a royal judicial system and a sophisticated process of handling appellant cases. Individuals actually preferred royal justice to the customary courts because the former was more efficient, more capable, and more humane. Therefore, both Kim and de Schepper contend, from the standpoint of law, not only the prince but also the individual came to triumph over the local community in the sixteenth century.

Historians writing even before Max Weber had identified modernizing tendencies in the Protestant Reformation. Because of Weber's pervasive influence, it has become a truism that Protestantism, and, more recently, post-Tridentine Catholicism, fostered a sense of secular vocation, ascetic self-discipline, and privatized faith, the hallmarks of modern religious experience and the basis of a capitalistic labor force. The essays by Ulrike Strasser and Susan Karant-Nunn certainly fall within this broad historiographic tradition, yet they call attention in different ways to critical transitions and changing dynamics between individuals and communities in the sixteenth and seventeenth centuries.

Noting that early modern historians generally regard religious women as relics of a medieval past, Strasser contends that nuns, individually and communally, played a crucial transitional role in the path to modernization by performing social services in Protestant lands, participating in institutional rationalization in Catholic lands, and promoting empire building in overseas lands. As such, female religious embodied the Middle Ages and advanced modernity, casting questions of individual and community in a new light.

Also drawing attention to the modernizing tendencies in religious discipline, Karant-Nunn explores the changing relationship between pastors and their congregations within German Protestantism as a result of increasing confessionalization in German churches. She claims that initially the Reformation integrated clergy into lay religious communities as never before, yet that integration proved transitory in large part because of pastoral efforts in disciplining their congregations. What Karant-Nunn sees as a process of reclericalization (i.e., the reassertion of clerical control) distanced pastors from their communities once again and, as a consequence, enabled ministers to impose discipline more effectively. Strasser and Karant-Nunn thus point to the disciplinary mechanisms in Catholic and Protestant traditions that promoted modernization in the early modern age.

Kathryn Reyerson, Donald Harreld, and Markus Vink examine the development of mercantile associations from the Mediterranean in the 1400s to the Low Countries in the 1500s and to the Indian Ocean in the 1600s. Collectively they posit that commercial organization did not develop in a linear fashion from medieval communal associations to modern individualistic endeavor during this period. Reyerson traces the activity of a single French merchant, Jacques Coeur, who worked largely as a free agent and only formed alliances for specific ventures in the Mediterranean. For Reyerson, Coeur's activity bears a basic likeness to the mercantilistic and capitalistic exchanges of the seventeenth and eighteenth centuries. Harreld pinpoints an important transition in that most medieval of organizations, the guild, in Antwerp in the first half of the sixteenth century. Merchants, so Harreld argues, came to depend less on corporate organization because new economic practices (freight terminals, payment cycles, merchant witnesses) enabled individuals to forge their own paths. As the economic instrumentality of the guilds waned, however, the social functions of merchant nations took on added significance, indicating that individual action and corporate cooperation continued to coexist during the sixteenth century. Vink also posits the ongoing coexistence of collective cooperation and individual action in the seventeenth century, based on his work on the VOC. Challenging long-held notions that the VOC became the first modern corporation, Vink, like Harreld, argues for a particularly transitional and early modern view of economic organization. The VOC straddled the divide between the collective and the individual, the impersonal and the affective, the innovative and the traditional—in essence the company bridged the medieval and modern worlds.

The variety and breadth of these essays reveal the intricate interactions between individuals and the collective associations that encased them in the early modern period. The construction of individuality took place within the corporate structure of early modern life that both circumscribed and empowered individual action. These essays represent exactly the sort of contrast, comparison, and cultural contact that resides at the heart of James Tracy's vision of early modern history. As a whole, this volume reveals how European experiences can be contextualized in a global setting, a fitting tribute to Jim and the generation of historians who created the early modern period.

Notes

1. See Wallace Ferguson, *The Renaissance in Historical Thought: Five Centuries of Interpretation* (New York: AMS, 1981).

2. See Fernand Braudel, *Civilization and Capitalism 15th–18th Century*, vol. 1, *The Structures of Everyday Life: The Limits of the Possible*, trans. Siân Reynolds (New York: Harper & Row, 1981); Eric R. Wolf, *Europe and the People without History* (Berkeley and Los Angeles: University of California Press, 1982).

3. John Martin, "Inventing Sincerity, Refashioning Prudence: The Discovery of the Individual in Renaissance Europe," *American Historical Review* 102 (1997): 1311. This entire paragraph is indebted to the insights of this article.

4. Martin, "Sincerity," 1322.

5. I would like to thank Markus Vink for this insight.

6. Quoted in "James Tracy Named as First Union Professor of Early Modern History," *University of Minnesota Department of History Annual Newsletter* 6 (2002): 13.

I
STRUCTURES

2

Early Modern Europe and the Early Modern World

Jerry H. Bentley

IN THE EARLY 1960S HISTORIANS BEGAN to speak frequently of early modern Europe, meaning the period from the Renaissance to the French Revolution, as a distinct and coherent era of European history. Since the mid-1980s the notion has emerged that the period from approximately 1500 to 1800 formed a distinct and coherent era of global history commonly referred to as the early modern world. The constructions of these parallel and yet intertwined conceptions of early modernity are very interesting historiographical developments, and they reflect some ways in which changes within the community of professional historians have influenced understanding of the European and global past. While exploring these points, this essay argues that a coherent conception of early modern Europe presupposes a conception of a larger early modern world. It also sketches a vision of the early modern world not as a stable site defined by a set of static traits or specific characteristics, but rather as an evolving product shaped by a cluster of dynamic historical processes that promoted intense cross-cultural interaction and exchange. The essay holds further that these interactive processes did not yield a homogeneous early modern world. Rather, they brought quite different effects to the various lands that they touched. It is particularly appropriate to consider the notions of early modern Europe and the early modern world together in this essay because James D. Tracy, the honoree of this volume, has made conspicuous contributions to the understanding of both conceptions.

For the first hundred years of professional historical scholarship, from the mid-nineteenth to the mid-twentieth century, professional historians generally adopted the periodization scheme advanced by Francesco Petrarca and other Renaissance humanists, who divided time into ancient, medieval, and modern periods. This tripartite periodization guided the massive efforts of scholars in the early twentieth century to compile definitive works such as the Cambridge histories of the ancient, medieval, and modern eras.[1] It also shaped the agenda of the American Historical Association in 1931 when it sought to identify future research needs and convoked conferences of specialists in ancient history, medieval history, modern European history, and American history to address the matter.[2] The community of professional historians was able to embrace the tripartite periodization scheme partly because historians restricted their studies almost exclusively to the Mediterranean basin, Europe, and Europe's offshoots in the Western Hemisphere. Working under the influence of G. W. F. Hegel, they regarded Europe as the site of genuine historical development, dismissing other regions as lands imprisoned by tradition and mired in stagnation. Thus it did not matter much that the tripartite periodization scheme did not apply well to Asian, African, American, and Oceanic societies because professional historians mostly left those regions to the tender mercies of Orientalists and anthropologists until the mid-twentieth century.

While working within the tripartite periodization framework, professional historians nevertheless edged gradually toward the notion that the early modern era constituted a recognizable period or subperiod of European history. A search of JSTOR archives on the Internet will show that the term *early modern* made sporadic appearances, mostly in book reviews and conference reports rather than formal articles, already in the early years of the twentieth century. Most early occurrences of the term came in debates on economic history and the development of capitalism, but a few appeared in discussions of European history more generally. The vast majority of these references reflected casual and even loose usage, however, by which the term *early modern* simply referred to the early centuries of the modern era rather than a coherent period with distinctive characteristics.[3]

The earliest instance I have noticed in which the term *early modern* reflected a considered category of periodization in European history comes from a textbook published in 1926 by Lynn Thorndike. If 1926 seems precociously early for the deliberate invocation of an early modern construct, there is no mystery about the purposes terminology served in this work: Thorndike, the great medievalist, transparently adopted the term *early modern* with an eye toward debunking the notion that the Renaissance and Reformation were meaningful historical periods, or even significant historical movements. To emphasize the point further, in April 1927 he published two scholarly articles that again relied on the concept of early modernity to undermine the significance of the Renaissance and Reformation.[4] Thorndike's incipient notion of early modern Europe thus had implications for intramural debates within the community of professional historians, particularly for their conceptions of the relationship between medieval and modern times. For the next quarter century, however, during an era of global depression and world war, historians seem to have found little time for debates over fine points of periodization.

About the mid-twentieth century, references to early modern Europe became more common among professional historians, particularly among those working in North America. William J. Bouwsma once suggested that the field of early modern Europe held special appeal for scholars in the United States because the era "roughly coincides with the colonial period of American history, when 'Americans' were still more or less Europeans."[5] This judgment is plausible enough, but it is relevant to note also that the notion of early modern Europe found its following during an era of unprecedented expansion in North American higher education. During the late 1950s and 1960s, the leading graduate schools ramped up their production of Ph.D.'s to staff newly created positions for historians. With a rapidly expanding population, the community of professional historians embarked on a round of intense scholarly specialization. The notion of early modern Europe was a principal beneficiary of this specialization. Scholars like Garrett Mattingly, E. H. Harbison, Crane Brinton, Wallace K. Ferguson, Louis Gottschalk, John B. Wolf, J. H. Hexter, and others produced the scholarship that defined early modern Europe as a field of study. They also made the field a staple in both undergraduate and graduate curricula in history. Their students wrote dissertations that fleshed out the details of early modern Europe and established the field in colleges and universities throughout the United States and Canada.

Meanwhile, the notion of early modern Europe attracted only limited interest in Europe itself. By the 1970s the concept of *frühe Neuzeit* had found a following among some German historians, but only after battling two decades of suspicion that it represented pernicious American influence. Elsewhere, European historians largely did without the term *early modern*, even as many of them made distinguished contributions to the understanding of European history during the centuries North American scholars considered the early modern era.[6] Differences between national communities of professional historians no doubt help explain this uneven recognition of early modern Europe as a distinct and coherent era. Strong traditions of national historiography discouraged European scholars from efforts to explore a larger European past, while North American historians were more willing to construe larger patterns as they looked at European history from transatlantic distance.

In any case, for a term that captured the imagination of professional historians rather quickly and spread widely throughout the academic world, at least in North America, it is remarkable that the concept of early modern Europe for a long time generated little critical discussion and no discernible debate on its coherence. For decades after its establishment as a commonly recognized period, historians made few efforts that I am aware of to reflect on the concept of early modern Europe in sustained fashion or to define its geographical and chronological boundaries. Still less did they subject the term to critical examination, interrogate its coherence, or question the limits of its usefulness. Rather, they simply took *early modern* as a term of convenience for a broadly construed postmedieval and prerevolutionary Europe, or some part thereof. Thus Garrett Mattingly dealt with European diplomatic history of the seventeenth century under the rubric "early modern diplomacy," but as one who worked by both habit and inclination in classic idiographic mode, he allowed historical data to drive his analysis and did not turn his attention to the abstraction of early modernity.[7]

To be sure, Mattingly and other historians provided thoughtful characterizations of early modern Europe, and their works communicated clearly enough their understanding of the early modern concept. In his popular synthetic work, for example, Eugene F. Rice Jr. treated the Renaissance and Reformation era as an age of early modern transition—not a transition from medieval to modern, but rather from medieval to "traditional" Europe, meaning prerevolutionary and preindustrial Europe.[8] Even if this formulation begged some questions, Rice offered a nuanced analysis of the various continuities and ruptures that characterized early modern Europe, with particular emphasis on cultural and religious developments. Similarly, H. G. Koenigsberger had little to say about the concept of early modernity as such, but he provided a judicious synthesis, studded with insightful observations, of Europe from the Reformation to the French Revolution.[9] Koenigsberger viewed early modern Europe basically through the lens of political organization, but he made generous space also for social, economic, and cultural developments in a succinct and pithy account. Herbert H. Rowen's detailed textbook for undergraduate survey courses also provided a meaty introduction that found occasion to stress the emergence and development of capitalism as a particularly salient feature of early modern Europe.[10]

So far as I am aware, the first careful discussion in the English language of early modern Europe as a historiographical concept appeared only in 1994. In the introduction to their handbook on early modern Europe, Thomas A. Brady Jr., Heiko A. Oberman, and James D. Tracy identified three main themes of European history from 1400 to 1600: the cycle of late medieval economic and demographic collapse followed by recovery in the fifteenth and sixteenth centuries, the rupture of Christendom and emergence of sovereign national states, and the establishment of European seaborne empires that organized global networks of production and exchange. As the trio summarized their argument: "Depression and recovery, Christendom and the states, Europe and the empires—these are three profoundly important changes specific to this era of late medieval-to-early modern transition."[11]

Granting that this formulation reflects great learning and wisdom on the part of three distinguished scholars, it also bespeaks the difficulty of framing a vision of a coherent and bounded early modern Europe. The problem of geographical boundaries in particular raises questions. What were the boundaries of Europe in the early modern era? All three of the Brady-Oberman-Tracy criteria clearly imply that early modern Europe is comprehensible only in the context of a larger early modern world. The cycle of depression and recovery from 1400 to 1600 was not peculiar to Europe, after all, but rather was, to some greater or lesser extent, a hemispheric phenomenon in which Europe participated along with other lands. The consolidation and centralization of powerful states was also a hemispheric phenomenon, and European state building depended heavily on resources and technologies, such as silver and gunpowder weapons, that flowed to Europe from the larger world. Meanwhile, the creation of maritime empires eventually linked the experiences and fates of almost all the earth's peoples with their counterparts in distant lands. To the extent that the Brady-Oberman-Tracy criteria draw attention to some distinctive features of early modern Europe, it appears that any coherent conception of early modern Europe entails the notion of a larger early modern world.

Indeed, by the time the Brady-Oberman-Tracy statement made its appearance, the notion of early modernity had already escaped European orbit and found its way to distant parts. The earliest published invocation of the term *early modern* in connection with the world beyond Europe that I have noticed dates to 1940, in the first edition of William L. Langer's *Encyclopedia of World History*.[12] Langer did not explain the periodization of his encyclopedia, nor did he attribute any distinctive features or characteristics to the periods he recognized. He simply established the early modern period as a category for events that took place between about 1500 and 1800 in the Americas, Africa, and Asia, as well as Europe. (Oceania did not appear in the early modern section of Langer's work, although it did draw attention in other sections.) It seems clear enough that Langer and his colleagues simply extended the writ of early modernity from European to global scale without fashioning a fully fleshed conception of a coherent early modern world: Crane Brinton, the distinguished historian of early modern Europe, was responsible for compiling and organizing most of the data in the encyclopedia's section on "The Early Modern Period."

By the 1980s historians and historical sociologists were beginning to generate deeper and more substantive conceptions of early modernity beyond Europe. When applied to the larger world, the notion of early modernity has

taken at least three distinct forms. One group of scholars has extended the notion of an early modern period to individual lands beyond Europe with historical experiences ostensibly similar or comparable to those of early modern
Europe. Thus Conrad Totman devoted a very important book to early modern Japan, by which he meant the Tokugawa era. He did not explicitly justify
his use of the specific term *early modern*, but processes like state building and
urbanization that shaped Tokugawa Japan were certainly comparable to similar processes at work in early modern Europe.[13] Similarly, working under the
influence of the alternative modernities project, Shmuel N. Eisenstadt and
colleagues organized a special issue of the journal *Daedalus* around the theme
"Early Modernities" that were noticeable in Asian as well as European lands,
with special attention to the issues of civil society and the public sphere.[14]

   While decoupling the notion of early modernity from Europe, this approach almost inevitably takes European experience as the starting point, if
not the standard, for the analysis of early modernity. It represents a straight-
forward extension of European historical categories to the larger world rather
than the construction of a more global notion of an early modern era that developed according to an identifiable set of historical dynamics. Thus it opens
itself to the kind of critique recently articulated by On-cho Ng, who argued
that traits associated with early modern Europe differed fundamentally from
those noticeable in seventeenth-century China, hence that the notion of early
modernity did not travel well beyond Europe.[15]

   A second group of scholars has pushed the notion of early modernity beyond individual lands and envisioned transregional Eurasian orders in the
early modern era. In his influential study on revolutions and rebellions, for
example, Jack A. Goldstone argued that "robust processes" such as demographic growth, inflation, and social mobility influenced the experiences of
societies throughout Eurasia during the early modern era.[16] Similarly, Victor
Lieberman argued that processes of territorial consolidation and political integration worked throughout early modern Eurasia, and he devised an elaborate program of comparative analysis to test his hypotheses.[17] Some empirical studies lend support to the notion of a Eurasian early modernity. One
salient recent example is Laura Hostetler's study of the Qing dynasty's methods of establishing colonial rule in southwest China. Hostetler argued that
Qing agents relied on cartography and ethnography in the same way as their
contemporaries in France and Russia, and moreover that the transregional
circulation of cartographic and ethnographic techniques strengthened the
hands of expansionist and imperialist powers throughout much of Eurasia.[18]
Another example is Stephen Frederic Dale's study of Indian merchants,
whom Dale portrayed as representatives of a larger Eurasian commercial
order.[19]

A theoretical statement on behalf of this second approach to early modernity beyond Europe appeared as early as 1985. This was the work of Joseph F. Fletcher, a prominent historian of central Asia and China, whose wide-ranging research encouraged him to understand historical developments in large, transregional contexts. In a posthumously published essay, Fletcher argued for an early modern Eurasia on the basis of what he called "interconnections" and "horizontal continuities." By "interconnections" he meant the spread of influences, such as trade items or religious ideas, via direct contacts that linked two or more societies. By "horizontal continuities" he meant parallel experiences of two or more societies that did not communicate directly with one another but that nevertheless participated in the same larger historical processes. Examples might be the growth of cities and urban commercial classes in the Ottoman Empire and Japan—lands that had little or no direct connection but that both responded to the larger rhythms of Eurasian history. Taking this approach, Fletcher suggested, it would become clear that "Japan, Tibet, Iran, Asia Minor, and the Iberian peninsula, all seemingly cut off from one another, were responding to some of the same, interrelated, or at least similar demographic, economic, and even social forces."[20]

The logic of this argument points well beyond Eurasia, of course, and Fletcher himself made some tentative claims for its global significance. It is possible that, given more time, he might have developed his argument further and offered a fully fleshed portrait of an early modern world. As it happened, however, Fletcher's essay remained unfinished at the time of his death, so he had no opportunity to extend his analysis beyond Eurasian horizons. Several of the features Fletcher considered to be the hallmarks of early modernity—such as the rise of urban commercial classes, religious revival and reform, rural unrest and rebellion, and the decline of nomads—would seem to apply awkwardly to the world beyond Eurasia, and indeed would have little resonance at all in some regions. Furthermore, several features that would seem to be prominent characteristics of a global early modernity—such as the construction of global trade networks, global exchanges of biological species, and the organization of transcontinental migrations—make little or no appearance in Fletcher's essay. Even if he entertained the notion of an early modern world, the formidable scholar of central Asia and China sketched only the outlines of an early modern Eurasia. While arguing persuasively for the need to recognize larger contexts in which European and Asian histories unfolded, Fletcher did not have the opportunity to explore larger contexts of Eurasian history itself.

Meanwhile, a third approach has extended the tentacles of early modernity beyond both Europe and Eurasia to genuinely global dimensions. James D. Tracy and Stuart B. Schwartz have both edited volumes that assumed a recognizable early modern world on the basis of surging long-distance trade, increasing economic integration, and rampant cross-cultural interaction.[21] John F. Richards has published a powerful analysis of global environmental history that takes increasing economic integration of the early modern world as its most basic assumption.[22] Many other studies have supported the notion of a global early modernity, particularly from the perspectives of environmental and economic history, though without necessarily invoking the term *early modern* or drawing implications specifically for historical periodization.[23]

Like the concept of early modern Eurasia, the notion of an early modern world has generated theoretical discussion. Richards has addressed the issue of periodization most explicitly by arguing for a coherent early modern era in world history during the period about 1500 to 1800 on the basis of six global processes: the creation of global sea-lanes and transportation networks; the emergence of a global economy; the consolidation of large centralized states; the doubling of world population; the intensification of land use, particularly on settler frontiers; and the global diffusion of powerful technologies.[24] If widely accepted, this vision of an early modern world, or a modified conception such as the one outlined below, would constitute a solid foundation for studies that seek to locate early modern Europe and early modern Eurasia in global context.

Even though it has made its way into numerous studies, the notion of early modernity is not without its critics. Jack A. Goldstone has lodged an objection against the concept, in both European and global contexts, largely on grounds of terminology. If the term *modern* refers to an era distinguished by traits such as religious freedom, mechanical industry, and constitutional government, Goldstone argued, then the centuries before 1800 were neither modern nor even an early stage of modernity. Rather, borrowing the formulation of E. A. Wrigley, Goldstone suggested the phrase "period of advanced organic societies" as a more apt characterization of the era.[25]

Goldstone offered some cogent points in his critique of the specific term *early modern*, but many scholars would not likely agree to reduce all the complexity of modernity to religious freedom, mechanical industry, and constitutional government. If the presence of large Euro-American and African American populations in the Western Hemisphere is also a characteristic of the modern world, for example, then large-scale European and African migrations might well justify an "early modern" label for the period 1500 to 1800. Similarly, if the global exchange of biological species is a prominent feature of the modern world, then the Columbian exchange might well justify use of the term *early modern* for the centuries following 1492. If the creation of global markets counts as a salient characteristic of the modern world, then the period 1500 to 1800 certainly deserves recognition as an early modern era. In any case, leaving aside the merits of the specific term *early modern*, what is perhaps more important is that Goldstone's critique applies to the term rather than the substance of the era that it refers to: Far from denying the notion that the period about 1500 to 1800 constituted a reasonably distinct and coherent era of world history, Goldstone himself explicitly recognized the fundamental integrity of that globally linked yet still preindustrial world.

Might there be sociological considerations that help explain the emergence of this concept of an early modern world? Genealogically, the idea of an early modern world clearly derived from the notion of early modern Europe. Yet the emergence of the new concept was not simply a natural occurrence in the normal development of historical scholarship. Rather, it reflected changes within the community of professional historians. Just as the notion of early modern Europe benefited from a round of intense scholarly specialization fueled by a rapidly expanding population of historians during the 1960s, so the concept of an early modern world also flourished in a particular scholarly environment. By the 1980s, when scholars were applying the term *early modern* to the world beyond Europe, several developments were influencing the substance of historical scholarship. For one thing, the accumulated results from several decades' worth of area studies scholarship were bringing a vast amount of information about the larger world to the attention of professional historians. Furthermore, the community of professional historians in North America, where the notion of early modern Europe was most popular, was becoming increasingly diverse, as scholars of African, Asian, and Latin American ancestry sharply increased their numbers in the North American academy. At the same time, offerings in the history curriculum were becoming correspondingly diverse, as scholars developed and deepened fields of study beyond European and U.S. history. Meanwhile, historians in North America and Europe were communicating much more closely than in earlier times with their colleagues in other lands, particularly with those in Asian and Latin American universities. Finally, world history was emerging as a distinct subfield in the larger discipline of history. In combination, these developments encouraged some historians to view the European and American pasts in larger contexts. As historians noticed historical parallels between Europe and other lands, they stretched concepts originally devised for Europe and applied them more broadly throughout Eurasia. As they became more aware of the numerous global links that served as avenues for cross-cultural interaction and exchange, they ventured even further and formulated conceptions of a distinct and coherent early modern world.

Indeed, from the larger perspective of world history, the period roughly 1500 to 1800 was an age of cross-cultural interaction on a previously unprecedented

scale. Increasingly during these centuries, cross-cultural interactions and exchanges influenced the ways peoples led their lives and organized their societies
in almost all parts of planet earth. It was most certainly not the case that cross-
cultural interactions had their origins in the early modern era: Peoples of the
Eastern Hemisphere, the Western Hemisphere, and Oceania had all crossed political and cultural boundary lines since the early days of human presence on
the earth, although before 1500 there was limited interaction between the
world's largest geographical regions. Yet the early modern era brought almost
all the world's peoples into frequent, intense, and sustained interaction with
one another. The early modern age differed from earlier eras in that networks
of cross-cultural interaction and exchange extended well beyond the boundaries of the Eastern Hemisphere, the Western Hemisphere, and Oceania to embrace the entire world. It also differed markedly from the nineteenth and twentieth centuries—the age of national states, mechanized industry, and global
empires—when European and Euro-American peoples dominated world affairs through political, military, technological, and economic power. Thus by
the term *early modern world* I mean the era about 1500 to 1800, when cross-
cultural interactions increasingly linked the fates and fortunes of peoples
throughout the world, but before national states, mechanized industry, and industrial-strength imperialism decisively changed the dynamics governing the
development of world history.[26]

In this conception of things, the early modern era was a genuinely global
age not so much because of any particular set of traits that supposedly characterized all or at least many lands, but rather because of historical processes
that linked the world's peoples and societies in increasingly dense networks of
interaction and exchange, even if those interactive processes produced very
different results in different lands. As I see things, three primary global
processes drove the development of the early modern world, while several
spinoff effects of the three primary global processes also exercised their influences on large transregional scales. The three primary global processes that
drove the development of the early modern world included the creation of
global networks of sea-lanes that provided access to all the world's shorelines,
global exchanges of biological species that held massive implications for
human populations as well as natural environments, and the forging of an
early capitalist global economy that shaped patterns of production, distribution, consumption, and social organization around the world. These three
processes did not unfold separately and independently, but rather overlapped
and reinforced one another. Indeed, they all stemmed from the largely European impulse to establish long-distance trading relationships. Since they unfolded in different ways and on somewhat different schedules, however, it is
useful for analytical purposes to consider them as distinct processes.

At least seven large-scale developments followed from the three primary global processes: demographic fluctuations, large-scale migrations, intensified exploitation of natural environments, technological diffusions, consolidation of centralized states, imperial expansion, and global cultural exchanges. These spinoff effects affected different lands in very different ways, but they nevertheless reflected the participation of the world's peoples in larger global processes of interaction and exchange. As in the case of the three primary global processes, these seven subsidiary effects were not separate and distinct developments. Rather, they overlapped, influenced, complicated, contradicted, and reinforced one another in myriad ways: Early modernity was a messy affair. Nevertheless, in combination, the three primary global processes together with their various spinoff effects constituted a cluster of historical dynamics that profoundly influenced the development of individual societies and the world as a whole. The early modern world was the evolving and ever-changing product of the interactive processes driven by this cluster of historical dynamics.[27]

It is clearly impossible in short compass to trace the workings of the three primary global processes and the seven spinoff effects just mentioned, but the following paragraphs will attempt to outline in sketchy fashion their operation in the early modern world. The establishment of global networks of sea-lanes providing access to all the world's shorelines was a precondition for the other large-scale processes of early modern times. Without reliable maritime highways, it is self-evident that intense and sustained interaction between the peoples of the Eastern Hemisphere, the Western Hemisphere, and Oceania was impossible. After the opening of the world's oceans, relatively cheap transportation and communication facilitated interactions between peoples from distant parts of the earth. Two sets of considerations help to explain why European mariners were most active in establishing global networks of sea-lanes. First, Europeans had stronger incentives than most other peoples to explore the world's oceans. Their motives included the prospect of prospering from direct participation in the hemispheric economy centered on the Indian Ocean basin as well as a powerful missionary impulse and a desire to establish connections with Christian communities beyond Europe. Second, through a combination of borrowing, adaptation, tinkering, and outright invention, Europeans accumulated a remarkable tool kit of maritime technologies. By the mid-sixteenth century, their nautical hardware was the most effective, their naval armaments the most formidable, and their navigational expertise the most reliable in the world. By the end of Captain James Cook's voyages in the late eighteenth century (1768–1779), European navigators and cartographers had compiled a reasonably accurate understanding of almost all the world's shorelines, excepting those of the polar regions, and European vessels were routinely calling at ports around the world.

Once European mariners established transoceanic connections, a largely unplanned process of biological exchange began to unfold. The Columbian exchange—the global diffusion of agricultural crops, wild plants, domestic animals, feral species, and disease pathogens that took place over newly established sea-lanes—was much more massive and consequential than earlier processes of biological exchange.[28] The Columbian exchange resulted in the transfer of numerous food crops and animal species—including sugar, wheat, vines, cattle, pigs, sheep, goats, dogs, horses, rabbits, and others—from the Eastern Hemisphere to the Western Hemisphere and Oceania. Meanwhile, American crops like maize, potatoes, sweet potatoes, manioc, tomatoes, peppers, beans, peanuts, and tobacco also crossed the oceans en route to new homes in African and Asian as well as European lands. In combination, newly introduced food crops and animal stocks enriched diets and helped to fuel population growth from east Asia to Europe and sub-Saharan Africa. Yet biological exchanges were not always kind to human populations: In the Americas and Oceania, the most dramatic effects of biological exchange were the firestorms of epidemic disease sparked by introduced pathogens that brought about the disastrous collapse of indigenous populations.

While the Columbian exchange sponsored global diffusions of biological species, the creation of an early capitalist global economy helped to structure societies and economies by influencing patterns of production, distribution, consumption, and social organization around the world. A well-known list of commodities circulated globally: silk and porcelain from China, spices from Southeast Asia, pepper and cotton from India, and sugar and tobacco from the Americas. The crucial role of silver in the early modern global economy has recently received a great deal of scholarly attention. It is now clear that American silver not only provided European merchants with the resources they needed to trade in Asian markets but also lubricated Asian economies themselves.[29] Much of the early modern era's long-distance trade was in the hands of European merchants, who profited handsomely from their efforts, particularly after the organization of chartered trading companies like the English East India Company (founded in 1600) and the Dutch Vereenigde Oost-Indische Compagnie or VOC (established in 1602). Yet the global flow of commodities had deep implications also for lands beyond Europe. The production of textiles, porcelain, spices, cash crops, and other commodities in quantities sufficient to meet the demands of world markets was possible only because of changes in local social and economic organization. In many cases these changes involved the expansion or intensification of existing practices: increasing the numbers of Indian cotton weavers, for example, or establishing new facilities for the production of Chinese porcelain. In other cases, however, changes involved wrenching social adjustments and brutal coercion of labor forces, as in the organization of mining operations in Mexico and Peru or the establishment of plantations to produce cash crops in the Americas and the islands of Southeast Asia.

These three primary global processes had numerous ramifications. One spinoff effect was dramatic fluctuation in world population. The human population of the world as a whole approximately doubled between 1500 and 1800, from about 450 million to about 900 million—an increase due partly, though certainly not entirely, to enhanced diets that followed from the Columbian exchange of food crops.[30] Yet demographic experiences differed sharply from one region to another. While Asian and European populations surged, and while African population also expanded despite the Atlantic slave trade, the indigenous peoples of the Americas and parts of Oceania experienced severe depopulation due mostly to the epidemic diseases sparked by the Columbian exchange of pathogens. Differential demographic experiences help to explain a second spinoff effect of the three primary global processes— migrations during the early modern era of about 2 million Europeans and 12 million Africans across the Atlantic Ocean to the Western Hemisphere. Thus demographic fluctuations help to account for the establishment of European colonies and African diasporas in the Americas. Meanwhile, the general global surge of human population resulted in sharply increased pressures on the natural environment: John F. Richards has recently documented the intensification of land use on environmental frontiers, the explosion of commercial hunting, and the increasing scarcity of energy and natural resources that characterized the early modern world.[31]

Further and somewhat differently related spinoff effects of the three primary global processes included technological diffusions, the consolidation of centralized states, campaigns of imperial expansion in several world regions, and global cultural exchanges. Numerous technologies moved around the world, including printing, nautical technology, and agricultural methods that accompanied food crops and animal species transported across biological boundary lines. The technological cluster that arguably had the most significant immediate impact, however, was that of gunpowder weaponry, which reinforced state-building efforts that were already underway while also supporting campaigns of imperial expansion in the early modern world. Because of their expense, large cannons strengthened the hands of central rulers who could build arsenals that subordinates and potential rivals could not easily afford or readily match. Gunpowder facilitated the consolidation of states and imperial expansion in Asia, Europe, and the American regions dominated by Europeans: Ming and Qing China, Mughal India, the Ottoman Empire, Muscovite and Romanov Russia, the Habsburg Empire, the Dutch Republic, and the first English Empire all depended on gunpowder technologies. Tokugawa rulers also relied on gunpowder weapons to unite Japan, then banned them in order to deny effective weapons to potential rivals. Toward the end of the early modern era, gunpowder even enabled conquering chiefs to consolidate centralized kingdoms in the Hawaiian Islands, Tahiti, and Tonga.[32] Finally, alongside biological species, trade goods, migrants, and sophisticated technologies, ideas and religious beliefs also circulated throughout the early modern world, promoting a round of intense global cultural interaction. In many cases interactions continued processes already underway long before early modern times and so featured little if any European involvement. Muslim merchants and missionaries, for example, continued to attract converts to Islam, especially in Southeast Asia and sub-Saharan Africa, like their predecessors since the eighth century. Since European peoples were so prominent in global trade, however, it is not surprising that they also played conspicuous roles in global cultural interactions of early modern times, particularly in their efforts to spread Christianity around the world.[33]

The three primary global processes and their various spinoff effects intertwined and influenced one another in multifarious ways during the early modern era. It would take a long book rather than a short essay to trace their interdependence, interconnections, and interrelationships. Nevertheless, it is clear enough in general terms that long-distance voyaging over newly established sea-lanes expedited cross-cultural trade and biological exchanges, for example, while cross-cultural trade facilitated both technological diffusions and cultural exchanges, and expansive gunpowder states sponsored large-scale migrations as well as cross-cultural trade. Similarly, it is clear in general terms that biological exchanges had implications for differential demographic fluctuations and migrations, while European migrations promoted imperial expansion and African migrations played crucial roles in the creation of a global economy. Again, it is clear in general terms that population growth in some regions combined with the creation of global markets to place unprecedented pressures on natural resources and natural environments, while these pressures themselves encouraged ambitious rulers to embark on campaigns of state consolidation or imperial expansion. There can be no question of reducing the early modern world to any set of particular traits, specific characteristics, or even any simple historical dynamic operating in mechanical fashion. Rather, the early modern world was a messy and ever-changing affair, a constantly evolving product shaped by a cluster of powerful, intertwining, interactive historical processes combined with human agency in the forms of individual wills and collective efforts.

European peoples were certainly among the most prominent actors in this early modern world. European merchants and mariners linked the world's various regions, and they both launched and sustained many of the processes that shaped the early modern world. By virtue of their participation in far-flung global networks, European peoples were in position to take best and most immediate advantage of economic and political opportunities that arose during early modern times. By establishing offshoots of their societies in the Western Hemisphere, they gained access to American resources and wealth that financed constantly increasing European intervention in the larger world. In many ways the fruits of this activity strengthened European societies and contributed to the construction of the historical formation that historians call early modern Europe. By no means did European peoples dominate other lands and peoples as they did in a later age when national states, mechanized industry, and industrial-strength imperialism gave rise to a new set of dynamics driving world history. During early modern times, outside Europe itself and European colonies in the Western Hemisphere, European peoples pursued their interests mostly on sufferance of local authorities and largely on terms set by others. It may well be the case, as several scholars have recently implied, that European experience in the early modern era was crucial for the later development of national states, mechanized industry, and global empire.[34] Yet to the extent that it is possible to recognize early modern Europe as a distinct and coherent historical formation, it is clear that early modern Europe itself is only conceivable because of European participation in the affairs of a much larger early modern world.

Notes

1. J. B. Bury et al., eds., *Cambridge Ancient History*, 12 vols. (Cambridge: Cambridge University Press, 1923–39); *Cambridge Medieval History*, 8 vols. (Cambridge: Cambridge University Press, 1911–36); John Emerich Edward Dalberg-Acton et al., eds., *Cambridge Modern History*, 13 vols. (Cambridge: Cambridge University Press, 1902–12).

2. American Historical Association, *Historical Scholarship in America: Needs and Opportunities* (New York: American Historical Association, 1932).

3. See the results for the term *early modern* using the search function at www.jstor .org. If the search embraces the field of economics as well as history, thus it will turn up additional uses of the term, mostly in reviews of books on economic history.

4. Lynn Thorndike, *A Short History of Civilization* (New York: Crofts, 1926). Thorndike gave part seven of this work the subtitle "Early Modern Times." On no less than four occasions he referred to "the so-called Italian Renaissance": 186, 295, 386, and 434. At several other points he conspicuously aired his view that the Renaissance and Reformation were backward-looking movements that did not inaugurate a new historical era: See especially 295–97 and 348–49. See also Thorndike's essays "The Survival of Mediaeval Intellectual Interests into Early Modern Times," *Speculum* 2 (1927):

147–59; and "The Blight of Pestilence on Early Modern Civilization," *American Historical Review* 32 (1927): 455–74.

5. William J. Bouwsma, "Early Modern Europe," in *The Past before Us: Contemporary Historical Writing in the United States*, ed. Michael Kammen (Ithaca, NY: Cornell University Press, 1980), 78.

6. See Wolfgang Reinhard, "The Idea of Early Modern History," in *Companion to Historiography*, ed. Michael Bentley (London: Routledge, 1997), 281–92; and Randolph Starn, "The Early Modern Muddle," *Journal of Early Modern History* 6 (2002): 296–307, especially 300–301 on the fortunes of the concept of early modernity in Europe.

7. Garrett Mattingly, *Renaissance Diplomacy* (Boston: Houghton Mifflin, 1955), 181–256. For another example see Sir George Clark, *Early Modern Europe from about 1450 to about 1720* (New York: Oxford University Press, 1960), who also did not find it useful to explain or examine the term *early modern*.

8. Eugene F. Rice Jr. and Anthony Grafton, *The Foundations of Early Modern Europe, 1460–1559*, 2nd ed. (New York: Norton, 1994), especially xiii–xiv. This work builds on Rice's first edition (1970) under the same title.

9. H. G. Koenigsberger, *Early Modern Europe, 1500–1789* (London: Longman, 1987).

10. Herbert H. Rowen, *A History of Early Modern Europe, 1500–1815* (New York: Holt, Rinehart and Winston, 1960).

11. Thomas A. Brady Jr., Heiko A. Oberman, and James D. Tracy, "Introduction: Renaissance and Reformation, Late Middle Ages and Early Modern Era," *Handbook of European History, 1400–1600: Late Middle Ages, Renaissance and Reformation*, vol. 1, ed. Thomas A. Brady Jr., Heiko Oberman, and James D. Tracy (Leiden: Brill, 1994–95), xvii. The intention of this chapter was not to deal with early modern Europe as a whole, but rather to focus attention on the transition from late medieval to early modern Europe in order to seek alternatives to the categories of Renaissance and Reformation in analyzing the earlier stage, as it were, of early modern Europe.

12. William L. Langer, ed., *An Encyclopedia of World History: Ancient, Medieval, and Modern, Chronologically Arranged* (Boston: Houghton Mifflin, 1940). Subsequent editions of this work retained the early modern category. The work that served as a foundation of Langer's encyclopedia did not refer to an early modern era. Rather, it recognized three main historical eras—ancient, medieval, and modern—and subdivided modern history into five chronological periods, of which the first two (1492–1648 and 1648–1789) corresponded roughly to Langer's early modern era. See Karl Julius Ploetz, *Ploetz' Manual of Universal History from the Dawn of Civilization to the Outbreak of the Great War of 1914* (Boston: Houghton Mifflin, 1915) and subsequent editions.

13. Conrad Totman, *Early Modern Japan* (Berkeley and Los Angeles: University of California Press, 1993). See also Totman's more recent book *A History of Japan*, 2nd ed. (Oxford: Blackwell, 2005), especially 143, 174, 203–314.

14. See especially Shmuel N. Eisenstadt and Wolfgang Schluchter, "Introduction: Paths to Early Modernities: A Comparative View," *Daedalus* 127 (1998): 1–18; and Björn Wittrock, "Early Modernities: Varieties and Transitions," *Daedalus* 127 (1998): 19–40, as well as other essays in the same issue.

15. On-cho Ng, "The Epochal Concept of 'Early Modernity' and the Intellectual History of Late Imperial China," *Journal of World History* 14 (2003): 37–61.

16. Jack A. Goldstone, *Revolution and Rebellion in the Early Modern World* (Berkeley and Los Angeles: University of California Press, 1991), especially 50–62.

17. Victor Lieberman, "Introduction: Eurasian Variants" and "Transcending East-West Dichotomies: State and Culture Formation in Six Ostensibly Disparate Areas," in *Beyond Binary Histories: Re-imagining Eurasia to c. 1830*, ed. Victor Lieberman (Ann Arbor: University of Michigan Press, 1999), 1–18 and 19–102, respectively. See also the other essays in this volume, most of which test Lieberman's model against the experiences of individual lands. For Lieberman's more recent synthesis, see his *Strange Parallels: Southeast Asia in Global Context, c. 800–1830* (Cambridge: Cambridge University Press, 2003), with a second volume to follow.

18. Laura Hostetler, *Qing Colonial Enterprise: Ethnography and Cartography in Early Modern China* (Chicago: University of Chicago Press, 2001).

19. Stephen Frederic Dale, *Indian Merchants and Eurasian Trade, 1600–1750* (Cambridge: Cambridge University Press, 1994).

20. Joseph F. Fletcher, "Integrative History: Parallels and Interconnections in the Early Modern Period, 1500–1800," in *Studies on Chinese and Islamic Inner Asia* (Brookfield, VA: Variorum, 1995), p. 3.

21. James D. Tracy, "Introduction," in *The Rise of Merchant Empires: Long-Distance Trade in the Early Modern World, 1350–1750*, ed. James D. Tracy (Cambridge: Cambridge University Press, 1990), 1–13. See also James D. Tracy, ed., *The Political Economy of Merchant Empires: State Power and World Trade, 1350–1750* (Cambridge: Cambridge University Press, 1991); and Stuart B. Schwartz, ed., *Implicit Understandings: Observing, Reporting, and Reflecting on the Encounters between Europeans and Other Peoples in the Early Modern Era* (Cambridge: Cambridge University Press, 1994).

22. John F. Richards, *The Unending Frontier: An Environmental History of the Early Modern World* (Berkeley and Los Angeles: University of California Press, 2003).

23. A recent synthesis lending support to this view is J. R. McNeill and William H. McNeill, *The Human Web: A Bird's-Eye View of World History* (New York: Norton, 2003). For works that substantiate the notion of an early modern world on environmental grounds, see Richards, *The Unending Frontier*, and two books by Alfred W. Crosby: *The Columbian Exchange: Biological and Cultural Consequences of 1492* (Westport, CT: Greenwood, 1972) and *Ecological Imperialism: The Biological Expansion of Europe, 900–1900* (Cambridge: Cambridge University Press, 1986). For works that substantiate the notion on economic grounds, see Andre Gunder Frank, *ReOrient: Global Economy in the Asian Age* (Berkeley and Los Angeles: University of California Press, 1998); Kenneth Pomeranz, *The Great Divergence: China, Europe, and the Making of the Modern World Economy* (Princeton: Princeton University Press, 2000); and Robert B. Marks, *The Origins of the Modern World: A Global and Ecological Narrative* (Lanham, MD: Rowman and Littlefield, 2002).

24. John F. Richards, "Early Modern India and World History," *Journal of World History* 8 (1997): 197–209. This view informs Richards's more recent environmental history of the early modern world, *The Unending Frontier*.

25. Jack A. Goldstone, "The Problem of the 'Early Modern' World," *Journal of the Economic and Social History of the Orient* 41 (1998): 249–84.

26. For a periodization that places the early modern era in the larger context of world history, see Jerry H. Bentley, "Cross-Cultural Interaction and Periodization in World History," *American Historical Review* 101 (1996): 749–70. See also the response by Patrick Manning, "The Problem of Interactions in World History," *American Historical Review* 101 (1996): 771–82.

27. So far as I am aware, there is no scholarly work that discusses the early modern world in quite this same way. One approach that is congenial, however, is that of McNeill and McNeill, *The Human Web*. World-system scholars have of course treated the global political economy of early modern times, albeit from a somewhat narrower perspective: see especially Immanuel Wallerstein, *The Modern World-System*, 3 vols. (New York: Academic Press, 1974–89); and Eric R. Wolf, *Europe and the People without History* (Berkeley and Los Angeles: University of California Press, 1982). The vision of the early modern world sketched here draws inspiration from several works mentioned earlier, particularly the essays of Fletcher, "Integrative History," and Richards, "Early Modern India and World History." Yet it differs from earlier views in both substance and organization, and rather than seeking to identify some particular set of distinctive traits or characteristics of early modernity, it seeks to bring focus to the interactive historical processes that drove development of the early modern world.

28. The best guides to this process are Crosby's two volumes: *The Columbian Exchange* and *Ecological Imperialism*. The largest round of biological exchange prior to early modern times was probably that associated with the Islamic green revolution. See Andrew M. Watson, *Agricultural Innovation in the Early Islamic World: The Diffusion of Crops and Farming Techniques, 700–1100* (Cambridge: Cambridge University Press, 1983).

29. See especially two articles by Dennis O. Flynn and Arturo Giráldez: "Born with a 'Silver Spoon': The Origin of World Trade in 1571," *Journal of World History* 6 (1995): 201–221; and "Cycles of Silver: Global Economic Unity through the Mid-Eighteenth Century," *Journal of World History* 13 (2002): 391–427.

30. Colin McEvedy and Richard Jones, *Atlas of World Population History* (Harmondsworth, UK: Penguin, 1978), 349. Like Richards, "Early Modern India and World History," I have revised the McEvedy and Jones figure for 1500 up to adjust for the authors' low estimate of the American population.

31. Richards, *The Unending Frontier*.

32. On this cluster of issues, see especially William H. McNeill, *The Pursuit of Power: Technology, Armed Force, and Society since 1000 A.D.* (Chicago: University of Chicago Press, 1983); Arnold Pacey, *Technology in World Civilization: A Thousand-Year History* (Oxford: Blackwell, 1990); and Geoffrey Parker, *The Military Revolution: Military Innovation and the Rise of the West, 1500–1800*, 2nd ed. (Cambridge: Cambridge University Press, 1996).

33. For a sampler of recent essays, see Schwartz, *Implicit Understandings*. For an imaginative essay arguing for the circulation of ideas and mental constructs in early modern Eurasia, see Sanjay Subrahmanyam, "Connected Histories: Notes towards a

Reconfiguration of Early Modern Eurasia," in *Beyond Binary Histories: Re-imagining Eurasia to c. 1830*, ed. Victor Lieberman (Ann Arbor: University of Michigan Press, 1999), 289–316.

34. See especially Frank, *ReOrient*; Pomeranz, *The Great Divergence*; and Marks, *Origins of the Modern World*.

3

German Burghers and Peasants in the Reformation and the Peasants' War

Partners or Competitors?

Thomas A. Brady Jr.

IN THE SUMMER OF 1499 KING MAXIMILIAN CAME up the Rhine from the Low Countries to take command of the war against his Swiss subjects, who had refused to submit to new imperial laws adopted four years earlier. His manifesto declared the rebels to be "wicked, crude, contemptible peasants, who despise virtue, nobility, and moderation in favor of arrogance, treachery, and hatred of the German nation."[1] These "peasants" comprised in fact an alliance of city-states and rural federations, many of whose leaders were certainly not peasants by any modern definition. Nor did Maximilian mean that they were. He called them peasants because they were opposed to the king and his nobles, and in their vocabulary, "peasant" was another name for what people called "the common man," that is, all who lacked the elements of true lordship—honor, descent, and wisdom. As the Nuremberg lawyer Christoph Scheurl (1481–1542) explained: "The common folk have no power. It does not belong to their estate, since all power comes from God, and good government belongs only to those who have been endowed with special wisdom by the Creator of all things and nature."[2] All those whose nature it was not to rule but to be ruled belonged to "the common man."

Then as now, the word *common* had another set of meanings: mutual dependence, sharing, togetherness, and solidarity. The body of citizens in a town or village was the commune (*Gemeinde*), which derives in both German and English from the word *common* (*gemein*). Yet so differently were the historical roles of town and village construed in modern historical literature that for a long time any argument based on their similarities, even solidarities, made little if any headway against a heavy historiographic sea. Today, the medieval countryside and town are less frequently held to have represented two entirely different, even opposed, historical forces: stasis and hierarchy on the one side, dynamism and freedom on the other. Few today would defend Henri Pirenne's confident declaration that the town and its burghers alone constituted the engine of historical change. "To the middle class," he wrote, "was reserved the mission of spreading the idea of liberty far and wide and of becoming, without having consciously desired to be, the means of the gradual enfranchisement of the rural class."[3] The burgher's engine pulled the train in which the peasants rode as passengers.

Pirenne's view nonetheless represented a significant correction of the nineteenth-century liberal view that the burghers comprised a protobourgeoisie that had brought down feudalism and fashioned modern civilization. Still, his belief in commerce as "the principal and almost exclusive cause for the reinvigoration of urban life in the middle ages," and hence for social change *tout court*, has undergone a radical revision since his day, and today "an exaggerated distinction between town and village does not appear to be very useful historically."[4] This view goes back to Max Weber, who expressed skepticism about separating radically town from countryside, the economic roles of which he defined in terms of complementarity: "The relation of the city as agent of trade and commerce to the land as producer of food comprises one aspect of the 'urban economy' and forms a special 'economic state' between the 'household economy' on the one hand and the 'national economy' on the other."[5] Weber rejected, moreover, the tendency to see the medieval city à la Pirenne in economic terms alone and proposed that "hidden non-economic dimensions" made it "time to expand the concept of the 'city' to include extra-economic factors." This led him to integrate the Western city and its burghers, just like those of antiquity, into a particular stage of history, which denied to the medieval burghers any but an indirect relationship to the modern world.

Marxist historians, too, had to struggle with the problem of the city and the social and economic forces it housed. Their view of history required the burghers to explain the beginnings of capitalist accumulation, but the empirical research on medieval urban history revealed the burghers to have possessed few if any characteristics of a protobourgeoisie. This problem was discussed with great vigor in the early 1970s by historians in the German Democratic Republic, who, because of the interpretation of the German Peasants' War of 1525 as the peak of an "early bourgeois revolution," could not deny the burghers an importance to antifeudal movements.[6] The outcome of the discussions proved in the end inconclusive, for while some argued that the burghers were too diverse to form a class, others held that they coalesced into a class during struggles against the feudal powers. Both parties, however, agreed that even as a separate class, the burghers were closely integrated into the feudal order as links between different feudal units.

On the western side of the Iron Curtain, too, the Cold War nourished a retrenchment from the thesis of the medieval burghers as a protobourgeoisie. The Austrian Otto Brunner (1898–1982), a historian of radical temperament and tainted political past, fashioned a vision of "Old Europe," a conservative, aristocratic society on an agrarian basis and formed around the household as an economic unit, which had existed continuously since ancient times.[7] This social order began to collapse around 1800, in Brunner's view, in the face of new forces: capitalism, socialism, the bureaucratic state, and democracy. A deep continuity runs between the book Brunner published on late medieval Austria (subsequently heavily revised) and his ideas in the post-1945 era, for his chief targets remained the old ones: liberalism and capitalism.[8] From the ancient Greeks to the French Revolution, "Old Europe" organized itself not in classes defined by wealth but in status groups defined by law and resting on the common basis of the household. This concept of old status-based society (*altständische Gesellschaft*)[9] held that the burghers were merely one estate among many in a society organized into orders. Peter Laslett formulated a similar view in 1965, and several years later Roland Mousnier argued for a radical distinction between a medieval and early modern "society of orders" (*société des ordres*) and a modern "society of classes" (*société des classes*).[10]

In the 1970s a younger generation of social historians of late medieval and early modern Europe began to steer a middle course between the antimodernism of Brunner and Mousnier and liberal historiography's radical modernism. The German-speaking world proved especially fertile in theses, the most original of which is arguably the communalization thesis. It holds that between the disintegration of the manorial economy of the High Middle Ages and the rise of the absolutist state in the seventeenth century, Europe in general and the German lands in particular experienced the growth of small, corporately organized units of self-administration and even self-government by means of communes. My article examines the debate on one central postulate of the communalization thesis—the similarity and solidarity of burghers and peasants as political agents—in the late medieval German lands.[11] A concluding reflection briefly expands the contrast to the religious component in "the reformation of the common man."

Burghers and Peasants as Political Partners

Peter Blickle has framed and grounded theoretically the modern discussion of communalism. His thesis holds that the burghers and peasants of the late

medieval and early modern German lands possessed a common political culture and a common history, which can be recognized first in the isomorphism of their institutions and second in their collaboration in the German
Peasants' War and the religious reformation of the sixteenth century. The first
point, the structural similarity of urban and rural institutions, had been discovered long ago by two German jurists, Georg Ludwig Maurer
(1790–1872)[12] and, following him, Otto von Gierke (1841–1921),[13] who derived them from the ancient Germanic community of the march association
(*Markgenossenschaft*). In 1957 another historian of law, Karl Siegfried Bader,
wrote that most historians of medieval Germany had abandoned this derivation and held that the rural commune arose since about 1300 in village communities' struggles against their seigneurs.[14] Rural and urban communes
possessed, therefore, similar structures and functions but neither a common
derivation nor a common chronology. Urban communes formed much earlier, in the twelfth century when seignurial power was at its peak, while rural
ones formed later, in the early fourteenth century when this power was beginning to disintegrate. A little later, a medieval lawyer was moved to note
that "only a fence or a wall divides burgher from peasant."[15]

Blickle took up this line of argument in the mid-1970s. He had already published a large study of peasants' participation in south German parliamentary
regimes.[16] Ranging across a series of southern territorial principalities, his
work established that the peasants, far from being condemned to political si-
lence or insignificance after 1525, participated routinely in territorial parliaments. Blickle's discovery formed the first step toward his communalization
thesis. The second step came with the 450th anniversary of the Peasants' War
in 1975. Blickle postulated a political collaboration between burghers and
peasants in an "insurrection of the Common Man as a Revolution." The "common man," he wrote, "was the peasant, the miner, the resident of a territorial
town; in the imperial cities he was the townsman ineligible for political office."[17] Their common actions in 1525 proved that the "commonness" of
burghers and peasants lay not in their betters' prejudices alone but in what
they had in common in the sense of "shared."

In subsequent studies, Blickle assembled the spatial and legal evidence for
similarly constituted structures in medieval towns and villages. Following
Bader, he downplayed the significance of walls, long held to be a mark of the
town's distinction from the village, in favor of "the comparability of village
and urban residential and economic spaces" as "a specially protected zone of
peace and peacekeeping."[18] Moving from spaces to institutions, Blickle established "a parallel development from first to last" in town and village in the
forms of communal assemblies, legislative authority, and judicial powers.
These supplied evidence not of a common genesis but of analogous relation-

ships to feudal society. The burghers had secured their liberties from their lords by means of negotiation, purchase, and armed force; later on, the peasants exploited the ambivalence of the basis of servitude—the person or the land—and the recession of direct seigneurial management to assert their own claims to the freedom to dispose of their own labor.[19] In this union of liberty and labor—the formulation is mine—burghers and peasants acquired by separate paths a new moral basis for their lives and hence a capability for solidarity and political action. Diachronic but parallel actions in the two social milieus created a new form, the commune, and a new politics based on the principles of representation, election, and consent.

Having once established the spatial and institutional isomorphism of town and village, Blickle mapped anew their common struggle for emancipation from feudal power in the context of the Reformation. Their communal norms converged, he argued, in the idea of the commune as a religious community. Here he took a leaf from the historians of the urban reformation. In the early 1960s the Göttingen church historian Bernd Moeller had identified the sacral commune as the enabling idea in the burghers' enthusiastic reception of Martin Luther's message.[20] Two decades later, Blickle and his collaborators methodically uncovered a "peasants' reformation," contemporary with and parallel to that of the burghers. It expressed the highest stage of rural communalization, to which the Protestant Reformers' theology of the church provided the catalyst. Here, at last, parallel, nonsimultaneous developments merged in the ideas and acts of a joint communal reformation. Blickle called it a "people's reformation," a term he took from the Soviet historian M. M. Smirin (1895–1975). This movement, Smirin had written in the 1940s,

> which found its clearest expression in the doctrine of Thomas Müntzer, took as its goals the transformation of material life, the extirpation of evil in the world by means of the revolutionary power of the people, and the establishment of a "kingdom of God" on earth in a society which, free of princes, magnates, or boundaries, lived from the sweat and blood of the people.[21]

In Blickle's account—hotly disputed by the Protestant church historians—the Reformers' message, at once theological and ethical, both justified and ideologically unified the movement of burghers and peasants to establish a communally constituted world.[22]

It remained only to fuse forms and acts of reformation into a single narrative. In *The Communal Reformation* (1985), Blickle traced popular reformations in towns and districts of south Germany and Switzerland, portraying them ensemble as a capstone on the movement for communal autonomy that had begun in the fourteenth century.[23]

Of the interpretations that German-speaking historians have advanced since 1960 about the passage from medieval/feudal to early modern/absolutist society, Blickle's is the most ambitious theoretically and most solidly grounded in the sources. It reconfigures time and space in highly original ways. Temporally, it offers a new periodization for German history based on the genesis, course, and fate of communalization. Spatially, it moves outward from the southern German-speaking lands into Europe as a whole. Blickle and his collaborators have established a bid for communal organizations as the Pan-European fundament of a popularly based politics, obscured but not destroyed by absolutist and other authoritarian forms of governance.

The thesis and all of its corollaries are summed up in Blickle's two volumes on *Communalism* (2000), which undertakes nothing less than a reconstruction of Europe's elemental social constitution and its history.[24] All the threads come together in a story which begins with the common people's origins in the feudal age as "those who work" (*laboratores*); it continues through the rise of the common people's communal world and its subsequent subjection to absolutist regimes; and it debouches finally on the ravaged plain of modern European politics, where it signals the way to a future better than the past. "Where the community becomes the ruler," Blickle summarizes, "it paves the way to modernity with a solid surface. Demands for a constitution were voiced long before the nineteenth century, and this wherever authoritarian elements became too strong and, copying the politics of secrecy proper to monarchies, threatened at its core the communal constitution of society."[25] Blickle also sees "progress toward modernization" in communal rebellion against lordship, for the contemporary definition of territorial assemblies "resembles, though not identical with, the understanding of political representation in nineteenth-century parliamentarism."[26] Thus communalism— Blickle's final judgment—"stands considerably closer to modernity than feudalism did."

The practice of communalism, Blickle argues, is the common heritage of Europe's peoples. It consisted in "the local organization of every day life by all heads of households gathering together and exercising their right to define local norms, to exercise government, and to choose representatives."[27] If such practices were especially powerful in central Europe, they were by no means absent in other lands.[28] Communalism both contributed to the positive elements of state formation and nourished oppositions to absolutist state formation, and it supplied "continuities of principle [which] underlie the [modern] constitutions and parliaments." Blickle does not conclude that "modern democratization is the direct continuation of the communalization of older, status-based societies" but that, despite the Enlightenment, French Revolution, and liberalism, "the nineteenth century did not reinvent the wheel."[29]

Modern democracy is the fruit not of a modern political parthogenesis but of the common people's long march out of the deep past. In these ranks, burgher and peasant finally become one.[30]

Burghers and Peasants as Competitors

An intellectual edifice so firmly fixed in the sources and so conceptually cut from a single cloth as Blickle's work on communalism does not yield easily to attack. The earliest indirect criticism targeted not Blickle's analysis of the Peasants' War but Moeller's concept of the sacral commune, which eventually became a key mental element in the possibility for direct burgher-peasant collaboration. In 1975, the jubilee of the Peasants' War, the Australian historian Bob Scribner declared, basing himself on two seminal studies of Erfurt and Cologne,[31] that "serious social analysis of the Reformation has scarcely begun."[32] Others chimed in with doubts about conducting social history in terms of concepts in general and the explanatory power of the ideal of the sacral commune in particular.[33] Taking unity as a postulate that masked the fact of disunity, historians argued that the urban communes were in fact oligarchies, and the burghers possessed unity in law but not in social fact. About the same time, similar arguments about the villages appeared, mainly from English-speaking historians, who dwelt upon the social tensions within villages caused by population growth and land hunger.[34] Not accidentally, until very recently Blickle's arguments and conclusions were discussed, not without criticism, with greatest interest by English-speaking historians.

The most searching examination of Blickle's argument about the common cause of burghers and peasants in the Peasants' War and the Reformation has been undertaken by Tom Scott. No one is better equipped to understand the scope and complexity of Blickle's vision. Scott's monographs on local and regional economies, urban networks, two-land relations, the Reformation, and the Peasants' War overlap Blickle's main themes;[35] and his comprehensive work on German social and economic history from 1300 to 1600 is almost certainly the finest work ever written on the subject.[36] Others have criticized one or another aspects of Blickle's interpretations, but none with greater authority.

Scott's heaviest caliber targets Blickle's interpretation of the economic history of the late medieval German lands. His misconceptions, Scott contends, have led Blickle to identify an economic basis for positive peasant-burgher collaboration that is without basis in fact. Whereas Blickle locates the causes of the Peasants' War in the worsening of peasant-seigneurial relations by the late medieval "agrarian crisis,"[37] Scott argues for a quite different picture of a rural economy undergoing a widespread and profound commercialization.[38] This change had three strands: the commercialization or commodification of landholding and property rights; the growth of a rural artisan economy; and the putting-out system and early capitalism. Each strand embodied, on the one hand, an intensification of market forces and their effects on the lives and work of its peasant-producers and, on the other, a growing integration of rural and urban economies. Towns and land were fusing into economic units—the lesson of Scott's on work the regional histories of southwestern Germany.[39] The process produced not a partnership of town and land but the countryside's progressive subjugation to the burghers' economic interests, which were not those of the peasants. According to Scott, there existed no economic basis for collaboration between burghers and peasants.[40] Where political alliances did appear between peasant forces and towns during the Peasants' War, they were always based on political opportunism, not on a solidarity rooted in a perceived identity of interests and feelings.[41]

Such political ties were, in Scott's view, fleeting and trivial when measured against the growth of the market. The great transformation of this era was not the Peasants' War and the Reformation but "the shift from medieval regions, only loosely defined by an urban hierarchy, to early modern regions which are driven by a generative urban system."[42] To this change the peasants related principally through their engagement in the market, for, just as much as the burghers, they pursued objectively rational interests. "Leaving aside the now somewhat sterile debate on the economic motivation of producers in predominantly agrarian societies," Scott writes, "we can quietly agree that peasants will engage in the market provided that the perceived risks are not too great." Their markets were "partially commercialized, and increasing exposed to the impact of regional or even international markets," which drove "a partially commercialized economy."[43]

The great changes around 1500 were, therefore, neither political nor religious but economic, and for the "degree and nature of market exchange . . . 'structural transformation' seems an altogether more appropriate term than 'crisis.'"[44] The regionally consolidating structures could "accommodate retrenchment (sometimes no doubt painful) and healthy contraction, without implying that economic agents were so mesmerized by demographic and productive adversity that they were incapable of responding imaginatively."[45] Scott notes that the Marxist historians presented a generally gloomy picture of late medieval rural life and emphasized a late medieval "crisis in feudalism"— the Marxist version of the "agrarian crisis." But not all, for one French Marxist, the medievalist Guy Bois, discovered in fifteenth-century Normandy a new spirit of agricultural individualism and initiative.[46] In the opinion of Scott, Bois, and other recent writers, the fifteenth century was an age of new initiatives, entrepreneurial activities, and recovery from the late medieval economic depression.[47]

Scott also criticizes Blickle's concept of communalism. He believes that the alleged unifying and egalitarian faces of communalism were at best masks for conflict and inequality. While Scott admits that "a welter of recent research has emphasized, corporative values reigned supreme," we may not conclude that "the rural communes' corporate sense of identity was fundamentally collective and egalitarian."[48] Just as in the towns, there were "perceptible differences of status and power within villages and rural settlements, and the corporative principle could be as exclusive as in the towns." The general rule in the village was that "peasant proprietors held the whiphand in village affairs."[49] Moreover, the decades just prior to the Peasants' War witnessed "an increasing differentiation . . . within the rural economy and society between peasants in possessions of farms, and cottars or day-laborers," which in turn opened up a gap "between those with full rights as members of the village commune, and those with lesser rights, or those who were excluded from the commune altogether." This process contained a "socially explosive potential" that formed a standing threat to all forms of collaboration and a standing rebuke to all notions of equality.[50] For Scott the solidarity and egalitarianism attributed to village communes turns out to be a myth that cannot stand up to the demographic and economic facts of rural life. It may well be that Scott here exaggerates the argument of Blickle, who has never insisted so emphatically on the egalitarian or democratic character of village life as his critics have sometimes assumed.[51]

For the same reasons, it seems to Scott too obvious to require argument that the town sustained less solidarity and equality than the village did. The structure of urban society, he argues, "was by no means as communal as it seemed (and as many modern historians have argued)." The community of citizens was "an ideological construct, [and] corporative sentiments were most directly articulated by specific interest-groups rather than by the community at large—craft guilds, parish and wards, rifle and archery clubs, religious confraternities, all of which employed vs. the council the triad of familiar maxims—peace, justice, and the commonweal."[52] Communalist values may have been genuine enough among such folk, but "from the lips of the urban elites, eager to underpin their hegemony, they should be taken with a hefty pinch of salt. But even within the interest-groups themselves an invocation of corporative-communal values should not be mistaken for a general commitment to fraternity, let alone egalitarianism."[53]

A third criticism aims at Blickle's assertion that "what united the common project of peasants and townsmen was the gospel, or more precisely, the transformation of Reformation theology into a political theology."[54] Theology, political or not, Scott believes, played no significant role in the political relations between burghers and peasants in the Peasants' War, when the explicit alliances of town magistrates with rebel armies were driven more by the search for local political advantage than by any sympathy based on shared values or religious sensibilities.[55] Scott believes Blickle's communalist theology to be a will-o'-the-wisp. Far from communalist even in sentiment, the Protestant Reformers, from Martin Luther on one wing to the radical Tyrolean Michael Gaismair (1490–1532) on the other, were remarkably responsive to and realistic about the market's growing importance for the whole society.[56] The decisive point is not their negative attitudes toward the great firms and usury but "their underlying endorsement of petty capitalism," which in Scott's view formed the main field of economic initiative and innovation.[57] Luther and Gaismair were not pioneers of mercantilism, much less of classical economics, but neither were they guardians of a hardy communalist flame.

Popular Politics, Popular Religion

The Blickle-Scott debate is a discussion about history of a classical kind. It turns not on disagreements about particular documents and events, but on a clash of ideas. It presents two very different conceptions of how history works and, just as important, how history can be known. Seen in this light, the stakes are considerable.

Blickle's view of German and European history is dialectical. It begins with the emancipation of the burghers and the peasants—by two distinct routes—from feudal lordship, and it leads to their local political empowerment during the economic upheavals after 1300 and the political struggles of the late fifteenth and the first quarter of the sixteenth century. Then began their political defeat by a reconstituted lordship that can be called *absolutist* or *protoabsolutist*.[58] Yet the story does not end there, for the springs of communalism—household practice—remained, and the common people return for another round in the modern fight against aristocratic power in the Old Regime. This time they acquire and keep more or less full political rights and access to cultural resources. This grand, three-phased scheme is populist in mood, and though it owes something to historical materialism, Blickle's purpose is moral in the classical sense of the term: the betterment of public life. He aims not so much to chronicle the continuity of European history—of which the principles, but not the route, can be fully understood—as to display the historic ideal of community that requires to be completed in its particulars of equality, fraternal respect, defense of the common good, human rights, and, in a word, democracy.

Scott's conception of European history, implicit in his writings, is utilitarian in economics and realistic in politics: not because he denies the lives of burghers and peasants as thinking, moral subjects, no more than Blickle does, but because he believes that these—the useful and the real—are the terms in which can be comprehended historically the actions of social groups over time and in space. To say that historical change depends ultimately on forces and factors that can best be analyzed in economic terms is not, at least for Scott, to argue that only economic matters count. What can be charted with some certainty, however, is the slow expansion of the market and the increasingly complex division of labor it produced. The story of the market and its consequences can yield a comprehensible continuity between earlier and later times. The narrative they suggest is not necessarily progressivist, though greater aggregate wealth does allow elements of civilization to flourish that could not have existed in a more nearly agrarian society. There is no overriding narrative of social replacement, for the nobles do not become obsolete, the burghers do not evolve into a capitalist bourgeoisie, and neither burghers nor peasants consciously strive for full political autonomy. History moves slowly, often silently and unpredictably. Although Scott takes concepts and suggestions evenhandedly from many sides, his larger vision of slow, incremental, environmentally configured change reminds one somewhat of Fernand Braudel's vision of the slow, often unnoticed evolution of a civilization toward prosperity.

The debate thus comes down to the old question of the burghers' place in late medieval and early modern German (and European history). Were they partners with the peasants in a coalition against feudal power? Were they competitors of the peasants in a recovering market? Or do these alternatives form *une question mal posée*? Though their arguments imply two very different grand narratives of German (and European) history, on the ground, in the trenches in which the historical record has to be excavated, neither a convergent (Blickle's) nor divergent (Scott's) model of the relationship of mentality to behavior is inherently preferable. We have learned to accept, rather, the relationship's plasticity and to surrender the welcome assumption that there was only one great drama in which the people, peasants and burghers, were playing their *real* parts.

The issue of reality turns, of course, on accepting or discounting what people said as a reliable access to the causes, though not the consequences, of their actions. The very different positions of Blickle and Scott on this issue emerge from their evaluation of the role of religion in the great actions of the Peasants' War and the Reformation. The contrast is quite dramatic.

Scott is quite right, of course, to doubt that mentality or ideology can yield a clear picture of the rationality of human actions, just as Blickle is right to mistrust the reduction of mentality to a kind of superficial chatter in spaces dominated by economic rationality. Here the contrast between Scott's view and that of Blickle is quite dramatic. Always cool—like Brunner—to the notion of the

church's historical agency, Blickle accords a significance to religion only insofar as the Protestant Reformers' teachings provided a legitimizing and galva-
nizing ideology for the raising of the communal idea to a conscious, fully political level.[59] His view, that "the progressive theology of the sixteenth century"
served the need of communalism—albeit unconsciously—"to be heard as an
intellectual position,"[60] represents a fargoing instrumentalization of religion in
the service of an objective process. It serves neither the market nor the absolutist state but communally constituted or reconstituted polity. The Christian-
ization of the commune and communal life represented the burghers' and
peasants' coming to a self-conscious understanding of their communal ideas, a
process the Protestant Reformers' theology willy-nilly enabled. In the early
1520s the political struggle became ideologically heated by new calls for a break
with the old church, so that popular aspirations could achieve their fullest ex-
pressions. The concept of the communal reformation, therefore, presupposes a
high degree of compatibility and even identity between the laity's understanding of reform and the religious intentions of the Protestant Reformers.

Initially, perhaps, Scott shared Blickle's coolness toward religion as an explanatory factor in historical change. In his book on *Freiburg and the Breisgau*
(1986), he wondered "whether the peasants' understanding of those doctrines
may not have been as instrumental—serving the subjective aims of communal defence—as idealistic—committed to objective truths valid for all Christian everywhere."[61] More recently, he has accepted that there was a communal
reformation but holds that it could have reached its goals without a widespread knowledge and acceptance of evangelical theology on the part of the
laity—Blickle's indispensable catalyst. "I believe," he said in 1990, "that it was
possible to achieve a Communal Reformation without the introduction of
evangelical religion."[62] He thereby acknowledges the fundamental importance
of untheologized lay religion, the religious practice of the people, to the events
of the 1520s in the German lands. In this Scott shares the insight of the late
Bob Scribner about the fundamentally religious character of popular practice
and mentality before—and after—those events.

Finally, it would be wrong to leave the impression that an unbridgeable gulf
stands between Blickle's and Scott's accounts of these great events. On the crucial issue—relations between burghers and peasants in the mid-1520s—there
is a middle ground between a distillation of them into a notion of general solidarity and a dismissal of them as opportunistic. The evidence is ambiguous,
and it cannot be adequately treated by either Blickle's historical sociology or
Scott's political economy alone.

The point can be illustrated by two texts from Alsace. The first is a passage
in an anonymous Strasbourg chronicle that describes the fate of the leaders of
the conspiracy called the Bundschuh, the Upper Rhenish prelude to the Peas-

ants' War.[63] In the year 1493, the burgher says, "many wicked persons in Alsace . . . secretly gathered on the Hungersberg. . . . They aimed to conquer all Alsace, killing all who opposed them, and they called the Swiss to their aid. They began this action in Holy Week. But God prevented this, and the authorities decided that the principal conspirators would be quartered, the others punished as each deserved."[64] The rebels were simply bad men, their defeat was God's punishment.

Very different was the judgment of another burgher, Hans Stolz, who from 1502 to 1540 served as city secretary of Guebwiller, a small town in south-central Alsace.[65] A witness to many events of the Peasants' War, he placed principal blame for the whole affair not on the rebels but on Martin Luther, whose agitation caused "unbelief to began to spread among the common man."[66] The insurrection's background lay in the long-standing local hatred and envy that fueled actions by rebels—including burghers from other towns—against the men of Guebwiller, but also among citizens of the town—the local guilds split four-to-three on whether to reject or accept the rebels' demands. The Peasants' War here was thus as much between burghers as between peasants and burghers.[67]

Religion weighs heavily in Stolz's explanations of the causes of 1525. The insurrection's chief cause was "unbelief"—Luther's heresy—for the spread and consequences of which he blames "bad priests" and burghers, not their peasant dupes. His comment about the beginnings of the reformation at Basel is characteristic. "As the diabolical, contemptible cause of Lutherism was now gaining supporters in Basel," he writes, "it would wring tears from a stone to see how those cursed people, as bad as pagans, insulted the gracious Savior when the most worthy Sacrament was carried through the streets to someone who was ill."[68] The "Lutherist scoundrels at Basel," by contrast, "when they lay on their deathbeds, cried 'hang me on the gallows, throw me into the Rhine or out into the fields, so that I won't be buried in a churchyard.' This shows how much in error the scoundrels were." God punished them, Stolz reports with some satisfaction, when on October 9 lightning struck an arsenal, and the explosion "destroyed many houses and part of the walls," killing thirty and maiming many others.[69] He records no comparable satisfaction in relating the disastrous failure of the Peasants' War, which he sees as one phase of a religious war, a struggle for the true faith and the true church. The anonymous chronicler of the Bundschuh saw God's punishment visited on the peasants; Stolz saw it visited on the burghers of Basel.

The issues raised by the debate on communalization cannot be resolved by appeals to specific texts and anecdotes. As it runs through much of historical thinking over the past 150 years, it probably cannot be resolved at all. Not even Max Weber could create a safe path between Karl Marx and Wilhelm Dilthey.

We may end with clear statements of the alternatives. In 1912 Ernst Troeltsch (1865–1923) spoke for the primacy of explanation. "No science can escape," he wrote, "from the conditions imposed by the constitution of the thinking mind which gives it birth."[70] More recently, the case for understanding over explanation has been stated as follows: "Instead of a sociological history that looks in the past for institutional forms that can be used to predict the future, we need . . . a historical history, one that takes the kaleidoscopic shifting of events *on its own terms, looking not for explanations of human behavior in general, but for an understanding of specific outcomes in the past.*"[71]

Notes

This text expands on a paper read to the Sixteenth Century Studies Conference at Pittsburgh on October 30, 2003. I am grateful to the colleagues who offered comments on it, also and in particular to Peter Blickle and Tom Scott.

1. Hermann Wiesflecker, *Kaiser Maximilian I. Das Reich, Österreich und Europa an der Wende zur Neuzeit*, 5 vols. (Munich: R. Oldenbourg, 1971–86), 2: 337, 5: 76.

2. Christoph Scheurl, "Epistel über die Verfassung der Reichsstadt Nürnberg (1516)," 791, lines 24–28, quoted by Hans-Christoph Rublack, "Political and Social Norms in Urban Communities in the Holy Roman Empire," in Peter Blickle, Hans-Christoph Rublack, and Winfried Schulze, *Religion, Politics and Social Protest: Three Studies on Early Modern Germany*, ed. Kaspar von Greyerz (London: George Allen & Unwin, 1984), 44.

3. Henri Pirenne, *Medieval Cities, Their Origins and the Revival of Trade*, trans. Frank D. Halsey (Garden City, NY: Doubleday, 1956), 154.

4. John H. Mundy, introduction to Henri Pirenne, *Early Democracies in the Low Countries: Urban Society and Political Conflict in the Middle Ages and the Renaissance*, trans. J. V. Saunders (New York: Harper & Row, 1963), xiv, xxiii.

5. Max Weber, *The City*, trans. Don Martindale and Gertrud Neuwirth (New York: Collier, 1962), 78–79.

6. Andreas Dorpalen, *German History in Marxist Perspective: The East German Approach* (Detroit: Wayne State University Press, 1985), 94, who supplies a brief account with references.

7. Otto Brunner, *Adeliges Landleben und europaischer Geist. Leben und Werk Wolf Helmhards von Hohberg, 1612–1688* (Salzburg: O. Muller, 1949); *Neue Wege der Verfassungs- und Sozialgeschichte*, 3rd ed. (Göttingen: Vandenhoeck & Ruprecht, 1980).

8. See Howard Kaminsky and James Van Horn Melton, "Otto Brunner's Land and Lordship," in Otto Brunner, *Land and Lordship: Structures of Governance in Medieval Austria*, trans. Howard Kaminsky and James Van Horn Melton (Philadelphia: University of Pennsylvania Press, 1992), xiv–lviii; James Van Horn Melton, "From Folk History to Structural History: Otto Brunner (1898–1982) and the Radical-Conservative Roots of German Social History," in *Paths of Continuity: Central European Historiog-*

raphy from the 1930s to the 1950s, ed. Hartmut Lehmann and James Van Horn Melton (Cambridge: Cambridge University Press, 1994), 263–92; "The Ideological Origins of *Begriffsgeschichte*," in *The Meaning of Historical Terms and Concepts,* ed. Hartmut Lehmann and Melvin Richter (Washington, DC: German Historical Institute, 1996), 21–34. A strongly and (in my view justifiably) critical note is struck by Gadi Algazi, "Otto Brunner—'Konkrete Ordnung und Sprache der Zeit,'" in *Geschichtsschreibung als Legitimationswissenschaft 1918–1945,* ed. Peter Schoettler (Frankfurt: Suhrkamp Taschenbuch Verlag, 1997), 166–203.

9. The entire scheme is laid out by Dietrich Gerhard, *Old Europe: A Study of Continuity, 1000–1800* (New York: Academic Press, 1981); in German: *Das Abendland 800–1800; Ursprung und Gegenbild unserer Zeit,* trans. Tilla Stumpf (Freiburg: Verlag Ploetz, 1985). The German title expresses the concept more precisely, as *Abendland* (the West) conveys the mood of the time of the book's composition.

10. Peter Laslett, *The World We Have Lost* (London: Methuen, 1965); Roland Mousnier, *Les hierarchies sociales de 1450 à nos jours* (Paris: Presses Universitaires de France, 1969); in English: *Social Hierarchies, 1450 to the Present,* trans. Peter Evans, ed. Margaret Clarke (New York: Schocken, 1973).

11. I use this term as the most usual expression from that era, useful because it expresses the actual plurality and diversity of the lands rather than a fictive unity.

12. His titles reveal the tendency of his thinking: *Geschichte der Markenverfassung in Deutschland* (Erlangen: F. Enke, 1856); *Geschichte der Fronhöfe, der Bauernhöfe, und der Hofverfassung in Deutschland* (Erlangen: F. Enke, 1862–63); *Geschichte der Dorfverfassung in Deutschland* (Erlangen: F. Enke, 1865–66); and *Geschichte der Städteverfassung in Deutschland* (Erlangen: F. Enke, 1869–75).

13. Otto von Gierke, *Das deutsche Genossenschaftsrecht,* 4 vols. (Berlin: Weidmann, 1868–1913; reprint, Graz: Akademische Verlagsanstalt, 1954). Sections of the work have appeared in English, of which the most useful selection in this context is *Community in Historical Perspective: A Translation of Selections from Das deutsche Genossenschaftsrecht (The German Law of Fellowship),* trans. Mary Fischer, ed. Antony Black (Cambridge and New York: Cambridge University Press, 1990).

14. Karl Siegfried Bader, *Das mittelalterliche Dorf als Friedens- und Rechtsbereich,* 3rd ed. (Cologne and Vienna: Böhlau Verlag, 1981), 1–20.

15. "Einen burger und einen gebuer/scheit nicht me wen ein czuhin und ein muer." From a gloss (before 1368) to Article 72 of the Saxon feudal code, quoted by Hans Planitz, *Die deutsche Stadt im Mittelalter von der Römerzeit bis zu den Zunftkämpfen,* 2nd ed. (Graz and Cologne: Böhlau-Verlag, 1965), 229.

16. Peter Blickle, *Landschaften im Alten Reich: Die staatliche Funktion des gemeinen Mannes in Oberdeutschland* (Munich: C. H. Beck, 1973).

17. Peter Blickle, *Die Revolution von 1525,* 2nd ed. (Munich: R. Oldenbourg, 1981); in English: *The Revolution of 1525: The German Peasants' War from a New Perspective,* trans. Thomas A. Brady Jr. and H. C. Erik Midelfort (Baltimore: Johns Hopkins University Press, 1981), 124.

18. Peter Blickle, *Deutsche Untertanen. Ein Widerspruch* (Munich: C. H. Beck, 1981); in English: *Obedient Germans? A Rebuttal,* trans. Thomas A. Brady Jr. (Charlottesville: University Press of Virginia, 1997), 33. Blickle acknowledges a debt to Bader

and also to Franz Steinbach (1895–1964), whom he quotes at the same place to the effect that in the Rhineland "the laws on communal constitutions prescribe no difference between urban and rural communes."

19. Blickle, *Obedient Germans*, 34.

20. Bernd Moeller, *Reichsstadt und Reformation*, Schriften des Vereins für Reformationsgeschichte, vol. 180 (Gütersloh: Gerd Mohn, 1962), 11–15; in English: "Imperial Cities and the Reformation," in *Imperial Cities and the Reformation: Three Essays*, trans. H. C. Erik Midelfort and Mark U. Edwards Jr. (Philadelphia: Fortress, 1975), 44–49. For comment, see Thomas A. Brady Jr., "From the Sacral Community to the Common Man: Reflections on German Reformation Studies," *Central European History* 20 (1987): 29–45.

21. M. M. Smirin, *Die Volksreformation des Thomas Müntzer und der große Bauernkrieg*, 2nd ed., trans. Hans Nichtweiss (Berlin: Dietz Verlag, 1956), 5–6. For Blickle's treatment of Smirin, see *Die Reformation im Reich*, 3rd ed. (Stuttgart: Eugen Ulmer, 2000), 169–71; "Bauern und Reformation. Positionsbestimmungen," in *Zugänge zur bäuerlichen Reformation*, vol. 1, ed. Peter Blickle and Peter Bierbrauer, Bauer und Reformation series (Zurich: Chronos, 1987), 11–13, where he grapples with Marxist historiography of the Reformation.

22. Most characteristically, Blickle, *Die Reformation im Reich*, 3rd ed. 46–85. His most provocative move was to amalgamate Luther and Müntzer with the urban reformers, Huldrych Zwingli and Martin Bucer, as theorists of the people's reformation.

23. Peter Blickle, *Gemeindereformation. Die Menschen des 16. Jahrhunderts auf dem Weg zum Heil* (Munich: R. Oldenbourg, 1985); in English: *The Communal Reformation: The Quest for Salvation in Sixteenth-Century Germany*, trans. Thomas Dunlap (Atlantic City, NJ: Humanities, 1992).

24. Peter Blickle, *Kommunalismus. Skizzen einer gesellschaftlichen Organisationsform*, 2 vols. (Munich: R. Oldenbourg, 2000).

25. Blickle, *Kommunalismus*, 1: 158.

26. Blickle, *Kommunalismus*, 1: 158–59.

27. Blickle, *Kommunalismus*, 2: 374.

28. Peter Blickle, ed., *Gemeinde und Staat im Alten Europa*, Historische Zeitschrift, supplements, new series 25 (Munich: R. Oldenbourg, 1998); *Resistance, Representation, and Community* (Oxford: Clarendon, 1997), which also appeared in French.

29. Blickle, *Kommunalismus*, 1: 159.

30. See Peter Blickle, *Von der Leibeigenschaft zu den Menschenrechten* (Munich: C. H. Beck, 2003), a narrative informed by the communalization thesis.

31. R. W. Scribner, "Civic Unity and the Reformation in Erfurt," *Past and Present* 66 (1975): 29–60; and "Why Was There No Reformation in Cologne?" *Bulletin of the Institute of Historical Research* 48 (1975): 217–41, reprinted in R. W. Scribner, *Popular Culture and Popular Movements in Reformation Germany* (London: Hambledon, 1987), 185–216, 217–42. On R. W. Scribner (1941–1998), see Thomas A. Brady Jr., "Robert W. Scribner, a Historian of the German Reformation," in R. W. Scribner, *Religion and Culture in Germany (1400–1800)*, Studies in Medieval and Reformation Thought, vol. 81, ed. Lyndal Roper (Leiden: Brill, 2001), 9–26.

32. R. W. Scribner, "Is There a Social History of the Reformation?" *Social History* 4 (1977): 483–505; "The Reformation as a Social Movement," in *The Urban Classes, the Nobility and the Reformation: Studies on the Social History of the Reformation in England and Germany*, ed. Wolfgang J. Mommsen, Peter Alter, and R. W. Scribner (Stuttgart: Klett-Cotta, 1979), 49, reprinted in Scribner, *Popular Culture*, 145–74.

33. Thomas A. Brady Jr., "The 'Social History of the Reformation' between 'Romantic Idealism' and 'Sociologism': A Reply [to Bernd Moeller]," in *The Urban Classes, the Nobility and the Reformation. Studies on the Social History of the Reformation in England and Germany*, Publications of the German Historical Institute London, vol. 5, ed. W. J. Mommsen, P. J. Alter, and R. W. Scribner (Stuttgart: Klett-Cotta, 1979), 40–43; "From the Sacral Community to the Common Man."

34. Similar arguments about social tensions in the villages, caused by population growth and land hunger, were initially raised by David Warren Sabean, *Landbesitz und Gesellschaft am Vorabend des Bauernkrieges. Eine Studie der sozialen Verhältnisse im südlichen Oberschwaben in den Jahren for 1525*, Quellen und Forschungen zur Agrargeschichte, vol. 26 (Stuttgart: G. Fischer, 1972). See also David Martin Luebke, *His Majesty's Rebels: Communities, Factions, and Rural Revolt in the Black Forest, 1725–1745* (Ithaca, NY: Cornell University Press, 1997).

35. Tom Scott, *Freiburg and the Breisgau: Town-Country Relations in the Age of Reformation and Peasants' War* (Oxford and New York: Clarendon, 1986); *Regional Identity and Economic Change: The Upper Rhine, 1450–1600* (Oxford: Clarendon; New York: Oxford University Press, 1997); and the important volume *Regions and Landscapes: Reality and Imagination in Late Medieval and Early Modern Europe*, ed. Peter Ainsworth and Tom Scott (Oxford: Oxford University Press, 2000). Scott had already produced a study of the revolutionary theologian Thomas Müntzer (d. 1525). Tom Scott, *Thomas Müntzer: Theology and Revolution in the German Reformation* (Houndmills, UK: Macmillan, 1989).

36. Tom Scott, *Society and Economy in Germany, 1300–1600* (Houndmills, UK, and New York: Palgrave, 2002).

37. Blickle adopts this concept from Wilhelm Abel, *Agrarkrisen und Agrarkonjunktur. Eine Geschichte der Land- und Ernährungswirtschaft Mitteleuropas seit dem hohen Mittelalter*, 3rd ed. (Hamburg and Berlin: Parey, 1978); in English: *Agricultural Fluctuations in Europe from the Thirteenth to the Twentieth Centuries*, trans. Olive Ordish (New York: St. Martin's Press, 1980).

38. Most recently, Tom Scott, "The German Peasants' War and the 'Crisis of Feudalism.' Reflections on a Neglected Theme," *Journal of Early Modern History* 6 (2002): 265–94.

39. Scott, *Regional Identity and Economic Change*.

40. This point, it seems to me, does not speak against Blickle's argument, as he does not argue that common economic interests united burghers and peasants.

41. Tom Scott, "Südwestdeutsche Städte im Bauernkrieg. Bündnisse zwischen Opportunismus und Solidarität," in *Stadt und Revolution*, Veröffentlichungen des Südwestdeutschen Arbeitskreises für Stadtgeschichtsforschung, vol. 27, ed. Bernhard Kirchgässner and Hans-Peter Becht (Stuttgart: Thorbecke, 2001), 10–36.

42. Tom Scott, *Freiburg and the Breisgau*, 7.

43. Scott, *Regional Identity*, 7.

44. Scott, *Regional Identity*, 7; "German Peasants' War," 272.

45. Scott, "German Peasants' War," 272–73.

46. Guy Bois, *Crise du féodalisme: économie rurale et démographie en Normandie orientale du début du 14e siècle au milieu du 16e siècle*, Cahiers de la Fondation nationale des sciences politiques, no. 202 (Paris: Presses de la Fondation nationale des sciences politiques, 1976), here from *The Crisis of Feudalism: Economy and Society in Eastern Normandy c.1300–1550* (Cambridge and New York: Cambridge University Press; Paris: Editions de la Maison des sciences de l'homme, 1984), 352.

47. The degree to which thinking has changed about a crisis of feudalism may be seen in the most recent general work on the "transition problem." Robert S. Duplessis, *Transitions to Capitalism in Early Modern Europe* (Cambridge: Cambridge University Press, 1997), 21: "Conditions in mid-fifteenth-century rural Europe . . . smiled on the majority of peasant families."

48. Scott, *Society and Economy*, 48–49.

49. Scott, *Society and Economy*, 49.

50. Scott, "The German Peasants War," 281.

51. If so, Scott's exaggeration is mild compared to those of some other (especially German) critics of Blickle, who accuse him of arguing for something like a village Jacobinism. See Robert von Friedeburg's highly polemical review, "*Kommunalismus. Skizzen einer gesellschaftlichen Organisationsform*, by Peter Blickle," *English Historical Review* 116 (2001): 141–43. His exaggerations quite miss the depth and subtlety of Blickle's argument in general, for example, his concepts of the analogical and pedagogical relationships between household practice and communal practice and of the importance of serfdom to his concept of how rural communalism began.

52. Scott, *Society and Economy*, 41.

53. Scott, *Society and Economy*, 41.

54. Blickle, *Revolution of 1525*, 115.

55. See Scott, "Südwestdeutsche Städte im Bauernkrieg," 10–36.

56. Tom Scott, "The Reformation and Modern Political Economy: Luther and Gaismair compared," in *Die deutsche Reformation zwischen Spätmittelalter und Früher Neuzeit*, Schriften des Historischen Kollegs, Kolloquien, vol. 50, ed. Thomas A. Brady Jr. (Munich: R. Oldenbourg, 2001), 173–202.

57. Scott, "The Reformation and Modern Political Economy," 200.

58. His view of the relationship between feudal and absolutist rule is reminiscent of Perry Anderson's remark that "the Absolutist State was . . . the new political carapace of a threatened nobility." Perry Anderson, *Lineages of the Absolutist State* (London: NLB, 1974), 18.

59. Peter Blickle, "Communal Reformation and Peasant Piety: The Peasant Reformation and Its Late Medieval Origins," *Central European History* 20 (1987): 216–28.

60. Blickle, *Gemeindereformation*, 203–204.

61. Scott, *Freiburg and the Breisgau*, 234.

62. Tom Scott, "The Communal Reformation between Town and Country," in *The Reformation in Germany and Europe: Interpretations and Issues/Die Reformation in*

Deutschland und Europa: Interpretationen und Debatten, ed. Hans R. Guggisberg and Gottfried G. Krodel, (Gütersloh: Gütersloher Verlagshaus, 1993), 192.

63. On the Bundschuh, see now Thomas Adam and Peter Blickle, eds., *Bundschuh: Untergrombach 1502, das unruhige Reich und die Revolutionierbarkeit Europas. Bundschuhbewegung und Bauernkrieg im 16. Jahrhundert* (Stuttgart Steiner, 2004).

64. Strasbourg, Bibliothèque Municipale, Ms. 630 ("Städel-Chronik"), vol. 2:1059–60.

65. There is no adequate study of Stolz and his chronicles. Parts of his biography are strewn through Wolfram Stolz's introduction to *Die Hans Stolz'sche Gebweiler Chronik. Zeugenbericht über den Bauernkrieg am Oberrhein* (Freiburg: Edition Stolz, 1979), 7–70. My thanks to Katherine Brun for her unpublished study of this text.

66. Hans Stolz, *Gebweiler Chronik,* 135, 142–45, 160.

67. Georges Bischoff, "La Haute-Alsace et la Guerre des Paysans," in *La Guerre des Paysans 1525. Études et documents,* ed. Alphonse Wollbrett (Saverne: Société d'Histoire et d'Archéologie de Saverne et Environs, 1975), 111–20.

68. Hans Stolz, *Gebweiler Chronik,* 210.

69. Hans Stolz, *Gebweiler Chronik,* 213.

70. Ernst Troeltsch, *Protestantism and Progress: The Significance of Protestantism for the Rise of the Modern World* (New York: G. P. Putnam, 1912), 17.

71. James D. Tracy, "The Background War of the Early Modern Era: Christian and Muslim States in Contest for Dominion, Trade, and Cultural Preeminence," an unpublished paper quoted here with the author's permission (emphasis mine).

4

A Tale of Two Brothers

Corporate Identity and the
Revolt in the Towns of Holland

Henk van Nierop

I N FEBRUARY 1567 THE TOWN OF AMSTERDAM WAS on the brink of civil war. It was the aftermath of the Wonder Year, an episode marked by iconoclastic riots and a short-lived efflorescence of religious freedom for the fledgling Calvinist churches in the Low Countries.[1] Yet by the beginning of 1567, Philip II's regency government in Brussels was gaining the upper hand. The Amsterdam Calvinists were ordered to evacuate the church of the Franciscans' convent, where they had been holding their religious services. The three citizens' militia companies had to be disbanded, while the town's Catholic burgomasters were authorized to enlist an additional three hundred mercenary soldiers in addition to two hundred men previously levied. These measures, if implemented, would cause a significant shift in the town's balance of power, for it was only due to the protection of the civic militias that Amsterdam's Calvinists had been able to conduct their religious services. The burghers feared that the magistrates, with the help of the city soldiers, would open the gates for a government army, expel the Calvinists, and have one or two hundred citizens put to death.[2]

These rumors caused an insurrection, which must have involved the entire adult male population of Amsterdam. The insurgents, estimated by contemporaries at some eight or nine thousand men, secured control over most of the town. Calvinists could have formed only a minority; many among the rebels must have been traditional Catholics who wished to defend the right of the urban community to conduct its own religious business. The supporters of the magistrates were estimated at no more then two thousand men. They occupied the town's central Dam Square to assist the mercenary soldiers in defending the town hall.[3] "Never before had the city to such an extent been divided," wrote Laurens Jacobszoon Reael, one of the Calvinist leaders, in his memoirs, and he continued:

> One saw the father file to one party, the son to the other one; one brother to Dam Square, the other one with the burghers. Two brothers in one house helped each other donning their armor. One of them asked: "Brother, where will you go?" "To Dam Square," he replied, "to the ancient Catholics." "And I," said the other one, "shall go to the most ancient Catholic Christians of all [i.e., the Calvinists] in the streets, but if it comes to fighting, do not have mercy on me; I shall not spare you."[4]

This chilling conversation—"miserable to hear," wrote Reael—may well have taken place in reality, yet at the same time Reael must have used it as a metaphor for the condition of the city itself. The different political choices made by the two brothers magnify the discord gripping the urban community.

The tale of the two brothers reminds us that the Revolt was not a war of national liberation but a civil war, comparable to the conflicts that were being played out in France at the same time.[5] The story also addresses the problem of the relations between individual and community in the early modern world, the theme of this volume. Jacob Burckhardt, had he known of our two brothers, would have had no problem explaining their dialogue.[6] Each of the two brothers tore away the veil of tradition and corporate identity to make an individual choice of allegiance. "Here I stand" is what each of the brothers might have said. They were acting as individuals, not as members of a family, a corporate body, or an urban community.

Yet different interpretations of the same story are imaginable. One might argue that the two brothers confronted each other as representatives of confessional groups, that is, totally novel types of organization, which potentially undermined the civic solidarity of town burghers. Another argument might present each brother as believing that he was the one who was best serving the interests of the entire urban community. According to this interpretation, the Catholics assembled on Dam Square were convinced that they, by defending the magistrates and the ancient Catholic Church, prevented the community from slipping into chaos and anarchy; while the opposition similarly held that they were the ones who stood for authentic communal values by preventing foreign troops from entering the town and the central government from meddling with its internal affairs.

This chapter explores the role of communal values and civic identity in the province of Holland during the Revolt of the Netherlands. Historians have underscored religion, the defense of privileges, and the economic crisis of the 1560s as key factors explaining the Revolt.[7] It will be argued here that we can only begin to understand the outbreak of the Revolt if we fully appreciate the impact of corporate identity, and in particular perceptions of the role of the elites in the urban community.[8] However, if a sense of urban identity was a factor in the outbreak of the Revolt, it was also its victim. The Revolt tended to undermine the solidarity of town burghers on an unprecedented scale, for only by extraditing large numbers of politically and religiously suspect citizens could urban communities weather the storm of the Revolt. The Revolt presented a set of rival loyalties to urban citizens and thereby caused a crisis of communal identity in the towns. The conclusion of this chapter suggests a number of factors to explain why the towns were eventually able to overcome this crisis.

Corporate Bodies and Corporate Identity

Identity is a slippery term.[9] First of all, there is no hard bedrock of *identity*, while *national identity* is a notion as mythical as *national character* or *race*. Identity is a cultural construction, and *urban identity* is as much an "imagined community" as any other community.[10] Yet members of a community, insofar as they believe in such constructions, also tend to act in accordance with them. Hence a sense of urban solidarity turns from a belief into a practice, which, in turn, will feed feelings of identity. Second, there was no single, dominant sense of identity in early modern Europe. Early modern society should rather be regarded as a cascade of overlapping communities, each of them claiming an individual's loyalty. As James Tracy has suggested, European society threw up many kinds of tightly organized groups and thereby created so many occasions for individuals to play out the game of deciding who they were.[11] Third, while we do know that individuals were part of many interlocking corporate groups (a religious brotherhood, a craft guild, a parish, a town, etc.), little is known about the actual experience of such multiple group identities. We can only study the acts of town burghers and try to make sense of them by assuming an underlying sense of identity. We do know, however, that early modern Europeans tended to identify with small groups rather than large ones. A recent volume studying the shifting uses of the concept of "fatherland" or *patria* in the Netherlands suggests that this term was often used for an individual's hometown or the town where he was born rather than to the province where he was living, and very rarely indeed for the Netherlands as a whole.[12]

What, then, is *corporate identity*? The social fabric of early modern Europe consisted of a large number of overlapping corporate bodies, social groups imagined as consisting of "members" and a "head" to which the members

owed obedience.[13] The numerous towns of the Low Countries are good examples of such corporate bodies, but the towns also harbored numerous
smaller corporate groups within their walls, such as craft guilds or religious
fraternities. Each of these smaller communities was thought of as a corporate
body in itself, yet together they made up the larger corporate body of the
urban community. From a legal point of view, urban communities were defined by privileges, special rights conceded by the prince or his ancestors, usually in exchange for a sum of money.[14] The members of the urban communes,
the burghers or citizens, collectively had a share in these privileges. Citizenship had significant legal, political, economic, social, military, moral, cultural,
and religious dimensions.[15] Heinz Schilling has argued that urban citizens
shared an ideology of urban republicanism, a code of behavior rarely written
down but expressed in urban practices such as processions, joyous entries, or
patterns of urban revolts.[16]

The pre-Reformation urban community was also a sacred community. Processions carrying the Holy Sacrament or relics of the town's patron saint frequently filed through the streets, with magistrates, militiamen, craft guilds,
and local clergy participating in the ceremony. They thereby marked the identity of the various corporate groups making up the body politic of the city,
while at the same time inscribing the unity and concord of the community as
a whole into the public space.[17]

Historians have described urban communities as "quasi kin groups," whose
members were bound to assist, aid, and protect one another. Its members had
mutual claims and obligations to assistance and protection. Burghers constituted a sworn community (*coniuratio*), a brotherhood in arms, ready to defend their privileges, their modes of self-government, and their freedom. Key-
words of the early modern commune were peace, friendship, brotherly love,
unity, and concord.[18]

Such lofty notions, however, usually were an ideal rather than a reality. First
of all, not all individuals living in a town were full citizens. Full citizens would
be looking down on mere inhabitants, while both groups mistrusted outsiders
and strangers. It was widely felt that a town could rely only on its full citizens.
Thus in 1572, when the town was under attack by rebel forces, the magistrates
of Amsterdam decreed that all inhabitants who were not full citizens must
swear the citizens' oath or leave at once.[19]

Second, economic differentiation within the citizenry tended to undermine
social cohesion, especially when elites of wealthy burghers monopolized government offices.[20] The urban middle classes were usually prepared to accept
the elite's monopoly of town administration. Holding offices became ever
more complicated and time consuming as a result of urban growth, the development of long-distance trade, and the development of the dynastic state.

It had been a commonplace since antiquity that only the rich were immune to the seductive powers of corruption; yet from a more practical point of view, shopkeepers and artisans were simply not in a position to close up their workshops and dedicate their precious time to administrative duties. Only those who enjoyed an independent income from capital invested in trade, manufacture, or government bonds—in other words, those who were absolved from working with their hands, an infallible mark of lowly origin—had the opportunity to serve their town as magistrates.[21] The single condition set by commoners on the power monopoly of the elite was that the latter represented and defended the interests of the urban community. The elite were usually prepared to play out this role, but this was not always a simple matter with the Habsburg government bent on enlarging its legal and political prerogatives at the cost of the independence of the towns.

Hence, rebellions were a recurring feature of urban life. Historians have discerned two interlocking traditions of revolt in the Netherlands between the twelfth and the late eighteenth century, a "great" and a "little" tradition.[22] The "great" tradition consists of revolts of the towns against the prince, while rebellions of the common people against the town elites form the "little" tradition. Both types of revolts interacted; local revolutionary movements often fueled the "great" revolts against the prince. If the elite were divided, the common people might revolt against the incumbent faction and bring to power a rival faction that might better defend the interests of the town against the prince. Thus urban elites were in a delicate position, poised between the demands of the central authorities and those of their own populations. The Habsburg government demanded that the town elite carry out royal policies; in return it offered elites support against pressure exerted by commoners. The urban community, on the other hand, expected the elites to defend urban privilege against the encroachments of princely rule. The elite had to preserve a balance between the demands of the prince and those of their own constituents. They might find support from the common people in presenting their demands with the central authorities; yet at other times they accepted the help of the prince in suppressing unrest among their fellow citizens.[23]

Corporate Identity Under Duress, 1520–1572

Corporate solidarity in the towns came under increasing pressure after the first introduction of evangelical ideas in the early 1520s. The collapse of religious conformity threatened to undermine civic unity. The Holy Sacrament, once a symbol of the integrity of the entire corpus of the town, was scoffed at when it was solemnly carried around during Corpus Christi processions. Priests were being abused and lampoons were pasted on church doors and altars. In Amsterdam, people feared that burghers "beat each other on the head for Luther's sake."[24] Catholics generally showed restraint in the face of religious aggression, but they too would sometimes pose a threat to civic order. A Catholic crowd chased two women through the streets of Gouda, shouting "Lutheran whore, Lutheran whore, burn, burn!"[25] In Amsterdam people jeered at a group of evangelicals returning from a conventicle ("Heretics, heretics, you hold school in your houses!"), and women threw dung at the windows of a house where illegal religious meetings were being held.[26]

Since 1521 heresy had been a crime punishable according to secular law and by ordinary urban law courts. Yet the town magistrates were reluctant to crack down on alleged heretics. They issued local ordinances against conventicles and public name calling with no other aim than maintaining public order, upholding urban solidarity, and preventing bloodshed.[27] The first edict issued against religious dissenters in Amsterdam, in November 1523, stated its goal not to be the restoration of religious concord, but the reestablishment of civic unity. "Good cities," it said, "are strengthened by concord, but injured by discord and feuds."[28]

Their lenient attitude brought the town magistrates into conflict with the emperor's officials in the Netherlands.[29] Charles V insisted on treating heresy as an "enormous" or "reserved" crime, which implied that in heresy cases the privileges of the town were considered null and void. A great number of conflicts between the urban and the central authorities suggest that the town magistrates generally regarded the infringement on their privileges as a more serious threat than the incidence of heresy itself. Only in cases where heresy led to serious disruption of public order, as was the case with the 1535 Anabaptists' uprising in Amsterdam, were the magistrates willing to play along with the authorities and act firmly. Yet the magistrates, as soon as the crisis had passed, fell back to their previous tolerant attitude. Even in Amsterdam, where in the aftermath of the Anabaptist rebellion the government had bypassed local privileges to replace the overly tolerant ruling party with a "sincerely Catholic faction," did repression of heresy come to an end in the 1550s. In Haarlem and Rotterdam, feelings of communal solidarity became evident when burghers rioted in an attempt to prevent the execution of Anabaptists in 1557 and 1558.[30]

The Wonder Year brought a crisis of civic solidarity.[31] In April 1566 a group of nobles, both Calvinists and Catholics, forced the regent Margaret of Parma to suspend the antiheresy legislation, cease the persecution of religious dissenters, and allow a measure of religious toleration. The slackening of repression encouraged the Calvinists to organize public open-air sermons, and this in turn eventually led to iconoclastic riots. Holland's town magistrates relied on the civic militias to disrupt illegal sermons and suppress image breaking, but they found that the militias were unwilling to use force against their fellow citizens. In Leiden, Delft, and Amsterdam, it was the militias who brokered an agreement between the Calvinists and the magistrates that went far beyond anything the regent was willing to concede. In Amsterdam a college of six (later nine) "captains in chief" (*opperkapiteinen*) from the militias mediated between the magistrates and the Calvinists; they came to be regarded as representatives of the urban middle classes, who had no voice in the town council. Such experiments in citizens' representation soon came to an end when the central government gained the upper hand and revoked the concessions granted to the Calvinists. By the spring of 1567 the government had regained full control, and a stream of Calvinists and others who had been involved in the "time of troubles" fled the Low Countries.

From the point of view of urban solidarity, the significance of the Wonder Year was twofold. First, massive attendance of the open-air sermons and the failure or unwillingness of Catholics to act against Calvinist aggression and their appropriation of public space suggests that many burghers were prepared either to go along with the Calvinists and accept a German-type Reformation in which the entire town's church would undergo a "reformation" in some form or the other, or expected a settlement that would guarantee religious freedom for the adherents of both religions. Second, polarization had gone so far that the magistrates became unable to play out their usual intermediate role between the urban community and the central government. The citizens simply did not trust them to stand for the interests of the town, especially in towns where faction and strife were endemic and where public confidence in the magistrates had already been undermined by previous feuds, as was the case in Delft and Amsterdam. The civic militias profited from this situation by stepping into the power vacuum and setting up ephemeral structures of popular representation that had hitherto been absent. The significance of the role of the magistrates for the preservation of urban solidarity and public order is underlined when we consider Gouda and Dordrecht. In these conservative towns no iconoclasm took place at all due to the prudent stance of the Catholic magistrates, who remained loyal to the central government, but whose moderate attitude also gained them the support of the citizens.[32]

Civic unity was brutally restored during the regime of Philip II's new regent, the Duke of Alba (1567–1573). His Council of Troubles, an extraordinary tribunal, punished individuals who had been involved in the troubles of 1566 by sentencing them to death if arrested and to eternal banishment if they were so lucky as to escape. Yet if the disappearance of the Calvinists from the towns facilitated the restoration of the monopoly of the Catholic Church, it did not take away the essential political bone of contention between the towns and the central government. Alba introduced new policies that strengthened the position of the central authorities while undermining urban autonomy. A notorious case was the Tenth Penny, a sales duty that, if introduced, would have taken away taxation from the control of the provincial states, thereby severely limiting the political leverage of the franchised towns. Alba's policies made high demands upon the political suppleness of the magistrates, who again found themselves uncomfortably squeezed between the demands of the central authorities and the expectations of their own citizens. Magistrates in some towns won credit from their constituents by fiercely resisting the unpopular new taxes (e.g., in Gouda, Delft, and Amsterdam), while easily giving way elsewhere (e.g., in Dordrecht), thus earning the scorn of the burghers.[33] The burgomasters of Amsterdam gained respect and loyalty from the citizens by preventing the construction of a citadel commanding the town, which would have spelled the end of the city's independence.[34]

Corporate Identity and the Revolt

To what extent did feelings of urban identity define a town's relation to the Revolt when it broke out in the towns of Holland in 1572?[35] There are three interconnected areas of communal ideology that shed light on the attitude of the towns. First, citizens were highly averse to taking in a garrison of government troops. Quite apart from the very real and tangible problem of the economic burden caused by garrisons, which were routinely billeted on the inhabitants, burghers believed that an urban community ought to rely on its armed citizens for the defense of its freedom, privileges, and autonomy. They regarded the civic militias as the core of the community's citizens-in-arms.[36]

Second, burghers believed that the magistrates failed to defend the true interests of the community. This became evident in Dordrecht, where the burghers mistrusted the burgomasters who had shown insufficient mettle in resisting the introduction of the Tenth Penny tax, or when the burghers of Enkhuisen, rightly or wrongly, suspected that the burgomasters were making preparations to take in a garrison of government troops. Here, the burghers rose in rebellion, stormed the town hall, deposed the burgomasters, and brought Enkhuisen to the side of the rebels.[37]

Third, burghers widely believed that the civic militias somehow represented the urban community, and that the militias therefore needed to be consulted in all matters of importance. In Hoorn the burghers prevented the burgomasters from employing mercenary soldiers against the Orangist rebels in neighboring Enkhuisen, but they resisted, on the other hand, taking in a garrison of rebel troops. While Hoorn thus hovered between the twin evils of taking in government soldiers or rebel soldiers and anxiously strove to preserve its neutrality, a new representative "broad council" was instituted, in which burgomasters and *Vroedschap* (the existing town council, in which elite families were represented) consulted with the militia officers and the headmen of the craft guilds. When pressure increased, this relatively democratic organ voted in favor of opening the gates for the rebel troops, thus bringing the town to the side of the Revolt, with the representatives of the middle classes outvoting the more conservative elite members.[38]

The counterexample of Amsterdam suggests how an ideology of civic republicanism determined a town's position toward the Revolt.[39] Amsterdam, in the face of mounting pressure exerted by the rebels, remained loyal to the government. Its magistrates had been extremely unpopular with the burghers at an earlier period. They nonetheless succeeded in turning around public opinion and mobilizing broad popular support by stubbornly resisting both the introduction of the Tenth Penny and the building of a citadel and, significantly, by refusing to take in a garrison of government soldiers. Their consistent antigovernment stance convinced the burghers of Amsterdam that the magistrates stood for authentic civic values. The magistrates were aided by the circumstance that Amsterdam's militias had been disbanded and that they had successfully prevented the return of Calvinist exiles into the city. Without the militias and the Calvinists, there was simply no rallying point for the opposition.

The Crisis of Urban Corporate Identity

If a sense of civic identity in the towns was one of the factors fueling the Revolt, the Revolt itself also caused an unprecedented crisis of solidarity among the citizens. A huge stream of Catholic and loyalist refugees, as soon as the first towns sided with the rebels, abandoned the rebel towns and poured into such towns as had remained loyal to Philip II's government. These so-called *glippers* (literally "slippers" or "sneakers," because they had secretly slipped over the town walls and joined the enemy) traditionally had a bad press among contemporary supporters of the Revolt as well as among its more recent historians. Some *glippers* are indeed known to have been engaged in plots to open the gates for the Spanish and bring their hometown back under government rule. More recently historians have argued for a more balanced view.[40] Many *glippers* were former magistrates who had been ousted from office during the rebellions in the towns in 1572. The Catholic clergy, both secular and regular, who were cruelly persecuted and in some cases murdered by the advancing rebel soldiers, formed another category. Other fugitives were faithful Catholic laypeople, who felt they could not live in their hometowns after the abolition of the Mass and the suspension of the sacraments. Others again were simply war refugees; many inhabitants of Holland, especially after the massacre of the town of Naarden, considered it prudent to follow events from a safe distance. Hundreds of the citizens of Alkmaar, when an advance party of the Spanish army appeared before the town's gates in July 1573, fled to prevent being trapped during a siege; the authorities sent them back from the neighboring town of Hoorn under the threat of severe punishment.[41]

It is impossible to estimate the number of *glipper* fugitives. The military commander Bernardino de Mendoza in a stunning passage in his memoirs describes how the Spanish army evacuated The Hague and the surrounding countryside accompanied by

> four thousand people, carried on seven hundred wagons; they were the Council of Holland, the clergy, the members of the religious orders, noblemen and ladies and burghers of the party of His Majesty, who for living as Catholics and fulfilling their duty as faithful vassals of His Majesty sacrificed the natural affection that one has for his *patria* and one's property.[42]

The new rebel regime ordered all fugitives to return to their hometowns, but many of them remained in Amsterdam, Utrecht, and other loyalist towns, waiting for a victory of the Spanish army. The rebel authorities in due course had the fugitives' property confiscated and sold, thereby encouraging the remaining burghers to take a material interest in an eventual Protestant settlement that included the permanent extradition of their Catholic and royalist fellow citizens.[43]

Thus the entire corporate structure of Holland's urban society, with its strong traditions of mutual solidarity, became fatally undermined. The Revolt created a society that became increasingly split along party lines, with the adherents of Calvinism and the Revolt on one side and those who wished to remain faithful to church and king on the other. Both Calvinist rebels and Catholic royalists offered a focus of loyalty and an ideology that was incompatible with urban corporatism, which was simply based on local patriotism.[44] A significant part of the population, of course, preferred not to declare their allegiance at all and keep a low profile until either of the two parties would have gained the upper hand. Yet in the circumstances of polarization and civil war they had no other choice than conforming at least outwardly to whichever party was in power.[45]

The burghers of the towns of Holland were keenly aware that their traditional corporate world was in shambles. This is how Wouter Jacobszoon, a former prior of the Augustinians' convent at Stein near Gouda—the same convent where Erasmus had begun his career as a monk[46]—and himself a war refugee living in Catholic Amsterdam, described the plight of his fellow fugitives:

> Ah! One saw so many a distressed person walking in the streets, lost in themselves. The good Catholic people who had run away from their towns because they did not want to mingle with such ungodliness as was perpetrated by the rebels—the distress they suffered can hardly be described. They had always been people of honor. They were used to affluence, and had never sojourned anywhere against their will when traveling abroad for pleasure. And now they found themselves in a completely different condition, because they saw they had been expelled from their towns almost as exiles, as villains, with little hope of soon coming back to their own people. In addition, the money they had to live from became very scarce and they saw no means to find more [money], since everyone during this time was abandoned by his friends and relatives. And, on top of that, they experienced that they were not at home but among strangers, because they missed the service of their family on which they were accustomed to rely. And, finally, it cost them great effort to keep a place in the towns where they wished to settle, as a result of the scarcity of provisions everywhere and because of the multitude of exiles now leaving all towns. Whoever has any sense can understand the distress and anxiety these good people must have been experiencing during this time. Yet everybody had to go on with his charge, as imposed by God, and maintain his patience.[47]

Brother Wouter's journal is a moving document that paints in stark colors the plight of his fellow refugees, a gloomy picture of atomized individuals thrown back onto their own resources, apparently abandoned by their God. Holland's fugitive Catholic burghers had forfeited their snug, safe corporate world of solidarity and mutual aid, a world that, to all appearances, had vanished forever.

Corporate Identity Restored

The astonishing fact about the Dutch Revolt is that civic harmony, after more than four years of bitter civil war, was eventually restored. In November 1576 the rebel provinces of Holland and Zeeland concluded a peace treaty with most of the other provinces, the Pacification of Ghent, in which they agreed to forget their differences and undertake a joint effort to expel the Spanish army. The very first article of the Pacification proclaimed a general amnesty by stating that "all offences, injuries, unlawful acts and damage done during the disturbances between the inhabitants of these provinces as are involved in the present treaty . . . shall be forgiven, forgotten and regarded as not having occurred, so that no one may mention them or may be sued for them"; another clause made provisions for compensation for confiscated and alienated properties.[48] Both parties saw it as their principal task to reconcile the country's deeply divided inhabitants. Yet this was easier said than done, and the question remains: How did they do it?

Reconciliation of the deeply divided population of the Netherlands was never to be an easy task. It was obstructed by many factors, such as the triumphalist attitude of the public Reformed Church; the official proscription of the Mass, of the administration of the sacraments, and of all gatherings of Catholics; the widespread suspicion that Catholics might act as traitors in the ongoing struggle with Spain; and the discrimination against Catholics in many fields, notably their inability to serve in significant government or magisterial offices. Catholics in the Dutch Republic were not persecuted, but they were second-rate citizens: mistrusted, discriminated against, and sometimes harassed. Scholars have rarely addressed the problem of reconciliation and reconstruction after the Revolt, nor have contemporaries reflected on it in exactly these terms. Just how Dutch society succeeded in burying its hatchets is a question that requires further research. By way of conclusion, I should like to suggest three possible factors.

First, reconciliation may have been aided by the tremendous upsurge of the economy beginning in the 1590s. The spectacular boom in trade and manufacture was inaugurated by the fall of Antwerp, the closure of the Scheldt River, and the influx of yet another wave of war refugees, mainly Calvinists this time from the southern provinces. Economic growth is not a panacea, but it may have helped to heal the wounds of the past. The newly found wealth lubricated the mechanisms of reintegration by enabling religious dissenters to deploy themselves successfully as merchants, entrepreneurs, artisans, or artists.

Second, the specific nature of the religious settlement in the Dutch Republic facilitated the integration of former adversaries. This may seem paradoxical, for the Dutch Republic was in many ways a confessional state, with a privileged position for the Reformed Church and strong mechanisms for the political, social and moral exclusion of dissenters. Nevertheless, the Union of Utrecht (1579), which laid down the constitutional ground plan for the Dutch Republic, guaranteed freedom of conscience for every individual, even if it stopped short of granting freedom to conduct religious services.[49] The Reformed Church became the public church, yet it remained the church of a minority. If some of its more self-righteous ministers were not always aware of this fact, the town magistrates certainly were, and they set about imposing a religious settlement upon the towns that was Christian without being confessionally Protestant.[50] The policy of the magistrates of the towns of Holland was to play down confessional differences while at the same time fostering communal values. They encouraged a sense of civic identity by promoting civic ritual and commissioning ambitious artistic programs for the decoration of public space. Their policy was to promote civic peace and unity rather than doctrinal orthodoxy. On top of that, almost every individual in the Dutch Republic had friends and relatives who were adherents of some different religion. The logic of everyday confessional conviviality often made them private friends even if they were public enemies.[51] In practice, the town magistrates connived at much that was officially forbidden, including celebration of the Mass and administration of the other Catholic sacraments in Holland's many clandestine "house churches."[52]

A third factor that reinforced the coherence of Dutch society was the resilience and vitality of traditional corporate structures and corporate identities, and the essentially corporate organization of the Dutch Republic. The success of the Revolt against the relatively centralized Spanish monarchy gave birth to a state based on what has been called "the politics of particularism."[53] The Revolt resulted in a consolidation and strengthening of the corporate order of society and an articulation of local and regional rather than national identities. The Dutch Republic, even if it was "the first modern economy,"[54] was based on essentially medieval principles of corporate organization. The outcome of the Revolt was a surprisingly open society with the urban middle classes playing a key role in political culture and in the process of decision making. The civic militias in the seventeenth century had not forgotten the part they had performed during the Revolt. Although excluded from official political authority, they regarded themselves as the embodiment of civic identity and they sometimes violently interfered when they felt that the magistrates did not represent the town's interests as they interpreted it.[55] Ordinary citizens and their associations influenced local policies on a scale larger than is sometimes assumed by frequently handing in written petitions to the elite dealing with a wealth of topics of local interest.[56] Holland's literate urban middle classes relished discussing all sorts of political matters. The precondition for this "discussion culture" was diversity of opinions, not ideological conformity.[57] This climate of corporate solidarity and open discussion provided the breeding ground for the reconciliation of former enemies. The spectacular successes in many fields of the Dutch Republic during its golden age proved what most Catholics and Protestants had doubted during the Reformation era: that the corporate order of the towns could survive without the monopoly of one single church.

Finally, the reader will want to know what happened to the two brothers with whom this chapter began. In the end, they never had to confront each other on the barricades, and they were thus spared the grueling decision whether or not to kill each other. With both parties armed to their teeth, the militia's *opperkapiteinen* brokered one last agreement between the magistrates and the insurgents. The burgomasters were to renounce levying additional mercenary soldiers, while the insurgents had to lay down their arms. In this sense, the tale of the two brothers, a story that began with a civil war and ended with a compromise, is also a metaphor for the birth of the Dutch Republic.

Notes

1. On the Wonder Year see Guido Marnef, "The Dynamics of Reformed Militancy in the Low Countries: The Wonderyear," in *The Education of a Christian Society: Humanism and the Reformation in Britain and the Netherlands (Papers Delivered to the Thirteenth Anglo-Dutch Conference, 1997)* ed. N. Scott Amos, Andrew Pettegree, and Henk van Nierop (Aldershot: Ashgate, 1999), 193–210; Geoffrey Parker, *The Dutch Revolt* (London: Allen Lane, 1977), 68–99; Phyllis Mack Crew, *Calvinist Preaching and Iconoclasm in the Netherlands* (Cambridge: Cambridge University Press, 1978), 5–38. On events in Holland see Alastair Duke, *Reformation and Revolt in the Low Countries* (London and Ronceverte, PA: Hambledon, 1990), 125–51.

2. Jan Ter Gouw, *Geschiedenis van Amsterdam*, 8 vols. (Amsterdam: 1879–93), 6: 147–61.

3. In 1567 Amsterdam had about thirty thousand inhabitants at most, including women and children. The number of adult males cannot have exceeded ten thousand. Hubert Nusteling, *Welvaart en werkgelegenheid in Amsterdam 1540–1860: een relaas over demografie, economie en sociale politiek van een wereldstad* (Amsterdam and Dieren: De Bataafsche Leeuw, 1985), 234.

4. Gemeentearchief Amsterdam, Archief Marquette (archive nr. 231), inv. nr. 130, p. 30. The brothers are identified as Jan and Cornelis, the sons of Pieter, living in a house called Deventer. Pieter Cornelisz. Hooft, *Nederlandsche historiën*, 2 vols., ed. W. Hellinga and P. Tuynman (Amsterdam: Amsterdam University Press, 1972), 1: 136–37.

5. H. A. Enno van Gelder, "De Nederlandse adel en de opstand tegen Spanje," in *Van beeldenstorm tot pacificatie. Acht opstellen over de Nederlandse revolutie der zestiende eeuw* (Amsterdam and Brussels: Agon Elsevier, 1964), 138–69; Henk van Nierop, "Similar Problems, Different Outcomes: The Revolt of the Netherlands and the Wars of Religion in France," in *A Miracle Mirrored: the Dutch Republic in European Perspective*, ed. Karel Davids and Jan Lucassen (Cambridge: Cambridge University Press, 1995), 26–56; Philip Benedict et al., eds., *Reformation, Revolt and Civil War in France and the Netherlands 1555–1585* (Amsterdam: Royal Netherlands Academy of Arts and Sciences, 1999).

6. Jacob Burckhardt, *Die Kultur der Renaissance in Italien*, 2 vols. (Leipzig: Alfred Kröner Verlag, 1919), 1: 111.

7. Henk van Nierop, "Alva's Throne: Making Sense of the Revolt of the Netherlands," in *The Origins and Development of the Dutch Revolt*, ed. Graham Darby (London and New York: Routledge, 2001), 30–33.

8. On the role of the towns in the Revolt, see Guido Marnef, "The Towns and the Revolt," in *The Origins and Development of the Dutch Revolt*, ed. Graham Darby (Lon-

don and New York: Routledge, 2001), 84–106; J. J. Woltjer, "Stadt und Reformation in den Niederlanden," in *Kirche und gesellschaftlicher Wandel in deutschen und niederländischen Städten der werdenden Neuzeit,* ed. Franz Petri (Cologne: Böhlau, 1980), 155–68.

9. Willem Frijhoff, "Identiteit en identiteitsbesef. De historicus en de spanning tussen verbeelding, benoeming en herkenning," *Bijdragen en Mededelingen betreffende de Geschiedenis der Nederlanden* 107 (1992): 614–34.

10. Benedict Anderson, *Imagined Communities: Reflections on the Origin and Spread of Nationalism,* rev. ed. (London: Verso, 1991).

11. James D. Tracy, *Europe's Reformations 1450–1650* (Lanham, MD: Rowman & Littlefield, 1999), 230.

12. N. C. F. van Sas, ed., *Vaderland. Een geschiedenis van de vijftiende eeuw tot 1940* (Amsterdam: Amsterdam University Press, 1999).

13. Tracy, *Europe's Reformations,* 342, n. 66.

14. J. J. Woltjer, "Dutch Privileges, Real and Imaginary," in *Britain and the Netherlands,* vol. 5: *Some Political Mythologies (Papers Delivered to the Fifth Anglo-Dutch Conference),* ed. J. S. Bromley and E. H. Kossmann (The Hague: Martinus Nijhoff, 1975), 19–35.

15. Joost Kloek and Karin Tilmans, eds., *Burger. Een geschiedenis van het begrip burger in de Nederlanden* (Amsterdam: Amsterdam University Press, 2002); Maarten Prak, *Republikeinse veelheid, democratisch enkelvoud* (Nijmegen: SUN, 1999), especially 33–136.

16. Heinz Schilling, "Gab es im späten Mittelalter und zu Beginn der Neuzeit in Deutschland einen 'städtischen Republikanismus'? Zur politische Kultur des alteuropäischen Bürgertums," in *Republiken und der Republikanismus im Europa der Frühen Neuzeit,* ed. Helmut G. Koenigsberger (Munich: Oldenbourg, 1988), 101–43; in English: "Civic Republicanism in Late Medieval and Early Modern German Cities," in Heinz Schilling, *Religion, Political Culture and the Emergence of Early Modern Society: Essays in German and Dutch History* (Leiden: Brill, 1992) 3–59.

17. Mervyn James, "Ritual, Drama and Social Body in the Late Medieval English Town," *Past and Present* 98 (1983): 3–29.

18. Eberhard Isenmann, "Norms and values in the European city, 1300–1800," in *Resistance, Representation, Community (The Origins of the Early Modern State in Europe: 13th to 18th Centuries),* ed. Peter Blickle (Oxford: Clarendon, 1997) 185–215.

19. Henk van Nierop, *Het foute Amsterdam. Rede uitgesproken bij de aanvaarding van het ambt van hoogleraar in de Nieuwe Geschiedenis aan de Universiteit van Amsterdam op vrijdag 13 oktober 2000* (Amsterdam: Vossiuspers UvA, 2000), 16–17; Henk van Nierop, "Confessional Cleansing: Why Amsterdam Did Not Join the Revolt (1572–1578)," in *Power and the Cities,* ed. Wim Klooster and Wayne te Brake (Leiden: Brill, 2006), 85–102. On citizenship in Amsterdam, see Erika Kuijpers and Maarten Prak, "Burger, ingezetene, vreemdeling: burgerschap in Amsterdam in de 17e en 18e eeuw," in *Burger. Een geschiedenis van het begrip burger in de Nederlanden,* ed. Joost Kloek and Karin Tilmans (Amsterdam: Amsterdam University Press, 2002), 113–32.

20. George Huppert, *After the Black Death: A Social History of Early Modern Europe* (Bloomington and Indianapolis: Indiana University Press, 1986), 41–55.

21. The *schepenen* (aldermen) of 's-Hertogenbosch for example were active every other day during their term in office. Anton Schuttelaars, *Heren van de raad. Bestuurlijke elite van 's-Hertogenbosch in de stedelijke samenleving, 1500–1580* (Nijmegen: Nijmegen University Press, 1998), 126.

22. Marc Boone and Maarten Prak, "Rulers, Patricians and Burghers: The Great and Little Traditions of Urban Revolt in the Low Countries," in *A Miracle Mirrored: The Dutch Republic in European Perspective*, ed. Karel Davids and Jan Lucassen (Cambridge: Cambridge University Press, 1995), 99–134.

23. An example of how the central government, the town magistrates, and the urban people interacted is the unrest that broke out in Amsterdam in October 1541. James D. Tracy, "Habsburg Grain Policy and Amsterdam Politics: The Career of Sheriff Willem Dirkszoon Baerdes 1542–1566," *Sixteenth Century Journal* 14 (1983): 300.

24. *Corpus documentorum inquisitionis haereticae pravitatis Neerlandicae. Verzameling van stukken betreffende de pauselijke en bisschoppelijke inquisitie in de Nederlanden*, 5 vols., ed. Paul Fredericq (Ghent and The Hague: Vuylsteke; Martinus Nijhoff, 1889–1906), 4: 246.

25. Duke, *Reformation*, 35.

26. *Corpus documentorum inquisitionis*, 5: 32, 329–30.

27. Duke, *Reformation*, 36.

28. *Corpus documentorum inquisitionis*, 4: 239–40.

29. James D. Tracy, *Holland under Habsburg Rule, 1506–1566: The Formation of a Body Politic* (Berkeley and Los Angeles: University of California Press, 1990), chap. 6; James D. Tracy, "Heresy Law and Centralization under Mary of Hungary: Conflict between the Council of Holland and the Central Government over the Enforcement of the Placards," *Archiv für Reformationsgeschichte* 73 (1982): 284–308.

30. Tracy, *Holland*, 200–203.

31. Duke, *Reformation*, 125–51.

32. J. C. Boogman, "De overgang van Gouda, Dordrecht, Leiden en Delft in de zomer van het jaar 1572," *Tijdschrift voor Geschiedenis* 57 (1942): especially 88, 94; C. C. Hibben, *Gouda in Revolt. Particularism and Pacifism in the Revolt of the Netherlands* (Utrecht: Hes, 1983) 32–33; Jan van Herwaarden et al., *Geschiedenis van Dordrecht tot 1572* (Hilversum: Verloren, 1996) 359.

33. Boogman, "De overgang," 88, 89, 105; Ter Gouw, *Geschiedenis van Amsterdam*, 6: 385–86.

34. Ter Gouw, *Geschiedenis van Amsterdam*, 6: 359–67.

35. For the rebellions in Gouden, Dordrecht, Leiden, and Delft, see Boogman, "De overgang"; for Rotterdam, H. ten Boom, *De reformatie in Rotterdam 1530–1585* (Amsterdam: De Bataafsche Leeuw, 1987), 135–38; for Haarlem, Joke Spaans, *Haarlem na de Reformatie. Stedelijke cultuur en kerkelijk leven, 1577–1620* (The Hague: De Bataafsche Leeuw, 1989), 40–44; for the towns in North Holland, Henk van Nierop, *Het verraad van het Noorderkwartier. Oorlog, terreur en recht in de Nederlandse Opstand* (Amsterdam: Bert Bakker, 1999), 63–83.

36. On the role of the civic militias in the Revolt see Paul Knevel, *Burgers in het geweer. De schutterijen in Holland, 1550–1700* (Hilversum: Verloren, 1994), especially 82–91; J. C. Grayson, "The Civic Militia in the County of Holland, 1560–81: Politics

and Public Order in the Dutch Revolt," *Bijdragen en Mededelingen betreffende de Geschiedenis der Nederlanden* 95 (1980): 35–63.

37. Boogman, "De overgang," 93–99; Van Nierop, *Het verraad*, 72–75.

38. Van Nierop, *Het verraad*, 76–77.

39. Van Nierop, *Het foute Amsterdam*.

40. Louis Sicking, *Geuzen en glippers. Goed en fout tijdens het beleg van Leiden* (3 Oktoberlezing 2003, The Hague: SDU Uitgevers, 2003).

41. H. J. Wytema, "Alkmaar voor de keuze: 16 juli 1573," *Alkmaars Jaarboekje* 6 (1970): 96–100.

42. Quoted by Van Gelder, "De Nederlandse adel," 169.

43. James D. Tracy, "Émigré and Ecclesiastical Property as the Sheet-Anchor of Holland Finance," in *Reformation, Revolt and Civil War in France and the Netherlands 1555–1585*, ed. Philip Benedict et al. (Amsterdam: Royal Netherlands Academy of Arts and Sciences, 1999), 255–66.

44. H. G. Koenigsberger, "The Organization of Revolutionary Parties in France and the Netherlands during the Sixteenth Century," in *Estates and Revolutions: Essays in Early Modern European History* (Ithaca, NY, and London: Cornell University Press, 1971), 224–52.

45. J. J. Woltjer, "Political Moderates and Religious Moderates in the Revolt of the Netherlands," in *Reformation, Revolt and Civil War in France and the Netherlands 1555–1585*, ed. Philip Benedict et al., eds. (Amsterdam: Royal Netherlands Academy of Arts and Sciences, 1999), 185–200.

46. James D. Tracy, *Erasmus of the Low Countries* (Berkeley and Los Angeles: University of California Press, 1996), 19.

47. *Dagboek van Broeder Wouter Jacobsz (Gualtherus Jacobi Masius) Prior van Stein. Amsterdam 1572–1578 en Montfoort 1578-1579*, 2 vols, ed. I. H. van Eeghen (Groningen: J. B. Wolters, 1959–60) 1: 158–59.

48. E. H. Kossmann and A. F. Mellink, eds., *Texts concerning the Revolt of the Netherlands* (Cambridge: Cambridge University Press, 1974), 127.

49. Kossmann and Mellink, *Texts*, 170.

50. Spaans, *Haarlem*, 227–32.

51. Judith Pollmann, *Religious Choice in the Dutch Republic: The Reformation of Arnoldus Buchelius (1565–1641)* (Manchester and New York: Manchester University Press, 1999) 169–78; "Public Enemies, Private Friends: Arnoldus Buchelius's Experience of Religious Diversity in the Early Dutch Republic," in *The Public and Private in Dutch Culture of the Golden Age*, ed. Adele Seeff and Arthur Wheelock (Newark, NJ: University of Delaware Press, 2000), 181–90; Willem Frijhoff, "The Threshold of Toleration," in *Embodied Belief: Ten Essays on Religious Culture in Dutch History* (Hilversum: Verloren, 2002), 39–65.

52. Christine Kooi, "Paying Off the Sheriff: Strategies of Catholic Toleration in Golden Age Holland," in *Calvinism and Religious Toleration in the Dutch Golden Age*, ed. Ronnie Po-chia Hsia and Henk van Nierop (Cambridge: Cambridge University Press, 2002), 87–101; Benjamin J. Kaplan, "Fictions of Privacy: House Chapels and the Special Accommodation of Religious Dissent in Early Modern Europe," *American Historical Review* 107 (2002): 1031–64.

53. J. L. Price, *Holland and the Dutch Republic in the Seventeenth Century: The Politics of Particularism* (Oxford: Clarendon, 1994).

54. Jan de Vries and Ad van der Woude, *The First Modern Economy: Success, Failure, and Perseverance of the Dutch Economy, 1500–1815* (Cambridge: Cambridge University Press, 1997).

55. Knevel, *Burgers*, chap. 10.

56. Henk van Nierop, "Popular Participation in Politics in the Dutch Republic," in *Resistance, Representation, and Community*, ed. Peter Blickle (Oxford: Clarendon, 1997), 272–90.

57. Willem Frijhoff and Marijke Spies, *1650: Bevochten eendracht* (The Hague: SDU Uitgevers, 1999), 218–24.

5

Family and Community in the Spanish World

Carla Rahn Phillips

THE DISCONTINUITIES OF INDIVIDUAL AND COMMUNAL IDENTITY loom large in much scholarly work on the religious and political upheaval that marked sixteenth-century Europe. Continuities interest me more than discontinuities, however, especially the continuities that defined what can be called the Spanish world—the collection of territories in Europe and around the globe administered by the Spanish monarchy from the fifteenth through the early nineteenth century. The notion of a Spanish world is not simply an imaginary umbrella sheltering the disparate peoples involved. Elements of unity and cohesion justify thinking of it as a reality, rather than simply as a verbal construct. At a conference in February of 2003 I surveyed elements of that cohesion, including dynastic rule, bureaucracy, navigation and trade, religion, law, local governance, and loyalty and reciprocity in human relationships. All of these elements help to explain how the Spanish Empire in the Americas held together for more than three centuries.[1] In this chapter, I will focus on two elements that seem to me fundamental to all the others: notions of family (including kinship) and community.

Family and community are often neglected by scholars interested in modern political topics. Benedict Anderson argues that the "imagined communities" we know as modern nations began to be conceptualized in the late eighteenth century and developed thereafter as legally defined agglomerations of myriad individuals with a central government. In earlier times, according to Anderson, dynastic and religious identity provided the foundation for a sense of community and loyalty, but those foundations had to crumble before the "imagined communities" that developed into modern nations could rise in their place.

Anderson's argument leaves the impression that pre-eighteenth-century concepts of community and nation and loyalty are somehow inferior or less worthy of attention than their modern counterparts. That is not Anderson's fault. It is inherent in the often unexamined assumptions that change necessarily means progress, and that individual identities are more modern than collective identities. A more serious failing from my point of view is that Anderson barely mentions familial or local identities as a basis for community and national identities and loyalties in the early modern period. I would argue instead that only by understanding the tight network created by family and local ties can we understand the strength and tenacity of the dynastic and religious identity that Anderson discusses. In many parts of Europe, political and doctrinal upheavals undercut dynasty and religion as unifying forces. In Spain and its empire, by contrast, loyalty to the ruling dynasty and the Roman Catholic Church served as a defining characteristic of the population through the early modern period. That loyalty rested on the network of local ties created by family and community identity.

A distinguished roster of scholars has documented the importance of family and community in early modern Europe.[2] As interest in family history burgeoned in the 1980s, pioneers such as Peter Laslett in historical demography, Tamara Hareven in social history, and Andreas Plakhans in anthropology helped to shape the field.[3] In a groundbreaking book, Plakans argued for the need to flesh out the bare bones of genealogical relationships in the historical record so as to better understand the social roles of kinship.

Plakhans argued that we can make reasonable assumptions about the roles played by fathers and sons, mothers and daughters, and other kin to fill in the lives of the real individuals we encounter only for a moment in the records. As a basis for his argument, he discussed four general principles regarding the social role of kinship. First, kinship roles "achieve meaning only in the context of reciprocity." Second, "kinship roles are enacted through time. That is, a relationship which is identifiable, at a moment in past time . . . can be assumed to have lasted throughout the lifetime of these individuals." Third, "an individual can possess many kinship roles simultaneously—and enact them simultaneously and separately." And fourth, for the purposes of family history, individuals are better understood through their roles in kinship networks than as isolated beings with a unique blend of character traits.[4]

With Plakhans's principles in mind, once we know the genealogical relationships linking a group of individuals together, we can reasonably assume some of the social roles they played over the course of their lifetimes, whether or not we have documentary proof of those roles. None of this obviates the need to interrogate each document carefully and to ascertain—if possible—when, where, why, and by whom it was written, with due attention to the vocabulary used to describe kinship links. Nor do Plakhans's general principles permit us to overrule contradictory evidence when we find it in the historical record. Instead, his notions provide us with a logical framework for thinking about the social roles of kinship in Europe, particularly when we have sparse and limited documentary evidence at hand—rather like imagining a full head of hair when all we have in sight are a few scattered tufts and a bad comb-over.

The potential for documentary gaps increases when we broaden our sphere of inquiry to study Europeans and their communities outside Europe. One of the great benefits of studying Spain and its empire is that there is a sufficient documentary base to study family and community throughout the Spanish world.[5] In the early modern centuries, the bureaucracy of the Habsburg monarchy in Spain and its empire generated an enormous flow of documents, recording information about virtually every aspect of public and private life. In the eighteenth century, the Bourbon dynasty ascended the Spanish throne and reorganized the royal bureaucracy, but the creation of paperwork continued unabated.

Spain comprised about 8.5 million people at the end of the sixteenth century, and nearly 11 million at the end of the eighteenth century. During the latter period, the Spanish Empire consisted of more than 15 million people, as a conservative estimate. The Spanish government kept track of their numbers, the taxes they paid, their religious orthodoxy, and their military service, among other characteristics. At the local level, municipal, religious, occupational, and social institutions recorded the mundane activities of daily life, capturing with ink and paper individuals who might otherwise have escaped the historical record altogether.[6] And private citizens wrote or dictated letters in an effort to stay connected to family, friends, and associates near and far. Spanish scribes, bureaucrats, and private citizens elsewhere in Europe and overseas created the same types of documents, in virtually identical form wherever they were written.[7] Vast archives in Spain and throughout the Spanish Empire were organized to house state papers, and countless municipal, episcopal, institutional, occupational, and private archives and libraries also served as depositories for the documentary legacy of lives recorded.

Virtually every document, whatever its purpose, includes information that can be used to study family and kinship roles, whether or not the document was created with that purpose in mind. In recent decades, historians of Spain and Spanish America have mined the archives to ask new questions about family, kinship, and community in the Spanish world.[8] What defined those notions in Spain during the early modern period? How did Spaniards act out their social roles of kinship and community membership? And how—if at all—did Spanish norms of family, kinship, and community change when Spaniards left home for various outposts around the globe? A range of recent scholarship provides solid evidence about these questions and helps us to understand the cohesiveness of the Spanish world in the early modern centuries.

Marriage between a man and a woman formed the hub of family and social relations in Spain as in other parts of Europe, so it is not surprising that scholars have focused on marriage as a key to understanding society as a whole.[9] In the early modern centuries, the choice of a marriage partner depended on the appropriateness of the match as well as on the ties of real or potential affection between the contracting parties. Appropriateness could be defined in a variety of ways, however. Members of ruling elites typically looked for marriage partners at the same social level or higher. Farther down the social scale, the impulses were similar. Bureaucrats and other professionals typically sought marriages that could enhance professional advancement. Merchants and artisans married with an eye toward consolidating their family businesses, and landowners at all levels of society often married to gain more land or to connect disparate family properties.[10]

The Roman Catholic Church prohibited marriage between individuals who were closely related by blood, although dispensations could be granted by the ecclesiastical authorities for marriages within the prohibited degrees of kinship.[11] Beyond the moral dimension, modern genetics teaches us that such strictures would avoid the transmission of recessive genes carrying undesirable physical or mental traits. Yet marriages to relatives could consolidate family properties and ensure the continuity and strength of a lineage. The Habsburg dynasty repeatedly arranged marriages between close relatives in Spain and central Europe to maintain the strength and solidarity of the dynasty as a whole. The strategy worked well for nearly two centuries, until recessive genetic traits finished off the Spanish Habsburgs. At all social levels, marriages between close relatives also aimed to enhance the strength of the family.

On the other hand, families and communities in early modern Spain seem to have been aware of the benefits of variety in marriage partners. If marriages between close relatives consolidated family property, they also restricted the possibilities for expanding a kinship network. In other words, there were logical reasons for the heads of families to seek a balance between marriages inside and outside the kinship network. Similar impulses may have driven community norms as well. In rural Catalonia, for example, marriages between third cousins, as well as multiple marriages between the same families, were discouraged by villagers, even though such marriages were permitted by the church. Community norms had the effect of pushing families to look outside their villages for marriage partners, bringing in new blood, literally and figuratively, and linking the village to the outside world.[12] We know that families in villages and small towns elsewhere also sought outside marriages by choice as well as necessity.

Overall, marriage can be understood as a business contract with sentimental overtones.[13] The best marriages from the point of view of families and their communities combined economic and affective ties in a harmonious blend, because that was the best way to ensure that the marriage would fulfill its assigned roles in the family and the community. Spanish ecclesiastical authorities took quite seriously the stricture that a valid marriage required the free will of both parties, however, regardless of family strategies. Clergymen in Spain and Spanish America frequently intervened when parents tried to prevent their child from contracting what they considered an inappropriate marriage, or, conversely, tried to force an unwilling child into a socially or financially desirable marriage. The principle of free will overruled the principle of parental authority, when the validity of the sacrament of marriage was at stake.[14]

Once the marriage bond had been forged, Roman Catholic ideals prescribed that it could be broken only by death. Given Spain's religious orthodoxy, many scholars assume that Spaniards adhered closely to religious ideals regarding marriage. In practice, however, Spaniards who found themselves in an unhappy union often found ways to escape, with or without ecclesiastical permission. During the early modern centuries, Spain fought nearly continuous wars in defense of the Habsburg dynasty and the Catholic religion, so the crown had a chronic need for soldiers and sailors. Military service provided one escape route for men who wanted to distance themselves from unhappy marriages, just as it provided income for poor married men who were devoted to their wives. The same can be said of migratory occupations such as muleteering, seasonal agricultural work, itinerant peddling, herding, and a number of other occupations that separated men from their wives for at least part of the year.

Women had fewer occupational outlets than men for escaping unhappy marriages, but both men and women could petition the ecclesiastical authorities for a legal separation or divorce (*separación de matrimonio*).[15] The grounds varied, and it is not always clear how cases were decided. Under canon law, refined at the Council of Trent in the late sixteenth century, heresy, abandonment, or adultery alone were not valid grounds for separation or divorce; there had to be some other complicating factor or factors that would make the marriage invalid in the eyes of the church—for example, if one of the parties had been forced into the marriage.

Scholars find petitions for the dissolution of marriages in a variety of archives—for example, among diocesan or judicial papers and in notarial records, because notaries drew up the legal documents. Women filed the majority of petitions found to date, most often claiming mistreatment (*maltratos*), the impossibility of maintaining the marriage, or adultery by their husbands (often linked to mistreatment). Most of the petitions for separation or divorce filed by men claimed adultery by their wives and the resulting mistreatment and damage to their honor and good name. The economic stakes were high. If a marriage was dissolved, under Spanish law the woman regained her dowry, plus any interest accrued to it during the course of the marriage.

Faced with the expense and bother of using legal action to end an unhappy marriage, many Spaniards simply behaved as if their marriage vows no longer bound them. They took lovers while continuing to live with their spouses, sometimes openly cohabiting with them. If they continued to live in the same community, such behavior would bring the disapproval of their neighbors, as well as sanctions from church authorities, including excommunication. To avoid such complications, some unhappily married Spaniards abandoned their hometowns and went to live somewhere else, where they might take up residence with new partners, or even contract new marriages, presumably hoping that no one ever found out they were already married. In fact, instances of bigamy came to official notice with some frequency. Because bigamy was an offense against the sacrament of marriage, the officials who most often dealt with it were attached to the Spanish Inquisition. In a monumental study of 44,000 inquisitorial cases in Spain from 1540 to 1700, Jaime Contreras and Gustav Henningsen found 2,645 cases of bigamy, or about 6 percent of the cases overall.[16]

We should not assume that all of the instances of bigamy were intentional. Many bigamists married a second time in the sincere belief that their spouses had died. Emigration to America made such honest mistakes more likely. If a man left his wife behind in Spain and traveled to the Indies, she might reasonably assume that he had died if he did not return after a period of years; she might even hear indirect reports of his death. At that point, she might petition to have her marriage declared at an end and then remarry, only to learn later that her first husband was still alive. By the same token, a man who emigrated might hear that his wife in Spain had died. He might then marry in America, only to find that the reports of his first wife's death had been mistaken—or perhaps he had fabricated them. Not surprisingly, individuals accused of bigamy often claimed "truthful ignorance" in order to escape the charges, leaving the ecclesiastical authorities to sort things out.[17] As in many other aspects of Spaniards' lives, there was much more flexibility than we might assume regarding the application of rules. Spaniards who migrated overseas to America or Asia carried with them legal and customary norms governing marriage and family relations, but it is fair to say that those norms underwent a sea change in the process.

Although many early Spanish migrants to America were young unmarried males (including clergymen), whole families and marriageable women were always part of the migratory stream. The government encouraged royal officials to take their families with them, not only on moral grounds but also to prevent them from identifying too closely with the societies they were supposed to govern. Women accounted for nearly 30 percent of Spanish migrants to America in the late sixteenth century, and about 60 percent of those women were unmarried. Most of the latter quickly found husbands among the Spanish and Creole population already there.[18]

There were never enough Spanish women to fully supply the marriage market in the Americas, however. From the earliest days of the empire, Spanish men married or established informal sexual unions with local women. At the highest political level, the leading Spanish *conquistadores* (conquerors) paired with Aztec and Inca royalty, both formally and informally, in effect creating a merger between the preconquest and postconquest elites. It is fair to say that the hoped-for outcome of these marriages, and those farther down the social scale, was very similar to expectations for marriages in Spain: to enhance the economic, political, and social status of the contracting parties.[19] A Spaniard who married a local Indian woman in New Spain (Mexico), for example, would acquire access to his wife's property or to her family's connections in manufacturing, trade, or other occupations. The children of such a marriage, usually designated as *mestizos* (literally, "mixed"), had access to positions in the emerging colonial society that were more difficult for their Indian counterparts to obtain. In Perú, the male children of similar mixed marriages often enjoyed tax benefits because of their part-Spanish heritage.[20] The female children, especially if they were carefully raised and educated in convent schools, became valuable assets in the marriage markets of colonial society.

The preconquest norms of sexual behavior in the Americas seem to have been rather different from those in Spain, especially regarding temporary liaisons and multiple marriages. Medieval Christian warriors had sometimes adopted the Muslim custom of polygamy to seal political alliances during the Spanish reconquest of the peninsula, but the Catholic Church had always condemned the custom. In the Americas prior to contact with Europeans, temporary sexual liaisons also served as a form of diplomatic courtesy or hospitality, and many Spanish men easily adapted to such local customs.[21] Moreover, although sexual promiscuity was common enough in Spanish society, it is probably fair to say that it was not considered acceptable behavior to the extent that it was in the Americas, both before and after the European invasion.

The great importance of emulation in Spanish society, in which the middle and lower classes adopted the manners and values of the elite along with their fashions and amusements, had unexpected echoes in Spanish America. Foreign travelers commented upon what, to them, was unseemly behavior by the "lower orders" in Spanish America. To cite just one example, the English

Dominican Thomas Gage, who later defected to the Puritans in England, wrote disapprovingly of the "attire of this baser sort of people of black-amoors and mulattoes (which are of a mixed nature, of Spaniards and black-amoors)" in Mexico City—attire that included silver and gold lace and fancy imported cloth adorned with pearls and gems.[22] By adopting the trappings of wealth and status, as well as flouting moral strictures against vulgar ostentation, diverse individuals in Spanish America behaved as if they enjoyed a higher status than their birth accorded them, and also redefined the standards of proper elite behavior.

Moreover, just as domestic servants and nursemaids in Spain transmitted a certain amount of popular culture to their well-born charges, household servants in Spanish America did the same. In Spain, the close relationship between nursemaids and children bridged the gap between disparate levels of society; in the Americas it also bridged the gap between different cultural traditions.[23] This may have contributed to more relaxed standards for public sexual behavior at all social levels in Spanish America than in Spain. During the colonial period, foreign travelers routinely commented upon the lascivious behavior of well-born Spanish and Creole residents of Mexico City, Lima, and elsewhere—both male and female.[24]

At the highest levels of both Spanish and Spanish colonial society, however, traditional Mediterranean notions of honor and shame continued in force, and may even have grown stronger over time, perhaps to separate the most distinguished families from the rest of society. Honor belonged only to families that maintained an unblemished record of ecclesiastically sanctioned marriages and legitimate births, plus at least the appearance of upright moral behavior. Reality often fell short of appearances, but a family's honor could be protected from shame—or restored—by keeping private indiscretions away from public view, or by "doing the right thing" in the end—such as marrying the mother of one's illegitimate child.

Another possibility short of marriage allowed a young woman who had been seduced to seek legal redress. If she could prove that her lover had seduced her with promises of marriage (*estupro por palabras de futuro*), the authorities could symbolically restore her lost honor and assess monetary damages for the offense. The young woman could then contract an honorable marriage (with the dowry supplied by her ex-lover), and the young man was free to marry someone else, all with the blessings of the ecclesiastical authorities. Such cases were fairly common in both Spain and Spanish America, which contradicts many of our assumptions about the power of religious orthodoxy and moral precepts in the Spanish world.[25]

In contrast to the continued importance of marriage and legitimacy at the upper levels of society, informal unions and illegitimacy were common at lower levels in Spanish America and some parts of Spain, much to the dismay of the Catholic clergy.[26] Presumably, the partners involved saw no need to be married because it brought them no particular economic benefits, their residential communities did not disapprove of such unions, and religious precepts about sexual behavior were not strong enough to overrule local customs.

If we broaden the focus from marriage and family outward, we can see Plakhans's "social roles of kinship" in action, both in Spain and in Spanish America. The first and most important kinship link was that between parents and children. Uncles and aunts formed the next line of protection and defense for the younger generation, and god parentage (*compadrazgo*) extended the ranks of protectors more broadly into the kinship network and beyond. Those relationships remained in force even when family members emigrated overseas and closely related individuals became separated by vast oceans. I recently examined the applications of two young noblemen and brothers to enter one of Spain's prestigious military orders in the late seventeenth century. Their uncle sponsored their application and wrote to them affectionately over the course of several years as he assembled the necessary paperwork—a complicated task, as he lived in Spain and his nephews lived in Mexico City.[27]

There were several reciprocal links involved in that case. The young men were children of the senior member of the family; their sponsor was their father's younger brother. In fulfilling his avuncular duties, he also earned his older brother's gratitude; he might even have been paying back an earlier favor. Ironically, because of their father's seniority in the family, the young men outranked their uncle in the Spanish noble hierarchy. They stood higher still after they entered the Order of Santiago, because their uncle belonged to the less prestigious Order of Alcántara. For the purpose of sponsorship, their uncle acted as their patron; as their social inferior, however, he might have hoped to benefit as a client from their higher status sometime in the future. Every act of reciprocity would reinforce the ties of kinship and affection that bound them all together.

Marriage alliances reinforced the primary links of kinship when they led to similar acts of reciprocity. In Spain, as in many other parts of Europe, marriage alliances served as a standard tactic for family advancement, a pattern borne out by countless family histories. The pattern applied at all levels of society, and among every social group defined by lineage, occupation, ethnic identity, or religious affinity in early modern times.[28] When Spaniards traveled abroad, either elsewhere in Europe or to the Americas, kinship networks served the same function, helping individuals to adapt and flourish in their new environment. Although early emigration streams came in large part from the western and southern parts of Castile, eventually every province in Spain played a role in colonizing the Americas.[29] Correspondence back and forth across the Atlantic helped to maintain the migrants' ties to their kinship network back home.

When they died, emigrants habitually left bequests to relatives and to charitable and religious foundations in Spain. A favored few had returned to their hometowns wealthy, providing a living example of the prosperity that lay across the ocean.[30] Others had made lives for themselves of no particular distinction in Spanish America and remained there for the rest of their lives. Still others had died young, or poor, or both, and had very little to bequeath.[31] Yet even poor sailors who died on board ship or in the Indies would leave their few articles of clothing and personal effects—or the proceeds from their sale—to relatives back home. In other words, as their last official acts on earth, individuals in the Spanish world continued to reinforce the ties of kinship, wherever they happened to live and die. Scholars continue to study the activities of Spaniards and their extended families at home and abroad, and their findings provide overwhelming evidence for the strength and resiliency of kinship ties, even when they were stretched for thousands of miles.

Just as marriage and family provided the foundation for kinship networks, affinity groups of various sorts provided other foundations for community in the Spanish world. In Spain, the place of residence provided one important focus for individual and group identity, and most often that place of residence was a municipality of some sort. Town life and town citizenship are perhaps the most common denominators among Spaniards, as there is almost no land in Castile that does not fall under the jurisdiction of a municipality of some sort.[32] Ancient notions of urban life as the source of culture and the rule of law took root in Spain along with the towns founded by Phoenicians, Greeks, Carthaginians, and Romans. By extension, the separation between the relatively dense population within the towns and the unpopulated hinterland also marked the separation between the safety of communal life and the dangers of the open countryside. Christian ideals of spiritual brotherhood and religious establishments based in towns reinforced the idea that an orderly town, based on Christian principles, provided an orderly life for its citizens and inspired them to good behavior.

During the centuries of medieval frontier warfare between Christians and Muslims in Spain, new towns were founded to protect the citizenry and their Christian settlements along the frontier. The dichotomies of town versus countryside, communal life versus isolation, safety versus danger, and Christianity versus Islam persisted long after the final conquest of Muslim Spain in 1492, strengthening the importance of towns in Spanish life.[33]

Law and custom defined three sorts of town inhabitants: official citizens (*vecinos*), resident sojourners (*residentes*), and outsiders (*forasteros*). Individuals passing through a town for one reason or another might appear in documents as being there (*estantes*), but they were invisible for official purposes. Citizens alone enjoyed the full range of benefits and responsibilities. The norms of citizenship were very similar in large cities and tiny villages alike, so Spaniards as a whole grew up with the experience of living in structured municipalities.[34] In a village or small town, adult male householders all took turns holding the various municipal offices; in larger towns they elected municipal officials and had the right to hold office. In addition, they shared in communal benefits such as the right to graze livestock on the municipality's common land or to collect a share from the sale of communal assets such as timber. The citizens were collectively responsible for paying taxes assessed on the town and for meeting the town's quotas in military levies as well. Resident sojourners typically paid certain taxes but enjoyed no political or financial benefits. Outsiders were just that—peripheral to the life of the commune.

Throughout the year, a regular round of civic festivals brought the citizens together, and additional gatherings might be arranged as well—for example, to celebrate the birth of a royal heir or to make a religious procession to pray for rain during a drought. Many civic occasions had a religious dimension as well, because the rituals and ceremonies of the Roman Catholic Church punctuated and defined the daily lives of Spaniards, and religious and civic life were virtually inseparable. The countless disputes between ecclesiastical and municipal officials, often occasioned by community gatherings, prove that closeness. Whenever the citizens gathered together, they reenacted their collective identity, defined by their attachment to the municipality and its communal life.

In the unknown vastness of the Americas, towns continued to signify order, safety, and collective identity in a dangerous world, but the definitions of all of those concepts had to be adapted to the new reality. In the Americas, the outside dangers included uncontrolled Indians, runaway slaves, and others who did not live in an urban setting. Spanish colonial authorities, like their counterparts at home, believed that urban structure would naturally inspire citizens to live orderly, peaceable, and hardworking lives. That was the driving idea behind settling Indians into their own towns, whether or not a particular Indian group had a tradition of settled urban life. In Indian towns the population was more or less homogeneous, though that did not mean the residents adopted Spanish norms of town life more easily; the reverse was probably closer to reality. Nonetheless, officials believed that the Indian populations would become civilized, prosperous, happy Christians and loyal subjects of the crown if they could be shaped by the structures of orderly urban life under their own leaders.

In non-Indian municipalities in America, the community was anything but homogeneous. Visitors to large colonial cities such as Havana, Mexico City,

Cartagena de Indias, and Lima were impressed by the variety of people they saw, including Spaniards, Creoles, others of European ancestry, Indians, Africans, and a growing population of mixed ancestry. It is fair to say, however, that the administrative, social, and cultural norms of urban life were closer to Spanish models than to any other. When they migrated, Spaniards carried with them a sense of how to shape and run a town.

Spaniards who settled elsewhere in Europe often maintained a sense of their separateness in the first several generations after their arrival, but eventually they assimilated into the local population—for example, in Bruges, Rouen, or Rome.[35] In America, where Spaniards formed themselves into new municipalities before they did almost anything else, they replicated the structures and rituals that defined town life in Spain rather than adjusting to local customs. In so doing, they consciously reproduced not only the familiar forms and rituals of a municipality but also the customs that town life implied. Lavish celebrations for the birth of a royal heir might take place in Madrid, Seville, Mexico City, and Lima with only minor variations. Over time, the customs and rituals of Spaniards abroad inevitably incorporated elements of local culture as well, while preserving the importance of Spanish identity that those customs and rituals represented.

Some of the key issues in shaping Spanish colonial society in the Americas involved the definitions of citizenship and nativeness (*naturaleza*). In an important new study, Tamar Herzog discusses these issues on both sides of the Atlantic.[36] According to her research, although municipal citizenship was carefully regulated during the early modern period in Castile, towns readily welcomed outsiders and even foreigners as citizens, as long as they established residence and displayed the will to become part of the community and share in its communal life. Not everyone could become an official citizen, however; only Catholic male householders over the age of twenty-five qualified, and women held citizenship through their male relatives.

Individuals had to obtain permission from the Spanish crown to travel to America, which is how the authorities hoped to control religious orthodoxy and social stability in the colonies. Once there, however, they might establish residence virtually anywhere that accepted them as citizens. In Spanish America, as in frontier Spain during the Middle Ages, many towns were founded on paper, traced out, and populated with citizens before any physical town existed. Early on there were distinctions among citizens, sojourners, and outsiders, as there were in Spain. Over time, however, municipal citizenship in Spanish America came to be almost identical to residence, so that all the residents of a town, however temporary their sojourn, were considered citizens, paying taxes and enjoying the benefits of citizenship.

Absent the legal distinctions between citizens and noncitizens, other distinctions gained importance. Sixteenth-century decrees that restricted public office holding, ecclesiastical benefices, and direct relations with Spanish America to "natives of the kingdom of Spain" gave rise to debates about what constituted the status of nativeness. Although one might assume that nativeness could be acquired only by birth, it could also be acquired by voluntary integration, which generally meant becoming a resident sojourner or citizen in a Spanish municipality. Thus, in practice local communities had control over certifying foreigners as integrated natives of Spain.

In Spanish America local definitions of citizenship had to deal with a more diverse body of potential citizens, and the definitions could vary as well. In seventeenth-century Caracas, for example, the body of citizens became much more exclusive over time. Indians and *mestizos* were considered ineligible for citizenship because they were supposed to reside in their own towns; Africans might be ineligible because they had been forced to immigrate; mulattoes and other individuals of mixed ancestry were ineligible because they were not considered to behave or to live like proper citizens should. In Buenos Aires the legacy of border wars with the Portuguese led to citizenship being restricted to "natives of the kingdom of Spain" alone, though with all the complexity that nativeness in Spain invoked.[37] By contrast, many Spanish American municipalities welcomed virtually anyone who had the money to purchase the privilege of permanent residence, as long as they were willing to share in the communal life of the town.[38]

In time, and especially during the early eighteenth century, Spanish communities became more restrictive in granting citizenship, frequently demanding continuous residence, regardless of an individual's claims of loyalty to the municipality. In other words, citizenship became more a matter of legal requirements than of loyalty and emotional attachment to the commune. As the century wore on, the Bourbon monarchy asserted its right to grant nativeness to foreigners, rather than continuing to leave such questions to local authorities. Instead of requiring would-be citizens to demonstrate their good faith by settling into a municipality before gaining legal status, the crown allowed them to establish the privileges of nativeness simply by declaring their intention to settle. Many Spanish municipalities resented having to accept as citizens foreigners who showed up with letters of naturalization but no other proof of their good faith and trustworthiness. Nonetheless, if the newcomers settled down and behaved like good citizens, they were eventually accepted as such in fact as well as in law. Overall, although the norms for acceptance as citizens in Spain and Spanish American municipalities varied and changed over time, the duties and expectations of communal citizenship remained remarkably stable.

Municipalities thus continued to be an important source of social identity and—arguably—social stability on both sides of the Atlantic.

Emigrants from the same region in Spain often tended to cluster together in Spanish American towns, which made it easier for their traditional networks to continue functioning in the new environment. In an important recent study, Ida Altman traced emigrants from Brihuega, a small town in central Spain, who settled in the Mexican town of Puebla, which grew to be the second most important municipality in New Spain.[39] Even as Puebla grew far beyond its colonial beginnings, residents linked to Brihuega continued as a recognizable affinity group in the city, preserving their identity through marriage alliances, business partnerships, and place of residence, among other means. They also used their communal ties to help one another in countless demonstrations of reciprocity.

Brihuega was small enough so that virtually every family rotated in and out of power on the municipal council. In Puebla, by contrast, the Brihuega group did not have much influence on local politics, in which descendants of *conquistadores* and others who held grants of Indian labor services also held political power. The distinction between nobles and common people, crucial in Spanish society, seems to have had less importance in America, leaving an opening for the emergence of an elite based largely on wealth. A few families in the Brihuega group managed to penetrate the political elite in Puebla, but overall they seem to have been less concerned with power than with preserving their communal identity.

In addition to their familial and communal identity, residents at all levels of Spanish society joined voluntary affinity groups, often based in the parish where they lived. In each parish, religious confraternities devoted to a particular saint or to a particular representation of the Virgin Mary or Jesus Christ each had special days of prayer and celebration during the year, bringing their members together. Confraternity members would also participate as a group in civic and religious activities that involved the municipality as a whole. Such ritual activities reinforced the links among members of a given confraternity and bound them collectively to the broader community, and ultimately to the crown.

Rivalries among the various confraternities in a given parish, and among the various parishes in a town, had the potential to divide the citizenry. Nonetheless, these rivalries played themselves out within carefully defined norms of behavior and were subordinated to collective goals. I would argue that this tended to tame their divisive potential and to provide an intermediate focus of loyalty between the family and the commune. Something similar seems to have occurred with regard to differences in wealth and status. Just as kinship networks included a range of "haves" and "have-nots," so did most

Spanish parishes. Confraternities defined by the wealth and status of their members were nonetheless part of the same parish and could be expected to work together and to help one another. Moreover, some Spanish confraternities cut across lines of wealth and status, so that they functioned much like an extended kinship network, binding together a diversity of brothers and sisters (*cofrades*).[40] To a certain extent, therefore, confraternities, like kinship networks, could foster patron-client relationships and ameliorate social tensions and rivalries.

When Spaniards crossed the ocean to America, they often established branches of the same confraternities that they belonged to in Spain. It was not uncommon for parish confraternities in Spain to list hundreds of members living in America, many of whom had been away for years, if not decades. This suggests that the members retained their sense of common identity with the confraternity despite their separation in distance and time.[41]

Affinity groups based on occupation—craft guilds or merchant consulates, for example—functioned much like confraternities, both in Spain and abroad. Typically, guilds had their own patron saints and sponsors, and the members reinforced their collective identity with a round of ritual observances and acts of mutual assistance. One well-known function of craft guilds involved providing aid to their members in case of illness, injury, and death, as well as group participation in the funerals of departed members of the guild.

If family, citizenship, and voluntary associations shaped collective identities, they did not necessarily thwart personal ambition. A desire to move up the social ladder in status and wealth marked society in both Spain and Spanish America. Advantageous marriage, military service, or a career in the church provided avenues for upward mobility in both venues. In addition, we know of individuals in Madrid, Seville, and other large cities who simply pretended to a higher social status, hoping that no one from their hometowns exposed their real origins. The likelihood of turning pretense into reality became easier the farther one traveled. Countless tales of immigrants claiming a higher status in America than they had enjoyed in Spain suggest that individual identities were highly malleable once their owners traveled overseas. Such behavior seems to have been typical of frontier societies in many periods. Late medieval Spain and colonial Spanish America were both frontier societies in which new avenues for advancement could penetrate traditional social boundaries.

Overall, the individual and collective identities shaped by family, kinship, geographical origins, and group affiliations provided social cohesion for communities as well as support for individual ambition. I would argue that the proven value of traditional forms of family and community, and the ability of individuals at all levels of society to manipulate those forms to their advantage, helped to stabilize society over the vast territories that comprised the Spanish world. The various intermediate affinity groups did not weaken loyalty to the monarchy but rather strengthened it, given that the monarch served as the ultimate source of patronage and sponsorship for society as a whole.

Notes

1. Carla Rahn Phillips, "The Organization of Oceanic Empires: The Iberian World in the Habsburg Period and a Bit Beyond" (plenary address, Seascapes, Littoral Cultures, and Trans-Oceanic Exchanges, conference organized by the American Historical Association and other scholarly organizations, Washington, DC, February 2003). A selection of revised papers will be published by the University of Hawai`i Press in 2006.

2. Useful syntheses include Jean-Louis Flandrin, *Families in Former Times: Kinship, Household and Sexuality*, trans. Richard Southern (Cambridge: Cambridge University Press, 1979); James Casey, *The History of the Family* (Oxford and New York: Oxford University Press, 1989); Beatrice Gottlieb, *The Family in the Western World from the Black Death to the Industrial Age* (Oxford and New York: Oxford University Press, 1993); Michael Anderson, *Approaches to the History of the Western Family 1500–1914* (Cambridge and New York: Cambridge University Press, 1995); *Family Life in Early Modern Times, 1500–1789. The History of the European Family*, ed. David I. Kertzer and Marzio Barbagli (New Haven, CT: Yale University Press, 2001); and *Sixteenth Century Journal* 34, no. 2 (Summer 2003), a special issue devoted to "Marriage in Early Modern Europe."

3. Tamara Hareven and Andrejs Plakans, eds., *Family History at the Crossroads: A Journal of Family History Reader* (Princeton, NJ: Princeton University Press, 1987), in particular Peter Laslett, "The Character of Familial History, Its Limitations and the Conditions for Its Proper Pursuit," 264–84.

4. Andrejs Plakans, *Kinship in the Past: An Anthropology of European Family Life, 1500–1900* (Oxford and New York: Basil Blackwell, 1984), 88–91.

5. For a discussion of sources for Spanish family history, see Pablo Rodríguez and Annie Molinié-Bertrand, eds., *A través del tiempo. Diccionario de fuentes para la historia de la familia* (Murcia: Colección Mestizo-Universidad de Murcia, 2000).

6. The Spanish bureaucracy plays a central role in Juan Luis Castellano, Jean Pierre Dedieu, and María Victoria López-Cordón, eds., *La pluma, la mitra, y la espada: Estudios de historia institucional en la Edad Moderna* (Madrid: Marcial Pons, Ediciones de Historia, S.A., 2000).

7. For personal correspondence, see James Lockhart and Enrique Otte, eds., *Letters and People of the Spanish Indies* (Cambridge: Cambridge University Press, 1976); and Réné Salinas Meza and Igor Goicovic Donoso, "Cartas privadas," in *A través del tiempo. Diccionario de fuentes para la historia de la familia*, ed. Pablo Rodríguez and Annie Molinié-Bertrand (Murcia: Colección Mestizo-Universidad de Murcia, 2000), 53–56.

8. David I. Kertzer and Caroline Brettell. "Advances in Italian and Iberian Family History," in *Family History at the Crossroads: A Journal of Family History Reader*, ed. Tamara Hareven and Andrejs Plakans (Princeton, NJ: Princeton University Press, 1987), 87–120.

9. Francisco Chacón Jiménez is a key figure in studies about the economic and social context of marriage in Spain. Examples of his work include Francisco Chacón Jiménez, ed., *Historia social de la familia en España* (Alicante: Universidad de Alicante, 1990); Francisco Chacón Jiménez, J. Hernández Franco, and A. Peñafiel Ramón, eds., *Familia, grupos sociales y mujer en España (Siglos XV–XIX)* (Murcia: Universidad de Murcia, 1991); and Francisco Chacón Jiménez and Juan Hernández Franco, eds., *Poder, familia, y consanguinidad en la España del Antiguo Régimen* (Barcelona: Anthropos, 1992).

10. Antonio Pérez Ortiz, "Mayorazgo," in *A través del tiempo. Diccionario de fuentes para la historia de la familia*, ed. Pablo Rodríguez and Annie Molinié-Bertrand (Murcia: Colección Mestizo-Universidad de Murcia, 2000); Fernando Mikelarena Peña, "Modelos de matrimonio y regímenes de herencia en Navarra a finales del siglo XVIII," *Príncipe de Viana* 53, no. añejo 16 (1992): 19–33; M. Dolors Comas d'Argemir, "Matrimonio, patrimonio, y descendencia. Algunas hipótesis referidas a la Península Ibérica," in *Poder, familia, y consanguinidad en la España del Antiguo Régimen*, ed. Francisco Chacón Jiménez and Juan Hernández Franco (Barcelona: Anthropos, 1992), 157–76; Francisco García González, ed., *Tierra y familia en la España meridional, siglos XIII–XIX* (Murcia: Universidad de Murcia, 1998).

11. Angel Rodríguez Sánchez, "El poder y la familia: Formas de control y de consanguinidad en la Extremadura de los tiempos modernos," in *Poder, familia, y consanguinidad en la España del Antiguo Régimen*, ed Francisco Chacón Jiménez and Juan Hernández Franco (Barcelona: Anthropos, 1992), 15–34; Annie Molinié-Bertrand, "Dispensas de matrimonio," in *A través del tiempo. Diccionario de fuentes para la historia de la familia*, ed. Pablo Rodríguez and Annie Molinié-Bertrand (Murcia: Colección Mestizo-Universidad de Murcia, 2000), 77–78.

12. Joan Bestard Camps, "La estrechez del lugar. Reflexiones en torno a las estrategias matrimoniales cercanas," *Poder, familia, y consanguinidad en la España del Antiguo Régimen*, ed Francisco Chacón Jiménez and Juan Hernández Franco (Barcelona: Anthropos, 1992), 149–52.

13. For marriage contracts in Spain, see Annie Molinié-Bertrand, "Capitulaciones matrimoniales," in *A través del tiempo. Diccionario de fuentes para la historia de la familia*, ed. Pablo Rodríguez and Annie Molinié-Bertrand (Murcia: Colección Mestizo-Universidad de Murcia, 2000), 43–44.

14. Patricia Seed, "The Church and the Patriarchal Family: Marriage Conflicts in Sixteenth- and Seventeenth-Century New Spain," in *Families in the Expansion of Europe, 1500–1800*, ed. María Beatriz Nizza da Silva (Brookfield, VT: Ashgate, 1998), 29–39.

15. Allyson M. Poska, "When Love Goes Wrong: Getting Out of Marriage in Seventeenth-Century Spain," *Journal of Social History* 29 (1996): 871–82; Annie Molinié-Bertrand and Alicia Nieto López, "Demandas de divorcio," in *A través del tiempo. Diccionario de fuentes para la historia de la familia*, ed. Pablo Rodríguez and Annie Molinié-Bertrand (Murcia: Colección Mestizo-Universidad de Murcia, 2000), 69–72.

16. Jaime Contreras and Gustav Henningsen, "Forty-Four Thousand Cases of the Spanish Inquisition (1540–1700): Analysis of a Historical Data Bank," in *The Inquisition in Early Modern Europe: Studies on Sources and Methods*, ed. Gustav Henningsen and John Tedeschi in association with Charles Amiel (DeKalb: Northern Illinois University Press, 1986), 114. For bigamy charges in northwestern Spain, see Allyson M. Poska, "When Bigamy Is the Charge: Gallegan Women and the Holy Office," in *Women in the Inquisition: Spain and the New World*, ed. Mary Giles (Baltimore: Johns Hopkins University Press, 1998), 189–205.

17. Alexandra Parma Cook and Noble David Cook, *Good Faith and Truthful Ignorance. A Case of Transatlantic Bigamy* (Durham, NC: Duke University Press, 1991); Richard Boyer, *Lives of the Bigamists: Marriage, Family, and Community in Colonial Mexico* (Albuquerque: University of New Mexico Press, 1995).

18. In this chapter, I use the term *Creole* as the equivalent of the standard Spanish meaning of *criollo*—an individual born to European parents in the Americas. Peter Boyd-Bowman used the official passenger registries at the Archive of the Indies in Seville to launch a new subfield of inquiry about Spanish migration. See Peter Boyd-Bowman, *Indice geobiográfico de cuarenta mil pobladores españoles de América en el Siglo XVI* (Bogotá: Instituto Caro y Cuervo, 1964; Mexico: Editorial Jus, 1968), extended in "Patterns of Spanish Emigration to the Indies, 1579–1600," *The Americas* 33 (1976): 78–95. Many other scholars have followed his lead. See Antonio Eiras Roël, "Introducción: Consideraciones sobre la emigración española a América y su contexto demográfico," in *Emigración española y portuguesa a América: Actas del II Congreso de la Asociación de Demografía Histórica* (Alicante: Instituto de Cultura Juan Gil Albert, 1991), 9–32.

19. See, for example, Edgar F. Love, "Marriage Patterns of Persons of African Descent in a Colonial Mexico City Parish," in *Families in the Expansion of Europe, 1500–1800*, ed. María Beatriz Nizza da Silva (Brookfield, VT: Ashgate, 1998), 279–91.

20. Karen Spalding, "Social Climbers: Changing Patterns of Mobility among the Indians of Colonial Peru," in *European Intruders and Changes in Behavior and Customs in Africa, America and Asia before 1800*, ed. Murdo J. MacLeod and Evelyn S. Rawski (Aldershot, UK, and Brookfield, VT: Ashgate-Variorum, 1998), 57–76, especially 74–75.

21. Solange Alberro, "L'acculturation des Espagnols dans le Mexique colonial: Déchéance ou dynamisme culturel?" in *European Intruders and Changes in Behavior and Customs in Africa, America and Asia before 1800*, ed. Murdo J. MacLeod and Evelyn S. Rawski (Aldershot, UK, and Brookfield, VT: Ashgate-Variorum, 1998), 173–87.

22. Thomas Gage, *The English-American his travail by sea and land: or, A new survey of the West-India's* (London, 1648), 56–57.

23. Alberro, "Acculturation des Espagnols dans le Mexique colonial," 183.

24. See, for example, Gage, *English-American*; and Amédée François Frézier, *Relation du voyage de la Mer du Sud aux côtes du Chily et du Perou* (Paris, 1716).

25. Abigail Dyer, "Seduction by Promise of Marriage: Law, Sex, and Culture in Seventeenth-Century Spain," *Sixteenth Century Journal* 34 (Summer 2003): 439–55; Ann Twinam, "Honor, Sexuality, and Illegitimacy in Colonial Spanish America," in *Families in the Expansion of Europe, 1500–1800*, ed. María Beatriz Nizza da Silva (Brookfield, VT: Ashgate, 1998), 95–132.

26. Allyson Poska, *Regulating the People: The Catholic Reformation in Seventeenth-Century Spain* (Leiden: Brill, 1998) analyzes Galicia in northwestern Spain, an area with an illegitimacy rate of 5 to 10 percent of all live births. See also Sarah Cline, "The Spiritual Conquest Re-examined: Baptism and Christian Marriage in Early Sixteenth-Century Mexico," in *Families in the Expansion of Europe, 1500–1800*, ed. María Beatriz Nizza da Silva (Brookfield, VT: Ashgate, 1998), 213–40, especially 237; and José Abel Ramos Soriano, "Expedientes de la Inquisición," in *A través del tiempo. Diccionario de fuentes para la historia de la familia*, ed. Pablo Rodríguez and Annie Molinié-Bertrand (Murcia: Colección Mestizo-Universidad de Murcia, 2000), 87–91.

27. Archivo Histórico Nacional, Madrid, Sección de Ordenes Militares (OO.MM.), Expedientillos, 5496.

28. Jack Goody, Joan Thirsk, and E. P. Thompson, *Family and Inheritance in Rural Western Europe, 1200–1700* (Cambridge: Cambridge University Press, 1976). As an entry point into the literature about Spain, see the various works by Chacón Jiménez and Casey cited above. Examples of the hundreds of published local and regional studies include Isidro Dubert García, *Historia de la familia en Galicia durante la Época Moderna, 1550–1830* (Santiago de Compostela: Edicios do Castro, 1992); Paloma Fernández Pérez, *El rostro familiar de la metrópoli: Redes de parentesco y lazos mercantiles en Cádiz 1700–1812* (Madrid: Siglo XXI, 1997); and Estrella Garrido Arce, "La imposible igualdad: Familia y estrategias hereditarias en la huerta de Valencia a mediados del siglo XVIII," *Boletín de la Asociación de Demografía Histórica* 10 (1992): 83–104.

29. For emigration and transatlantic ties related to southwestern Spain, see the series titled *Andalucía y América* (Seville: Escuela de Estudios Hispano-Americanos de Sevilla, 1983–). For Basque migration, see A. R. Ortega Berruguete, "Población y familia (siglos XVII–XIX)," in *Gran Atlas Histórico del Mundo Vasco* (Bilbao: El Mundo del Pais Vasco, 1994), 225–40.

30. Ida Altman, *Emigrants and Society: Extremadura and America in the Sixteenth Century* (Berkeley and Los Angeles: University of California Press, 1989); "A New World in the Old: Local Society and Spanish Emigration to the Indies," in *"To Make America": European Emigration in the Early Modern Period*, ed. Ida Altman and James Horn (Berkeley and Los Angeles: University of California Press, 1991), 30–58.

31. Carlos Alberto González Sánchez, *Dineros de ventura: La varia fortuna de la emigración a Indias (siglos XVI–XVII)* (Seville: Univeridad de Sevilla, 1995).

32. Helen Nader, *Liberty in Absolutist Spain: The Habsburg Sale of Towns, 1516–1700* (Baltimore: Johns Hopkins University Press, 1990).

33. Richard L. Kagan, *Urban Images of the Hispanic World, 1493–1793* (New Haven, CT: Yale University Press, 2000), discusses these issues, as well as providing a magnificent array of maps, plans, and views of the Spanish world. See also the same author's "Cartography and Community in the Hispanic World," in *Visions of Community in the Pre-Modern World*, ed. Nicolas Howe (South Bend, IN: University of Notre Dame Press, 2002), 153–58.

34. Susan Tax Freeman, *Neighbors: The Social Contract in a Castilian Hamlet* (Chicago: University of Chicago Press, 1970.)

35. William D. Phillips Jr., "Local Integration and Long Distance Ties: The Castilian Merchants in Bruges in the Sixteenth Century," *Sixteenth Century Journal* 17

(Spring 1986): 33–48; Carla Rahn Phillips, "Spanish Merchants and the Wool Trade in the Sixteenth Century," *Sixteenth Century Journal* 14 (1983): 259–82; Christiane Demeulenaere-Douyère, "Les marchandes étrangers à Rouen au XVIe siècle (vers 1520–vers 1580): Assimilation ou ségrégation?" (thesis, École des Chartes, Paris, 1973); Gayle K. Brunelle, "Immigration, Assimilation and Success: Three Families of Spanish Origin in Sixteenth-Century Rouen," *Sixteenth Century Journal* 20 (1989): 203–20; Thomas James Dandelet, *Spanish Rome, 1500–1700* (New Haven, CT: Yale University Press, 2001), 150–59.

36. Tamar Herzog, *Defining Nations: Immigrants and Citizens in Early Modern Spain and Spanish America* (New Haven, CT: Yale University Press, 2003).

37. The above discussion relies heavily on the analysis in Herzog, *Defining Nations*, 101–106.

38. Ann Twinam, "Gracias al sacar," in *A través del tiempo. Diccionario de fuentes para la historia de la familia*, ed. Pablo Rodríguez and Annie Molinié-Bertrand (Murcia: Colección Mestizo-Universidad de Murcia, 2000), 107; Fernán Vejarano, "Expedientes de naturalización," in *A través del tiempo*, 93–96.

39. Ida Altman, *Transatlantic Ties in the Spanish Empire: Brihuega, Spain, and Puebla, Mexico, 1560–1620* (Stanford, CA: Stanford University Press, 2000).

40. Maureen Flynn, *Sacred Charity: Confraternities and Social Welfare in Spain, 1400–1700* (Ithaca, NY: Cornell University Press, 1989). For confraternities elsewhere in Catholic Europe, see Nicholas Terpstra, ed., *The Politics of Ritual Kinship. Confraternities and Social Order in Early Modern Italy* (New York and Cambridge: Cambridge University Press, 1999).

41. For Basque confraternities, see William A. Douglass and Jon Bilbao, *Amerikanuak: Basques in the New World* (Reno: University of Nevada Press, 1975), 107–11.

II
INTERACTIONS

6

Individual and Community among the Medieval Travelers to Asia

William D. Phillips Jr.

I N 1340 FRANCESCO BALDUCCI PEGOLOTTI PRODUCED La pratica della mercatura, a manual cataloguing the merchandise available in the markets of
the Mediterranean and the Black Sea. It included a brief but detailed guide for
travel between Italy and China. Though he never personally traveled to Asia,
Pegolotti used the commercial connections he gained as an employee of the
Bardi trading company of Florence to learn much about the routes to Asia,
based on information Pegolotti collected from merchants and other travelers
who had made the journey and had returned to describe it. Pegolotti set forth
itineraries and offered practical advice regarding mounts and pack animals,
provisions, and safety precautions.[1] His informants traveled to Asia and returned to Europe, as did the missionaries, many of them Franciscan friars.
This chapter examines their experiences, in which they mainly traveled and
worked in groups, and their accounts, which often give the misleading impression that they acted alone.

Excursions as far as Asia were unusual for Europeans of the period, but medieval people tended to travel far more frequently than we think, especially
after the eleventh century.[2] Jean Verdon has grouped medieval travelers into
four major categories.[3] Some traveled on their own account. These included
merchants and students, monarchs and nobles. Many young noblemen traveled widely as knights-errant as they sought to prove their prowess and see a
bit of the world. In some cases they did so to avoid conflict with their fathers
as they waited for their inheritances. In German the apt term for these noble
excursions is *Rittersreisen*.[4] Others traversed the roads of Europe at the orders
of a king or other lord. These included ambassadors and other envoys, agents,

and messengers. Farther down the social scale, artisans and peasants sought new and better opportunities by relocating, when the laws that governed them permitted it. Troubadours and other entertainers were almost always on the move, but, like those of the artisans and peasants, their travels left little impression on the written record. Still others had religious motivations. The pious or the penitent made pilgrimages to local shrines or to the principal Christian centers of Jerusalem, Rome, or Santiago de Compostela.[5] Before the 1290s, crusaders traveled to the eastern Mediterranean. Missionaries traveled wherever they were accepted. Some few traveled beyond the bounds of Europe and the Mediterranean to seek passages to Asia, beginning with the missionaries and merchants who followed the Mongol routes to Asia—men such as John of Plano Carpini and Marco Polo—or sought uninterrupted ocean pathways to India and Cathay—with Christopher Columbus and Vasco da Gama in the vanguard.

This chapter focuses on the contemporaries of Pegolotti's informants, travelers who visited parts of Asia during the *Pax Mongolica*, the relatively peaceful period in the thirteenth and fourteenth centuries when the Mongols imposed their sovereignty over the lands of the Asian landmass from the Black Sea to the Sea of Japan, and when Latin Christians could travel to Asia and return successfully.[6] The travelers' experiences increased Western knowledge of Asia and inspired still more Western interest in approaches to the peoples and riches of Cathay and India. The *Pax Mongolica* guaranteed the safety of travelers for more than a century along the overland routes spanning the Mongol Empire. Asian goods, and Asia itself, came within the reach of Europeans. Merchants explored the possibilities for direct trade with the markets of Asia. Missionaries dreamed of converting the huge Asian populations to Christianity. Popes and princes became aware that, beyond the Islamic world lived other peoples who might be willing to form alliances against the Muslims of the Middle East. A remarkable number of European missionaries and merchants traveled to Asia and returned to tell their stories.[7] Their accounts, produced between the 1240s and the late fourteenth century, gave Europe a view of Asia that inspired merchants and missionaries for two centuries more. Except for Marco Polo and his relatives, the merchants left far fewer traces than the missionaries, but there are a few tantalizing glimpses of the social world of the European merchants in Asia. Columbus, among many others, read Marco Polo and tried to calculate the distance necessary to sail across the western ocean to Asia.[8] Europe's seaborne expansion of the late fifteenth century seems to have owed much to the reports of those who followed overland caravan roads during the *Pax Mongolica*.

All this was an unintended consequence of the Mongol conquests. Early in the thirteenth century, a young nobleman called Temujin rallied the Mongols and a number of related tribes. Taking as his new name Genghis Khan, "ruler of the universe," he led his followers on a career of conquest that spanned the breadth of Asia.[9] The Mongols invaded north China, took Beijing by 1215, and entered Russia and Persia in 1223. By the death of Genghis Khan in 1227, Mongol power stretched across Asia to the eastern fringes of Europe. In the late 1230s the Mongols overran the Russian principalities and in 1240 devastated Kiev. In the next year they entered Poland, Silesia, Bohemia, Moravia, and Hungary. Many western Europeans perceived them as a major threat. In 1240 Matthew Paris, writing from the comparative safety of England, called them "inhuman and of the nature of beasts, rather to be called monsters than men. . . ."[10] Conveniently and surprisingly, at the very height of its danger to western Europe, the Mongol threat abruptly subsided. In 1241 the khan Ogodei died, and the Mongol leaders left the frontiers to assemble to elect his successor, obviously and immediately reducing pressure on Europe.

As knowledge of the Mongols filtered through to the West, several popes saw important reasons for seeking contacts with the Mongol Empire. The Mongols were a distant threat, despite the chilling news about them. They might prove useful against a much closer threat—the Muslims. Pope Innocent IV (1243–1254) came to consider them as potential allies. He was especially concerned because the fall of Jerusalem to the Muslims in 1244 exposed the remaining crusader holdings in Syria and Palestine to further Muslim threats and demanded a bold response by the leader of Western Christianity. Consequently, the pope assembled an embassy to send to the court of the Mongol khan with instructions to ask the khan to recognize the pope's religious supremacy and to suggest the possibility of a military alliance against the Muslims.[11]

John of Plano Carpini led the embassy. A Franciscan friar who had worked as a missionary in northern and eastern Europe, he was joined by Lawrence of Portugal and a Polish Franciscan named Benedict. The expedition went by land from Kiev to the Mongol court near Karakorum, where its members witnessed the coronation of Guyuk Khan. Nothing came of papal plans for a military alliance with the Mongols, and the khan even called on Plano Carpini to lead the kings of the West to the khan's court to render him homage. Europeans at least gained more knowledge about Asia from the expedition, and hope remained that the Mongols could one day be brought into an alliance. Plano Carpini returned with a written account, which he developed into his *Historia Mongolorum*, including the first Western description of China. His account was copied into a history of the world by Vincent of Beauvais,[12] court historian of King Louis IX of France (1226–1270).

Innocent IV in 1247 sent a second mission to the Mongols, led by a Dominican, Brother Ascelino of Cremona (1247), and four companions. They reached the headquarters of the Mongol chieftain in the West, Baiju, west of the Caspian Sea, but unfortunately succeeded in angering their host. Fortuitously, Aljigiday, a lieutenant of the Great Khan, arrived and sent the Latin embassy back with two Mongol envoys to the pope and to the leader of the western crusaders, Louis IX of France, who was then residing on Cyprus.[13]

Louis, who eagerly sought allies against the Muslims, sent two embassies to the Mongol court. The first, led by Andrew of Longjumeau in 1249–1251, failed to obtain an alliance and received instead a Mongol demand that Louis and his fellow Western kings render homage to the Mongols. The second embassy, headed by William of Rubruck, also reached the Mongol court, but with no greater success. Rubruck, however, produced one of the best and most appealing accounts of travel through the Mongol lands.[14]

John of Monte Corvino, a Franciscan, left Rome in 1289, commissioned as a papal envoy to the Mongol court. On his way to China he passed through India, where his companion, Nicholas of Pistoia, died, and Monte Corvino made the last leg of the trip to China with the Italian merchant Peter of Lucalongo. The rest of his life was spent in successful missionary activity, primarily in Khanbalik (Beijing). He was designated as the first Latin Christian bishop of Beijing, and other Western bishoprics soon developed elsewhere in China, staffed by Western friars. Monte Corvino's accounts are valuable for showing the details of his missionary work. He announced that he had baptized thousands of new Christians and proudly reported on the churches he built, including two in Beijing. His letters helped build the European impression of the significance of the Mongol Empire and, not incidentally, Monte Corvino's place in it: "Concerning the lands of the Orientals and especially the empire of the Lord Chaan, I declare that there is none greater in the world. And I have a place in his court and the right of access to it as the legate of the Lord Pope, and he honours me above the other prelates, whatever their titles."[15]

Monte Corvino nonetheless complained about loneliness and reported that he was the lone Franciscan in China for eleven years before he was joined by Arnold of Cologne, a German Franciscan. In 1308 a new mission reached Khanbalik, made up of Gerard Albuini, Pellegrino of Città di Castello, and Andrew of Perugia. From this group came the establishment of a second bishopric in China, this one in the port city of Zayton (or Zaitun, Ch'üan-chou or Quanzhou).[16] By 1326 Brother Andrew wrote that he was the bishop and that he was the last survivor of his companions.[17]

Another Franciscan, Odoric of Pordenone, wrote a spirited account of his journey to Asia. Designated a missionary to China in 1320, Odoric traveled through Persia, then sailed to India and Ceylon (on Muslim vessels), and visited Sumatra, Borneo, and Java before reaching China in 1325. After several years, he returned to the West, traveling along the overland caravan routes through northern Asia.[18]

Still another Franciscan, John of Marignolli, left Avignon in 1338 as a member of a missionary team to China. He reached Beijing in 1342 after traversing the caravan routes. After visiting the Franciscan establishment in Zayton, he left China in 1347 and returned by way of India, reaching Avignon in 1353. His disjointed account offered a description and location of the terrestrial paradise (in or near Ceylon, he said), but it also shows his rational views and dismissals of some of the stock tales about "wonders of the east." After listing all the supposed monstrous races that people have said to exist, he discarded the stories. As for those

> who have but one foot which they use to shade themselves. . . . [The Indians] are in the habit of carrying a thing like a little tent roof on a cane handle, which they open out at will as a protection against sun and rain. This they call a *chatyr* [from the Persian for umbrella]. I brought one to Florence with me. And it is this which the poets have converted into a foot.[19]

Marignolli was emphatic about his views dismissing monstrous races. "I have travelled in all the chief countries of the earth, and in particular to places where merchants from all parts of the world do come together . . . and yet I never could ascertain that such races of men really do exist. . . . The truth is that no such people do exist as nations, though there may be an individual monster [by which he meant a victim of genetic mutation] here and there."[20]

In direct contact with Asia, Italian merchants were at least as active as missionaries, but their economic ventures have not produced as many lasting accounts. Marco Polo is the most famous of them, and his account is the most familiar. Nonetheless, his trip, just as the earlier one by his brother and father, was not simply a commercial effort, but had connections with the papacy and diplomatic overtones as well.

In 1260 the Venetian merchants Niccolo and Maffeo Polo departed from Constantinople for the Crimean Peninsula on the Black Sea, where Italian (especially Genoese) merchants had been established for some time. From there they traveled through Mongol lands on a trading expedition and reached the camp of Barka Khan, Mongol leader in the West, on the Volga River. Military campaigns in the area prevented them from going back along the same route. Instead, they penetrated deep into Mongol territory, and at Bukhara joined a party on its way to Kublai Khan's court in China. The Great Khan designated them as his envoys to the pope, and he requested through them that the pope send "up to a hundred men learned in the Christian religion, well versed in the seven arts. . . . Furthermore the Great Khan directed the brothers to bring oil from the lamp that burns above the sepulchre of God in Jerusalem."[21]

The Polo brothers returned to Acre in the crusader states in 1269, and found that the pontifical office was vacant following the death of Clement IV the previous year. They reported to the papal envoy in the crusader states, Teodoldo Visconti, and when Visconti was elected pope, taking the papal name Gregory X, he authorized them to return to China with the pope's gifts and greetings for Kublai Khan. The Polos returned, taking Niccolo's son Marco with them.

Marco Polo lived for eighteen years in China, serving as a bureaucrat in the court of Kublai Khan. He traveled throughout China and visited India as well before returning to Europe. His return journey brought him back by sea from India, which gave him a view of the vast trade around the Indian Ocean that linked India with the Red Sea and the Persian Gulf.[22]

After Marco Polo returned to Venice in 1292, he fell victim to the seemingly endless wars among the Italian city-states. Captured by the Genoese, he spent 1298–1299 as a prisoner of war. In his enforced leisure, Polo recounted his experiences in China and the East to his fellow prisoner, Rustichello of Pisa, a writer much influenced by French romances. Rustichello wrote a book based on Polo's account, embellishing in places and not completely understanding all of it, but nonetheless preserving a tale that might otherwise have been lost forever. The book is not a merchant's manual, and Polo's personal history seldom intrudes. Rather, it is about the wonders of Asia that Polo witnessed or heard described, along with what resembles a gazetteer outlining the politics and economic potential of numerous cities and provinces. As all of it is filtered through Rustichello's prose, it is impossible to tell what Polo actually viewed or learned of China and its neighboring regions.[23]

The works of the missionaries and Marco Polo were known to a lesser or greater degree during the late Middle Ages, and modern scholarship has certainly not neglected them. For two centuries, geographers and historians have mined their riches straightforwardly, for what they reveal about the travelers and the places they traveled.[24] In this chapter we can see how the accounts fit into the idea of the interplay between the individual and community and show some degree of the authors' assimilation to the languages and customs of the host societies.

These travelers have often been presented as heroic individuals, something they may have been, and as people who traveled and did their missionary activity alone, which they certainly did not. In part this comes from the fact that many of them wrote in the first person, often in the first person singular. Marignolli used *we* but failed even to name his companions. Rubruck used *we* in many sections but only occasionally mentioned the actions of his colleagues. In crucial sections, he uses *I*. Monte Corvino, as we saw, really was alone for eleven years, in the sense of being the only Latin Christian clergyman, so the first person singular is appropriate for his report.

The emphasis on the individual is understandable but prevents our full comprehension of the framework in which the travelers operated. Sometimes there were well-defined contexts in which they operated and there were communities of fellow Christians to aid them, yet they chose to present their own narrative as the key element in their accounts. In part this may have arisen because the authors were thinking of what they wrote as direct communications with their sponsors and superiors back in Europe.

In their journeys and as they established themselves in enclaves in Asian cities, Western missionaries and merchants had several sources of potential aid, though some of the sources turned out to be less than useful. There were many other Christians in Asia, mainly Nestorians, followers of a variant of Christianity that took its name from the fifth-century theologian Nestorius, based in Antioch in Syria. Over the centuries, Nestorians had taken their form of Christianity first to Persia, and from there Nestorian missionaries had spread it throughout Asia: to India, along the Silk Road into central Asia, and to China by the late Middle Ages. The Latin Christian missionaries, far from considering the Nestorians to be coreligionists and allies, almost universally denounced them as pompous and ill informed and only grudgingly recognized them as Christians at all.[25]

Rubruck encountered Armenian and Nestorian priests on his travels to the Mongol court at Karakorum in Mongolia, and on several occasions they aided his progress. He was contemptuous, nonetheless, of the general run of the Nestorians in central Asia and north China.

> The Nestorians there are ignorant. They recite the office and have their Holy Scriptures in Syriac, a language they do not know, so that they chant like the monks among us who know no [Latin] grammar. . . . [They] are usurers and drunkards, and some of them, furthermore, who live among the Tartars, have several wives just as the Tartars have. On entering the church they wash their lower members, in the Saracen manner; they eat meat on Fridays and follow the Saracens in having their feasts on that day. The bishop takes his time about visiting those parts, [doing so] perhaps hardly once in fifty years. On that occasion they have all the male children, even those in the cradle, ordained as priests. As a result almost all of their men are priests. Thereafter they marry, which clearly contravenes the degrees of the Fathers.[26]

John of Monte Corvino found the Nestorians of Beijing to be his serious rivals and obstacles to his missionary work.

> [The] Nestorians, who call themselves Christians, but behave in a very unchristian manner, have grown so strong in these parts that they did not allow any Christian of another rite to have any place of worship, however small, nor to preach any doctrine but their own. . . . [The] Nestorians, both directly and by the

bribery of others, have brought grievous persecutions upon me. . . . And this intrigue lasted about five years, so that I was often brought to judgment, and in danger of a shameful death. But at last, by God's ordering, the Emperor came to know my innocence and the nature of my accusers.[27]

The communities of Western Christians that developed in India and China during the late Middle Ages were sizable but have left a surprisingly slight imprint on the historical record. We must rely on indirect evidence and on the almost parenthetical remarks of the authors of the main accounts. Certainly, the Latin Christian missionaries who visited Asia late in the thirteenth and fourteenth centuries found communities of Western Christian merchants present and able to offer them support.

The Western, mainly Italian, merchants in China and other parts of Asia during the *Pax Mongolica* probably made up what Philip Curtin described as a merchant diaspora or trade settlement. "Commercial specialists would remove themselves physically from their home community and go to live as aliens in another town . . . important in the life of the host community. There, the stranger merchants could settle down and learn the language, the customs and the commercial ways of their hosts. They could then serve as cross-cultural brokers, helping and encouraging trade between the host society and the people of their own origin who moved along the trade routes."[28] The Western merchants did exactly this in Zayton and other Chinese cities, aided by the Mongols' distrust of their Chinese subjects and their need for foreigners as administrators and intermediaries. The Vilioni family, which first surfaced in Venice in the twelfth century, provides one line of evidence. In 1264 Pietro Vilioni wrote his will in Tabriz, near the Black Sea on the famous Silk Road. The tombstones of two other members of the family, Catarina Vilioni (who died in 1342) and her father, Domenico Vilioni, were uncovered in 1951 when the city walls of Yangchow in China were being torn down. For J. R. S. Phillips, this shows a family's involvement "in the commerce of Asia for the better part of a century, as well as evidence for the existence of a European community in China that was well enough established and sufficiently secure to have unmarried women in its midst."[29] Phillips even suggests that Marco Polo had a connection with the Vilionis, for it was in Yangchow that Polo is supposed to have served in the Chinese bureaucracy. If true, it would illustrate a pattern that historians of trade have often found: Merchants in faraway places relied on networks of fellow countrymen and relatives in order to conduct their business. Although the ruling political power in an area controlled the initial access, merchants had to create their own opportunities for trade once they arrived. Unfortunately, the sources available do not permit a full examination of the activities of the European merchants.

However, we can use the sources they produced to understand at least part of how the travelers reacted and adjusted to the alien societies into which they ventured. Their reactions to the peoples they encountered were on a different plane from the reactions of Europe's oceanic explorers of the fifteenth and sixteenth centuries. Unlike Columbus in the Western Hemisphere or Albuquerque in South Asia, they had no technological advantage in China—quite the contrary. They traveled in small groups, mostly unarmed, and often were dependent on the goodwill and protection of the Mongol authorities. Consequently, both missionaries and merchants had to act circumspectly merely to be allowed to remain in China. To pursue their goals, they needed to assimilate to some degree into their host society. To succeed, they could not rely exclusively on the intermediation of their hosts but sought to establish direct communication, and that required the acquisition of the local language. Surprisingly, not all the travelers' accounts mention language, and those that do often mention it very briefly. Equally surprisingly, modern scholars seem to have neglected this most basic component of the challenges that faced the travelers. The Europeans in Mongol lands faced far greater linguistic hurdles than their fellow merchants who traded with the Muslims in the Mediterranean ports.[30] Europeans in Asia confronted problems unknown to the famous Muslim traveler Ibn Battuta, who made his way from Morocco to Asia and back in the same period. He covered more ground than Marco Polo, but many of the lands he traversed shared Islamic culture and Arabic as a common language. When he left the lands under direct Muslim control, he could still find Arabic speakers to aid him.[31]

Pegolotti's guidebook, which distills a century's experience by Italian merchants, approaches the question of language forthrightly. After telling prospective travelers to China to let their beards grow long, his first piece of practical advice, he counsels: "At Tana [in the Crimea] you should furnish yourself with a dragoman [interpreter]. And you must not try to save money in the matter of dragomen by taking a bad one instead of a good one. For the additional wages of the good one will not cost you so much as you will save by having him."[32] That statement no doubt rests on a series of complaints that Pegolotti heard from those who had made the trip.

William of Rubruck would certainly have agreed with Pegolotti. When he reached the main Mongol encampment, he was prepared with copies of the French king's letter that he had had translated into Syriac and Arabic in Acre in the crusader states.[33] Both languages were familiar at the Mongol court. For day-to-day business, nonetheless, Rubruck rued his inability to speak the language of the Mongols almost as much as he regretted hiring his particular interpreter, who was named Abdullah.

I was especially vexed by the fact that whenever I wanted to do some preaching to them my interpreter would say, "Do not make me preach, since I do not know how to express these things." He was right. Later, when I acquired some little knowledge of the language, I noticed that when I said one thing he would say something totally different, depending on what came into his head. After that I realized the danger of speaking through him, and chose rather to say nothing.[34]

As his journey progressed, Rubruck and his companions had greater access to high-ranking Mongols who traveled in the same caravan. The ecumenical Mongols asked the Westerners to pray for them, and Rubruck obliged. "Had I been possessed of a good interpreter, this would have given me an opportunity of sowing much good seed."[35]

Rubruck made efforts to learn Mongol languages, but he continued to need interpreters. His final interpreter in the court of the khan Möngke (or Mangu) in Karakorum was the adopted son of a French goldsmith. The smith's name was William Buchier; members of Buchier's family were jewelers in Paris and he himself had been captured and enslaved in Hungary. He lived well in Karakorum, even though he was the khan's slave. He had married a Hungarian woman, also a slave. They entertained Rubruck while he was in Karakorum, and their son acted as Rubruck's interpreter in his final meetings with the khan.[36] Buchier was an involuntary resident of Karakorum, but his skills made him a valued artisan at the khan's court. His family, particularly his son, were learning the ways of the Mongols and gaining a command of their language, enabling them to serve as intermediaries for Rubruck in his dealings with the khan and his entourage.

John of Monte Corvino, the missionary who became the first Christian bishop of Beijing, had greater skills in languages. For his missionary work, he used the local languages and also used other stratagems.

> Also I have gradually bought one hundred and fifty boys, the children of pagan parents, and of ages varying from seven to eleven, who had never learned any religion. These boys I have baptized, and I have taught them Greek and Latin after our manner. Also I have written out Psalters for them, with thirty Hymnaries and two Breviaries. By help of these, eleven of the boys already know our service, and form a choir and take their weekly turn of duty as they do in convents, whether I am there or not.[37]

He learned one of the Mongol languages, which according to Christopher Dawson could have been Uighur or Jagatay or Mongol.[38] As Monte Corvino explained his life's work:

> I have myself grown old and grey, more with toil and trouble than with years; for I am not more than fifty-eight. I have got a competent knowledge of the lan-

guage and character, which is most generally used by the Tartars. And I have already translated into that language and character the New Testament and the Psalter, and have caused them to be written out in the finest penmanship they have. . . . And I had been in treaty with the late King George, if he had lived, to translate the whole Latin ritual, that it might be sung throughout the whole extent of his territory; and whilst he was alive I used to celebrate mass in his church, according to the Latin ritual, reading in the before-mentioned language and character the words of both the preface and the Canon.[39]

Monte Corvino thus gained a command of the language necessary for him to preach among the Mongol elite.

His fellow Franciscan missionary Pascal of Vitoria learned the Coman dialect for his work in central Asia in the early fourteenth century. As he reported:

I was determined first to learn the language of the country. And by God's help I did learn the Chamanian language, and the Uigurian character; which language and character are commonly used throughout all these kingdoms or empires. . . . [F]rom the time I acquired the language, by the grace of God I often preached without an interpreter both to the Saracens and to the schismatic and heretical Christians.[40]

The other merchants and missionaries do not mention problems with language or translators. Like Marco Polo's book, their accounts are travel literature, designed to present the places they visited and the wonders they beheld. They are not intended to display the difficulties their authors may have experienced in understanding their hosts or making themselves understood. In Polo, the main mention of languages comes in Rustichello's introductory chapter, not in the body of the book. Rustichello reported that Polo "acquired a remarkable knowledge of the customs of the Tartars and of their languages and letters. I assure you for a fact that before he had been very long at the Great Khan's court he had mastered four languages with their modes of writing."[41] Modern scholars agree that Chinese did not count among these four languages. As for the others, they may have been the Coman dialect of Turkish, Persian, the Mongol dialect of the khan's court.[42]

Polo was remarkable in his abilities, as perhaps was Monte Corvino. Their contemporaries had, to be fair, lesser advantages than Polo, who began his Chinese sojourn as a favorite of Kublai Khan. Monte Corvino also did not know Chinese. After all, his preaching was directed not toward the Chinese, but only toward the Mongols and other non-Chinese. That is characteristic of the other Western missionaries as well. It is therefore easily understandable why the Western Christian presence would not outlast the collapse of the

Mongol Empire and its replacement by a native Chinese dynasty, and why the Western contact with east Asia had to be rebuilt beginning in the sixteenth century. Through their personal efforts and with the support of coreligionists and communities along the ways to Asia, missionaries and merchants contributed to greater Western understanding of the lands lying between Europe and China. Although their accounts often display them as solitary voyagers, they were heavily indebted to those who traveled with them and the communities of Christians, Nestorians, and other Eastern (and later Western) Christians, as they traveled.

Notes

1. Francesco Balducci Pegolotti, *La Pratica della Mercatura*, ed. A. Evans (Cambridge, MA: Harvard University Press, 1936; reprint, 1970). Evans's edition contains the Italian text of the book. A partial English translation is available in *Cathay and the Way Thither, Being a Collection of Medieval Notices of China*, trans. and ed. Henry Yule, rev. ed Henri Cordier (London: Hakluyt Society, 1914), 3:143–71. A better, but still partial, translation is in Robert S. Lopez and Irving Raymond, eds., *Medieval Trade in the Mediterranean World* (New York: Columbia University Press, 1961), 355–58.

2. Hans-Werner Goetz, *Life in the Middle Ages, from the Seventh to the Thirteenth Century*, trans. Albert Wimmer (Notre Dame, IN: University of Notre Dame Press, 1993), 12.

3. Jean Verdon, *Travel in the Middle Ages*, trans. George Holoch (Notre Dame, IN: University of Notre Dame Press, 2003). For an additional formulation, see J. E. Ruiz-Domènec, "El viaje y sus modos: Peregrinación, errancia, paseo," in *Viajes y viajeros en la España medieval* (Madrid: Polifemo, 1997), 85–94.

4. Margaret Wade Labarge would place these in her category of adventurers among medieval travelers. *Medieval Travelers* (New York: Norton, 1983), 177–94.

5. For Christian pilgrimage, see Jonathan Sumption, *Pilgrimage: An Image of Mediaeval Religion* (Totowa, NJ: Rowman & Littlefield, 1975); and Pierre-André Sigal, *Les marcheurs de Dieu: Pèlerinages et pèlerins au Moyen Age* (Paris: Colin, 1974).

6. And perhaps Jewish travelers as well. See *The City of Light: the Hidden Journal of the Man Who Entered China Four Years before Marco Polo*, supposedly the work of Jacob d'Ancona as translated by David Selbourne (New York: Citadel Press, 2000). Many scholars have not accepted this book as an authentic account. S. D. Goitein, in his massive study *A Mediterranean Society: The Jewish Communities of the World as Portrayed in the Documents of the Cairo Geniza*, 6 vols. (Berkeley and Los Angeles: University of California Press, 1976–1993), has numerous citations of Jewish merchants and traders active in India, but few if any references to others in East Asia, but the Geniza documents have an eleventh-century bias.

7. Jerry H. Bentley places their activities in the wide context of the medieval Eurasian world in *Old World Encounters: Cross-Cultural Contacts and Exchanges in Pre-*

Modern Times (Oxford: Oxford University Press, 1993), 153–63. See also Richard C. Foltz, *Religions of the Silk Road: Overland Trade and Cultural Exchange from Antiquity to the Fifteenth Century* (New York: St. Martin's Griffin, 2000), 117–34.

8. For a discussion of the background of Columbus's geographical ideas, see William D. Phillips Jr. and Carla Rahn Phillips, *The Worlds of Christopher Columbus* (Cambridge: Cambridge University Press, 1992); and William D. Phillips Jr., "Columbus and European Views of the World," *American Neptune* (1993).

9. For the Mongols, see J. J. Saunders, *A History of the Mongol Conquests* (London: Routledge & Kegan Paul, 1971); David Morgan, *The Mongols* (Oxford: Oxford University Press, 1986); René Grousset, *The Empire of the Steppes: A History of Central Asia*, trans. Naomi Walford (New Brunswick, NJ: Rutgers University Press, 1970).

10. *Matthew Paris's English History from the Year 1235 to 1273*, trans. J. A. Giles, 3 vols. (London, 1852; reprint, New York: AMS, 1968), 1:312–13.

11. The most easily available edition of Plano Carpini's *Historia Mongolorum* is Chritopher Dawson, ed., *Mission to Asia: Narratives and Letters of the Franciscan Missionaries in Mongolia and China in the Thirteenth and Fourteenth Centuries*, trans. a nun of Stanbrook Abbey (New York: Harper & Row, 1966). Alternate title: *The Mongol Mission.*

12. See Gregory G. Guzman, "Vincent of Beauvais," in *Trade, Travel, and Exploration in the Middle Ages: An Encyclopedia*, ed. John B. Friedman and Kristin Mossler Figg (New York: Garland, 2000), 633–34.

13. On Louis's crusading career, see William C. Jordon, *Louis IX and the Challenge of the Crusade* (Princeton, NJ: Princeton University Press, 1979).

14. *The Mission of Friar William of Rubruck: His Journey to the Court of the Great Khan Möngke, 1253–1255*, trans. Peter Jackson; introduction, notes, and appendices by Peter Jackson and David Morgan (London: Hakluyt Society, 1990).

15. John of Monte Corvino's letters, together with letters of his fellow missionaries, are in *Cathay and the Way Thither.* Excerpts, better translated, appear in Dawson, *Mission to Asia.* The quotation comes from *Mission to Asia*, 230.

16. Ian Gilman and Hans-Joachim Kilmkeit, *Christians in Asia before 1500* (Ann Arbor: University of Michigan Press, 1999), 301.

17. Andrew of Perugia, in *Cathay and the Way Thither*, 3:74–75.

18. The Travels of Friar Odoric are to be found in *Cathay and the Way Thither*, vol. 2. Yule's translation is reproduced in a new edition, *The Travels of Friar Odoric* (Grand Rapids, MI: William B. Eerdmans, 2002), with a useful introduction by Paolo Chiesa.

19. Marignolli's account can be found in *Cathay and the Way Thither*, vol. 3. This quotation is on 256. See also Paolo Chiesa in *Travels of Friar Odoric*, 25, and Gilman and Klimkeit, *Christians in Asia*, 301.

20. Marignolli in *Cathay and the Way Thither*, 3:256.

21. *Travels of Marco Polo*, 36.

22. K. N. Chaudhuri, *Trade and Civilisation in the Indian Ocean: An Economic History from the Rise of Islam to 1750* (Cambridge: Cambridge University Press, 1985).

23. The latest comprehensive account is John Larner, *Marco Polo and the Discovery of the World* (New Haven, CT: Yale University Press, 1999). See also Jacques Heers, *Marco Polo* (Paris: Fayard, 1983); Leonardo Olschki, *Marco Polo's Asia* (Berkeley and

Los Angeles: University of California Press, 1960); *The Travels of Marco Polo*, trans. R. E. Latham (Harmondsworth, UK: Penguin, 1958; reprint, 1982).

24. For an early nineteenth-century account, see Hugh Murray, *Historical Account of Discoveries and Travels in Asia, From the Earliest Ages to the Present Time* (Edinburgh and London: A. Constable, 1820), 1:69–197. Other more recent studies include C. Raymond Beazley, *The Dawn of Modern Geography*, 3 vols. (Oxford, 1897–1906; reprint, New York: Peter Smith, 1949); Arthur Percival Newton, *Travel and Travellers of the Middle Ages* (London: A. and C. Black, 1926; reprint, Freeport, NY: Books for Libraries Press, 1967); John Kirtland Wright, *Geographical Lore in the Time of the Crusades* (New York: American Geographical Society, 1925; reprint, New York: Dover, 1965); Pierre Chaunu, *L'expansion européenne du XIIIe au XVe siècle* (Paris: Presses Universitaires de France, 1969); James Muldoon, *Popes, Lawyers, and Infidels: The Church and the Non-Christian World, 1250–1550* (Philadelphia: University of Pennsylvania Press, 1979); James Muldoon, ed., *The Expansion of Europe: The First Phase* (Philadelphia: University of Pennsylvania Press, 1977); Michel Mollat, *Les explorateurs du XIIIe au XVIe siècle* (Paris: J. C. Lattès, 1984); J. R. S. Phillips, *The Medieval Expansion of Europe*, 2nd. ed. (Oxford: Oxford University Press, 1998). The anthropologist Mary Helms has put the travel stories into a category of the enhancements that knowledge provides to power. Mary W. Helms, *Ulysses' Sail: An Ethnographic Odyssey of Power, Knowledge, and Geographical Distance* (Princeton, NJ: Princeton University Press, 1988). Mary Campbell, a professor of English literature, analyzes over a thousand years of European travel writing to show how the features of descriptions of visits to distant lands and exotic people evolved into a variety of genres: the novel and the autobiography, ethnology and anthropology. Mary B. Campbell, *The Witness and the Other World: Exotic European Travel Writing, 400–1600* (Ithaca, NY: Cornell University Press, 1988).

25. The most comprehensive recent survey of Christianity in premodern Asia is that of Gilman and Kilmkeit, *Christians in Asia*.

26. *Mission of Friar William of Rubruck*, 163–64.

27. Monte Corvino, in *Mongol Mission*, 224–25.

28. Philip D. Curtin, *Cross-Cultural Trade in World History* (Cambridge: Cambridge University Press, 1984).

29. J. R. S. Phillips, *Medieval Expansion*, 104–105.

30. Kathryn L. Reyerson has mentioned the ways Mediterranean merchants overcame linguistic barriers, "The Merchants of the Mediterranean: Merchants as Strangers," in *The Stranger in Medieval Society*, ed. F. R. P. Akehurst and Stephanie Cain van D'Elden (Minneapolis: University of Minnesota Press, 1997), 1–13.

31. Ross E. Dunn, *The Adventures of Ibn Battuta: A Muslim Traveler of the 14th Century* (Berkeley and Los Angeles: University of California Press, 1986, 2005).

32. *Cathay and the Way Thither*, 3:151.

33. *Mission of Friar William of Rubruck*, 118.

34. *Mission of Friar William of Rubruck*, 108.

35. *Mission of Friar William of Rubruck*, 141–42.

36. *Mission of Friar William of Rubruck*, passim. See also Leonardo Olschki, *Guillaume Boucher: A French Artist at the Court of the Khans* (Baltimore: Johns Hopkins University Press, 1946).

37. *Cathay and the Way Thither*, 3: 46–47.

38. Dawson, *Mission to Asia*, xxxiii.

39. *Cathay and the Way Thither*, 3:50.

40. Pascal of Vitoria, in *Cathay and the Way Thither*, 3:82–83.

41. *Travels of Marco Polo*, 40.

42. Larner, *Marco Polo*, 41, 64; *Travels of Marco Polo*. The translator, R. E. Latham, commented: "Marco probably knew both Mongol and Turkish, which are related (Altaic) languages, and it is not always clear which form he was trying to reproduce . He also seems to have had some knowledge of Persian; but it is doubtful which was the fourth language he claimed to have mastered. It can scarcely have been Chinese" (p. 28). Leonardo Olschki offered a series of conjectures about how, when, and to what extent the Polos acquired their Asian languages. *Marco Polo's Asia*, 81, 86, 89, 100.

7

Settle or Return

Migrant Communities in
Northern Europe, ca. 1600–1800

Douglas Catterall

Migrants and Outsider Status in Early Modern European Society

In the last decades, scholars have shown that premodern Europe and its cultures resulted fundamentally from migration. More importantly, historians have demonstrated that migrants exercised cultural influence through complex and durable networks of considerable social breadth.[1] Some states and communities even incorporated migration and migrant networks and institutions into their policies, attempting to manage, not just frustrate, movements of people into and through their territories, with the result that outsider groups could sometimes achieve an accommodation with a host community on terms acceptable to them.[2] This work has also revealed the incredible adaptability of venerable institutional forms such as the *natio* to the demands of migrant group, host community, and individual newcomer alike.[3] Consequently, it is no longer sufficient to frame questions of migrant identity in terms of group cohesion or normative conformity. Individual migrants' strategic positioning within the normative world(s) they inhabited and their capacity to influence community institutions has rightly come to the fore.[4]

Yet this deeper understanding of migrants' roles in premodern Europe and of their potential for agency in their adopted communities has made imperative a reevaluation of their outsider status. For if migration was integral to all European cultures, specifying what separated migrants from and joined them to their host societies cannot, as Donna Merwick has shown in her work on colonial New York, be a matter of an insider/outsider divide.[5] Similarly, categories that predetermine a migrant's decision to settle or leave a new home, such as refugee or exile, lose some of their viability. A putative exile or refugee can easily decide on permanent settlement or a life between the host community and the community of origin.[6] Even diaspora, which allows migrants multiple identities, implies that the migrant(s) in question maintain links with some time/place of origin, however tenuous.[7] But applying the notion of diaspora to Europe's *converso* migrants, for example, is difficult, because historians have had trouble deciding which homeland should count and how.[8]

Abandoning these terms altogether would be foolish. They capture important dimensions of migrant identity. Yet I want to suggest that a greater emphasis on how migrants and communities negotiated and interacted with one another would enrich current discussions of the migrant's place in premodern Europe. In this chapter, I argue that for migrants in an established migration tradition,[9] the decision to settle hinged in part on the outcome of two dialogues that occurred on arrival in a new place: one with the host community, focused on corporate rights and privileges; and one with their fellows in the host community, rooted in the migrants' own networks. These two discourses intertwined in different ways for any given migrant group, reflecting the degree of formalization in the ties between the migrants and the host community and the migrant group's institutionalization in the host society. Formal relations with the host community signaled that a migrant group had achieved public status, while migrants dependent on ties to their own group or individual members of the host society lived either as members of an unofficial foreign enclave or, in essence, as members of the host society. Consequently, the migrant's world depended on whether and how he could negotiate a place with his fellows and/or the local authorities; the migrant lived not in a world of exile and return, of outsiders and insiders, but in one of settle or return, in which migrant status was often ambiguous. This is what the fates of the four groups I discuss below—the Sephardim of Amsterdam, Rotterdam's Scots community, and the Dutch/Flemish and Walloon/French migrants of southeast England—suggest.[10]

Following a Traveled Path: Migrants and Precursor Communities

With the exception of Amsterdam's *converso*/Sephardi[11] migrants, all of the groups under consideration had established presences in the places to which they were migrating by the sixteenth century. Even Amsterdam's *converso*/Sephardi newcomers, who did not have a precursor community to welcome them, formed part of a well-established migration tradition.[12] Thus Amsterdam's *converso*/Sephardi migrants quickly generated much of what the precursor communities of Scots, Dutch/Flemish, and Walloon/French migrants could offer their newly arrived fellows: information about the host community, employment, and a cultural and social net. A given immigrant's access to aid depended on individual circumstances, but sketching the mechanisms involved gives a sense for the decisions migrants faced when the dialogue with the host community was informal and ties to the group of origin predominated.

Precursor Communities

For Scots migrants to Rotterdam, the regional trades linking Rotterdam to Scotland, England, and France provided a supportive social milieu. Some among Rotterdam's Scots merchants hailed from one of the commercially privileged royal burghs. As importers of luxury goods into Scotland and exporters of coal, salt, wool, and textiles, these men maintained active ties to Scotland and the Dutch Republic, giving them ample opportunity to decide whether Rotterdam would suit them. Still other merchants, as well as sailors and skippers, came either from the royal burghs or the smaller ports along the Firth of Forth, often with ties to coal production on noble estates. With Scots enclaves across the North Sea zone, settlement of these individuals in Rotterdam hinged in part on choosing the best economic opportunities. Very likely ties of family or friendship to sailors, skippers, merchants, or already established compatriots drew Scots craftsmen to Rotterdam. Making use of the same maritime world, soldiers migrated to Rotterdam in response to recruitment efforts in Scotland.[13]

Scots in Rotterdam also shared religious, linguistic, and neighborhood bonds, which made for a tight-knit enclave that strongly determined the lives of most newcomers. Initially, most Scots joined either the Dutch Reformed Church in Rotterdam or one of the English-speaking Protestant congregations active in town. The distinctiveness of the Scots language brought newcomers together too, although the power of its pull remains unclear in the sources bearing witness to its presence. There is better evidence of social solidarity among Scots in Rotterdam. By the 1630s a Scots neighborhood, replete with Scots boarding houses catering to Scots sailors and prominent kin-driven networks, had crystallized. And as early as the 1620s Scots also participated in the municipal regulatory apparatus for the coal trade with Scotland.[14]

Like Rotterdam, London had heavy migrant settlement, although distributed across several districts. In 1550 these included East Smithfield, Aldgate, Langborne, Tower, Billingsgate, Dowgate, Langborne, St. Martin le Grand, and Southwark. As in Rotterdam, migrants from a particular region often lived near one another. Two other qualities marked the districts where Dutch/Flemish and Walloon/French migrants lived: their poverty and their suburban or near suburban location, with some enjoying an independent status (as liberties) that allowed migrant craftsmen to practice their trades free of London guild interference.[15]

In sharp contrast to Rotterdam, however, London circa 1500–1550 presented the migrant with a larger, more polyglot conurbation, allowing migrants some freedom to decide how they would live. Some fifty thousand inhabitants called London home in 1500, and about eighty thousand by 1550. Conservatively estimated, the migrant share of this population never rose above 4 or 5 percent in the sixteenth century.[16] Nevertheless, because of London's sizeable total population, aliens always numbered into the thousands. According to Andrew Pettegree, "London's foreign community was in many respects a very open one," in which religious ideas flowed easily.[17] London's migrants were among the trendsetters of England's Reformation, with some promoting Protestantism, and some of them facing execution for their trouble. Because migrant settlement in London remained diffuse, though, migrants could also remain Catholic. London migrants also differed from their Rotterdam counterparts in their motivation for migration, which focused more narrowly on the skills differential favoring Dutch, Flemish, and French-speaking craftsmen over their English brethren. And if we can credit the charges of London artisans, newcomers acted in solidarity, suggesting that some were recruiting their countrymen after establishing themselves.[18]

Negotiating with Host and Precursor Communities before the Emergence of a Public Enclave

Preexisting migrant communities offered migrants options, and without access to such communities dealings with the host community could become complicated, as Amsterdam's first *converso*/Sephardi migrants found. Still, precursor communities had no official status. Migrants claiming a public identity therefore had to work within the host community's system of privilege and status while avoiding clashes with the precursor community of their fellows.

Legal conditions for residency, citizenship, and access to corporate rights bulked large in a migrant's calculations, and absent an official migrant enclave, the host community held all the cards.[19] In the Dutch Republic, towns usually had the central role in determining their residency requirements, which in Amsterdam and Rotterdam amounted to proof of the capacity to find work within a fixed period after one's arrival.[20] Rotterdam's policing apparatus could not track every migrant, and the houses of burghers were free from search without special cause. If a newcomer could find an economic niche or some form of support, residency in the *Maasstad* presented little problem. After two years of residence a newcomer qualified as an indweller, which allowed access to municipal poor relief. Obtaining citizenship required surmounting some additional hurdles, but was not unattainable even for Scots sailors if they were skilled. It typically involved either marrying someone with citizenship or acquiring citizenship through purchase. Citizenship compensated those who made the effort to acquire it with certain legal immunities and protections as well as privileges such as the possibility of joining a guild. By the 1620s some Scots had obtained even this restricted privilege, becoming Sworn Brokers to the Scots coal trade.[21]

Amsterdam's early *converso*/Sephardi migrants, most of whom were merchants, had fewer problems than Rotterdam's Scots with the economic requirements of residency.[22] For them, adapting to a society that theoretically granted only Calvinists full civil rights proved more important and more difficult. In September 1598 Amsterdam's city fathers acquiesced in the newcomers' wish to acquire citizenship (*poorterschap*) "'trusting that [the Portuguese merchants] are Christians and will live an honest life as good burghers.'"[23] They could therefore practice only one religion publicly in Amsterdam, "'that [which is] practiced publicly in the churches [already],'" that is, Dutch Reformed Protestantism.[24] The city fathers had allowed the newcomers what they accorded disadvantaged Christian denominations: space to worship privately in a manner that did not compromise the republic's Calvinist identity, assuming their political loyalty was not in question. The newcomers probably expected this response, as their first request for *poorterschap* had come in March of 1597, and they had likely become familiar with official policies toward dissenting religious groups given that they had been arriving in Amsterdam even earlier in the 1590s.[25] Corporate status, then, did not become an issue until later.[26]

Turning to London and its environs, the area of concentrated Dutch, Flemish, Walloon, and French settlement prior to 1550, migrants had more limited choices regarding civil status. This would be one of the hallmarks of migration to England throughout the early modern period. First, only Parliament or the crown could grant anything approaching citizenship status in England. Although they did control access to certain rights and privileges within their jurisdiction by their power to grant or refuse urban citizenship (freedom of the city), localities did not have the power to control these matters as in the Dutch Republic. Second, a migrant usually required considerable effort and money to obtain a patent of denization from the crown or an act of naturalization from Parliament, and Parliament conceded the latter infrequently. Third, the officials of London and other English towns as well as the corporate entities in them (e.g., guilds) resisted or managed grants of privilege to foreigners. To make matters worse, early modern English/British monarchs willingly sacrificed privileges granted to migrants if they could thereby secure political or financial gain.[27]

Skilled as they were, then, some of London's migrants in the first half of the sixteenth century still had to contend with London's politically influential artisans. Some, such as skilled migrant brewers and coopers, found local guilds willing to protect and assist them. Even in the face of the Marian measures against foreigners, they survived handily. Other migrants, often those who pursued trades where English expertise existed, had to endure storms of nativist protest. The disputes between the London guilds, with the cordwainers taking a prominent role, and their migrant competitors circa 1513–1529 are emblematic. As a direct result of guild agitation in this period, the London guilds received the power to regulate their foreign competitors within the city of London itself. Freedom of the city, the only certain shield against this unwanted attention, required finding a sponsor and paying a fee or completing an apprenticeship to a freeman. Most foreign migrants in London preferred to seek out a district of the city with fewer regulatory hurdles.[28]

Religion posed migrants as many problems as civic status, although complications arose between different groups of migrants as well as between migrants and hosts. Thus, most Rotterdam Scots migrants adopted a Calvinist civic identity while still maintaining their Scottishness. A palpable number, however, participated in some of Rotterdam's grander religious experiments, which led to tension in the Scots community. Until the founding of an English congregation in 1619, Scots (most of whom were Protestants) had to worship in the Rotterdam Dutch Reformed congregation.[29] After 1619 some Scots almost certainly joined the newly formed English church and others that followed it.[30] A number of Scots members of the Scots Church of Rotterdam, in any case, had sympathies with the more experimental forms of Protestantism that Rotterdam's English churches sponsored in the 1630s and early1640s. They brought these proclivities with them into the newly formed Scots Church of Rotterdam in 1643 and a running battle with the Scots Church of Rotterdam's first, staunchly Covenanter minister Alexander Petrie ensued.[31] In all likelihood, however, a majority of Scots became members of Rotterdam's Dutch Reformed Church in the period prior to 1643. The marriages between these Scots and others, including Dutch partners, attest that these Scots were forging ties to become part of the civic community.[32] Becoming Rotterdamers did not, however, preclude a strong sense of Scottishness. Many founding members of Rotterdam's Scots Church had been members of the Dutch Reformed Church of Rotterdam.[33]

That these two groups in the Scots community managed to coexist later in the Scots Church of Rotterdam is further testimony to the existence of a strong sense of Scots ethnicity, which the Dutch themselves acknowledged through the concept of the Scots nation.[34] Nevertheless, Rotterdam's Scots community became embroiled in the debates on religion and community that often divided the city during the seventeenth century. For newly arrived migrants this would mean coming to terms with varying "Scots" and "Dutch" interpretations of communal norms.[35]

For Amsterdam's early *converso*/Sephardi migrants, religious affiliation did not imply commitment to the urban community. The city's leaders enjoined *converso*/Sephardi *poorters* to respect the Dutch Reformed religion as the city's public faith and defined Judaism as a private matter.[36] Even once the newcomers' Judaism became known (likely in 1603) and the first synagogue was operating (circa 1608), the Amsterdam city fathers ignored this. In their minds, Judaism remained a private choice to which no public benefits accrued.[37]

From the perspective of the migrants, becoming part of the Bet Jacob or, after 1612, the Neve Shalom synagogue had to do with personal religious views, on the one hand, and comfort with the way in which these synagogues defined membership on the other. According to David Swetschinski, the Neve Shalom synagogue had a close-knit membership defined by closely shared kinship, and both synagogues represented small groupings of individuals very aware of their Judaism. For most early *converso*/Sephardi newcomers, these exclusive clubs had little appeal. Indeed, one of the driving forces behind the earliest public dispute among Amsterdam's *converso*/Sephardi inhabitants (circa 1618–1619) involved divisions in the Bet Jacob synagogue driven by such insider-outsider dynamics. Only with this dispute resolved, and cooperation among Amsterdam's synagogues possible, could publicly Jewish life provide sufficiently attractive benefits to a broader cross-section of *converso*/Sephardi migrants. Earlier, individual personal networks defined the Amsterdam *converso*/Sephardi world.[38]

London's early to mid-sixteenth-century Flemish, Dutch, French, and Walloon migrants lived in a world between public and private participation in their adopted urban community.[39] As Christians they could participate in English religious life. Some of the migrants also had their own ideas as to appropriate worship, which, by the 1520s, included Lutheranism and Anabaptism. Thus, London's strangers, as the English called them, had several options, all of which attracted adherents. Some, it seems, remained Catholic.[40] By contrast, London's Hanse merchants, who had their own jurisdiction in the Steelyard, were worshipping as Lutherans by the 1520s, receiving attention from the English authorities only occasionally.[41] Yet other migrants, mostly Dutch, found themselves persecuted for their Anabaptism.[42] Only the late 1540s influx of Calvinist refugees caused the Dutch/Flemish and Walloon/French populations

to coalesce around anything resembling a dominant religious institution, re-
stricting the religious ambiguity they had known.[43]

Migrants and Public Community

The transition to public enclave, sometimes mistaken for a migrant enclave's
genesis, redefined the possibilities for individual migrants as well as the group.
Typically, corporate rights and privileges defined the enclave, which, in the
cases examined, included: (1) sanction for a designated religious institution;
(2) separate institutionalization of poor relief, other charity, and credit institutions; (3) access to alternative forms of law or dispute resolution; and (4)
group-specific definitions of rights and privileges. Enclaves founded for religious reasons did not differ in their form from those founded for other reasons.[44] Becoming public did not necessarily alter an enclave's economic basis,
but a leadership concentrated around the enclave's economic leaders, mercantile or artisanal, always emerged. Individual migrants now had more
choices to make. They confronted new rules for resolving disagreements, and
decisions about political and cultural loyalties when enclave moral discipline
became overly harsh. Sometimes enclave members chose to rely more on the
host society or leave the enclave altogether. But public enclaves also institutionalized a particular migration stream, and newcomers especially found
much greater support awaiting them.

The most crucial issues for migrants and hosts setting up a public enclave
concerned apportioning rights and responsibilities. Rotterdam's Scots began
this process by submitting a petition in 1642 requesting a church of their own
as well as monetary support for a minister's salary and church fabric. Rotterdam's city fathers received these requests of and granted them to "those of the
Scots nation [here in Rotterdam understood] as well as . . . the Scots skippers,"
that is, to a specific group of Scots corporately defined as a *natio* or *natie*.[45]
Other rights, jurisdiction, and responsibilities soon entered the picture. The
Scots minister Petrie requested permission to institute Scots church discipline
in Rotterdam and to impose it on all Rotterdam Scots, regardless of their ties
to his church! Rotterdam's city fathers and religious leaders wanted to prevent
the Scots from experimenting too vigorously with religious ideas and refused
this request.[46] In the 1650s they did, however, grant Rotterdam's Scots another
set of privileges limited to their number: a poor-relief subsidy, designed to
limit the city fathers' responsibility for the Scots poor.[47]

The Dutch/Flemish and Walloon/French enclaves in London, whose 1550s
founding opened the way to similar enclaves elsewhere in England, resulted in
a status as *unum corpus corporatum et politicum*.[48] The migrants also obtained

the right to worship separately from the Church of England and, ultimately, separate church buildings for the Dutch/Flemish and French-speaking groups.[49] Elizabeth I did not reauthorize the official corporate status of London's Dutch/Flemish and Walloon/French migrants. Effectively, though, the various enclaves that grew up in southeast England behaved and acquired rights as corporate groups. Ironically, given their status as the founding public enclaves, London's Dutch/Flemish and Walloon/French enclaves received the least favorable settlement from the Elizabethan regime. The two enclaves regained the use of their old churches (Austin Friars and St. Anthony's Chapel, respectively) and were ultimately able to have their members enrolled as denizens, but received no separate status or protections apart from those won after refounding.[50] They were therefore vulnerable to shifting political winds. Laws preventing strangers from exercising a craft or residing in London housing, not enforced in good times, often came back in bad.[51] For the outlying enclaves, which the London enclaves assisted the Elizabethan regime in founding, in contrast, letters patent usually specified residency rights, which were assigned to its members alone and could be extended to later migrants only on a limited basis. The newcomers also received a limited right to practice their crafts.[52]

Despite these limitations, England's Dutch/Flemish and Walloon/French enclaves evinced a corporate status in their behavior. At the regional and supraregional level of governance through meetings of ecclesiastical leaders, such as synods, colloquia, and the London *coetus*, and through the London-based enclaves' lobbying of the central government, the French-speaking and Dutch/Flemish migrants' leaders operated as representatives of each of their particular enclaves and of their two communities.[53] This was also true at the local level. The powers acquired either by church consistories or the so-called politic men (official migrant liaisons between host community and enclave) at the local level included enforcement of regulations applying to aliens, moral disciplining, mediation, dispute resolution, and notarial capacity.[54] Like their Rotterdam counterparts, local English authorities made the newcomers pay their own poor relief (and contribute to the English relief too). This minimized the costs of in-migration while enriching their communities with the considerable skills of the newcomers in the production and trading of textiles.[55]

Whereas Rotterdam's Scots enclave and England's Walloon/French and Dutch/Flemish enclaves arose from petitioning those in authority, Amsterdam's *converso*/Sephardi enclave became public through a mediation process. Between 1618 and 1619 members of Amsterdam's Bet Jacob synagogue came into conflict with each other and called on the Amsterdam city fathers and the Venetian Jewish community as judges. Their intervention involved a de facto recognition of the *converso*/Sephardi community as a *natio* (by Amsterdam's regents) and a religious entity (by the Venetian Jewish enclave's rabbinic court, the *bet din*).[56] This official recognition helped usher in the enclave's first official governing body, the *imposta* board, formed in 1622 from representatives of each of Amsterdam's then three synagogues (Bet Israel, Bet Jacob, and Neve Shalom). The *imposta* board regulated charity, judged disputes, and generally represented and made policy for the Amsterdam *converso*/Sephardi enclave. While the Amsterdam city fathers never specifically set the jurisdiction of the *imposta* board or the *Mahamad* of the combined synagogues, it acknowledged their legitimacy. The reason for the city fathers' policy comes through clearly in a 1683 decision by the burgomasters upholding the *Mahamad*'s *herem* (ban of excommunication), which they took to safeguard the *Mahamad*'s capacity to collect taxes from and care for the poor of the *converso*/Sephardi enclave. Decisions like this, rather than the few rights conceded to *converso*/Sephardi migrants (citizenship and some access to guild-regulated retail), effectively recognized in Amsterdam's *converso*/Sephardi enclave a corporately defined nation: the *Portugeesche natie*.[57]

Public enclaves divided migrant communities into three groupings: a leadership that maintained enclave privileges, rights, and responsibilities; migrants attached to the enclave; and detached migrants. The lay leaders of the enclaves were either merchants or involved in textile production. Clergy could also be crucial in the Christian enclaves, though not in *converso*/Sephardi Amsterdam.[58] Enclave leaderships faced three challenges: containing internal factionalization, ensuring that enclave members' behavior conformed to moral standards and did not conflict with the local population, and maintaining poor relief.

The enclave leaderships met with mixed success in controlling behavior. Success in guiding enclave members' actions depended on forces beyond a leadership's powers: migration patterns and the enforcement powers that the enclave's leadership received from the host society. Factional infighting, although frequently sparked by religious differences or matters of honor, had its roots in competitions for power between different waves of migrants to an enclave.[59] The main remedy for faction was time, as none of the enclaves possessed enough independent power or local influence to enforce judgments consistently against powerful, recalcitrant members. Not even multiple warnings and threats from the entire Walloon/French and Dutch/Flemish ecclesiastical hierarchy and a parliamentary committee, for example, could restrain the Huguenot minister Joseph Poujade in his crusade to retain his Canterbury position.[60] Consistent discipline of enclave members' behavior proved challenging for the same reasons, although relative cultural isolation (as in the *converso*/Sephardi enclave and the Dutch/Flemish community of London) or a close tie with the city fathers (as between the Norwich authorities and their Walloon and Dutch communities) could usually win the day.[61] Scots Rotterdam's leaders, on the other hand, had neither of these factors in their favor and found that within one generation of the enclave's attaining public status they could no longer control behavior consistently. Scots in Rotterdam chose to use the Dutch legal system rather than face the discipline of what many viewed as an overly regulatory Calvinist church council.[62]

In contrast, all of the enclaves under discussion succeeded in some measure with their poor-relief efforts due in part to their economic success. Merchants possessed far-flung personal/professional networks from which they could draw support.[63] Similarly, the more successful among the skilled Dutch, Flemish, and French-speaking artisans of England's southeast could generate the prosperity needed to support their less fortunate fellows.[64]

Given the mercantile (or artisanal) cast of their leadership, it is unsurprising to find these enclaves embedding poor-relief efforts in market-oriented infrastructures. Indeed, some of these enclave leaderships viewed poor relief as a necessary part of doing business, not just as a matter of keeping faith with enclave members and the host community.[65] To begin with Rotterdam, the Scots church there funded its poor relief in part from bequests derived from sailors to the East Indies that it had likely outfitted or assisted, loans made to sailors by lodging-house operators, and contributions from incoming Scots vessels.[66] In the 1640s and 1650s the consistory also made poor relief funds available as investment capital, although this occasioned friction that ended the practice.[67] The Amsterdam *converso*/Sephardi *imposta* board derived its funds from taxes on trade and, after the 1650s, once investment in the Dutch East India Company (VOC) and the Dutch West India Company (WIC) had become popular, from equities. The other main tax, the *finta*, was a clearly mercantile tax on wealth.[68] London's Dutch/Flemish and Walloon/French merchants maintained overseas trading involvements as well, and resident and itinerant merchants contributed significantly to poor relief; their regional counterparts became directly involved in export markets for cloth.[69] Cloth-manufacturing enclaves, such as those in Norwich and Canterbury, seem to have relied on standard collections and had no dominant merchant group. Their leaders could, however, employ poor relief funds as capital as their Scots Rotterdam counterparts did.[70]

The successful institutionalization of relief also institutionalized migration, drawing more migrants to these enclaves. True, the enclaves attempted to restrict short- and long-term relief in various ways to residents in good standing and those in need. Nevertheless, relief for those heading to another destination and periodic temporary migrants (e.g., sailors) became integral to relief practice in the enclaves; effective poor relief in these enclaves may actually have allowed migrants to maintain ties to an enclave and a place of origin.[71]

Obtaining ongoing support was another matter, as the Amsterdam *imposta* board's policy of refusing resources to nonmembers of the enclave suggests.[72] Still, the availability of resources in these enclaves eased the way of many migrants and accelerated migration to their host communities. That Rotterdam's Scots enclave and London's Dutch/Flemish enclave could collect resources from nonresident countrymen underscores the close tie between migration networks and enclaves that poor relief forged.[73] More striking are the London Dutch/Flemish and the Amsterdam *converso*/Sephardi enclaves' efforts to shape migration. The London enclave expended £12,510 between 1621 and 1640 assisting persecuted coreligionists from the Palatinate. The Amsterdam enclave sponsored dowries for poor *converso*/Sephardi women and transatlantic outmigration of enclave members as well as funding the repatriation of poor Ashkenazim.[74]

A public enclave's control of privileges, rights, and even jurisdictional powers also posed new questions concerning cultural and political loyalties. Members of a public enclave found resolving disputes with their fellows and responding to moral policing by the enclave's leadership particularly tricky. Even migrants living in a host community where they could avoid the public enclave of their fellows (e.g., London) did not willingly antagonize its members. It had connections with local authorities that commanded respect.

Where disputes were concerned, migrants weighed the advantages of the enclave's cultural familiarity against their perceptions of its fairness and the costs of using host community justice to their social position in the enclave. Going outside the enclave could create resentment: it created publicity, potentially embarrassed the enclave's leadership, and could lose the support needed by migrants later. This was especially true if enclave leaders had specified that disputes should remain internal, as the Dutch/Flemish consistory of Austin Friars had. Jan Sconinckx, an Austin Friars congregant, found that his willingness to sue fellow migrants in London's courts stripped him of his membership in the congregation and left him vulnerable to lawsuits from English opponents. This kind of isolation could force a migrant to move on. Alternatively, if, as was true in Amsterdam and Rotterdam, the easier availability of corporate rights and privileges made complete withdrawal from the enclave feasible, the enclave leadership could do little.[75]

Migrants had less chance, however, of countering an enclave leadership's disciplinary authority. Permission to exercise this authority came from the local community and could include policing and judicial support from the host community as well as specific judicial and/or policing powers granted to the enclave leadership. Moreover, enclave leaders and local authorities alike were committed to preserving honor for authority and the group. Finally, the foundation of disciplinary power for each of these enclave leaderships was rooted in a religious jurisdiction with all of the loaded symbolism that entailed. In short, the enclave leadership disciplined individuals to defend the honor of magistracy, the ethnos, and the divine.[76] The fate of Margaret Simson, a woman abandoned by her husband and the employer who had impregnated her, demonstrates this potent combination in action. Arriving in Rotterdam in the summer of 1643, Simson took service in the house of a couple who were members of the Scots Church of Rotterdam. When her pregnancy became evident, however, the minister Alexander Petrie began to ask questions. Simson fled to Dordrecht, where she died.[77]

Simson was not the last to flee the Scots Church of Rotterdam's jurisdiction, a strategy members of the other enclaves under consideration also perforce adopted.[78] Overall, though, the number of migrants ejected by disciplinary action was comparatively small in those cases where figures are available.[79] The real influence of enclave moral discipline was on the integration of migrants into the host community. To the extent that an enclave's jurisdiction was perceived as unduly oppressive and became labeled, ironically, as *foreign*, it drove migrants away. All of the enclaves under discussion struggled with this problem.[80]

Conclusion

None of the public enclaves discussed survived the eighteenth century without drastic change. Some disappeared. The Dutch/Flemish communities of seventeenth-century England melted into English society. Not even William of Orange's arrival in 1688 and the Dutch migrants he brought with him altered this. Without new migrants from France and the Dutch Republic throughout the seventeenth century, but especially after 1685, southeast England's Walloon/French community would have met a similar fate.[81] In contrast, Scots Rotterdam remained active well into the eighteenth century, although the Scots Church of Rotterdam's ties to it changed. Amsterdam's *converso/* Sephardi community survived the eighteenth century, but in a reduced state.[82]

In part, the forces of political economy explain the differing fates of these migration streams. After 1688 fewer political threats existed to make southeast England, Amsterdam, or Rotterdam enticing to the groups under discussion. Equally important, Dutch/Flemish and Walloon/French migrants had much to gain by joining the British Atlantic as did the more successful members of Amsterdam's *converso/*Sephardi enclave, whose departure for London, among other places, gravely diminished its prospects.[83] Scots, by contrast, could choose between the Atlantic, the North and Baltic Sea zone, and the Indian Ocean trades, so Rotterdam remained viable as a node within a complex system of Scots migration.[84]

At the same time, the disappearance or diminution of a public enclave's role did not augur a migration stream's elimination any more than the creation of one signaled its advent. Migration traffic between so-called places of origin and the migration destinations considered here never ceased, even for refugees from open and violent religious strife.[85] The forces of political economy worked through and were influenced by interactions within migrant communities, especially between different waves of migrants, and by legalized rights and privileges that societies historically extended to outsiders. These factors could change, but always with reference to the immediate and even the distant past as well as the particular situation of a local migrant community. In the above I hope to have given a preliminary mapping of migrant engagement with this past, exploration of which will bring migrants more fundamentally into the historical narratives of premodern Europe.

Notes

1. Robert Bartlett, *The Making of Europe: Conquest, Colonization and Cultural Change, 950–1350* (Princeton, NJ: Princeton University Press, 1994); Jan Lucassen, *Migrant Labour in Europe, 1600–1900: The Drift to the North Sea* (London: Croom Helm, 1987); Cynthia Truant, *The Rites of Labor: Brotherhoods of Compagnonnage in Old and New Regime France* (Ithaca, NY: Cornell University Press, 1994); Willem Frihoff, *Wegen van Evert Willemsz. Een Hollands weeskind op zoek naar zichzelf* (Nijmegen: Sun, 1995); Donna Merwick, *Death of a Notary: Conquest & Change in Colonial New York* (Ithaca, NY: Cornell University Press, 1999).

2. See Alexia Grosjean and Steve Murdoch, "The Scottish Community in Seventeenth-Century Gothenburg," in *Scottish Communities Abroad in the Early Modern Period*, ed. Alexia Grosjean and Steve Murdoch (Leiden: Brill, 2005), 192–93; Leo Lucassen, "Eternal Vagrants? State Formation, Migration, and Travelling Groups," in *Migration, Migration History, History: Old Paradigms and New Perspectives*, ed. Jan Lucassen and Leo Lucassen (Bern: Peter Lang, 1997), 229–40; Maria Bogucka, "Polish Towns Between the Sixteenth and Eighteenth Centuries," in *A Republic of Nobles: Studies in Polish History to 1864*, ed. and trans., J. K. Feorowicz, ed. Maria Bogucka and Henryk Samsonowicz (Cambridge: Cambridge University Press, 1982), 141–44; Laurence Fontaine, *The History of Pedlars in Europe*, trans. Vicki Whittaker (Durham, NC: Duke University Press, 1996), 22–28, 35–49; Jonathan Israel, *Diasporas within a Diaspora: Jews, Crypto-Jews and the World Maritime Empires (1540–1740)* (Leiden: Brill, 2002), 68–94; *European Jewry in the Age of Mercantilism, 1550–1750* (Oxford: Clarendon, 1985), 5–69, 87–206; David Swetschinski, *Reluctant Cosmopolitans: The Portuguese Jews of Seventeenth-Century Amsterdam* (London: Littman Library of Jewish

Civilization, 2000), 10–53, 102–64; Bernard Cottret, *The Huguenots in England: Immigration and Settlement, c. 1550–1700,* trans. Peregrine and Adriana Stevenson with an afterword by Emmanuel Le Roy Ladurie (Cambridge: Cambridge University Press, 1991), especially parts 1 and 2.

3. Swetschinski, *Reluctant Cosmopolitans,* 165–224, 241–49.

4. See Gayle K. Brunelle, "Migration and Religious Identity: The Portuguese of Seventeenth-Century Rouen," *Journal of Early Modern History* 7 (2003): 283–311.

5. Merwick, *Death of a Notary.*

6. Douglas Catterall, *Community without Borders: Scots Migrants and the Changing Face of Power in the Dutch Republic, c. 1600–1700* (Leiden: Brill, 2002), 344–45. The Covenanter minister John Livingston, for example, fled the harsh policies of Scotland's post-1660s Stuart regime with his family, a classic case of exile. John Livingston's son Robert Livingston, however, rejected Scotland and Rotterdam for New York, founding one of that state's colonial dynasties in the process.

7. The term *diaspora* has been the subject of scholarly debates touching, among other things, its precise historical background and development and its applicability to the experiences of different groups. Two recent discussions are Jon Stratton, "(Dis)placing the Jews: Historicizing the Idea of Diaspora," *Diasporas* 6 (1997): 301–29; Colin Palmer, "Defining and Studying the Modern African Diaspora," *AHA Perspectives* 36 (September 1998): 1, 22–25.

8. Miriam Bodian, *Hebrews of the Portuguese Nation: Conversos and Community in Early Modern Amsterdam* (Bloomington: Indiana University Press, 1999), 6–24, 76–151; Swetschinski, *Reluctant Cosmopolitans,* 165–224; Yosef Kaplan, *An Alternative Path to Modernity: The Sephardi Diaspora in Western Europe* (Leiden: Brill, 2000), 51–77; Israel, *Diasporas,* 41–96, 185–268; Jonathan Schorsch, "Portmanteau Jews: Sephardim and Race in the Early Modern Atlantic World," in *Port Jews: Jewish Communities in Cosmopolitan Maritime Trading Centres, 1550–1950,* ed. David Cesarani (London: Frank Cass, 2002), 60–70.

9. On migration traditions see Catterall, *Community without Borders,* 341–57.

10. In this chapter I focus chiefly on enclaves in London, Norwich, Canterbury, Southampton, and, to a lesser extent, Colchester, as the published primary and secondary source materials are richest for these communities.

11. Rather than the word *Sephardim,* I have opted for this more cumbersome term to capture the many relationships to Judaism that members of Amsterdam's Portuguese nation adopted, ranging from a publicly Sephardic identity (albeit with some twists unique to their *converso* origins) to an outwardly Christian stance to something in between. For some recent contributions to the complex debate on identity in the Portuguese nation, which I do not address here, see Bodian, *Hebrews,* 6–24, 76–151; Swetschinski, *Reluctant Cosmopolitans,* 165–224; Kaplan, *An Alternative Path,* 51–77; Israel, *Diasporas,* 41–96, 185–268.

12. See especially Swetschinski, *Reluctant Cosmopolitans,* 15–25, 54–101, 167–82.

13. Catterall, *Community without Borders,* 30–41, 125–26; T. C. Smout, *Scottish Trade on the Eve of Union, 1660–1707* (Edinburgh: Oliver & Boyd, 1963), 25–29, 72–115, 185–94, 205–38; Ian D. Whyte, *Scotland before the Industrial Revolution: An Economic & Social History, c. 1050–1750* (London: Longman, 1995), 68–71, 170–209;

W. H. K. Turner, "Burgh, State, and the Scottish Wool Textile Industry, c. 1500–c. 1840: Part I: The Role of the Royal Burghs," *Scottish Geographical Magazine* 101 (1985): 85–90; Margaret H. B. Sanderson, "The Edinburgh Merchant in Society, 1570–1603: The Evidence of their Testaments," in *The Renaissance and Reformation in Scotland: Essays in Honour of Gordon Donaldson,* ed. Ian B. Cowan and Duncan Shaw (Edinburgh: Scottish Academic Press, 1983), 188–97; Walter Makey, "Edinburgh in Mid-Seventeenth Century," in *The Early Modern Town in Scotland,* ed. Michael Lynch (London: Croom Helm, 1987), 192–97; Alexander Stevenson, "Medieval Scottish Associations with Bruges," in *Freedom and Authority, Scotland, c. 1050–c. 1650: Historical and Historiographical Essays Presented to Grant G. Simpson,* ed. Terry Brotherstone and David Ditchburn (East Linton, Lothian: Tuckwell, 2000), 93–107; David Ditchburn, *Scotland and Europe: The Medieval Kingdom and Its Contacts with Christendom, 1214–1560* (East Linton, Lothian: Tuckwell, 2000), 138–96, 205–32; John Davidson and Alexander Gray, *The Scottish Staple at Veere: A Study in the Economic History of Scotland* (London: Longmans, Green, 1909), 113–253; Steve Murdoch, *Britain, Denmark-Norway and the House of Stuart, 1603–1660* (East Linton, Lothian: Tuckwell, 2003), 25–36; Mathew Glozier, "Scots in the Dutch and French Armies during the Thirty Years' War," in *Scotland and the Thirty Years' War, 1618–1648,* ed. Steve Murdoch (Leiden: Brill, 2001), 124–37.

14. Keith Sprunger, *Dutch Puritanism: A History of the English and Scottish Churches in the Netherlands in the Sixteenth and Seventeenth Centuries* (Leiden: Brill, 1982), 162–80; Douglas Catterall, "The Rituals of Reformed Discipline: Managing Honor and Conflict in the Scottish Church of Rotterdam, 1643–1665," *Archive for Reformation History* 94 (2003): 205–208; *Community without Borders,* 95–115,195–202. For an early reference to the use of the Scots language in Rotterdam, see Gemeentearchief Rotterdam (hereafter GAR)/Oud Notarieel Archief (hereafter ONA)/431/ 133–135, 9-[3]-1640. The Forguns provide a good example of an early prominent Scots kin network: GAR/ONA/92/244; GAR/ONA/111/47; GAR/ONA/143/299; GAR/ONA/150/731; GAR/ONA/151/344; GAR/ONA/85/125; GAR/ONA/89/46; GAR/ONA/89/109; GAR/ONA/90/95.

15. Pettegree, *Foreign Protestant Communities in Sixteenth-Century London* (Oxford: Clarendon Press, 1986), 11–22; Laura Hunt Yungblut, *Strangers Settled Here amongst Us: Policies, Perceptions and the Presence of Aliens in Elizabethan England* (London: Routledge, 1996), 10–29, 36–60.

16. Here I have adopted Laura Yungblut's more conservative numbers as a floor for migrant numbers. Yungblut, *Stangers,* 10–29. For the end of the sixteenth century Irene Scouloudi has produced fairly precise figures for London's migrant population, pegging it at 3.69 percent, with a decline to between 1 and 2 percent by 1635. For the latter figures see Ole Peter Grell, *Dutch Calvinists in Early Stuart London: The Dutch Church in Austin Friars, 1603–1642* (Leiden: Brill, 1989), 16.

17. Pettegree, *Foreign Protestant Communities,* 18.

18. Pettegree, *Foreign Protestant Communities,* 11–22, 83–112; Yungblut, *Strangers,* 10–29, 36–60, 95–113; Eamon Duffy, *The Stripping of the Altars: Traditional Religion in England, 1400–1580* (New Haven, CT: Yale University Press, 1992), 454–59.

19. I leave aside the issue of vagrancy; migrants who could make a claim on a local enclave would be unlikely to fall into this category. See Douglas Catterall, "'Secondo il

resoconto di sua madre che ancora abita a Oostenhuysen . . .': Migranti e politiche sui flussi migratori nella società urbana nordeuropea," *Quaderni storici* 106, no. 36 (2001): 25–57.

20. Maarten Prak, "The Politics of Intolerance: Citizenship and Religion in the Dutch Republic (Seventeenth to Eighteenth centuries)," in *Calvinism and Religious Toleration in the Dutch Golden Age*, ed. R. Po-Chia Hsia and H. F. K. van Nierop (Cambridge: Cambridge University Press, 2002), 161–62; Catterall, "'Secondo il resoconto,'" 27–36; Lotte van de Pol, *Het Amsterdams hoerdom. Prostitutie in de zeventiende en achttiende eeuw* (Amsterdam: Wereldbibliotheek, 1996), 67.

21. Catterall, *Community without Borders*, 36–44, 78–84, 300–14.

22. Swetschinski, *Reluctant Cosmospolitans*, 10–11, 167–76; Miriam Bodian, *Hebrews*, 25–63; Israel, *Diasporas*, 73–96; Van de Pol, *Het Amsterdams hoerdom*, 110.

23. Hans Bontemantel, *Regeeringe van Amsterdam soo in't civiel als crimineel en militaire (1643–1672)*, ed. G.W. Kernkamp (The Hague: Martinus Nijhoff, 1897), 1:cxxxii, as quoted in Swetschinski, *Reluctant Cosmopolitans*, 11. The translation of Bontemantel is from Swetschinski's text.

24. Bontemantel, *Regeeringe*, 1:xcccii.

25. Swetschinski, *Reluctant Cosmopolitans*, 10–14. For a recent explanation of the origins of this approach to toleration, see Joke Spaans, "Religious Policies in the Seventeenth-Century Dutch Republic," in *Calvinism and Religious Toleration in the Dutch Golden Age*, ed. R. Po-Chia Hsia and H. F. K. van Nierop (Cambridge: Cambridge University Press, 2002), 77–85; Peter van Rooden, "Jews and Religious Toleration in the Dutch Republic," in *Calvinism and Religious Toleration*, 133–44. Van Rooden proposes that the treatment of Amsterdam's Jewish community, unique until the mid-seventeenth century, provided the paradigm for policies toward the republic's Christian dissenters thereafter.

26. Swetschinski, *Reluctant Cosmopolitans*, 20, 85–90, 167–87; Bodian, *Hebrews*, 43–52.

27. Yungblut, *Strangers*, 11–12, 61–94; Grell, *Dutch Calvinists*, 9–26, 149–75; *Calvinist Exiles in Tudor and Stuart England* (Aldershot: Scholar Press, 1996), 42–45; Cottret, *Huguenots*, 50–64; Lien Bich Luu, "Assimilation or Segregation: Colonies of Alien Craftsmen in Elizabethan London," *Proceedings of the Huguenot Society of Great Britain and Ireland* (36): Special Issue: *The Strangers' Progress: Integration and Disintegration of the Huguenot and Walloon Refugee Community, 1567–1889*, ed. Randolph Vigne and Graham C. Gibbs (1995): 160–64 (issue hereafter referred to as *Strangers' Progress*); Pettegree, *Foreign Protestant Communities*, 12–16, 140–49, 276–93.

28. Pettegree, *Foreign Protestant Communities*, 82–112; Yungblut, *Strangers*, 11, 25–29, 72–74, 77; Grell, *Dutch Calvinists*, 18–26.

29. Sprunger, *Dutch Puritanism*, 162–63, 175; *The Learned Doctor William Ames: Dutch Backgrounds of English and American Puritanism* (Urbana: University of Illinois Press, 1972), 215–18.

30. Sprunger, *Dutch Puritanism*, 175, 464. Unfortunately, it is hard to say how many Scots did. Membership lists for Rotterdam's early English churches do not survive.

31. Catterall, *Community without Borders*, 238–63; Sprunger, *Dutch Puritanism*, 164–80, 329–35.

32. Catterall, *Community without Borders*, 41.

33. GAR/Classis Schieland/5, 10-24-1642, 8-10-1643; GAR/Nederlands Hervormde Gemeente/1, 8-26-1643. How many Scots joined the Dutch Reformed Church of Rotterdam is uncertain, but the Classis of Schieland noted that there were three to four hundred Scots of the Reformed religion in Rotterdam in 1642 and the first minister of the church, Alexander Petrie, requested more than once that the Scots members of Rotterdam Dutch Reformed Church be allowed to come over to the Scots Church, suggesting that the number involved was significant.

34. GAR/Classis Schieland/5, 10-24-1642, e.g., refers to Rotterdam's Scots nation; for more on the concept of nation see below in section 3.

35. Catterall, *Community without Borders*, 233–93; Jori Zijlmans, *Vriendenkringen in de zeventiende eeuw. Verenigingsvormen van het informele culturele leven te Rotterdam* (Den Haag: Sdu Uigevers, 1999).

36. Swetschinski, *Reluctant Cosmopolitans*, 11.

37. Swetschinski, *Reluctant Cosmopolitans*, 11–14, 172; Bodian, *Hebrews*, 43–47.

38. Swetschinski, *Reluctant Cosmopolitans*, 172–87; Bodian, *Hebrews*, 30–43, 134–46. Cooperative efforts like the *Santa Companhia de dotar orfans e donzelas pobres* or *Dotar*, a society that provided dowries to poor *converso*/Sephardi women founded in 1615, preceded the resolution of the dispute I mention here. They did not, however, produce a public institutional form for the entire *converso*/Sephardi community. This happened in the 1620s (on this see below).

39. I have omitted consideration of the strangers outside London as their numbers were negligible. See Yungblut, *Strangers*, 12.

40. Pettegree, *Foreign Protestant Communities*, 17–18, 83–112; Duffy, *Stripping of the Altars*, 454–59.

41. Pettegree, *Foreign Protestant Communities*, 18–20.

42. Pettegree, *Foreign Protestant Communities*, 20.

43. Section 3 discusses the new jurisdictions created by the emergence of these public enclaves in London.

44. The public enclaves I am discussing all grew up around religious institutions, but this was only one pathway to a public enclave. All paths led to a similar form for most enclaves; the other developmental paths for public enclaves included merchant factory, group-specific rights granted in the charter of a local community, and enclaves built solely around shared territoriality through the *natio*. For examples of enclaves with these different origins see Heinrich Hitzigrath, *Die Kompagnie der Merchant Adventurers und die englische Kirchengemeinde in Hamburg, 1611–1835* (Hamburg: Verlegt bei Johannes Kriebel, 1904); Grosjean and Murdoch, "The Scottish Community," 191–223; Robert Sandberg, "Urban Landownership in Early Modern Sweden," in *Power, Profit and Urban Land: Landownership in Medieval and Early Modern Northern European Towns*, ed. Finn-Einar Eliassen and Geir Atle Ersland (Aldershot: Scolar Press, 1996), 179–193; Thomas Dandelet, "Spanish Conquest and Colonization at the Center of the Old World: The Spanish Nation in Rome, 1555–1625," *Journal of Modern History* 69 (1997): 479–511.

45. GAR/Oud Stadsarchief (hereafter OSA)/719/890v, 7-14-1642; GAR/OSA/719/918v-919r, 10-13-1642. On the corporate and ethnic dimensions of the *natio*, both of

which met in Rotterdam's *Schotse natie,* see Eric Hobsbawm, *Nations and Nationalism Since 1780* (Cambridge: Cambridge University Press, 1992), 14–17; Jeremy Black, "An English Identity?" *History Today* 48 (1998), 5, 4p, 1c, 4bw, http://80-search.epnet .com.argo.library.okstate.edu/direct.asp?an=340327& db=afh (accessed October 1, 2003); Guido Zernatto, "Nation: The History of a Word," *Review of Politics* 6(1944): 353–56; John Pope-Hennessey, *Cellini* (New York: Abbeville, 1985), 218; Dandelet, "Spanish Conquest and Colonization"; Swetchinski, *Reluctant Cosmopolitans,* 165–67; Brunelle, "Migration," 289–91. My thanks to Dr. Donald Harreld of Brigham Young University for sharing his expertise on the corporate meaning of *natie* in Antwerp.

46. Catterall, "Rituals," 205–207.

47. On Scots poor relief in Rotterdam, see GAR/OSA/721/480/ 8-2-1653; GAR/ Scots Church of Rotterdam (hereafter SCR)1/8-3-1653; GAR/SCR/40.

48. J. Lindeboom, *Austin Friars: History of the Dutch Reformed Church in London, 1550–1950,* trans. D. de Jongh (The Hague: Martinus Nijhoff, 1950), 7–10; Grell, *Dutch Calvinists,* 9–11.

49. Pettegree, *Foreign Protestant Communities,* 35–39.

50. Pettegree, *Foreign Protestant Communities,* 133–81. An example of privileges acquired later would be the collective exemption from apprenticeship requirements London's city fathers extended to members of Austin Friars (Grell, *Dutch Calvinists,* 78–80).

51. Pettegree, *Foreign Protestant Communities,* 276–95; Charles Littleton, "Social Interactions of Aliens in Late Elizabethan London: Evidence from the 1493 Return and the French Church Consistory 'actes,'" *Strangers' Progress,* 151–52; Luu, "Assimilation or Segregation," 162–64; Grell, *Dutch Calvinists,* 9–26, 149–75, 224–48.

52. For Norwich, Canterbury, and Southampton see John Miller, "Town Government and Protestant Strangers, 1560–1690," *Proceedings of the Huguenot Society of Great Britain & Ireland* 36 (1997): 578–86. Not that the outlying communities were immune to shifting political fortunes; Norwich's city fathers imposed on its Walloon and Dutch enclaves a Book of Orders.

53. On the *coetus,* the colloquia (a substitute for the *classis*), and the synods of the alien churches see Grell, *Calvinist Exiles,* 37–42. For the London-based enclaves' lobbying see Grell, *Dutch Calvinists,* 81–92; Cottret, *Huguenots,* 98–117.

54. On the politic men see Miller, "Town Government," 582; Grell, *Dutch Calvinists,* 86–87. On consistorial jurisdiction see W. J. C. Moens, *The Walloons and Their Church at Norwich: Their History and Registers, 1565–1832* (1887–88; reprint, Nendeln/Liechtenstein: Kraus Reprint, 1969), 1:47–57; Pettegree, *Foreign Protestant Communities,* 182–214; Grell, *Dutch Calvinists,* 74–89; John Campbell, "The Walloon Community in Canterbury, 1625–1649," (Ph.D. diss., University of Wisconsin, 1970), 41–42, 47–50.

55. Miller, "Town Government," 579–81. Predictably, migrants sometimes refused to pay parish rates. See Moen, *Walloons,* 61–63; John Miller, "The Fortunes of Strangers in Norwich and Canterbury, 1565–1700," in *Memory and Identity: The Huguenots in France and the Atlantic Diaspora,* ed. Bertrand van Ruymbeke and Randy Sparks (Columbia: University of South Carolina Press, 2003), 119.

56. Swetschinski, *Reluctant Cosmopolitans,* 12–13, 172–76; Bodian, *Hebrews,* 48–50.

57. Swetschinski, *Reluctant Cosmopolitans*, 10–25, 166–67, 172–87, 221–24; Bodian, *Hebrews*, 63–64. Although I use Swetschinski's work here, my conclusion that the *Portugueesche natie* was a corporate entity differs slightly from his. Earlier cooperative efforts like the *Dotar* predated the *imposta* board and the *Mahamad* (the governing board created when Amsterdam's three Jewish congregations merged in 1639). The *Dotar*, however, was no governing body, so I have not discussed it here.

58. Swetschinski, *Reluctant Cosmopolitans*, 102–104, 187–96, 204–206; Robert A. Houston, "Elders and Deacons: Membership of the Consistory of the Scots Church, Rotterdam (1643–1829) and Tolbooth Parish, Edinburgh (1690–1760)," *Tijdschrift voor Sociale Geschiedenis* 20 (1994): 282–308; Catterall, *Community without Borders*, 243–93; Moens, *Walloons*, iv, 25–37, 47–57, 67–85; Grell, *Dutch Calvinists*, 53–81; *Calvinist Exiles*, 36–37; Andrew Spicer, "A Process of Gradual Assimilation: The Exile Community in Southampton, 1567–1635," *Strangers' Progress*, 188, 190–91; Campbell, "Walloon Community," 32–45.

59. Catterall, *Community without Borders*, 73–78, 243–93; Swetschinski, *Reluctant Cosmopolitans*, 249–59; Moens, *Walloons*, 106–108; Pettegree, *Foreign Protestant Communities*, 149–81; Cottret, *Huguenots*, 123–58; Campbell, "Walloon Community," 154–80.

60. Campbell, "Walloon Community," 154–80.

61. Swetschinski, *Reluctant Cosmopolitans*, 213–77; Grell, *Dutch Calvinists*, 74–80; Moens, *Walloons*, 31–33, 55–57, 61–63.

62. Catterall, *Community without Borders*, 194–293.

63. Swetschinski, *Reluctant Cosmopolitans*, 102–64; Israel, *Diaporas*, 452–86; Catterall, *Community without Borders*, 77–78; Smout, *Scottish Trade*, 99–115; Grell, *Calvinist Exiles*, 6–28, 37.

64. Here I rely on data from Canterbury's Walloon/French enclave, assuming it to be representative of enclaves outside London given its economic similarities to Norwich's Dutch/Flemish and Walloon/French enclaves. Campbell, "Walloon Community," 56–110. Moens, *Walloons*, 27–30, 35–37, 71–85.

65. Catterall, *Community without Borders*, 115–29; Campbell, "Walloon Community," 90–93; Grell, *Dutch Calvinists*, 93.

66. Catterall, *Community without Borders*, 128–29, 148–51.

67. GAR/SCR/1.

68. Israel, *Diasporas*, 163, 191, 451–87; Swetschinski, *Reluctant Cosmopolitians*, 114–30, 182, 257–58; Tirtsah Levie Bernfeld, "Financing Poor Relief in the Spanish-Portuguese Jewish Community in Amsterdam in the Seventeenth and Eighteenth Centuries," in *Dutch Jewry: Its History and Secular Culture (1500–2000)* (Leiden: Brill, 2002), 71–79.

69. Grell, *Dutch Calvinists*, 43–53, 96–99, 292–307; Pettegree, *Foreign Protestant Communities*, 198–214; Moens, *Walloons*, 28–30, 74–79; Campbell, "Walloon Community," 63. For my statements on the French-speaking community I rely more on Andrew Pettegree's account of the late sixteenth century.

70. John Campbell, "Walloon Community," 56–59, 92–96; Moens, *Walloons*, 55–58, 60–63.

71. Grell, *Dutch Calvinists*, 93–105; Swetschinski, *Reluctant Cosmopolitans*, 182–87, 200–203; Bernfeld, "Financing Poor Relief," 63–67, 85–96; Catterall, *Community without Borders*, 115–29; Campbell, "Walloon Community," 88–92; Miller, "Town Governments," 578–81; Littleton, "Social interactions," 149–52.

72. Swetschinski, *Reluctant Cosmopolitans*, 182–87, 202; Kaplan, *An Alternative Path*, 60–107; Bernfeld, "Financing Poor Relief," 85–96. The success these measures had is debatable, as Tirtsah Levie Bernfeld has recently argued.

73. Catterall, *Community without Borders*, 128; Grell, *Dutch Calvinists*, 292–307.

74. Grell, *Dutch Calvinists*, 176–223; Swetschinski, *Reluctant Cosmopolitans*, 95–96, 126–29, 178–87, 202; Bodian, *Hebrews*, 47–48, 134–46; Kaplan, *An Alternative Path*, 60–107; Bernfeld, "Financing Poor Relief," 85–96.

75. Grell, *Dutch Calvinists*, 78–80; Swetschinski, *Reluctant Cosmopolitans*, 225–27; Catterall, "Rituals," 202–14; Catterall, *Community without Borders*, 43–44.

76. Moens, *Walloons*, 28–29, 47–57; Catterall, "Rituals," 205–14; Catterall, *Community without Borders*, 59–84, 115–29, 175–340; Robert A. Houston, "The Consistory of the Scots Church, Rotterdam: An Aspect of 'Civic Calvinism,' c. 1600–1800," *Archive for Reformation History* 87 (1996): 362–92; Swetschinski, *Reluctant Cosmopolitans*, 165–87; 213–77; Bodian, *Hebrews*, 76–151; Kaplan, *An Alternative Path*, 60–77, 108–42; Grell, *Dutch Calvinists*, 74–89; Miller, "Town Government," 579–84; Campbell, "Walloon Community," 41–42, 47–50; Francis W. Cross, *History of the Walloon & Huguenot Church at Canterbury* (1898; reprint, Nendeln/Liechtenstein: Kraus Reprint, 1969), 55–60; Littleton, "Social Interactions," 155; *idem*, "Acculturation and the French Church of London, 1600–circa 1640," in *Memory and Identity*, 2003, 91–104, 106–107.

77. Catterall, *Community without Borders*, 70–72.

78. GAR/SCR/1-2; Kaplan, *An Alternative Path*, 122–23; Grell, *Dutch Calvinists*, 74–80. Expulsions of common enclave members likely occurred in the other enclaves under discussion in addition to those for which I give citations here, but, unfortunately, less research has been devoted to this topic.

79. In Rotterdam's Scots community it appears that only one person was actually excommunicated and the leaders of the Dutch/Flemish public enclave in London showed a similar reluctance to impose this penalty. Amsterdam's *converso*/Sephardi leadership handed down excommunication sentences more often (at least forty men and women were excommunicated between 1622 and 1683). Still, the *parnasim* imposed excommunication reluctantly, often using its threat or withdrawing it within a few days to avoid harming the enclave's social cohesion. GAR/SCR/1–2; Grell, *Dutch Calvinists* 74–80; Kaplan, *An Alternative Path*, 110–54; Swetschinski, *Reluctant Cosmopolitans*, 225–77.

80. Catterall, *Community without Borders*, 73–78, 253–93; Kaplan, *An Alternative Path*, 109–10,133–39; Swetschinski, *Reluctant Cosmopolitans*, 15–16, 249–77; Pettegree, *Foreign Protestant Communities*, 192–93.

81. Grell, *Calvinist Exiles*, 34–36, 120–45; Moens, *Walloons*, 108–109; Cross, *History of the Walloon and Huguenot Church*, 143–76; Cottret, *Huguenots*, 8–21, 149–262; Daniel Statt, *Foreigners and Englishmen: The Controversy over Immigration and Population, 1660–1760* (Newark, NJ: University of Delaware Press, 1995), 19–98.

82. Catterall, *Community without Borders*, 341–45; Houston, "Consistory," 378–92; Levie, "Financing Poor Relief," 85–98.

83. Cottret, *Huguenots*, 185–90; Statt, *Foreigners and Englishmen*, 38–120, 194–222; Levie, "Financing Poor Relief," 85–98; Swetschinski, *Reluctant Cosmopolitans*, 126–30.

84. Catterall, *Community without Borders*, 341–45; Christian Koninckx, *The First and Second Charters of the Swedish East India Company (1731–1766)* (Kortrijk, Belgium: Van Ghemmert, 1980), 79–81, 82–107, 407–409; Murdoch, *Britain, Denmark-Norway and the House of Stuart*, 25–36; Ned C. Landsman, "Nation, Migration, and the Province in the First British Empire: Scotland and the Americas, 1600–1800," *American Historical Review* 104 (1999): 463–75.

85. Littleton, "Social interactions," 148–51; Grell, *Calvinist Exiles*, 1–33; Catterall, *Community without Borders*, 25–84; Swetschinski, *Reluctant Cosmopolitans*, 69, 85, 88–89.

8

Forcing the Doors of Heathendom

Ethnography, Violence, and the
Dutch East India Company

Sanjay Subrahmanyam

> But you, who presume that you have at last found the best religion, or
> rather, the best men to whom you have pledged your credulity, how do you
> know that they are the best out of all those who have taught other religions,
> are teaching them now, or will teach them in the future? Have you exam-
> ined all those religions, both ancient and modern, which are taught here
> and in India and throughout the whole world?
>
> —Spinoza to Alfred Burgh (1675)[1]

THIS CHAPTER IS INTENDED TO HONOR the contribution of James D. Tracy to
the historiography of the last quarter century and more, and when one reflects on his work, it is only natural eventually to gravitate—even if our route
takes us by the abodes of Charles V and Erasmus—to the problem of the *early
modern*. There are several—and even mutually contradictory—ways of defining the early modern period, of which two particular strands of definition
merit our attention here. The first of these stresses relatively massive and material aspects of the transformation from a medieval social formation to an
early modern one, and points to the opening of new geographical horizons
and trade routes; a worldwide monetary revolution; the so-called Columbian
exchange of plants, animals, and diseases; the construction of a new ecological regime on a world scale; and the attendant changes in the nature of state
power and state systems. Although European, or at least Eurocentric, in its
early predilections and first usage, this view need not necessarily mean that
the term *early modern* would be restricted to the western end of Eurasia, for
many of the phenomena listed above could be addressed from the Ottoman

Empire, Mughal India, or Tokugawa Japan. The second approach, shying away from the robust materialism of the first, would instead largely stress mental and sociocultural changes, and would hence concentrate on the "modern" part of the term *early modern*. In other words, the emphasis would be on the emergence of new and unprecedented forms of modern subjectivity, whether properly reflexive or not. This would go together with a new sense of individuality, presumably linked in turn to the capacity of the individual to liberate him- or herself to an unprecedented degree from received structures. Such a view has more in it, at first sight, of the vocabulary of the anthropologist and Taylorian sociologist than that of the historian, but appearances can be deceptive. For a little reflection shows that this view is not unrelated to a classic historian's formulation of the emergence of the modern, namely, that of Jacob Burckhardt.[2]

The two strands can be read either separately or together. If we choose the latter route, then attention needs to be paid not only to reflexive knowledge but also to the construction of knowledge about the world at large. In this context, the imperial traveler emerges as an excellent example of the "knowing subject" of the early modern period, preceding the Enlightenment proper by a century or two.[3] His conceit is that of the singular individual, yet his objects of attention are often communities—especially the communities of others. The traveler as ethnographer thus describes the collective behavior of the peoples whom he encounters, and at the same time poses himself as a sort of universal individual cast adrift from the familiar moorings of his own society. In this sense, the history of ethnography is an excellent place from which to study not only the early modern as a concept but also the complex relationship between individual and community as it was transformed between the medieval and early modern centuries.

The task described above is already well under way for the greatest of the early modern European empires—namely that of the Spanish Habsburgs. The subject has been approached from a variety of angles, whether the relatively classic "history of ideas" approach espoused by Anthony Pagden, or in more socially and culturally inflected works like those of Serge Gruzinski.[4] The same cannot be said, however, of the European nation that has most occupied James Tracy in his past work, namely the United Provinces of the Netherlands, which also had a world empire of sorts in the seventeenth and eighteenth centuries. True, things have changed even in Dutch East India Company (VOC) studies over the last two decades or so. In the 1980s, when I began my own work on the VOC, the principal focus was still on economic history, continuing the tradition established by Tapan Raychaudhuri and his student Om Prakash.[5] One could still live in a word where terms such as *representation* or *discourse*, and the names Edward Said or Stephen Greenblatt, were still distant specks on the horizon for the unreconstructed economic historian, whose main concern was whether or not VOC trade siphoned off the surplus of the economy, or actually promoted a form of export-led growth.[6]

Central still to the debates of that time was the work of J. C. van Leur, more Weberian sociologist than historian, but someone whose collected essays published posthumously marked a whole generation of scholars of Indian Ocean trade.[7] The Danish historian Niels Steensgaard in particular had brought Van Leur back into the center of the debate in the early 1970s, by way of contrasting the insecure functioning of Asian "peddlers" in uncertain markets to the sophisticated and rational organization of the European chartered companies. His work, which seemed greatly innovative at the time of its publication, appears in retrospect to be no more than a variant of very familiar "modernization theory," and quite continuous in most respects with the Weberian project, perhaps even more so than Van Leur, in whose work one can at least sense an attempt to positively valorize the cultural complex within which Asian economies of the pre-1800 period functioned.[8]

What this really implied for Asian economic history in the seventeenth and eighteenth centuries is a large and interesting subject, but one with which I cannot deal here. Instead, my primary intention is to reflect on what has happened in the studies of the last two decades concerning the relationship between Europeans and Asians, by focusing on the link between European expansion and the invention of ethnography. These studies have made considerable but uneven strides, as anyone who consults the volume from some years ago edited by Stuart Schwartz, entitled *Implicit Understandings*, will realize.[9] We are all clear in our minds today that the discipline of ethnography was either created or at least significantly modified in the centuries that are normally defined as those of European expansion, which is to say between the late fifteenth and the late eighteenth centuries. Yet what is less clear is the relationship between subsections of this period. How, for example, are we to evaluate the relative place of the sixteenth century, where European encounters with the non-European world are primarily in the hands of the Iberians, and the seventeenth century, which is that of what Jonathan Israel has evocatively termed *Dutch primacy in world trade*?[10] And, to enter into the heart of my subject, what does ethnography have to do with violence, when that violence is not the object of ethnography but rather a conditioning factor, a frame within which ethnographic observation takes place?[11] In order to enter into this latter question, it may be useful from the outset to define somewhat more clearly what I mean by some of the terms that I use. To begin with, let us take *ethnography*. I use this term here in preference to *ethnology*, because, as shall be seen presently, the bulk of the authors that I shall be looking at do not have an encompassing program in mind that may be compared to that of Bartolomé de las Casas or José de Acosta; their theoretical pretensions are lesser and the part of the empirical in what they set out is determining, even if what exactly their own notion of the empirical is can be debated.[12] So the materials that I mean to consider are notionally descriptions of this or that people in Asia or Africa, and more particularly south Asia, with a focus on their community mores, beliefs, habits, and customs, what in a typical mid-seventeenth-century text appears under such chapter titles as "Of the Heathens, and their God-worship," or "The Moorish character, clothing, houses and servants," or "Of the trading and diverse usages of the Benjans."[13]

A second brief clarification may be in order on the subject of violence. As is well known, the Dutch East India Company in the seventeenth century and a good part of the eighteenth century was not really a properly territorial colonial power in Asia. True, the VOC did control some territories, whether in Indonesia (in Maluku, and the region around Jakarta) or in Sri Lanka; and already in the 1670s some of its more bellicose employees, such as Cornelis Speelman, are said to have "believed that the Company should subject the existing Asian states to its authority, leaving them their internal autonomy, but exacting tribute from them."[14] But if we are to compare this situation with that of the Spaniards in Mexico and the Peruvian viceroyalty, or that of the Portuguese in Brazil, the contrast is apparent. European violence in Asia had not been institutionalized into the familiar forms of a colonial administration, with either its heavy secular apparatus or the missionary presence that one associates with the Latin American case. But does this mean that violence was in fact absent? Here, the historiography has been rather unhelpful in its definitions. In the immediate aftermath of the decolonization of India and Indonesia, the term *Vasco da Gama epoch* came to be much used in the wake of the writings an Indian diplomat and amateur historian called K. M. Panikkar, in order to define the long period from 1498 to 1945 as one where European violence was the determining factor in Asian history.[15] In this view, the Dutch presence in Asia after the foundation of the VOC would form a part of this continuum, running from Gama and Cabral, through Coen and Rijkloff van Goens, on to Clive and Hastings. It soon became apparent though from the writings of such Indian historians as Ashin Das Gupta (in the 1960s and 1970s) that such a position was empirically untenable, and certainly could not help us make sense of the history of the Mughal Empire, Qing China, or Mataram.[16] Some historians, notably under the influence of Holden Furber, hence proposed that one could still see the seventeenth and early eighteenth centuries as being an "Age of Partnership" that then gave way to an "Age of Empire" after about 1750; Furber himself had argued, it would be recalled, that "looking at the various forms of partnership between Europeans and Asians during these centuries I feel that those based on mutual respect may well outnumber those of a different and less pleasant character."[17] But truth be told, this is also singularly unhelpful in order to understand the nature of the violence that an organization like the Dutch East India Company embodied. I do not refer here only to the most dramatic aspects of this violence, such as the celebrated "ethnic cleansing" activities in the Banda Islands at the time of Jan Pieterszoon Coen in order to define and defend a monopoly of spice production. Rather, it is the far more banal use of violence by the VOC that we have to deal with, which stemmed from the fact that the company was a quasi state that made war and treaties, maintained armed vessels in Asian waters even in times when there was no major intra-European conflict on, and which from early on in its presence in India and Southeast Asia, also built up a chain of fortresses— ostensibly as a defense against Portuguese aggression but in fact usually directed against Asian polities. If we are to compare the activities of the VOC with those of the Venetians or Genoese in the Indian Ocean before 1450, we can easily see the different mix of violence and commerce in play in the former case as opposed to the latter one.

Some authors have argued that this use of violence by the Dutch was merely part of a commercial strategy and that it can be hence subsumed under the category of *rational violence* as opposed to the irrational violence practiced by, say, the Portuguese in the sixteenth century; in such a view, we must contrast the "pre-modern character of sixteenth century Portugal" to the situation of "different Europeans, people who were in the process of becoming 'modern,' people from countries where scientific and technological developments were beginning to lead to a qualitative change."[18] The assumption here is usually that the sadly premodern Portuguese gloried in using violence for its own sake, a thesis which gains support from the internal Portuguese chronicling tradition, in which authors such as João de Barros or Fernão Lopes de Castanheda speak of "the discovery and conquest of India," and the heroic "deeds" (*feitos*) of their Lusitanian heroes in this respect. True, the VOC did not have its Camões, and the work of the prosaic Pieter van Dam at the end of the seventeenth century does not really lend itself to an image of the glorious deeds of the Batavians in Asian waters. But first appearances can be deceptive here. The fact is that there was an ever present violence—whether acted out or potential—whenever the VOC appeared on the scene. The reader of Persian chronicles from eighteenth-century India, which deal with the *qaum-i walandez* (Dutch nation), is left in no doubt of this. Not only do the Dutch appear to be frequently under the influence of strong liquor, but they are also seen as inveterate troublemakers whose activities from their coastal fortresses are a constant thorn in the flesh of Indian polities, especially in peninsular India.

A constant but low-level violence was in a sense inscribed in the company's presence in India from the very start. To comprehend this, we can begin with a consideration of the account of the second voyage of the VOC's factors to the Coromandel coast of southeastern India, in the first months of 1606. The account thereof is anonymous but forms part of Isaac Commelin's *Begin ende Voortgangh van de Vereenighde Nederlantsche Geoctroyeerde Oost-Indische Compagnie*, published for the first time in 1646. The text appears as part of "The second voyage to the East Indies done by Steven van der Hagen," in the subsection entitled "Account and journal of the voyage done from Bantam to the Coast of Choromandel and other quarters of India by the chief merchant Paulus van Soldt," and is also termed "The voyage of the ship Delft to the Coast of Choromandel."[19] We may rehearse the broad lines of the account. In late March 1606, the Dutch vessel of van Soldt finds itself in Aceh on the north coast of Sumatra. It then sets out for the coast of Coromandel, attacking Portuguese country shipping on the way before arriving on April 25 near the port of São Tomé (today Chennai). Here, a further three ships are burnt by the Dutch, including one belonging in part to "a Portugalised Dutchman called Marten Tielmanssen van Neck, born in Enkhuisen." Van Soldt and his men then move up the coast to first the decadent port of Pulicat, and then Peddapalli (or Nizamapatnam), before arriving in the great Golkonda haven of Masulipatnam on May 17. The Dutch factors are received well enough, for the Dutch have paid a visit there the previous year and left a small factory in place. Van Soldt is received in the town, we are told, "by the most principal people of the town who had gathered at the toll-house," and once "the whores (*de hoeren*) who, according to the manner of the land were bedecked in costly gold and pearls, had danced," he is taken in a procession through the streets in the town to the Dutch lodgings. The VOC factors have occasion to recognize the complex ethnic landscape that they are faced with: their principal informant is a Jew called Arsalan, but they equally deal with Iranians from the Deccan, the odd Turk, as well as a number of Brahmin interpreters through whom they negotiate both at Pulicat and further north. But returning to the situation in the port of Masulipatnam itself, we may well ask what lay behind this sumptuous reception. Obviously we must bear in mind the fact that the Dutch could produce a counterviolence to that of the Portuguese, with whom the trading elite of Masulipatnam had been in intermittent conflict since at least the 1570s. Within a decade of van Soldt's visit, the Portuguese had been thoroughly marginalized in the trade of the area, with their violence having been quite comprehensively replaced by that of the VOC. True, the Dutch never managed to build a fortress in Masulipatnam, but through the 1620s a certain amount of ambient violence characterized the dealings between them and the authorities of the Sultanate of Golkonda at Masulipatnam. One of the Dutch chiefs of the factory, Abraham van Uffelen, was even killed in this ongoing tussle, allegedly from the torture to which he was subjected. The French physician François Bernier would describe these relations later in the century as follows. "Sometimes the Dutch presume to lay an embargo on all the Golkonda merchant-vessels in the port, nor will they suffer them to depart until the King complies with their demands. I have known them even to protest against the King because the Governor of Maslipatam [Masulipatnam] prevented them from taking forcible possession of an English ship in the port, by arming the whole population, threatening to burn the English factory, and to put all those insolent foreigners to the sword."[20] The nature of these tensions became further apparent in 1686 when the VOC for a time seized the main entrance from the landward side into the town of Masulipatnam, claiming that the Golkonda authorities owed it sums of money. On this instance, the town was handed back after an interval, but some forty years later, in 1729, the Dutch Council of the Coromandel was still discussing the need to "make ourselves master of one or the other suitable place in northern Coromandel, in which we could resist all sieges and assaults of the Moorish and Heathen governments which they continue to do regularly, and to that end following the example of the year 1686, the town Masulipatnam seems to be the best and most suitable."[21] Two conclusions can thus be arrived at directly, besides the somewhat obvious one that it is rather difficult to describe all this convincingly as an "Age of Partnership." First, it was not the Dutch alone who had recourse to violence, for Asian polities—whether in India, Iran, or elsewhere—could try and match threat by counterthreat and violence by counterviolence, thus creating a form of fragile equilibrium. Second, such a situation was bound to have an impact on the manner in which the Sultanate of Golkonda was portrayed in Dutch writings of the seventeenth century. In other words, the logic of violence is bound to affect the logic of political ethnography, as any reader of Daniel Havart's late-seventeenth-century text *Op- en Ondergang van Cormandel* can immediately perceive.[22] It is virtually impossible for Havart to portray the Golkonda Sultanate other than as a form of "Oriental Despotism." In a certain sense, one can find more virtues in a conquered people than in one that resists conquest.

The same logic holds in considerable measure for the Dutch portrayal of the Mughal domains. Several writers stand out here in the seventeenth century, among whom we must certainly mention Francisco Pelsaert, Wollebrant Geleynssen de Jongh, and Johan van Twist from the first half of the seventeenth century. All of these men were factors of the VOC who had experience in Gujarat and to a more limited extent in northern India, especially after about 1620. They produced a corpus of writings on the nature of the political and social system in Mughal India that had a mixed set of fortunes. Van Twist's work was published in the 1640s under his name, while Pelsaert's account was very largely drawn upon as the basis of the geographer and naturalist Johannes de Laet's *De Imperio Magni Mogolis*, published in 1631. Such texts as these were accompanied by the ever-greater production of maps of Asia. This production was itself not devoid of an ethnographic content, often portraying the peoples of different regions in the margins of the map. The contrast between the Dutch and the Portuguese is interesting here. Though a considerable corpus of materials on Asia was produced by the Portuguese in the sixteenth century, very little of it in fact went into print. Aside from the great chronicles of Barros, Castanheda, and Diogo do Couto, and some other apologetic texts devoted to the biographies of individual viceroys or captains, it is hard to find much that is published in Portugal itself. Garcia da Orta's work on drugs and simples was hence published in Goa, that of Cristóvão da Costa in Spain.[23] Indeed, Italians like Giambattista Ramusio did more to put out Portuguese ethnographic materials on Asia than the Portuguese themselves. In contrast, the links between the world of print and that of the Dutch East India Company appear far closer in places such as Amsterdam or Leiden. De Laet himself was involved in both the West India Company and the VOC, and was also closely associated with Heinsius. Later in the seventeenth century, texts like those of Abraham Rogerius and Philippus Baldaeus also enter print in a context that is closely linked with the company; these materials appear destined to drive out and discredit the Jesuit ethnography of Asia, which had held the high ground in the last decades of the sixteenth century. Even if this was not an entirely successful enterprise, the competitive element in this production of ethnography and the role of print in the seventeenth century cannot be ignored.

De Laet's own work, which was a major one amongst those listed above, appears divided into two parts, the first on the "Geography and Administration of the Mughal Empire," and the second "A Fragment of the History of India."[24] The source text used by him of Pelsaert also appears as a "Kroniek" on the one hand, beginning in the late 1530s and running to 1627, and a "Remonstrantie" on the other, with a mix of geographical, economic, and ethnographic information.[25] Under the last head, we find a wealth of detail concerning a series of social categories, in particular the Muslim elites, as also a reiteration of the common view of caste as we find it in Portuguese authors of the sixteenth century. Thus, Pelsaert writes that "the artisan can place his children in no other profession than the one that he himself is skilled in, and will also marry them into no other stock (*geslacht*)"—the word *geslacht* here standing in for what later texts would unhesitatingly call *caste*. Thus, we have the twin notions of endogamy and hereditary occupations as defining such groups as goldsmiths, carpenters, copper workers, and so on. If this is the lot of the common folk, who, so it is reported, are generally in a poor and miserable condition, it can only be contrasted with the flagrant luxury in which the elite, and particularly the Muslim elite, lives. As de Laet puts it, "The nobles live in indescribable luxury and extravagance, caring only to indulge themselves whilst they can, in every kind of pleasure. Their greatest magnificence is in their women's quarters (or Mahall), for they marry three or four wives or sometimes more: each of these wives lives separately in her own quarters with her handmaids or slaves, of whom she has often a large number . . . ." And naturally, all of this is linked in turn to an absence of laws to counterbalance the overweening weight of royal power. Thus, to quote Pelsaert again: "Of their laws little or nothing is maintained, for the rulers are absolute, even though they have law books preserved by their jurists, the cazis . . . . For who shall prescribe or demand of the governor, why do you judge us thus and so, when our law commands otherwise? Such a thing will never happen, though every city has its court (*ketschari*) or hall of justice, where, in the king's name, the governor meets daily, or four times a week for the settling of disputes, albeit that nothing is decided in which official greed does not play a role."

These were powerful images once they entered into print, which in the case of van Twist was a relatively simple process, and where Pelsaert was concerned was somewhat worsened by the fact that de Laet often further simplified and radicalized his propositions to make the contrast between East and West the more stark. A third text from the same broad period, namely the account of Wollebrant Geleynssen de Jongh, did not see its way into print at all until well into the twentieth century, but is in many respects the most subtle portrayal of the three. Geleynssen knew Gujarat in particular rather well, and his account begins with a description of *de stadt Brootchia*, or Bharuch, before moving on to a description of other major cities and towns such as Surat and Ahmadabad, as well as a set of broader reflections. Of Bharuch itself, we gather that "this town is pretty well-peopled with folk, Moors, Benjans and also Persians, who are born in this land itself; the said Benjans, who are here the most populous of the three nations, bring the most business into the town, as they control the greater part of the trade."[26] The *baniyas* directly inspire some comparative reflections ("this is a nation that is not unlike the Chinese in terms of covetousness, though not quite so fraudulent as the former"); but the Dutch factor is also adept at accumulating a series of small observations of one or the other sort, regarding the giving of alms, the maintenance of hospitals, and even sprinkles his text from time to time with an example of what he terms "the common Hindustani proverb." Naturally, the text is unable to escape from periodic reflections on the arbitrary character of the Mughal polity, the oppression of the poor, and the overall injustice, but Geleynssen can still surprise us from time to time. There is his claim, for example, that "no one is hindered or harassed in their beliefs or godly worship, but instead each one lives freely," a marked contrast to the European situation of the time. But Geleynssen is willing to go even further in his search for affinities between the Muslims and the religion of the greater part of the Dutch. Thus, a rather peculiar passage states:

> They like the Roman or Catholic religion a good deal less than the Reformed one, and this is because those Papists make use of images in their churches (which is against their [Muslim] law), as the Moors do not believe in honoring or making use of images, and so have no images at all in their temples, houses or places of worship that are made of wood, stone or other materials; they prefer a pile of silver or gold that they can sell, and make jewels or bracelets or such things with, in which respect too they agree very well with the Reformed [Dutch], who prefer silver and gold to stone and wooden images.[27]

This relatively favorable view can be quite easily contrasted to other writers, whether on India or the other parts of Asia with which the VOC had contact in these years. For, no matter how much some Dutch factors might grumble about this or that aspect of India, it is clear from even a rapid survey that their image of Safavid Iran was far more negative still. An excellent example of political ethnography in this instance comes from the 1620s, soon after the death of the long-reigning Shah 'Abbas I. The papers in question relate to the embassy of a certain Jan Smidt, sent out as the VOC's envoy to Isfahan between 1628 and 1630, and they are particularly revealing. Here for example is his description of how he was received by the young Shah Safi soon after his accession, on May 24, 1629.

> We rode out towards the court at about 10 o'clock. When we came there, we were taken through a courtyard and some rooms, and we came to a hall with an earthen floor of a fair size, laid with carpets, without any ornamentation; in its middle was a square place with water to keep the room cool. The King sat down below on a carpet in one corner of the room; around him sat various grandees, about a hundred in number it was said, but with little ceremony. I came before him with my entourage, made my bow, and I made a show of kissing his hand; those of my company kissed the hem of his garment, it being indicated that they should kiss his feet.[28]

Smidt then proceded to hand the shah a series of letters in Persian, from the states-general and the prince of Orange, and then stayed on for some three hours, twice drinking to the health of the prince of Orange. Yet the impression that one gathers is that he was anything but impressed by the Safavid court.

> We thus sat there for three hours, and from time to time we drank a round; behind the King there sat some players, with whom the king had various exchanges.

Meanwhile, he also drank tobacco and wine, and also played with some small apples, just as in our land children play at knucklebones (*bickelen*); in short, over here they care little for grandeur or kingly magnificence.

Besides the puerile character of the ruler, the quality of the banquet too did not meet the fastidious standards of the Dutch envoy, who wrote of how for the most part all they received to eat at first were "some fruits in keeping with the season . . . as also heads of salad and cucumbers." When the main part of the repast began, this too appeared rather substandard: "Around one o'clock, the fruit were taken away and around 2 or 3 o'clock the food was brought out; the plates were laid on damask cloth without napkins, plates or knives." Nor did the entertainment appear particularly civilized to his eye: "Meanwhile, rounds were drunk steadily; their players sang and played throughout but with little melody."

Another invitation was extended to the Dutch envoy some weeks later, by which time he had also had time to reflect on the city of Isfahan itself. Regarding this urban center, Smidt notes:

It is a town as large as Amsterdam with great external quarters or *faubourgs*, which if they were included would make it as large as Paris, full of folk and densely built-up; it lies close to the mountains, though it has many good valleys around it. The houses have a very poor external appearance, as they are made of earth and clay with very little chalk mixed in; they are somewhat better on the inside, when they are painted with chalk, as is the case with the principal houses.

Yet this grudging acceptance that not all was bad about the town is soon tempered once more by the experience of the *generael bancket* of June 15, when the Dutch envoys were made to wait three hours while Shah Safi was entertained with "the son of the Duke (*Hartoch*) of Syras [Shiraz]." Once the banquet began, the Dutch envoy's eye once more cast a disapproving gaze on proceedings.

The drinking goes on continually, though one is free to refuse. Dancing is not generally in use, and is only done by the whores and the sodomite young men, who are hired or invited for the purpose.

Reading this description together with other sections of the embassy account, as well as the accounts produced by other Dutch factors in about this time, we are left with the impression that the Iranian polity was corrupt through and through, run by moral degenerates, and also marked by an astonishing cruelty on a daily basis. Characteristic of this is Smidt's extensive obituary notice of Shah 'Abbas, where a promising beginning soon gives way to images of unbridled cruelty. Thus we are told at the outset that "this death [of the Shah] was extremely damaging for the whole position of the region of Persia, as he ruled his land very wisely and was greatly respected by the grandees." But we then learn of how the shah had killed his own son out of a fit of anger and mistrust (*"hy heeeft oock uyt jalousyen sijn eenige zoon doen ombrengen"*), and that he had also taken the Spanish ambassador Don García de Silva y Figueroa through Isfahan and shown him a street "where many of the grandees lay, whose hands and feet he had had hacked off, but who were still alive."

How does one interpret all these views and images, where the description of the character of an individual (the monarch) can rapidly yet imperceptibly become the means to evaluate the larger culture in which he is located? Are there some fundamental drives that inform the portrayal by the VOC, its factors, and its propagandists in the seventeenth century, of the polities and societies they encountered in Asia and southern Africa? One solution would be simply to argue, as some have done, that "the Dutch of the seventeenth and eighteenth centuries had little sense of cultural relativism; they took themselves as the absolute standard, generally rejecting out of hand anything that deviated from their own views and moral precepts."[29] Recently, James Tracy has proposed another view, namely that the fundamental tension in the portrayal may be organized around the axis of the hostility to Islam. He argues that "in this respect the practical-minded men who transacted Company business in Asia were not necessarily of a different mind than Europe's most noted scholars," and points to the fact that well-known European writers of the seventeenth century were still capable of such phrases as: "What is [Islam] but the scum of Judaism and Paganism sod together, here and there strewed over with a spice of Christianity?"[30] While Tracy's view undoubtedly can find·support in contemporary materials, I would nevertheless argue that Dutch views of India and Asia in the seventeenth century are not fundamentally informed by an anti-Islamic rhetoric. At least some important voices among company officials were relatively favorable to Islam, as we can see from Geleynssen's comparison of Protestantism with Islam (the two sharing features of austerity, an absence of idol worship, and care for the poor and destitute), while at the same time comparing Catholics with the Gentiles or Heathens of India. Rather than a clearly stated Islamophobia, as one finds with the Portuguese of the early sixteenth century, Dutch writers instead seem by the 1650s to be equally skeptical in regard of the Heathen or Gentile religion of India, what we would today call Hinduism. This was itself no doubt the outcome of a complex process of engagement. In a first stage, the VOC seems to have understood the Heathens in India to be organized around two groups, the Brahmins and the Baniyas. It is these groups which appear most prominently in Johan van Twist's *Generale Beschrijvinge van Indien*, even as they informed the work of the English Company's minister, Henry Lord, writing in the 1620s. But as we move into the latter part of the seventeenth century, matters appear more complex. From the Dutch presence in the area around Pulicat comes the text by the Dutch preacher Rogerius, which represents a rather intriguing collaboration between the Dutch author and a Smarta Brahmin called Padmanabha, who is often cited extensively in the text, both to bolster the authority and legitimacy of Rogerius when he enters into a discussion of Sanskrit (such as when he speaks of the classical author Bhartrhari), and when he discusses matters concerning local religion (the cult of Gangamma in the area around Tirupati), or left- and right-hand caste disputes in the town of Pulicat itself. Rogerius has sometimes been portrayed by recent writers as "remarkably dispassionate, even sympathetic" where the Heathens of India are concerned. His book has equally been termed "surely the most comprehensive and perceptive description European description of South Indian Hinduism up to that time, or more likely, up to the end of the nineteenth century."[31] This view, from the pen of Edwin van Kley, can simply not be sustained by a reading of the text in its context, namely of the VOC's relations with the Vijayanagara kingdom, which at that time was centered on the town of Chandragiri. For having listed the most famous temples in the "Carnatica kingdom," Rogerius enters into a detailed discussion in the tenth chapter of the second part of his work of the great temple of Tirupati, which—I have shown elsewhere—can hardly be seen as either dispassionate or sympathetic.[32]

The narrative of Rogerius in fact uses the authority of Padmanabha in order to present an image of a politico-religious complex that is composed of credulous devotees, and avaricious kings, all revolving around the central institution of the Heathen pagoda. I would hence argue that in the latter half of the seventeenth century, the primary hostility of the VOC was directed not solely against Islam but equally against the Heathen religions and potentates of Asia. We may develop this point by taking the Dutch portrayal of the Nayaka kingdom of Madurai in the 1660s, where they had just been engaged in a long, drawn-out, and violent dispute. In a document entitled "Reasons and causes of the commencement and continuation of the Madura War, conducted on the defensive, on the part of the Honourable Company," written by Laurens Pijl and Hendrik Adriaan van Rheede, the reader is informed in no uncertain terms that the reason for the war lay in the tyrannical nature of the Nayaka government, but also because "the peoples who inhabit the countries of Madura are by nature servile, lazy, distrustful, miserable and consequently low, cunning, faithless, lying, greedy, possessing least of all virtues as regards to honor and shame, overbearing in prosperity, slavish in adversity, cruel, merciless, only by compulsion good or beneficent."[33] Or again, the portrayal at much the same time of the Buddhist kingdom of Arakan (Mrauk-U) in northern Burma also followed a similar pattern; the kings Thado Mintara and Sandathudhamma were in the Dutch view tyrannical and cruel, the laws arbitrary and unjust, and the customs and beliefs of the people largely viewed by VOC factors with scorn and distaste.[34] It has been pointed out, however, that such portrayals in the case of mainland Southeast Asia were not always quite so one-dimensional; for example, Jeremias van Vleet's account of the Ayuthia kingdom, does claim that the ruler Prasat Thong "through crafty plots and many murders has succeeded in usurping the Crown," but then also goes on to state that "His Majesty has been a wise, careful and mighty Prince, who has possessed his Kingdom in prosperity and peace."[35] So rather than being simply "tyrannical or bloodthirsty," the Thai ruler is depicted as a monarch whose cunning attributes dominate all others.

Again, there were undoubtedly variations in terms of the portrayal of the religion of the "heathens" of Asia, ranging from the avowedly hostile, to the moderate, to the "friendly" attempt to build genealogical relations with the ancient past of Europe. At one extreme of the spectrum was the disciplining attitude of missionaries such as Robertus Junius to the "heathens" of Taiwan, which eventually led to the altogether disastrous outcome in the seventeenth century that has been studied by Leonard Blussé.[36] On the other hand, an example of the more genealogical viewpoint is to be found in the writings of a celebrated VOC employee, Engelbert Kaempfer, whose views on Indian religion can be cited even though he was not himself Dutch. Kaempfer writes:

> It is probable, that before the introduction of the present Paganism among the Indians, they had the same sort of worship with the neighboring Chaldeans and Persians. For as it cannot be suppos'd, that these sensible Nations liv'd without any Religion at all, like the Brutal Hottentots, it is highly probable, that they rever'd the divine Omnipotence by worshipping, according to the Custom of the Chaldeans, the Sun and other Luminaries of the Firmament, as such parts of the Creation, which most strike the outward senses, and fill the understanding with the admiration of their unconceivable proprieties.[37]

He further adds that the Heathens in India also preserved elements from the religion of the Egyptians, namely "the Transmigration of Souls, and a Veneration for Cows . . . . Both these Articles are still observ'd among the Asiatick Heathens, particularly those that inhabit the west-side of the Ganges." The generally measured and tolerant tone of these passages in Kaempfer may be contrasted to his brief reference above to the "Hottentots," and they also render the following passage regarding the Buddha all the more curious.

> This Saint being represented with curled Hairs, like a Negro, there is room to conclude, that he was no native of India, but was born under the hot climate of

Africa, considering that the Air in India produces on its black Inhabitants none of that curl'd wool, but long and black Hair, quite lank, and very little curl'd: And tho' the Siamites crop theirs, so as to leave it only of the length of a Finger; yet as it stands on end like bristles, it is easily distinguish'd from the woolly curls of a Negro, and consequently it is more probable, that Budha [*sic*] was of African, than of Siamite extraction.

But the tools of ethnographic persuasion also went beyond mere words and verbal arguments. Visual images, too, were produced, whether of cities and towns, or of kings in their courts, to accompany the words. The celebrated work of the Protestant minister Baldaeus, entitled *Naauwkeurige beschrijving van Malabar en Choromandel,* which appeared in 1672, offered a series of interpretations of the religion of the Heathens that seem to be taken from earlier authors, but also produced an important set of visual images, some of which derive from the Dutch artist Philip Angel, while others—such as his portrayals of Masulipatnam and Surat—are of more complex derivation. Discussions of such visual images have often taken up the question of the degree to which Indian styles of representation appear therein; thus Partha Mitter in a well-known work has argued that with Rogerius and Baldaeus, the monstrous stereotypes of Indian gods in earlier European works are finally replaced by depictions that are "of Indian inspiration."[38] The title page to Rogerius's book, *De Open Deure tot het Verborgen Heydendom* (which was published in 1651 in Leiden, and from which I draw for the title of this chapter) has it all: a temple where Ganesha is visible, a sati scene, and a scene of the Juggernaut, that is the temple chariot under which people fall by way of self-sacrifice.

The drive in these visual presentations is to define iconic scenes, rather than a focus on peoples, and thus the ethnographic route that is taken appears rather different here than that followed by the Dutch in Brazil at much the same time. As is well known, the presence of Johan Maurits of Nassau in Pernambuco produced two powerful sets of visual portrayals, those by Franz Post, and those by Albert Eckhout. The latter, of which we have a recent comprehensive discussion by Peter Mason, purport to depict a series of typical inhabitants of colonial Brazil, whether from among the indigenous people or the slave population and its descendants. Mason notes in this context that "if we consider the reception of Eckhout's paintings, especially in the twentieth century, the emphasis has been on the fact that, since he has 'been there,' his 'ethnographic portraits' must be taken at face value."[39] Rejecting this view, he then goes on to argue that "these paintings are portraits in which the intellect prevails over the eye, furnishing what the eye could not take in at any one moment." In

Mason's reading, then, "the Eckhout paintings [are] bearers of visual facts rather than . . . direct records of observation at any point in time." From this he concludes that, in general, such apparently ethnographic representation in fact "betrays the thrust of the colonial desire, eager to reduce the Other to Self, bent on using its eye to extend the dissemination of its power."

This viewpoint has been challenged by writers such as Siegfried Huigen in an analysis of Dutch writings and descriptions regarding southern Africa in the second half of the seventeenth century. The individual actors here are often the same as those whom we encounter further east, Rijkloff van Goens, Hendrik Adriaan van Rheede, and others. Focusing on a series of eleven expeditions sent from the Cape colony to the interior kingdom of Munhumutapa between 1659 and 1686, including one in which an artist named Hendrik Claudius participated, Huigen argues that whereas writers such as Mason (and Said) "would have us believe that representations of other worlds are never more than projections made by whoever is speaking about that other world," the pure empirical content of both the verbal and visual ethnography produced by the VOC cannot be quite so easily dismissed.[40] Instead, he claims that "the VOC desired the most accurate information possible about the interior of southern Africa. This desire could be seen in the orders, sent with the expedition, to encourage accurate observation." The clinching argument is hence a pragmatic one: "Continued belief in the imaginary notion of the interior would in all likelihood have lead [*sic*], after all, to financial fiasco."

It is probably not necessary to make such reductive appeals to the rationality of historical actors—who obviously must have been "accurate" because they were rational—in order to nuance or even contest the view defended by Mason. Recent researches by Marie-Odette Scalliet have turned up an important Asian equivalent of the portrayals of Eckhout, namely a series of paintings from seventeenth-century Southeast Asia, by Andries Beeckman—who has also left us some oil paintings of Batavia from the 1650s.[41] Beeckman provides us such characters from the Dutch Asian landscape as a *mestizo* in European dress, a Chinese merchant, a *mardijker*, or a Javanese, for which no counterpart has so far turned up in regard to the VOC's presence in India. I would point to three preliminary lines of research here. The first would be to compare the portrayals by Beeckman to earlier materials from Portuguese Asia, such as the celebrated Casanatense Codex from the mid-sixteenth century, which contains portrayals of "typical couples" from different parts of Asia, some scenes of daily life in the Deccan, and other elements having to do with the life of the Portuguese themselves in the tropics.[42] Second, and rather more speculatively, I would point to the contrast between the sort of ethnographic "realism" or pseudorealism of Beeckman, Post, and Eckhout and the obligatory passage through the elaborate mise-en-scène that seems necessary as a preliminary step to represent such societies as India or China visually. For Beeckman was operating in Asia in the closest equivalent that one can find to a colonial situation, namely Dutch Batavia. The relationship between the painter-ethnographer and the object was thus necessarily posed in terms that were different from those that one sees in societies where the balance of forces was of a different order. Third, it would be interesting to see how Beeckman's drawings came to be transformed when they passed into other hands, and were made to serve as illustrations to a text, as they did in the travel account of a German voyager, Caspar Schmalkalden.[43] This may also give us some clue as to processes of reception and manuscript circulation, in a situation where the book trade in Amsterdam was successfully able to represent "the world as a supremely seductive and wonderfully accessible place," that was "enchantingly, amenably, and reassuringly exotic."[44]

All in all, the nature of the relationship between the Dutch East India Company and its ethnographic objects in Asia cannot be understood by simply opposing two modes, one of conflict and another of collaboration or partnership. Instead, it is important to note that the two coexisted, interacted, or were superimposed. An example of this is the celebrated treatise on plants produced on the Malabar coast of southwestern India by van Rheede in the late seventeenth century entitled *Hortus Indicus Malabaricus*. While some writers have pointed to this text as a fine example of pure and cumulative knowledge produced in the context of the "Age of Partnership," which will "stand comparison with any major cooperative project supported by one of the great foundations of the present day," others have argued that it is a typical example of Indian knowledge robbed as it were, and transported into an alien context.[45] My own reading of this text, with its complex illustrations and systems of nomenclature (which combines Arabic, Malayalam, and Konkani with Latin), is that it is precisely one of those texts that emerge from the indeterminate equilibrium the period imposes. Van Rheede's problems are typical: How to produce a text that uses local knowledge, builds on the legitimacy of local informants, and yet goes beyond them to produce a metadiscourse of which they are not themselves seen as capable. The problem is not entirely different from that faced by Rogerius. The crucial difference lies, however, in the object that is chosen. When the subject is plants and their uses, the portrayal is surely charged in a rather different manner than when one wishes to portray social groups, their behavior, and their beliefs.

By way of conclusion, let me point to a rather curious chronological coincidence. The period when the materials that I have described above were being produced by the factors of the VOC was also the period when a new approach to the problem of comparative religion was beginning to gain ground in the

Netherlands. The relations between at least the three great religions from a European point of view—Christianity, Judaism, and Islam—were in the process of being reconsidered, by the circles that one associates with Spinoza, and by others who place themselves under the more or less ecumenical signs of various millenarian tendencies. How does one explain these changes, which are important not for the seventeenth century alone, but for the way in which they would influence the thinking of the eighteenth century? Where the latter period is concerned, Jürgen Osterhammel has attempted to provide an ambitious panorama of the nature of interrelations, although somewhat downplaying the continued importance of the Dutch presence.[46] But the seventeenth century still awaits a similar exercise. Can we assume that the Dutch Enlightenment is purely the product of intellectual developments internal to Europe, whether the rediscovery of ancient texts or the tussle between a secularizing Judaism and its Christian interlocutors? If not, what is the place of Asia? Can we really assume that the perception of Islam, as well as that of idolatry, remained immune to the materials that the VOC brought back from Asia, and which reached the world of print through the assiduous efforts of publishers in Amsterdam and Leiden?

I will freely confess that I am not in a position to provide a convincing answer to these questions at present, and I must also wonder why these questions are not even touched upon in a major recent work on Dutch modernity and comparative religion between 1650 and 1750.[47] What I can suggest is at least that there are some paths to be avoided. Among these is the view, made popular by writers such as Donald F. Lach and now increasingly brought to the fore by a certain number of younger historians, wherein the relationship between European knowledge and Asian conditions is seen as that of a simple "discovery," a process by which that which was veiled in 1500 came to be gradually unveiled by a simple process of empirical accumulation of data. Such writers, by reducing questions of knowledge and perception to the nearly trivial category of "information," refuse to admit into consideration the concrete conditions of the exercise of power and violence in which writings like those of Pelsaert or Rogerius were in fact produced.[48]

This said, I am nevertheless inclined to draw a distinction between the manner in which ethnographic views of Asian peoples were constructed by the employees—whether laypersons or religious—of the VOC and the manner in which the ostensibly similar exercise was carried out at the time when the Portuguese represented the principal European presence in Asia. Though this comparison may appear surprising at first sight, I would tend to assimilate the Portuguese to the English, while placing the Dutch in a different category. This is mainly because the Portuguese, like the English, represented a relatively decentralized form of organization, whereas the VOC practically from the outset insisted on its centralized character, which was perhaps more reflected in its discourse production than in its economic structure, where various activities that are lumped under the head of "corruption" actually provided major countercurrents to company policy. In the seventeenth and early eighteenth centuries, therefore, the Dutch East India Company repre-sented a powerful and effective producer of texts and images with regard to Asian peoples, and not simply an organization the function of which was to unload shipments of pepper, Moluccan spices, and Indian cottons onto the waiting wharfs of the Dutch Republic.

Four hundred years after the foundation of the VOC, there is undoubtedly a certain desire to be nostalgic about the "meeting of cultures" that the first generations of Dutchmen (and, it should be added, Germans) in Asian waters helped produce.[49] Here, as so often, the historian's task must be to play the devil's advocate, and to suggest that even before the age of high imperialism, other, more subtle forms of conflict and violence informed both the relation-ships and the consequent representations that emerged. Reading the account of an Iranian traveller to India or a Vietnamese visitor to Indonesia can help remind us that not all forms of early modern encounter were set in a context of powerful institutional violence, and they can thus help us come to terms with the many routes that have historically taken societies from the medieval to the early modern.[50] A too narrow and excessively teleological history of modernity may make it difficult for us to recognize this at first, even as it may make us take much too literally the oft-repeated Dutch claim to being the first truly modern society.

Notes

An earlier version of this text was presented as the Thirteenth Wertheim Lecture at the University of Amsterdam, in June 2002. I am grateful to several members of the audi-ence for comments.

1. Steven Barbone, Lee Rice, and Jacob Adler, eds., *Spinoza: The Letters*, trans. Samuel Shirley (Indianapolis: Hackett, 1995), 342.

2. See the useful reflection in Cemal Kafadar, "Self and Others: The Diary of a Dervish in Seventeenth-Century Istanbul and First-Person Narratives in Ottoman lit-erature," *Studia Islamica* 69 (1989): 121–50.

3. Cf. Mary Louise Pratt, *Imperial Eyes: Travel Writing and Transculturation* (Lon-don: Routledge, 1992).

4. Serge Gruzinski, *La colonisation de l'imaginaire: Sociétés indigènes et occidentali-sation dans le Mexique espagnol, XVIe-XVIIIe siècle* (Paris: Gallimard, 1988); Anthony Pagden, *European Encounters with the New World: From Renaissance to Romanticism* (New Haven: Yale University Press, 1993).

5. Tapan Raychaudhuri, *Jan Company in Coromandel, 1605–1690: A Study in the Interrelations of European Commerce and Traditional Economies* (The Hague: Martinus Nijhoff, 1962); Om Prakash, *The Dutch East India Company and the Economy of Bengal, 1630–1720* (Princeton, NJ: Princeton University Press, 1985).

6. For an excellent example of the persistence of this largely economistic worldview in an otherwise worthy general history, see F. S. Gaastra, *De geschiedenis van de VOC* (Leiden: Walburg Pers, 1991). In general, the ideology of seventeenth- and eighteenth-century Dutch expansion remains woefully understudied; see, in contrast, Anthony Pagden, *Lords of All the World: Ideologies of Empire in Spain, Britain and France, c. 1500–c. 1800* (New Haven, CT: Yale University Press, 1995).

7. J. C. van Leur, *Indonesian Trade and Society: Essays in Asian Social and Economic History*, trans. James S. Holmes and A. van Marle (The Hague: W. Van Hoeve, 1955); for a recent reconsideration, see Leonard Blussé and Femme Gaastra, eds., *On the Eighteenth Century as a Category of Asian History: Van Leur in Retrospect* (Aldershot, UK: Ashgate, 1998).

8. Niels Steensgaard, *Carracks, Caravans and Companies: The Structural Crisis in the European-Asian trade in the Early 17th Century* (Lund: Studentlitteratur, 1973).

9. Stuart Schwartz, ed., *Implicit Understandings: Observing, Reporting, and Reflecting on the Encounters between Europeans and Other Peoples in the Early Modern Era* (New York: Cambridge University Press, 1994).

10. Jonathan I. Israel, *Dutch Primacy in World Trade, 1585–1740* (Oxford: Oxford University Press, 1989).

11. Cf. E. Valentine Daniel, *Charred Lullabies: Chapters in an Anthropography of Violence* (Princeton, NJ: Princeton University Press, 1996); also Veena Das, ed., *Mirrors of Violence: Communities, Riots and Survivors in South Asia* (Delhi: Oxford University Press, 1990).

12. See for example Bartolomé de las Casas, *Historia de las Indias*, 3 vols., ed. Agustín Millares Carlo and Lewis Hanke, (Mexico City: Fondo de Cultura Económica, 1951).

13. These are chapter titles taken from Johan van Twist, *Generale beschrijvinge van Indien: Ende in't besonder kort verhael van de regering etc.* (Amsterdam: J. Hartgerts, 1648).

14. Luc Nagtegaal, *Riding the Dutch Tiger: The Dutch East Indies Company and the Northeast Coast of Java, 1680–1743* (Leiden: KITLV Press, 1996), 22.

15. K. M. Panikkar, *Asia and Western Dominance: A Survey of the Vasco da Gama Epoch of Asian History, 1498–1945* (London: George Allen & Unwin, 1953).

16. See his collected essays in Ashin Das Gupta, *The World of the Indian Ocean Merchant, 1500–1800: Collected Essays of Ashin Das Gupta* (Delhi: Oxford University Press, 2001).

17. Holden Furber, "Asia and the West as Partners Before 'Empire' and After," *Journal of Asian Studies* 28 (1969): 711-21.

18. M. N. Pearson, *The Portuguese in India* (Cambridge: Cambridge University Press, 1987), 133.

19. Isaac Commelin, *Begin ende Voortgangh van de Vereenighde Nederlatsche Geoctroyeerde Oost-Indische Compagnie, vervatende de voornaemste reysen by de inwoon-*

deren der selver Provincien derwaerts gedaen, 2 vols. (Amsterdam, 1646), 2: *Verhael* XII, 50–73. Also see the narrative account in H. Terpstra, *De vestiging van de Nederlanders aan de kust van Koromandel* (Groningen: De Waal, 1911).

20. François Bernier, *Travels in the Mogul Empire, AD 1656–1668*, trans. Irving Brock and Archibald Constable, rev. Vincent A. Smith (Delhi: Low Price Publications, 1989), 195–96.

21. For a discussion, see Sanjay Subrahmanyam, "Masulipatnam Revisited, 1550–1750: A Survey and Some Speculations," in *Gateways to Asia: Port Cities of Asia in the 13th–20th Centuries*, ed. Frank Broeze (London and New York: Kegan Paul International, 1997), 33–65.

22. Daniel Havart, *Op- en Ondergang van Cormandel (. . .)*, 3 parts (Amsterdam: J. ten Hoorn, 1693); also see the discussion of Havart in H. Terpstra, "Daniël Havart en zijn *Op- en Ondergang van Coromandel*," *Tijdschrift voor Geschiedenis* 67 (1954): 165–89.

23. Garcia da Orta, *Colóquios dos Simples e Drogas da Índia*, ed. Conde de Ficalho (Lisbon: Imprensa Nacional, 1891); Cristóvão da Costa, *Tratado das Drogas e Medicinas das Índias Orientais, no qual se verifica muito do que escreveu o Doutor Garcia de Orta*, ed. Jaime Walter (Lisbon: Junta de Investigações do Ultramar, 1964).

24. J. S. Hoyland and S. N. Banerjee, *The Empire of the Great Mogol: A Translation of De Laet's "Description of India and Fragment of Indian History"* (Bombay: D. B. Taraporevala Sons, 1927); also, Brij Narain and S. R. Sharma, *A Contemporary Dutch Chronicle of Mughal India* (Calcutta: Susil Gupta, 1957).

25. D. H. A. Kolff and H. W. van Santen, eds., *De Geschriften van Francisco Pelsaert over Mughal Indië: Kroniek en Remonstrantie* (The Hague: Martinus Nijhoff, 1979).

26. Willem Caland, ed., *De Remonstrantie van W. Geleynssen de Jongh* (The Hague: Martinus Nijhoff, 1929), 9–10; and, for a useful biographical study, H. W. van Santen, *VOC-dienaar in India: Geleynssen de Jongh in het land van de Groot-Mogol* (Franeker: Van Wijnen, 2001).

27. Caland, *De Remonstrantie*, 59–60.

28. "Reisverhael van Jan Smidt, 26 Juli 1628–14 Juni 1630," in *Bronnen tot de Geschiedenis der Oostindische Compagnie in Perzië, Eerste Deel (1611–1638)*, ed. H. Dunlop (The Hague: Martinus Nijhoff, 1930), 729–61. Again, a general narrative account is available in H. Terpstra, *De opkomst der westerkwartieren van de Oost-Indische Compagnie (Surratte, Arabië, Perzië)* (The Hague: Martinus Nijhoff, 1918).

29. Nagtegaal, *Riding the Dutch Tiger*, 29, citing the discussion in Jörg Fisch, *Hollands Ruhm in Asien: Françoys Valenteyns Vision des niederländischen Imperiums im 18. Jahrhundert* (Stuttgart: Steiner Verlag, 1986).

30. James D. Tracy, "Asian Despotism? Mughal Government as seen from the Dutch East India Company Factory in Surat," *Journal of Early Modern History* 3 (1999): 256–80.

31. Edwin J. Van Kley, "Asian Religions in Seventeenth-Century Dutch Literature," *Itinerario* 25 (2001): 57.

32. Willem Caland, ed., *De Open-Deure tot het Verborgen Heydendom door Abraham Rogerius* (The Hague: Martinus Nijhoff, 1915), 123–24.

33. For discussions, see Sanjay Subrahmanyam, "Noble Harvest from the Sea: Managing the Pearl-Fishery of Mannar, 1500–1925," in *Institutions and Economic Change*

in *South Asia*, ed. Burton Stein and Sanjay Subrahmanyam (Delhi: Oxford University Press, 1996), 146–47; and Markus Vink, "Church and State in Seventeenth-Century Colonial Asia: Dutch Parava Relations in Southeast India in a Comparative Perspective," *Journal of Early Modern History* 4 (2000): 13–15.

34. See Sanjay Subrahmanyam, "Slaves and Tyrants: Dutch Tribulations in Seventeenth-Century Mrauk-U," *Journal of Early Modern History* 1 (1997): 201–53.

35. Alfons van der Kraan, "On Company Business: The Rijckloff van Goens Mission to Siam, 1650," *Itinerario* 22 (1998): 50.

36. Leonard Blussé, "Retribution and Remorse: The Interaction between the Administration and the Protestant Mission in Early Colonial Formosa," in *After Colonialism: Imperial Histories and Postcolonial Displacements*, ed. Gyan Prakash (Princeton, NJ: Princeton University Press, 1995), 153–82.

37. Engelbert Kaempfer, *The History of Japan, together with a description of the Kingdom of Siam, 1690–1692*, 3 vols., trans. J. G. Scheuchzer (Glasgow: James Maclehose and Sons, 1906), 1: 66–67 (the first edition of the translation dates to 1727).

38. Partha Mitter, *Much Maligned Monsters: A History of European Reactions to Indian Art*, 2nd ed. (Chicago: University of Chicago Press, 1992), 48–72.

39. Peter Mason, *Infelicities: Representations of the Exotic* (Baltimore: Johns Hopkins University Press, 1998), 48ff.

40. Siegfried Huigen, "Travellers to Monomotapa: The Representation of Southern Africa by the Dutch in the Seventeenth Century," *History and Anthropology* 9 (1996), 207–30. Huigen refers here to earlier work by Peter Mason, not that cited in n. 39 above.

41. Marie-Odette Scalliet, "Une curiosité oubliée: Le 'Livre des dessins faits dans un voyage aux Indes par un voyageur hollandais' du marquis de Paulmy," *Archipel* 54 (1997): 35–62.

42. On this text, see the preliminary reflection in Sanjay Subrahmanyam, "O gentio indiano visto pelos Portugueses no século XVI," *Oceanos* 19/20 (1994): 190–96.

43. Wolfgang Joost, ed., *Die wundersamen Reisen des Caspar Schmalkalden nach West- und Ostindien, 1642–1652* (Leipzig: Acta Humaniora, 1983).

44. Benjamin Schmidt, "Inventing Exoticism: The Project of Dutch Geography and the Marketing of the World, circa 1700," in *Merchants and Marvels: Commerce, Science, and Art in Early Modern Europe*, ed. Pamela H. Smith and Paula Findlen (New York: Routledge, 2002), 364.

45. For the positive view, see Furber, "Asia and the West," 716; in contrast, see Richard Grove, "Indigenous Knowledge and the Significance of South-West India for Portuguese and Dutch Constructions of Tropical Nature," *Modern Asian Studies* 30 (1996): 121–43.

46. Jürgen Osterhammel, *Die Entzauberung Asiens: Europa und die asiatischen Reiche im 18. Jahrhundert* (Munich: C.H. Beck, 1998).

47. Jonathan I. Israel, *Radical Enlightenment: Philosophy and the Making of Modernity, 1650–1750* (Oxford: Oxford University Press, 2001).

48. The most recent example of this tendency is Gijs Kruijtzer, "Madanna, Akkanna and the Brahmin Revolution: A Study of Mentality, Group Behavior and Personality in Seventeenth-Century India," *Journal of the Economic and Social History of the Ori-*

ent 45 (2002): 232–67, which broadly follows the trend set by Joan-Pau Rubiés, *Travel and Ethnology in the Renaissance: South India through European Eyes, 1250–1625* (Cambridge: Cambridge University Press, 2000), adding to it a dash of "universalist" psychological theory to claim that "the 'othering' by Dutch sources was context dependent to the same extent as othering by early modern South Asians."

49. For an example, see Marion Peters (with André de la Porte), *In steen geschreven: Leven en sterven van VOC-dienaren op de Kust van Coromandel in India* (Amsterdam: Uitgeverij Bas Lubberhuizen, 2002).

50. For instance, see Muzaffar Alam and Sanjay Subrahmanyam, "Empiricism of the Heart: Close Encounters in an Eighteenth-Century Indo-Persian Text," *Studies in History* (N.S.) 15 (1999): 261–91.

9

Creating a Littoral Community

Muslim Reformers in the
Early Modern Indian Ocean World

Michael N. Pearson

Pᴇᴏᴘʟᴇ ᴀᴄᴄᴇᴘᴛ ᴀ ɴᴇᴡ ʀᴇʟɪɢɪᴏɴ when they find that their existing beliefs no longer enable them to cope with new challenges and opportunities. Often it is a trickle-down matter; an influential member of the elite, such as a Roman emperor, converts and the subjects follow. However, conversion is usually a process rather than an event. Even after the convert has accepted some central elements of the new faith, the drive toward a fuller observance of the norms of the faith continues. Religious authorities work to rectify the practice of ostensible believers, as seen, for example, in papal decrees, or the work of reformers in Hindu India today. Individuals are encouraged or constrained to accept the norms of their particular religious community as defined by some higher authority.

My chapter analyzes the ways in which the spread of Islam around the littoral of the Indian Ocean created important new forms of association; in other words, individuals became less particularistic and instead were given places in the wider community of Islam. This process began soon after the death of the Prophet. Over time the focus changed. Where once Muslim divines had worked to convert coastal people to their faith, by the period on which I will concentrate, roughly the sixteenth to eighteenth centuries, the effort was much more to rectify backsliding and bring already converted people closer to normative Islam. In the Indian Ocean world a "traditional" form of association, religious belief, was, if anything, being reinforced while at the same time in Europe it was being undermined or at least drastically changed. This is not to deny that all religious authorities see as one of their most important roles the effort to improve the quality of their followers' practice, as most obviously seen in pronouncements from the various popes. However, it does seem that in Europe religion was increasingly less important in creating forms of association. Economic and political matters were dominant. My argument is that in the early modern Indian Ocean religion remained much more significant.

Islam, however, cannot be separated out and made into something free floating or sui generis. As a form of association it intersected with several other factors, particularly economics and ethnicity. Yet despite tensions within each of these categories—differing interpretations of Islam, competition in the economic sphere, and ethnic rivalry—it is still possible to discern an Islamic community spread around the shores of the ocean. Over the early modern period this community was solidified, made more coherent and more differentiated from its neighbors, by the work of traveling Islamic religious specialists. In terms of the theme of this volume, there was continuity in the sense that there was an existing Muslim community spread around the shores of the ocean, but there was change in that slowly this community moved toward a more "pure" observance of Islam. This process continues today.

It was the coastal people all around the littoral of the Indian Ocean who converted most readily to Islam. In part this was because they increasingly found their existing folk beliefs inadequate as a wider world impacted them. These people obviously were most exposed to foreign ideas and foreign traders. One general way to look at this is to consider the influential theory of Robin Horton, who has studied conversions in Africa. He finds a two-tier cosmology and describes how the focus of many people shifts from the lower or second tier (that of lesser spirits) to the higher or first (that of the supreme being). This shift in focus and emphasis occurs because the latter, higher level was better able to help people cope with a wider world, and with intensified social change and disruption. The task for the missionary was to get such people to identify the higher level of their cosmology with the missionary's own supreme being, be it Allah or God. [1]

Arabs had traded in the western Indian Ocean before Islam. This trade continued after they were converted to the new religion. Inhabitants around the coasts of the Indian Ocean found that their already established interlocutors and their foreign business partners were now Muslim, and that they had things to communicate that made sense of an expanding and increasingly complex world. T. T. Spear and D. Nurse put this well for the Swahili.

> Many townspeople . . . operated in a wider world than the microcosm of the village, living in towns with other people, sailing from town to town along the coast, and trading with people from across the Indian Ocean. These people lived in a macrocosmic world inhabited by peoples speaking different languages, hav-

ing different ancestors, and working in different occupations. In this world the beliefs of the microcosm were too parochial; what was needed were beliefs that were universal. And so townspeople began to adopt Islam, and in so doing they adopted a set of beliefs and a framework for action that were held in common by others in the town, by people in other towns, and by people from the whole Indian Ocean world.[2]

I have sketched the spread of Islam elsewhere.[3] Put briefly, Islam very early reached the southern part of the Arabian Peninsula, that is Yemen and Hadhramaut, traveling to this region by land. Of the areas in the Indian Ocean that Islam reached by sea, we know that Muslims had arrived on the Swahili coast by the mid-eighth century,[4] though at first this was a matter of Muslim traders from the Red Sea and Hadhramaut visiting and erecting a mosque for their use. Over time some of these Arabs settled, and some of their neighbors in the port cities of this coast converted to Islam. This seems to have happened over the course of the eleventh to thirteenth centuries.

There is evidence of a similar process on the coasts of India occurring rather earlier. A traditional Muslim account of what happened in Malabar is normative and pious in tone, yet it reveals the typical process of the conversion of a coastal ruler, and then the religion "trickling down" to others in the area. The account claims that a group of Muslims, including a sheikh, arrived in Malabar, presumably from the Red Sea area:

> an intelligence of their arrival having reached the King, sending for them into his presence, he manifested towards them much kindness, conversing with them without reserve: and inquiring of them their circumstances and condition, the Sheikh, encouraged by the King's condescension, related to him the history of our prophet Mahomed (upon whom may the divine favour and blessing ever rest!), explaining also to the monarch the tenets of Islamism; whilst, for a confirmation of their truth, he narrated to him the miracle of the division of the moon [which purportedly Muhammad had done]. Now, conviction of the Prophet's divine mission, under the blessing of Almighty God, having followed this relation, the heart of the King became warmed with a holy affection towards Mahomet (on whom be peace!), and, in consequence of this his conversion . . . many others also became Muslims.[5]

Insular southeast Asia came later, from the end of the thirteenth century. The religion was spread more by Muslims who themselves were relatively recent converts from India, rather than people from the heartland in the Hijaz. Again the religion spread through the mediation of traders. Muslim trading groups would take with them their own spiritual preceptors, and these men, often members of Sufi (devotional) orders, would not only service their own merchants but also would spread the faith. So also with all traveling Muslims, for it would be incorrect to see a clear role differentiation between say a pros-elytizer and a merchant; rather, men oscillated between one role and the other, depending on circumstance. Even those who traveled and spread or reinforced Islam were a variegated lot. Some were men of the Book, adherents of the Qur'an, hadith, and, more generally, the sharia. Then there were Sufis, follow-ers of a more mystical version of Islam, and people more tolerant of devo-tionalism and saint worship or veneration than were the more orthodox. True that one cannot make a clear distinction between Sufis and orthodox *ulama* (religious scholars and guides)—most *ulama* were also members of Sufi orders—and true also that Sufi orders varied widely in their practice, yet the point is that traveling Muslims were by no means part of some rigid Islamic monolith. There was quite considerable diversity.[6]

Trade and politics often intersected, so that frequently the controller of a Southeast Asian port city would be pressured to convert by visiting Muslim merchants, who might even threaten to trade elsewhere unless this were done. The elite converted, and the religion then trickled down to the other residents of the ports, and then spread out to the countryside. The important conver-sion of the ruler of Melaka was briefly described by a Portuguese chronicler in an account that makes clear the merger of trade and religion: "Some ships ar-rived at Melaka from the ports of Arabia, and one year there came a *caciz* [Muslim divine] to preach the law of Muhammad in these parts." He was suc-cessful in becoming influential with the king, and impressed on him the grandeur of Islam. Conversion followed, and the king was honored by being given the name of the Prophet himself.[7]

So far, so good. It is simple to become a formal Muslim. One need only re-cite the *shahada*, the profession of faith: "There is no God but God, and Muhammad is his Prophet." However, Muslim travelers made it clear that many of the newly converted were lacking in their observance of even the most basic tenets of the faith. Within the Muslim "community" there was con-siderable dubiety expressed by those from the heartland of the Middle East to those on the edges, such as the Malay world, or even in Gujarat. The great nav-igator Ibn Majid wrote of his ostensible coreligionists in the Malay world that "[t]hey are evil people who follow no rules; the unbeliever marries the Mus-lim, and the Muslim the infidel woman . . . they publicly drink wine, and they do not pray before setting out on a voyage."[8] In 1556 a Jesuit in Mozambique claimed that he easily won a debate with a Muslim authority, for the latter was very ill informed. He thought Muhammad was the first man, even before Adam, and that the Prophet was of the same substance as God.[9] An unsuc-cessful Ottoman grandee in 1538 said that the local Gujarati Muslims were very slack: "at the time of prayer they simply play music; most of them are in-fidels."[10]

These people had converted, but retained folk practices from their pre-Islamic past. Similarly, Muslims who went to sea prayed to folk deities. Khwaja Khizr was dubiously Islamic but very influential. He was associated with fertility and so with water and fish. In times of peril, or even to preempt peril at sea, he was widely venerated and appealed to for intercession. On the Swahili coast the local fishers made elaborate sacrifices to sea spirits. The local Islamic teacher did not participate, for this was close to polytheism. David Parkin happily calls these fishers "intermediary Swahili," that is somewhere between "pure Islam" and folk belief. In a more general sense, Parkin notes different sorts of Islamic prayer: "the idea of prayer in the mosque connotes unambiguous Islamic piety, while that outside points towards the possibility of other kinds of worship."[11] A recent outstanding survey of the Swahili world similarly distinguishes between *din* (religion) and *mila* (custom); the two have a symbiotic relationship.[12]

A very early Portuguese account makes clear that the Mapillahs in Kerala, indigenous people who had converted, had by no means abandoned all their previous Hindu customs.

> And in this land of Malabar there are Moors in great numbers who speak the same tongue as the Heathens of the land, and go naked like the Nayres, but as a token of distinction from the Heathen they wear little round caps on their heads, and long beards . . . . These follow the Heathen custom in many ways; their sons inherit half their property, and their nephews (sisters' sons) take the other half. They belong to the sect of Mafamede, their holy day is Friday. Throughout this land they have a great number of mosques. They marry as many wives as they can support and keep as well many heathen concubines of low caste. If they have sons or daughters by these they make them Moors, and oft-times the mother as well, and thus this evil generation continues to increase in Malabar; the people of the country call them Mapuleres.[13]

Perhaps we know about the distribution and spread of Islam, but its consumption is much more difficult to study. Along the same lines, Parkin has suggested that it is more accurate to write of the "'acceptance' of Islam, which is likely to take longer and to be reciprocally inscribed in pre-existing custom and cosmology. The term conversion presupposes a shift from one to another unambiguously defined religion. Acceptance is less visibly dramatic and does not mean abandonment of a pre-existing cosmology. Yet it may well typify much Islamization in the region in allowing for Islamic and non-Islamic traits to inter-mingle steadily."[14] This means that we are looking at additive change much of the time, as opposed to substitutive change. The former implies that an existing body of belief is added to, while the latter means existing notions are cast aside and replaced. The Islamic community, initially loose knit and having very wide regional variations, slowly in the early modern period was purified, standardized, so that increasingly normative Islam, rather than region-specific folk practice, was most important.

This consolidation was achieved in two ways. First, a surprising number of people undertook the hajj to Mecca, which was the greatest movement of people on a routine basis in the early modern world, and indeed until the vast outflow of people from Europe, and later India, in the nineteenth century. I have estimated that in the early modern period some fifteen thousand made the trip from India each year. This had enormous implications for the propagation and consolidation of Islam, a matter which I have discussed elsewhere.[15] I will concentrate on the second process, the travels around the ocean of religious specialists, among whom those from the Islamic heartland were most important.[16] The great fourteenth-century traveler Ibn Battuta shows how by his time there was an identifiable "community" all around the shores of the ocean. He traveled about 120,000 kilometers in nearly thirty years, and all the time virtually was in a Muslim world, from West Africa to China. Everywhere he went he was welcomed as a person of religious authority hailing from the heartland. His account of his travels is replete with examples of Muslim networks. All around the littoral he called in at port cities and found Islamic authorities from all over the Muslim world: North Africa, the whole Middle East, and even further afield. A man he met on the west coast of India was a typical traveling authority. He was "a pious jurist from Maqdashaw [Mogadishu], called Sa'id, of fine figure and character. He used to fast continually, and I was told that he had studied at Mecca for fourteen years and for the same length of time at al-Madina, had met Abu Numayy, the Amir of Mecca, and Mansur b. Jammaz, the Amir of al-Madina, and had travelled in India and China."[17] In Kilwa the sultan was a lavish patron to visiting Muslim exemplars from Iraq and the Hijaz.[18] Ibn Battuta himself was often patronized and given important positions, such as in Delhi, and the Maldives, because of his prestige as a man who had visited the heartland of Islam and was a recognized authority.[19]

He describes a very well-traveled group of Muslims. The activities of these Islamic specialists created unity in the ocean in two ways: first, they themselves made up connecting links, and second, their activities, which continue today, have slowly increased adherence to a more normative, or standardized, Islam all around the littoral. As they left familiar Muslim areas they found different "Islams," ones indebted to local pre-Islamic practices that flourished beneath a veneer of adherence to stricter norms. They commented on this and strove to rectify it. In this process knowledge of Arabic was crucial for this gave access to the vast scriptural Arabic tradition, on which Islamic law and theology rested. One example of this is what happened late in our period on the Swahili coast. Where once a person who in Swahili terms was cultured or civilized was called *uungwana*, literally a freeborn urban person, by at least the nineteenth century it became *ustaarabu*, "to be Arab-like." At this time, that is, from the late eighteenth century, a large corpus of Arabic words entered the various Swahili dialects. The language in fact helped create unity around the ocean amongst its Islamic people. A modern authority says there are about five thousand words of Arabic origin in Malay, and more than that in Swahili. Revealingly, about 80 percent of these are common to the two widely separated languages.[20]

Stephen Dale's exemplary work on the Mapillahs of Malabar provides further detail. Scholars came to Kerala from Yemen, Oman, Bahrain, and Baghdad.[21] In the early sixteenth century Duarte Barbosa wrote about how many and how diverse they were: "There are many other foreign Moors as well in the town of Calecut, who are called *Pardesis*, natives of divers lands, Arabs, Persians, Guzarates, Curasanes and Daquanis, who are settled here. As the trade of this country is very large, they gathered here in great numbers with their wives and sons, and seem to have increased."[22] From Kerala Islam flowed on, to Southeast Asia, especially to the north Sumatran state of Aceh in the sixteenth century, and even to the Philippines. This contact was mediated through the port cities: "The city in Southeast Asia furnished the crucial link between international Islam and the local Muslim community whose bonds stretched far into the rural interior."[23]

Members of various Muslim Sufi orders, and of schools of law, traveled widely in a quite organized way to achieve greater observance. A typical rectifier would leave home to study in Mecca and Medina and other centers, and then go back to the periphery of the Muslim world, where they had very great prestige and where they sought to inculcate the normative Islam they had learned in the heartland. As an example, we know something of the career of 'Abd al-Ra'uf of Singkel, and this gives us a clear picture of the many ties and networks and connections established in seventeenth-century Islam, and of the centrality of the holy places in this process. He was born in North Sumatra around 1615, and in about 1640 moved to the Hijaz and Yemen to study. In Medina his main teacher was the Kurdish-born Ibrahim al-Kurani. He spent a total of nineteen years in Mecca and gained very considerable prestige. In particular, he taught hundreds, even thousands, of Indonesians there, and initiated many of them into the Sufi order of which he was a distinguished member, the *Shattariyya*. He returned to Sumatra, to Aceh, in 1661 and was a revered teacher there for nearly thirty years. He kept in touch with Ibrahim in Medina, and taught what he had learned from him to the many Indonesian—especially Javanese—pilgrims who stopped for a time in Aceh on the way to the Red Sea.[24]

Another Asian example stresses the role of Medina, and again shows the extreme cosmopolitanism of Islam, in this case in the eighteenth century. Muhammad Hayya, who was a teacher of the great reformer al-Wahhab, had himself been taught in Medina by scholars from India, Persia, Algiers, Morocco and other places. Apart from al-Wahhab, his students came from Turkey, India, Yemen, Jerusalem, Baghdad, Damascus and other Muslim cities. As John Voll says, "The Medinese scholarly community in general was able to contact people from throughout the world of Islam because of the Pilgrimage."[25] So also in India. Hajji Ibrahim Muhaddis Qadiri was born near Allahabad in northern India. He did the hajj and then studied in Cairo, Mecca, and Syria. He was away twenty-four years, but then returned to India, settled in Agra, and was a prestigious teacher until his death in 1593.[26] A final illustration of the wide ties and influence of these scholars again comes from Indonesia. Shaykh Yusuf was born in Makassar (on Sulawesi) in 1626, and was related to the ruling dynasty. He converted to Islam, and did a hajj at age eighteen. In typical fashion, he then studied in Mecca for several years before he went to Banten, where, with his Meccan prestige, he was a very influential religious leader to the sultan and court. In 1682 the Dutch East India Company (VOC) conquered Banten, and Yusuf led guerrilla resistance to them. Finally he surrendered and was imprisoned in Batavia. Then he was exiled to other parts of the VOC's dispersed maritime empire: first to Sri Lanka, and in 1694 to the Cape Colony along with two wives, other family, and twelve disciples, a total in all of forty-nine Muslims. The company tried to isolate him, but even so he was able to make a few converts before he died in 1699.[27]

Islam and trade were closely connected, as we have noted, but then there is a debate over whether or not a common religion engenders trust, a vital element in commerce. One view is that it is easier to generate trust in a group that has a religious identity, or, for that matter, a common ethnicity or place of origin. This primordialist view stresses the importance of established affective links, such as a common adherence to Islam. The opposed view is that rational calculation, based on an interlocutor's reputation, is more important. Yet trust based on reputation is more easily achieved within a group linked by affective ties, so the two are not necessarily opposed. One can assume that a common Muslim religion played some role in commercial matters: not, however, that Muslims would not compete vigorously with each other to drive the best bargain.[28]

Ethnicity, as many of the comments above show, was a divisive element. It seems that ethnicity could be transcended only if, again like many of the examples above, one learned Arabic and spent much time in the Muslim heartland, preferably in the holy cities or in Cairo and Damascus. In religion also there are levels and tensions. At the top is a corps of Arabic-knowing religious specialists, most of them from the heartland though they could take on others also. Below, if this be the correct term, is a much more complex variegated Islam, as again many of the examples above show. These people practiced Islam, but a regional one, which varied from place to place and was influenced to a greater or lesser degree by pre-Islamic customs. But there are value judgments here; we need not follow the intolerant lordly men from the heartland, or many Western Orientalists, in harsh denigration of the religious practice of others. What we see in the early modern period is a slow increment in the degree of orthodox observance among the Muslim community of the Indian Ocean littoral. Commonalities to do with living on the coast, hence being exposed to wide and cosmopolitan influences, merged with a common occupation where most coastal inhabitants were engaged in commerce, rather than being tribespeople or peasants, and with observance of some form or other of Islam to make these coastal people distinctive by location, by occupation, and most of all by religion. Indeed, this distinctiveness increased over our period as the process of the replacement of folk custom from the pre-Islamic past by a more pure Islam proceeded and a more close-knit community was created.

Notes

1. Robin Horton, "African Conversions," *Africa* 41(1971): 85–108; and "On the Rationality of Conversion," *Africa* 45 (1975): 219–35, 373–99. There are obvious value judgments in this schema, which I do not have the space to discuss or critique. For excellent comparative and theoretical discussions of conversions to Islam in India, see Richard M. Eaton, "Approaches to the Study of Conversion to Islam in India," in *Approaches to Islam in Religious Studies*, ed. Richard C. Martin (Tucson, AZ: Association for Asian Studies, 1985), 106–23; and P. Hardy, "Modern European and Muslim Explanations of Conversions to Islam in South Asia: A Preliminary Survey of the Literature," in *Conversion to Islam*, ed. Nehemia Levtzion (New York: Holmes & Meier, 1979), 68–99.

2. T. T. Spear and D. Nurse, *The Swahili: Reconstructing the History and Language of an African Society, AD 500–1500* (Philadelphia: University of Pennsylvania Press, 1984), 94–95.

3. See my *The Indian Ocean* (London: Routledge, 2003), 75–82; "Gateways to Africa: the Indian Ocean and the Red Sea," in *History of Islam in Africa*, ed. Randall Pouwels and Nehemia Levtzion (Athens: Ohio University Press, 2000), 37–59; and "Conversions in Southeast Asia: Evidence from the Portuguese Records," *Portuguese Studies* 6 (1990): 53–70.

4. Mark Horton and John Middleton, *The Swahili: The Social Landscape of a Mercantile Society* (Oxford: Blackwell, 2000), 49.

5. Zain-ud-din, *Tohfut-ul-Mujahideen*, trans. M. J. Rowlandson (London: Oriental Translation Fund, 1833), 48–50.

6. See works cited in n. 3, which also contain copious citations to original sources.

7. Diogo do Couto, *Da Asia* (Lisboa: Na Regia officina typografica, 1777–88), book 4, part 2, chap 1.

8. Luis Filipe F. R. Thomaz, "Malaka et ses communautés marchandes au tournant du 16ᵉ siècle," in *Marchands et hommes d'affaires asiatiques dans l'Océan Indien et la Mer de Chine 13ᵉ–20ᵉ siècles*, ed. Denys Lombard and Jean Aubin (Paris: Editions de l'Ecole des hautes études en sciences sociales, 1988), 42.

9. J. Wicki et al., *Documenta Indica*, 16 vols. to date (Rome: Institutum Historicum Societatis Iesu, 1948–), 3: 498–500. See also João dos Santos, *Ethiopia Oriental*, 2 vols. (Lisbon: Escriptorio da Empreza, 1891), 1: part 1, chap. 19.

10. Quoted in M. N. Pearson, *Pious Passengers: the Hajj in Earlier Times* (New Delhi: Sterling Publishers, 1994), 71.

11. David Parkin and Stephen C. Headley, eds., *Islamic Prayer across the Indian Ocean: Inside and Outside the Mosque* (London: Curzon, 2000), 1.

12. Horton and Middleton, *Swahili*, 180.

13. Duarte Barbosa, *Livro*, 2 vols. (London: Hakluyt, 1918–21), 2: 74–78.

14. Parkin and Headley, *Islamic Prayer*, 3.

15. See Pearson, *Pious Passengers*, 51–58 and passim for the significance of the hajj.

16. For a stunning analysis of such people in a later period, which, however, does not necessarily focus on the creation of unity around the ocean, see Anne Bang, *Sufis and Scholars of the Sea: Family Networks in East Africa, 1860–1925* (London and New York: Routledge Curzon, 2003). See also her web site at www.smi.uib.no/ab/abhome.html.

17. Ibn Battuta, *The Travels of Ibn Battuta*, 4 vols., trans. H. A. R. Gibb (Cambridge: Hakluyt, 1958–94), 4: 809

18. Ibn Battuta, *Travels of Ibn Battuta*, 2: 380.

19. Ibn Battuta, *Travels of Ibn Battuta*, 2: 272. See also Ross Dunn's excellent gloss on his travels: *The Adventures of Ibn Battuta* (Berkeley and Los Angeles: University of California Press, 1986).

20. Randall Pouwels, "The East African Coast, c. 780–1900 C.E.," in *History of Islam in Africa*, 265; Jan Knappert, "East Africa and the Indian Ocean," in *Africa and the Sea: Proceedings of a Colloquium at the University of Aberdeen, March, 1984*, ed. J. C. Stone (Aberdeen: University of Aberdeen Press, 1985), 125.

21. Stephen Dale, *Islamic Society on the South Asian Frontier: The Mapillas of Malabar (1498–1922)* (Oxford: Clarendon, 1980).

22. Barbosa, *Livro*, 2: 75–76.

23. J. Kathirithamby-Wells, "The Islamic City: Melaka to Jogjakarta, c. 1500–1800," *Modern Asian Studies* 20 (1986): 342, passim.

24. See two versions of his career by A. H. Johns: "Friends in Grace: Ibrahim al-Kurani and 'Abd al-Rauf al-Singkeli," in *Spectrum: Essays Presented to Sutan Takdir Alisjahbana on his Seventieth Birthday*, ed. S. Udin (Jakarta: Dian Rakyat, 1978), 471–72; and *The Gift Addressed to the Spirit of the Prophet* (Canberra: Australian National University, 1964), 8–11. Indeed, this latter work also shows other connections, for it consists of a study of a Javanese text on Sufism, which in turn was based on a seventeenth-century Arabic text from Gujarat to do with orthodox Sufism. See also B. G. Martin,

"Arab Migration to East Africa in Medieval Times," *International Journal of African Historical Studies* 7 (1975): 367–90.

25. John Voll, "Muhammad Hayya al-Sindi and Muhammad ibn 'Abd al-Wahhab: an analysis of an intellectual group in eighteenth century Madina," *Bulletin of the School of Oriental and African Studies* 38 (1975): 32–39.

26. S. A. A. Rizvi, *A History of Sufism in India*, 2 vols. (New Delhi: Munshiram Manoharlal, 1978–83), 2: 146–47, 294, 167, and passim for many other examples.

27. Robert C.-H. Shell, "Islam in Southern Africa, 1652–1998," in *History of Islam in Africa*, 328.

28. Claude Markovits, *The Global World of Indian Merchants* (Cambridge: Cambridge University Press, 2000), 260–61.

III
TRANSITIONS

10

Custom, Community, and the Crown

Lawyers and the Reordering of
French Customary Law

Marie Seong-Hak Kim

S OME THIRTY YEARS AGO THE FRENCH HISTORIAN Emmanuel Le Roy Ladurie proposed a "system of customary law." In his much celebrated article in *Annales ESC*, Le Roy Ladurie noted that regional customs, such as inheritance custom, in sixteenth-century France conferred on a particular locality its cultural identity that allows us to distinguish the various cultural regions.[1] He thus suggested that the ethnographer-historian "select a number of pertinent criteria whose presence, absence or diverse manifestations are associated with an entire family of cultural traits, which themselves give each customary region its specific configuration."[2] This approach to custom as "cultural traits" can help subsume peculiar characteristics of local communities and the collective conscience of their inhabitants under a structural system. But the problem remains, as has been pointed out by historians of law, that such a perspective tends to ignore the context of the codification of customs and also the degree of their effectiveness.[3] Custom acquires the force of law only when judicial courts acknowledge and enforce it. Doctrinal and jurisprudential approval is essential for the ordering of custom.[4] The juridical nature of custom thus limits the significance of custom as an element of cultural or social identity of a geographical community. Specifically, the ethnographical approach does not fully ascertain the fact that official codification of customary law in early modern Europe was not so much a spontaneous and autonomous manifestation of popular practices springing up in a local community as a product of deliberate and coherent reworking by professional jurists. In France, the late fifteenth and sixteenth centuries witnessed a massive campaign to record and reform local customs. Throughout the codification effort, led by the crown, French lawyers—advocates, judges, and legal scholars—played a prominent role in compiling, revising, and rationalizing custom, and reconciling different rules in localities to bring them, as much as possible, under a unified system of law. Together, their efforts represented a conscious movement toward creating a common customary law in France.

French customary law that emerged as the result of the codification enterprise in the sixteenth century revealed little resemblance to an organic artifact of community. However, the legislative contrivances inherent in the codification process crucially bore upon the local community's collaboration. The procedure of recording customary law had to be molded and adjusted in accordance with the ancient principles of the "public law of custom."[5] Since the king could not in principle create custom, the primary responsibility of gathering and consenting to customary practices was left to the population in local representative assemblies in each district. These popular assemblies were invariably dominated by local legal experts. The local community maintained its rights to consent to custom, but the legal instrument of codification revealed unmistakably professional aspiration and attributes that undermined popular and collective control of custom. The role of lawyers in the codification on behalf of the local population deserves attention because it provided means and support for the king to reform provincial customs while avoiding the appearance of open interference in private law. In the end, the local community's claims to ancient rights and privileges withered before the state's postulation of reason and equity embodying public good. The movement of revamping provincial custom thus resulted in an increasing approximation of customary law to royal legislation. Reordering customary law and linking it to statutory laws was an integral part of a state-building process in early modern Europe.[6] In France the determination of the royal government to pursue the codification project in the backdrop of the religious wars is a rare indication of the reformist ardor of the late Valois monarchs. This chapter argues that French lawyers fashioned in this codification process a critical nexus between the crown's assertion of legislative authority and the principle of representative institutions of the local community. The humanist legal professionals helped by creating a symbiotic relationship between the state and community. Examination of the role of lawyers in the systematization of customary law can shed important light on the evolving relations between local community and the emerging administrative monarchy in sixteenth-century France.[7]

In the late Middle Ages, French private law was largely composed of unwritten popular custom. Each local community, usually a *bailliage*, developed and applied its own customary usages. Unlike in England, the late medieval French kings did not attempt to use the royal courts to create a law common to the entire kingdom. Neither did France have a national common law, equivalent to Roman law in Germany. The initiative for official codification and reformation of local customs came from the king.[8] The ordinance of Montil-les-Tours (1454) noted that by writing customs down "lawsuits would be much shorter and the parties relieved of expenses and costs, and the judges would be able to render better judgments with greater certainty."[9] The crown thus ordered that "customary lawyers, practitioners and people of each of the said provinces in our kingdom" come to an agreement about their custom and codify it. In 1497 the letters patent included an important disposition: the royal commissioners delegated by the king to preside over the codification would not limit their role to registering custom hitherto observed; instead they would advise, after consultation with the three estates, on how to "correct, adjust, abridge or interpret" the custom that they deemed to be "hard, iniquitous and unreasonable."[10] Since the late Middle Ages, French kings had claimed that they had the power to declare, and possibly modify, custom. According to François Olivier-Martin, the king's power to abolish "bad" custom had been exercised without challenge from as early as the eleventh century.[11] It was largely accepted by the end of the fifteenth century that custom need not be substantiated in any exclusive manner; new custom could be introduced even if the contrary disposition had been observed the whole time.[12] By the middle of the sixteenth century the majority of the customs in the kingdom, including the custom of Paris, had been published.[13] Not long after the initial redactions of customs, however, there was a clamor among lawyers to modify and update those customs that had proved unjust or inadequate. The monarchy willingly enlisted these legal professionals in its effort to improve the legal system and to prevent disruption of existing social adjustments during the Renaissance by updating customary law. In 1555 a new campaign was launched under the direction of Christophe de Thou, the first president of the Parlement of Paris.[14] The main objective of this new undertaking was to revisit and reform the customs that had already been codified but proved inadequate. Between 1555, when the ancient custom of Sens was revised, and 1580, when the ancient Paris custom was reformed, eight local customs were reformed and seven customs were codified for the first time within the jurisdiction of the Parlement of Paris.[15]

The idea that the king could alter or dispense with the existing custom justified the periodic revision of customary law.[16] Yet it was generally accepted that he could amend or abrogate unjust or obsolete customary law only through a local consensus. French legists sharply distinguished between the realms of public law (royal edicts and ordinances) and of private law (custom). As the king increasingly behaved as the legislator, not merely the judge, the lines between ordinance and custom blurred, but the prevailing idea maintained that the domain of custom escaped the power of the king.[17] In order to reform customary law, the king therefore needed to resort to a special legislative instrument that was empowered by royal authority but was mainly subject to popular control. The king did not question the principle that the inhabitants of each locality were responsible for declaring their custom. The notion of popular consent of the three estates was consistently upheld throughout the reformation process. Royal commissioners, usually judges or advocates at the parlements, were delegated to preside over the proceedings, but their presence was meant primarily to arbitrate the possible conflict between different estates. Nevertheless, the king could not remain disinterested in the content of customary law; he had the duty to abolish bad custom. Distinguishing "good" custom from "bad" custom inevitably entailed the selection and reworking of customary terms by professional jurists sanctioned by royal authority. The role of legal practitioners, whose influence as a professional class had been steadily on the rise since the late Middle Ages, was crucial in the framing of customary law.

Lawyers in local jurisdictions enthusiastically supported the crown's campaign. The French legal profession had raised doubts about the published customs from early on. Charles Dumoulin's enormously influential commentary on the ancient Paris custom headed the criticisms of the lawyers about the old custom, in particular feudal custom, and their push for reform.[18] The official justification for prying into custom that had already been published several decades earlier was that these redactions remained useless because of the loss of their *procès-verbaux*. The *procès-verbal* was a report drawn up by the commissioners of the discussions or objections raised by the three estates during the redaction process. Without the *procès-verbal*, local inhabitants were again compelled to verify their custom by *turbes des témoins*, providing proofs by local inquest.[19] Understandably legal practitioners, as well as royal officials, did not like the *turbe* procedure. Whether or not the *procès-verbal* had indeed been lost was rather secondary in consideration, however, because no one denied that the principal reason for calling for customary reform was to change inequitable and unreasonable rules. To those who wondered why custom needed to be changed and reformed so often, Jean Brèche, *avocat* in Touraine, responded that custom ought to be "accommodated and doctored following the morals of the time and varieties among them."[20] Often initial steps were taken by local lawyers, who, having conceived the plan of republishing their custom, directly requested the king to delegate royal commissioners.[21] In Sens the local *avocat* Jean Pénon led the effort to petition the king for the reformation of its custom.[22] In Touraine a group of lawyers argued that several articles in their custom, officially codified in 1507, had "doubts and obscurities" leading to "endless lawsuits."[23] The custom of Auxerre had been compiled in 1507 and its *procès-verbal* was preserved, but the people of Auxerre claimed that they had lost it anyway.[24] Throughout the 1550s and 1560s the king was inundated with similar requests to authorize reformation of custom.

The codification process involved two phases. First, royal officials charged certain members of the local community to prepare a draft where there was no previous codification, or to propose changes to the existing custom. Legal practitioners dominated these preparatory proceedings because officials in the district usually selected *avocats* and *procureurs* who were better versed than others in the custom of their jurisdiction.[25] The substantiation of the custom relied on the testimony of local lawyers. The royal commissioners tended to give greater credence to the testimony of lawyers, even against the protest of laymen, in debates involving technical rules.[26] After the draft was prepared, the general assembly of the three estates met in the presence of the royal commissioners to discuss the proposed text article by article. Once debates revealed the opinions of the estates and the articles were agreed upon, the royal commissioners drew up the final text and declared the official publication of the articles on behalf of the king. The prerogative of authenticating the final text exclusively belonged to the crown.[27] The text was then sent to the Parlement for registration. When there were unresolved disputes over articles, the contesters reserved the right to appeal to the Parlement.[28] In the meantime, any attempts to propose custom other than the one officially proclaimed were explicitly prohibited. Throughout the process, royal commissioners were expected to play the neutral role of arbitrator. The direct defense of royal interests was assumed by the king's lawyers (*procureurs généraux* and *avocats généraux*) at each *bailliage* who frequently presented heated arguments on behalf of the king's rights.[29] Although the commissioners had no overt power to control the substance of the law, however, discussions found in many *procès-verbaux* evidenced the commissioners' considerable influence over the directions of the debate in the assemblies. In the 1560s, following the codifications in some *bailliages*, the Parlement of Paris heard a few cases in which local seigneurs accused the commissioners of overstepping their authority during the proceedings and challenged the validity of new articles or even the entire custom newly redacted. De Thou became the main target of such an attack in 1567 after the reformation of the custom of Amiens.[30] Interestingly enough, it was de Thou himself who presided over the court session in 1571 in which the final judgment was rendered, not surprisingly, in favor of the commissioners.[31]

The overhauling of the ancient custom of Paris in 1580 led by de Thou, which marked the crowning achievement of his reformation campaign, exemplified the codification process undertaken throughout the kingdom. Henry III, in the letters patent issued on December 15, 1579, commissioned first president de Thou to this momentous project.[32] The convocation of the estates of the *prévôté* and *vicomté* of Paris, the sole body competent to decide

the definite text of its custom, was preceded by elaborate preliminary procedures. The initial task of compiling the draft was undertaken by Pierre
Séguier, *lieutenant civil* of the *prévoté*, who presided over a commission of
lawyers at the Châtelet.[33] The Châtelet was the sanctuary of the Parisian custom. The provisional text was next circulated among the judges of the
Châtelet whose memoirs were gathered for further revisions of the draft. The
text adopted by the Châtelet judges was then submitted to a new commission
of *avocats* of the Parlement. The lawyers at the Parlement were not always of
the same mind as that of their Châtelet colleagues. Charged with pleading
cases on appeal from diverse provinces within the vast jurisdiction of the Parlement of Paris, they were accustomed to resorting to the jurisprudence of the
Parlement whenever their cases dealt with matters not explicitly regulated by
particular local custom. Therefore they were the natural interpreters of an
emerging common body of customary law, which the Parlement was progres-
sively delineating from different provincial customs.[34] Etienne Pasquier, *avocat* at the Parlement of Paris who participated in this second commission of
the Parisian reform project, described in detail the commission's activities.[35]
For eight days in January 1580, Pasquier joined his colleagues after midmorn-
ing meals at the house of *avocat* Pierre Versoris, which was close to the Palais
de Justice. There some of the most famous *avocats* of the time, including
Jacques Canaye, René Chopin, Jehan Durant, Guy du Faur de Pibrac, Mathieu
de Fontenay, Claude Mangot, and François de Montholon, worked together
"in order to bring their tribute and in order not to look idle in a public task."
Pasquier reported that each of them brought forth "all we have observed in
our memory about the decisions of the Parlement, not only in the *prévosté* and
vicomté of Paris but all other provinces, on general questions not attached to
particular local custom, and this way we accommodated the articles [of the
Parisian custom]."[36] The resulting draft was submitted to the assembly of the
three estates that gathered at the Châtelet on February 18, 1580. This assembly discussed and finalized the text, which was officially published a few days
later.

When one examines the *procès-verbaux* of local customs, one can detect a
certain continuum of innovations operating from the proposals of lawyers in
preparatory sessions through the dispositions of royal commissioners. A clear
program of systematic reforms can be found in areas ranging from property,
intestate succession, matrimonial property, personal capacity, to gifts and
wills. Many modifications introduced into different customs were often formulated in identical languages. The objective of reform was not changing established rules but removing injustice in custom that rendered the rules contrary to reason and equity. One custom of which the commissioners were
especially critical was the rule that denied children the right to represent their

deceased parents in intestate succession. This customary rule, which most likely originated in feudal society from the need for adult males to perform the military services of the fief, was consistently opposed by the royal commissioners.[37] All the reformations over which de Thou presided guaranteed the right of representation in the direct line. The same right was extended in a few localities to the collateral line despite heated resistance from the population.[38] Other reforms, also derived from the Roman law principle of equity, included augmenting the share of later-born children where local custom showed undue preference for the firstborn, and introducing the *légitime*, which guaranteed the children a minimum share of their parental properties so as to protect them against excessive liberalities of parents. Newly systemized customs required more strict formalities for the execution of wills, and wide variations in localities were reduced in favor of a uniform style. These were the reforms that had already been vociferously favored by legal practitioners. The lawyers wishing to lessen uncertainty and inequity in law they practiced found sympathetic supporters in the royal commissioners. In turn they proved themselves essential allies for the commissioners in carrying out their reforms.

The legal machinery of the local assemblies in which lawyers selected and clarified custom made it possible to reconcile the seemingly conflicting notions of the king's legislative authority and popular control of custom. Guy Coquille's formula that in France "it is the people who do the law" has been regarded as capturing the fundamentally popular aspect of customary law.[39] This lapidary phrase becomes less self-evident, however, when one considers that the word *people* includes professional jurists who played a preponderant role in the making and the remaking of the customs. Throughout the campaign of customary reforms, the king observed the notion that the sovereign did not meddle with customary law.[40] The requirement of popular consensus in local assemblies of the three estates has led some historians to emphasize the representative nature of the process.[41] But it was only part of the dynamics of the entire enterprise. While guaranteeing provincial particularities of local custom and fully respecting the notion that custom took its source and foundation from the consent of the three estates, the crown in fact asserted the plenitude of legislative power even in the areas belonging to private law.[42] Through all the solemnity of the codification process, the king confirmed the primacy of royal legislation and achieved deliberate changes of custom. The local assemblies, dominated by legal practitioners, became "a passive but willing instrument" in a program of reform.[43] After all, as Olivier-Martin justly pointed out, the king's attitude toward the custom of different intermediary groups was not one of hostility.[44] The myth of "consent" continued, but, by enlisting the assistance of legal professionals, the king implemented his legislative will.

The role of jurists in the reformation of customs reached far beyond the halls of the provincial assemblies. The reformed customs advocated by local lawyers were confirmed by the jurisprudence of the Parlement of Paris. Coquille remarked on the reformed custom of Paris: "The said articles of the new custom contain for the most part the verdicts arrived at concerning several difficulties and diversities of opinion among French jurisconsults, and even such as had been decided by solemn judgements."[45] All the *avocats* at the Parlement of Paris owned collections of court judgments, attested Pasquier, which they frequently consulted to clarify doubtful points during the redaction of the Paris custom.[46] Royal commissioners were certainly motivated to streamline customary law in accordance with the judgments of the Parlement, which had been authored by themselves or their colleagues. Numerous provisions added during the course of the customary reforms were simply solutions adopted by recent judicial interpretations. Lawyers' pleading in litigations at the Parlement of Paris over the interpretation of custom greatly contributed to articulating the customary provisions and related issues.[47] Where concrete questions as to the meaning of the customary rules were raised and adjudicated, the Parlement of Paris ordered its decrees to be published broadly in the districts "to govern other like cases" or "to serve as law for the future."[48] Large areas of customary rules were left to judicial practice to elaborate them in specific factual situations. Since the vast jurisdiction of the Parlement of Paris compelled its judges and lawyers to deal with the most disparate customs, they naturally looked for rapprochement among the customs and delineate common principles of private law.

The exercise of royal legislative power in private law involved not so much making or unmaking customary law as certifying on which points learned consensus had taken place in the developing body of opinions in the legal community. French doctrinal writers, especially legal humanists, many of whom were practitioners of private law, attempted a rational ordering of local customs. French customary law owed its doctrinal development to legal practitioners who, trained in civil law, searched for solving specific judicial problems drawing upon inspiration from classical scholarship.[49] The legal profession in sixteenth-century France, in particular in Paris, teemed with brilliant legal minds. Some of the most influential scholars, such as Antoine Loisel, du Faur, and Pasquier, were practicing lawyers who later became magistrates. The *quaestio vexata*, as Michel Reulos put it, for sixteenth-century legal practitioners was the fact that they were educated in Roman law in university but practiced customary law in court.[50] Historians have pointed out that legal science of the sixteenth century was the victim of its own success. Study of Roman law, *la raison juridique*, hardly had any rapport with legal practice based on custom and ordinances.[51] While academic legal humanists did little for the development of customary law, humanist legal practitioners devoted attention, by necessity, to expositions of customary law. They wrote procedural guides, commentaries on judicial decisions, and treatises, all based primarily on observation of court procedure and decisions.[52] Since they had to deal in their everyday practice as judges and lawyers with the multiplicity of precedents and rules in customary law that were often contradictory, they took up the task of matching and comparing local customs and tried to synthesize and reconcile them.

The French legal humanism of legal practitioners was essentially a humanism that studied the origin of custom and searched for the general principles of customary law, approaching them in the fundamentally same way as they approached Roman law.[53] For French humanist jurists, the reconstruction of Roman law had significance beyond certain cultivated pleasure in rediscovering an intellectual system of the past. Attempting to forge logical relationships between Roman law and customary law, legal humanists popularized the idea of Roman law as *droit supplétif.* Roman law was recognized as a written ensemble, supplying basic elements and rules of legal construction, without deforming customary law.[54] Since Roman law dispositions could not be applied to purely customary situations, however, practicing legal humanists had to find principles of customary law that could be used in juridical reasoning.[55] The dominant concern in the customary law literature was therefore to find common solutions by reconciling diverse customs. Loisel attempted in his *Institutes coustumières* to extract essential elements common to a number of customs and discern the common principles among them.[56]

While Loisel's work represented a search for the spirit of common customary law (*droit commun coutumier*), Dumoulin's *Orations on the Concord and Union of the Customs of France* was a de facto manifesto of the sixteenth-century French lawyers' reform movement.[57] Before Dumoulin, customary law had remained a chaotic mass of dispositions lacking coherent principles. He showed legal practitioners that French customary law had principles and maxims and that its applications to specific situations were not any less pertinent than those of Roman law rules. Above all, Dumoulin firmly linked equity and royal power. For him, the pursuit of just and equitable customary rules inevitably conjured up royal legislative will. This idea of Dumoulin's was faithfully put into practice by his former colleague de Thou.[58] De Thou's campaign marked the confluence of legal practitioners' search for a common customary law and the monarchy's quest for unified rules sanctioned by the crown. Throughout the reformation process, the contractual principle of custom was observed, but in every stage was present the implicit element of royal legislative authority. The crown extracted legislative power from the contractual framework.[59]

Reform of local customs was an integral part of the ambitious legislative movements in the late sixteenth century to bring French law more uniformity and reason. The endeavor of jurists to create a common customary law coincided with the growing attempt by the crown to promote the unity of the kingdom. In private law, French lawyers were provided with newly organized and rationalized law to practice, and, with better and more intelligent texts, they were prepared to adopt the principles of Roman law without being overwhelmed by it. In public law the monarchy attempted a sweeping reformation of justice. In fact, there existed certain parallels between royal edicts and reformed customs in the late sixteenth century.[60] In the second half of the sixteenth century, the crown issued a series of royal ordinances to instigate far-reaching reformation of justice. While sweeping ordinances and edicts issued by the monarchy were a clear assertion of the legislative power of the political sovereign, reformation of customary law represented a more nuanced expression of royal legislative authority. Occasionally the monarchy appeared to befuddle, perhaps not entirely unintentionally, the ancient distinction between royal law and custom. In 1567 the preamble of the famous edict of mothers, authored by Chancellor Michel de L'Hôpital, explicitly claimed the king's right to reform or altogether abrogate and abolish "the *laws and customs* [emphasis added] which . . . incur much inconveniences and harms the public good."[61] To be sure, such a bold statement attempting to link customary law to statutory law remained an exception rather than a norm in the sixteenth century. Nevertheless, it underscored an unmistakable tendency to redefine the spheres of public law and private law. In the reformation of customs, the third estate in various local communities resorted to the notion of equity to contest seigneurial rights, condemning them as being "unreasonable" and against the public good, and contrasting "particular interests" to the interests of the king and the "poor people."[62] The result was an extension of the sphere of public interest, represented by the king, at the expense of particular interests. In fact, the language of royal "nonintervention" in customary law appeared to be a mere formula intended to encourage reticent seigneurs to participate in the assemblies. The people of the estates were assured that, in participating in the process of customary reforms, they were the masters of the law that governed them.[63] While guaranteeing the principle of consent, however, the king succeeded in reforming customary law, achieving considerable progression in the unification of French law. When sweeping reform in public law often faltered before widespread resistance, customary reform largely sailed through.

Reforms that resulted were sympathetic in spirit but schematic in scope. There was a definite sign of the professionalization of French customary law. Various changes made in the reformed customs reflected the dominant professional opinion of the period. The custom of Paris was, as reported by Pasquier, nothing other than an "abridgment of the general climate of the court of the Parlement."[64] The spontaneity of custom was diminished and the Parisian custom took a form that was more learned, mature, and systematic. Almost every reformed custom exhibited the marks of a well-conceived program of innovation. The customary campaigns also brought about the professionalization of legislative process in France. The participation of the three estates in the reformation of the Paris custom in 1580 was much more limited than the original redaction at the beginning of the century. The project of 1510 had been the outcome of genuine provincial representation; in 1580 it was the work of competent practitioners, only timidly touched upon by the delegates of the Estates.[65] The personal intervention of royal commissioners, nearly insignificant in earlier codifications, grew prominently in later campaigns. The domination by professional lawyers of provincial assemblies is evidenced by the remarkable efficiency of the later publications. Once codified, customary provisions were extended, restricted, or refined by professional judges. Likewise, humanist legal practitioners provided doctrinal writings that they based on their everyday judicial practice, and their work was in turn closely watched and adopted by the courts. There was thus a constant and fruitful interaction, in which both doctrines and jurisprudence "progressed by the same steps along the same routes, each aiding the other, each sanctioning and confirming what the other had elaborated."[66] By the end of the sixteenth century, French customary law was rapidly withdrawn from direct popular control and enmeshed in all the complications of elaborate legal techniques. Custom underwent a gradual evolution from popular, empirical, and collective practices observed in a living community to a body of learned, reasonable, and equitable judicial rules sanctioned by the crown. When customary law metamorphosed to learned jurisprudence dominated by the professionals, the common people had significantly less means to interfere with it.

Finally, the reformation of custom gave a new impetus to the development of the French monarchy. Scholars have depicted official campaigns to standardize local custom as part of the state-building process in early modern Europe.[67] The essential aim of the codification of customs was to bring rationality and uniformity in law, and the new codes and procedures represented the instruments of state power to enforce the uniform rules in the realm. In sixteenth-century France, there was no dramatic expansion of governmental powers or bureaucratic apparatus as a result of the rationalization of French private law. The French codification of civil law as evidence of state building would have to wait until after 1789. Yet the codification movement in the sixteenth century exhibited a definite sign of the administrative monarchy moving into realms that had previously escaped royal power. The entire enterprise presupposed the acceptance of a common reference, namely, the state.

The reformation of custom in the sixteenth century was accomplished by the ingenious balance of the king's legislative power and the right of the three orders, a compromise worked out through the agency of the rising class of legal professionals. The spirit of customary common law sustained French jurists to continue the processes of harmonizing and reconciling law for the ultimate goal of the union and concord of French law. For the crown, it was an excellent means to remind the individuals in provincial communities of his authority, especially during the period of religious wars when they tended to be forgetful about it. Through customary reform, the king tackled the dangerous divisive tendencies of feudalism and local particularism. The local community willingly partook in the codification process, in which the assertion of particular rights of the subjects became increasingly subordinate to the public good represented by the king. This joint enterprise of the crown and community was overall a success, an achievement all the more remarkable when viewed in the background of civil conflict. The reordering of customary law marked an important development toward the unification of French law.

Notes

1. Emmanuel Le Roy Ladurie, "Système de la coutume. Structures familiales et coutume d'héritage en France au XVIe siècle," *Annales ESC* 27 (1972): 825–46; reprinted in *La Territoire de l'historien* (Paris: Gallimard, 1973), 222–51. This article was translated into English as "A System of Customary Law: Family Structures and Inheritance Customs in Sixteenth-Century France," in *Family and Society: Selection from the Annales: Economies, Sociétes, Civilization*, ed. Robert Forster and Orest Ranum (Baltimore: Johns Hopkins University Press, 1976), 75–103; and also in *Family and Inheritance: Rural Society in Western Europe, 1200–1800*, ed. Jack Goody, Joan Thirsk, and E. P. Thompson (Cambridge: Cambridge University Press, 1976), 37–70.

2. Le Roy Ladurie, "Système de la coutume," 826.

3. Louis Assier-Andrieu, "Penser le temps culturel du droit. Le destin anthropologique du concept de coutume," *L'homme. Revue française d'anthropologie* 160 (2001): 81–82.

4. Edouard Lambert, *La Fonction du droit civil comparé* (Paris: V. Girard & E. Brière, 1903), 799.

5. Substantive custom was within the realm of private law, but the matter of codifying custom constituted an area of public law.

6. James C. Scott, *Seeing Like a State: How Certain Schemes to Improve the Human Conditions Have Failed* (New Haven, CT: Yale University Press, 1998); Gerald Strauss, *Law, Resistance and the State: The Opposition to Roman Law in Reformation Germany* (Princeton, NJ: Princeton University Press, 1986).

7. The codification of custom and their reformation in early modern France was admirably studied by René Filhol: *Le Premier président Christofle de Thou et la réformation*

des coutumes (Paris: Librairie du Recueil Sirey, 1937); "La Rédaction des coutumes en France aux XVe et XVIe siècles," in *La Rédaction des coutumes dans le passé et dans le présent: Colloque organisé les 16 et 17 mai 1960 par le Centre d'histoire et d'ethnologie juridique sous la direction de John Gilissen* (Bruxelles: Institut de sociologie de l'Université libre de Bruxelles, 1962): 63–85; "The Codification of Customary Law in France in the Fifteenth and Sixteenth Centuries," in *Government in Reformation Europe, 1520–1560,* ed. Henry J. Cohn (London: Macmillan, 1971), 265–83. See also Henri Klimrath, "Etudes sur les coutumes," in *Travaux sur l'histoire du droit français,* 2 vols. (Paris: Joubert, 1848), 2: 133–338; J. van Kan, *Les Efforts de codification en France: Etude historique et psychologique* (Paris: Rousseau & Cie, 1929); John P. Dawson, "The Codification of the French Customs," *Michigan Law Review* 38 (1940): 765–800; P. Petot, "Le Droit commun en France selon les coutumiers," *Revue historique de droit français et étranger* 37 (1960): 412–29; Jean-Marie Carbassse, "Contribution à l'étude du processus coutumier: la coutume de droit privé jusqu'à la révolution," *Droits: Revue française de théorie juridique* 3 (1986): 25–37; Jean Hilaire, *La Vie du droit: coutumes et droit écrit* (Paris: Presses universitaires de France, 1994); Martine Grinberg, "La Rédaction des coutumes et les droits seigneuriaux: Nommer, classer, exclure," *Annales HSS* 52 (1997): 1017–38; Kathleen A. Parrow, "Provincial Estates and the Revision of Customary Law in Medieval and Early Modern France: Evidence from the *Procès-verbal* Narratives," *Parliaments, Estates & Representation* 21 (2001): 57–71; Marie Seong-Hak Kim, "Christophe de Thou et la réformation des coutumes: l'esprit de réforme juridique au XVIe siècle," *Tijdschrift voor Rechtsgeschiedenis* 72 (2004): 91–102.

8.   Private codifications of local customs existed but they were generally lacking in system and, of course, the official authority. The best-known compilation was the *Coutumes de Clermont en Beauvaisis,* composed by Philippe de Beaumanoir in 1283.

9.   Art. 125. François Isambert et al., *Recueil général des anciennes lois françaises,* 29 vols. (Paris: Belin-Leprieur, 1829), 9: 252.

10.   The letters patent issued at Amboise, March 15, 1497. The text is reproduced in the *procès-verbal* of the published custom of Touraine (1507). Charles A. Bourdot de Richebourg, *Nouveau coutumier général,* 4 vols.(Paris: Chez Michel Brunet, 1724), 4: 639–40.

11.   François Olivier-Martin, "Le Roi de France et les mauvaises coutumes au Moyen Age," *Zeitschrift der Savigny-Stiftung für Rechtsgeschichte. Germanistische Abtheilung* 58 (1938): 108–37; *Les Lois du roi* (Paris: Librairie générale de droit et de jurisprudence, 1988; reprint, 1997), 48, see also 97. In France, unlike England, equitable solutions were incorporated into the law at the Parlement without difficulty. There was no need in France to set up new courts to develop a body of special rules based on equity. John P. Dawson, "Remedies of the French Chancery before 1789," *Festschrift für Ernst Rabel,* 2 vols. (Tübingen: Mohr, 1954), 1: 99–140. The king delegated to the Parlement his right, along with his prerogatives of grace and mercy, to abolish bad custom. If the custom was not reasonable, justice required that it be quashed; if it was inadequate or too rigorous, equity required that it be completed and modified.

12.   See Klimrath, "Études sur les coutumes," 142; François Olivier-Martin, "Un document inédit sur les travaux preparatoires de l'ancienne coutume de Paris," *Nouvelle revue historique de droit français et étranger* 42 (1918): 202.

13. Early codification was led by Thibault Baillet, president of the Parlement of Paris. Jean Yver, "Le président Thibault Baillet et la rédaction des coutumes," *Revue historique de droit français et étranger* 64 (1986): 19–42; François Olivier-Martin, *Histoire de la coutume de la Prévoté et vicomté de Paris*, 3 vols. (Paris: E. Leroux, 1922–30; reprint, Paris: Éditions Cujas, 1972).

14. For de Thou's campaign seen as part of the reformist effort in sixteenth-century France, see Kim, "Christophe de Thou," 97–100.

15. Reformation of customs that had already been codified was undertaken in Sens (1555), Touraine (1559), Poitou (1559), Melun (1560), Auxerre (1561), Péronne (1567), Amiens (1567), and Paris (1580). New codification took place in Montfort (1556), Mantes (1556), Meullant (1556), Vermandois (1556), Étampes (1556), Dourdan (1556), and Grand Perche (1558). Three *parlementaires*, de Thou, Barthélemy Faye and Jacques Viole repeatedly served as commissioners extraordinary in these campaigns. After de Thou's death in 1582, the custom of Orléans (1583) was reformed by his son-in-law, Christophe de Harlay, president of the Parlement of Paris. The redaction of customs of Burgundy (1575), Brittany (1580), and Normandy (1585) was led by the commissioners from their respective parlements. Jean Yver, "La rédaction officielle de la coutume de Normandie (Rouen, 1583)," *Annales de Normandie* 36 (1986): 3–36.

16. François Olivier-Martin, *Histoire du droit français des origines à la Révolution* (Paris: Editions du Centre national de la recherche scientifique,1948), 423, n319.

17. Jurists such as Du Haillan and Le Caron emphasized that royal ordinances were mere regulatory power, and that the monarchy could intervene only with limited measures in fields directly related to the administration of justice, namely evidence and procedure. William F. Church, *Constitutional Thought in Sixteenth-Century France* (New York: Octagon, 1969), 112. The Ordinance of Villars-Cotterêts (1539) substituted French for Latin as the language of the administration of justice. The Ordinance of Moulins (1566) required written proof of obligations resulting from contracts over a certain amount.

18. Charles Dumoulin, *Commentarius in Priores Titulos antiquae consuetudinis Parisiensis* (1539). James Whitman argued that lawyers in the sixteenth century, including Dumoulin, struggled to preserve the customary feudal order, which was being threatened by the process of "romanization." James Q. Whitman, "The Seigneurs Descend to the Rank of Creditors: The Abolition of Respect, 1790," *Yale Journal of Law & Humanities* 6 (1994): 252. Many French lawyers objected to a blind worship of Roman law. But Whitman's assertion above needs to be balanced against the actual articles of the reformed customs, many of which clearly attacked seigneurial rights and privileges. Customary redaction in general weakened seigneurial rights. Grinberg, "La Rédaction des coutumes," 1028.

19. Letters patent of Henry II of August 19, 1555, issued for the custom of Sens, specifically mentioned this problem. Bourdot de Richebourg, *Nouveau coutumier général*, 3: 530.

20. Preface to the Coutume de Touraine, Tours (1560), cited from Filhol, *Le Premier président Christofle de Thou*, 169. See Bourdot de Richebourg, *Nouveau coutumier général*, 4: 643.

21. These initial steps taken by the locals are studied in Filhol, *Le Premier président Christofle de Thou*, 40–53.

22. It resulted in the letters patent of August 17, 1555, printed in the *procès-verbal* of the new custom of Sens, in Bourdot de Richebourg, *Nouveau coutumier général*, 3: 530.

23. Bourdot de Richebourg, *Nouveau coutumier général*, 3: 593.

24. The *lettres patent* by the king to de Thou said that the *procès-verbal* of the ancient custom of Auxerre had been lost, but the text is preserved in Bourdot de Richebourg, *Nouveau coutumier général* provided the *procès-verbal*, 3: 569. According to Filhol, it is likely that the people of Auxerre claimed the loss in order to obtain reformation of their custom. Twice the date was set for the reunion of the estates but both times commissioners had to delay their coming. In June 1561 Elie le Briois, *lieutenant particulier*, appeared before the queen mother in person and implored her not to frustrate his people. Filhol, *Le Premier président Christofle de Thou*, 148.

25. There seems to have been no fixed rule governing the composition of these preparatory assemblies. At the beginning only the delegates from the towns participated in the assemblies, but under Henry II and his successors rural parishes were invited to send their representatives. Albert Babeau, "La représentation du tiers état aux assemblées pour la rédaction des coutumes au XVIe siècle," *Revue historique* 21 (1883): 92. But the scope of the representation of the rural population is not clear.

26. *Gens de robe* tended to detach themselves from the third Estates in order to claim the fourth Estate. *Avocat du Roi* Baptiste Dumesnil stated in 1566 that "lawyers alone, separate from the third estate, cannot introduce custom," but this seemed to be an empty formula. See Filhol, *Le Premier président Christofle de Thou*, 87, n4.

27. Coquille stated: "Les coustumes prennent force de loy par l'autorisation que le Roy en fait par ses commissaires." Guy Coquille, *Les coutumes du pays et comté de Nivernois*, in *Oeuvres*, 2 vols. (Paris, 1665–66), 2: 313.

28. Contested cases were sent to the Parlement. The published text enjoyed binding force in the meantime, and in fact often permanently because, once the articles were published, objections raised at the time of the assemblies were rarely pursued.

29. The *procès-verbaux* of the reformed customs are full of the records of contentions between the king's lawyers and local seigneurs.

30. The specific challenge was lodged against the provision allowing representation in the collateral line. This case was analyzed in detail in Filhol, *Le Premier président Christofle de Thou*, 94–121. Claude Mangot and Pierre Versoris, two of the greatest *avocats* of the time, argued the case.

31. Archives nationales, X1a 1633, fol. 224, September 7, 1571, cited from Filhol, *Le Premier président Christofle de Thou*, 118.

32. The letters patent of Henry III charging de Thou with the reformation stated that Paris was "the capital of our kingdom, to the example of which other cities of the kingdom govern themselves and behave." Bourdot de Richebourg, *Nouveau coutumier général*, 3: 56. For the official *procès-verbal* of the reformation of the Paris custom, see Bourdot de Richebourg, *Nouveau coutumier général*, 3: 56–85. The two manuscripts of Simon Marion, *avocat* at the Parlement of Paris Bibliothèque nationale mss. fr. 5281 and 5282, provide a complete documentation on the progressive elaboration of the reformed text. See F. Olivier-Martin, "Les Manuscrits de Simon Marion et la coutume de Paris au XVIe siècle," *Travaux juridiques et économiques de l'Université de Rennes* 8 (1923): 13–240.

33. Bourdot de Richebourg, *Nouveau coutumier général*, 8: 75; Olivier-Martin, *Histoire de la coutume de la prévoté et vicomté de Paris*, 1: 122–26.

34. F. Olivier-Martin, *La Coutume de Paris: Trait d'union entre le droit romain et les législations modernes* (Paris: Recueil Sirey, 1925), 16.

35. Pasquier's letter to M. [Anne] Robert, written circa 1609, in *Les Oeuvres d'Estienne Pasquier, contenant ses recherches de la France* [. . .], 2 vols. (Amsterdam, 1723), 2: 578.

36. Pasquier, *Les Oeuvres*, 2: 578.

37. Jean Brissaud, *A History of French Private Law* (Boston: Little, Brown, 1915), 600–601.

38. The ancient custom of Paris had allowed the representation in the direct line only (Art. 138). The newly reformed Parisian custom recognized the right of representation in the collateral line as well (Art. 319). Filhol tells us an interesting fact that de Thou himself was the party to a lawsuit over the right of representation. De Thou's maternal uncle recalled him and his brothers in 1561 to represent their deceased mother in his succession, despite the fact that representation in the collateral line was not recognized in the old Parisian custom. A suit was filed by de Thou's aunt challenging this succession. The case was decided in favor of de Thou on September 7, 1564. See Filhol, *Le Premier président Christofle de Thou*, 225–26. Perhaps de Thou had a personal reason to feel indignant about denying children the right of representation in collateral succession.

39. "En effet, c'est le peuple qui fait la loy. Le roi, en autorisant et confirmant ces coutumes, y attribue la vie extérieurement, qui est la manutention et exercice de ce droit." Coquille, *Oeuvres*, 2: 153.

40. At the Estates General at Orleans in 1560, the nobility demanded in its *cahiers* that their temporary or lifetime leases be changed to those in perpetuity. The king replied that he "cannot justly infringe the conventions of people conforming to the law." Bibl. Nat., ms. fr. 4815, fol. 160, art. 31. Similar demands by the nobility in articles 24 and 25 drew the king's answer that "it is left to the customs of the localities. . . ." In February 1563 the *Conseil du Roi* received a request made "on behalf of the younger noble brothers of the regions of Anjou and Maine" to reform their customs, in particular demanding the change of the restrictions imposed by the right of primogeniture. After communicating for advice with the king's lawyers at the Parlement, the royal council declared that "one cannot touch custom except when remonstrance is made at the assembly of the Estates." Bibl. Nat., ms. fr. 18156, fol. 38, March 11, 1563. The king's answer was clear: The matter fell outside the royal domain for him to deal with in an ordinance.

41. Kathleen Parrow focused on claims to local rights and privileges as expressed in the *procès-verbaux* and emphasized the consultative nature of the codification process. Parrow acknowledged, however, that "[b]y the second half of the century, the local notables still retained their rights, but sometimes only as special exceptions to a law now changed under royal influence." Parrow, "Provincial Estates," 70.

42. Olivier-Martin, *Les Lois du roi*, 93.

43. Dawson, "The Codification of the French Customs," 790.

44. Olivier-Martin, *Les Lois du roi*, 84.

45. Coquille, *Oeuvres*, 2: 3. Coquille stated that newly published custom registered on many points "the most beautiful decisions rendered in the court rulings."

46. Michel Reulos, *Étude sur l'esprit, les sources et la méthode des Institutes Coutumières d'Antoine Loisel* (Paris: Recueil Sirey, 1935), 45.

47. For instance, the issue of representation was debated by Pierre Versoris and Claude Mangot in a case involving the Amiens customs in 1567, as discussed in detail in Filhol, *Le Premier president Christofle de Thou*, 94–121; the question of *don mutuel*, or gifts between spouses, in a marriage with or without a child, was argued by Canaye, Mangot, Augustin de Thou, and Versoris in a case at the Parlement of Paris in 1566. See Filhol, "Procès en parlement de Paris sur la coutume de la Rochelle (20 mai 1566)," *Études offertes à Jean Macqueron* (Faculté de droit et des sciences économiques d'Aix-en-Provence, 1970), 313–18; for the case on the renunciation to succession by endowed daughters, argued by Simon Marion and Choart in 1580, see Filhol, *Le premier président*, 207–208.

48. John P. Dawson, *The Oracles of the Law* (Ann Arbor: University of Michigan Press, 1968), 310–11.

49. For French legal humanists, see Donald Kelley, *Foundations of Modern Historical Scholarship: Language, Law and History in the French Renaissance* (New York: Columbia University Press, 1970); D. Kelley, "Civil Science in the Renaissance: Jurisprudence in the French Manner," in *History, Law and the Human Sciences: Medieval and Renaissance Perspectives* (London: Variorum Reprints, 1984), 261–76.

50. Michel Reulos, "L'importance des praticiens dans l'humanisme juridique," in *Pédagogues et juristes: Congrès du Centre d'études supérieures de la Renaissance de Tours, été 1960* (Paris: Librairie Philosophique J. Vrin, 1963), 121. François Hotman mused that a French lawyer entering a French court, after learning only Roman rules of property and succession (i.e., without taking account of the impact of feudal law on land holding), would be as well equipped as if he had arrived among the American savages." *Antitribonian*, cited in Peter Stein, "Legal Humanism and Legal Science," *Tidschrift voor rechtsgchiedenis* 54 (1986): 303.

51. Elie Barnavi and Robert Descimon, *La Sainte ligue, le juge, et la potence: l'assasinat du Président Brisson (15 novembre 1591)* (Paris: Hachette, 1985), 78.

52. Since in France Roman law was not treated as statutory law and customary law was free to depart from it, Roman law could be studied objectively without adapting it to practical concerns.

53. Reulos, "L'importance des praticiens," 124. French Romanists of the Renaissance period, such as Jacques Cujas and Hugues Doneau, focused on the textual analysis Roman law without attention to rules and principles useful to practitioners. Yet this kind of study brought attention to historical development of law from the origin to the compilation of Justinian. Loisel was a student of Cujas's.

54. Reulos, "L'importance des praticiens," 126.

55. In France, with the so-called *mos gallicus*, humanist jurists challenged the claims of the civil law to universal validity, and questioned whether it was justified to apply Roman law to contemporary France. In his *Francogallia*, Hotman demonstrated that each nation has its own ancient constitution and custom and that the Franks owed nothing to Roman law. R. E. Giesey and J. H. M. Salmon, eds., *Francogallia* (Cambridge:

Cambridge University Press, 1972), 62 ff. For French lawyers' efforts to neutralize any disruptive effect Roman law might have on French custom, see Whitman, "The Seigneurs Descend to the Rank of Creditors: The Abolition of Respect, 1790."

56. Antoine Loisel, *Institutes coustumières ou Manuel de plusieurs et diverses reigles, sentences et proverbes tant anciens que modernes du Droict coustumier et plus ordinaire de la France, 1607,* ed. M. Dupin and Edouard Laboulaye (Paris, 1846).

57. *Oratio de concordia et unione consuetudinum Franciae* (1546).

58. Dumoulin's views of customary rules were cited as authorities by the judges of the Parlement of Paris. Guy Coquille wrote: "the judges of the chambers of the Parlement for the most part adhered to the opinions of Dumoulin, and the majority of its notable *arrêts* and new articles of new custom were drawn from the opinions and resolutions of Dumoulin." *Oeuvres,* 224. As *avocats,* de Thou had daily contact with Dumoulin. It is possible that de Thou from early on had been influenced by Dumoulin's ideas.

59. Olivier-Martin, *Les Lois du roi,* 66: "du principe contractuel on aboutirait au pouvoir législatif."

60. In the sixteenth century the scope of legislation through ordinances expanded significantly, covering the matters of private law. The famous edict of July 1560 of *secondes noces* written by Chancellor Michel de L'Hôpital prohibited a remarrying widow from giving excessive gifts to her new husband to the detriment of her children from her first marriage. Isambert, *Recueil général des anciennes lois françaises,* 14: 36.

61. Isambert, *Recueil général des anciennes lois françaises,* 14: 222. The so-called Edict of Mothers contradicted the Roman law rules observed in the Midi concerning a widow's share in an inheritance, and provided that the widow would receive the usufruct of half her husband's estate, but could not deprive her sons of eventual inheritance. The parlements of the Midi refused to register the edict and the king, in 1739, abrogated it declaring that he did not want to encroach upon the private usages in his kingdom. Paul Viollet, *Histoire du droit civil français* (Paris: Larose and Tenin, 1905), 906.

62. Grinberg, "La Rédaction des coutumes," 1028.

63. Olivier-Martin, *Les Lois du roi,* 96.

64. Pasquier, *Les Oeuvres,* 2: 578.

65. According to Olivier-Martin, the custom of 1580 was much less respectful of the tradition than that of 1510. *La Coutume de Paris,* 12.

66. Edouard Meynial, "Sur le rôle joué par la doctrine et la jurisprudence dans l'œuvre d'unification du droit en France depuis la rédaction des coutumes jusqu'à la Révolution, en particulier dans la succession aux propres," *Revue générale du droit, de la législation et de la jurisprudence en France et à l'étranger* 27 (1903): 326, n2.

67. Strauss, *Law, Resistance and the State,* 289.

11

The Individual on Trial in the Sixteenth-Century Netherlands

Between Tradition and Modernity

Hugo de Schepper
(Translated by Elizabeth Bradbury Pollnow)

THE MAIN AMBITION OF THE EARLY MODERN MONARCH in the Low Countries was to achieve equity, peace, and order in society by acquiring a monopoly over constraint. In order to realize these goals, the sovereign had at his disposal above all the supreme power of justice (*justice retenue.*)[1] In the opinion of Charles the Bold, Duke of Burgundy, the proper administration of justice was "the soul and spirit of the public entity." And, according to the motto of a jurist from Visé, "an ounce of jurisdiction is worth more than a pound of gold."[2] Corresponding to that concept, the "supreme lord of the Netherlands and Burgundy," as was also the case with Charles V and Philip II of Spain, could legally inquire into any case in his territories, make a judgment on it, and carry out the sentence. To that end, the Burgundian and Habsburg prince placed a hierarchy of institutions at the disposal of the subjects, transforming the old courts of pre-Burgundian lords into his provincial councils and covering them with supraterritorial councils. They practiced only one kind of justice, that of the "sovereign chief of justice" or "sovereign judge," although judgments generally were pronounced without the prince's personal participation.[3] Nevertheless, without the benevolence of citizens—both physical persons and legal bodies—to make use of it, the ability of the sovereign to carry out justice would have been greatly limited. The question is at what point did *justiciables* (legal subjects)[4] wish to submit to his courts in order to lay claim to their rights or to defend them, in spite of the privileges of medieval autonomy in their natural communities? Or did they place more trust in the customary tribunals of local and regional authorities that had existed for centuries? Before answering, I will describe briefly the legal structure in the Netherlands along with its essential characteristics.

Traditional Tribunals

Rural Communities

In rural communities, the *hoofdschepenen* (head aldermen) and other regional tribunals functioned alongside feudal, freehold, and country courts, all in accordance with their own customary local law, which was fairly rudimentary and not based on a written tradition. The bailiff (titles differed according to region) took over repression of crimes and misdemeanors from private justice and other customary settlements between particular parties. His essential responsibilities were to arrest and prosecute offenders before the head aldermen or in other customary courts holding "high justice" over the countryside. It is through these types of officials that certain pre-Burgundian lords created an awareness of responsibility and guilt in matters of criminal law. Moreover, the new idea of "offense" as a disturbance of the common good emerged and the need to maintain public order increasingly prevailed over the notion of violence as private affair, to be settled through vengeance or through the victim (or his family) taking the law into his own hands. Feudal courts sometimes absorbed the responsibilities of the *hoofdschepenen* by recruiting aldermen from the feudal "men." In other cases, it was the head bench of aldermen in a district that absorbed the responsibilities of the feudal court.

In general, rural aldermen only exercised "low justice" and sometimes a "midlevel justice." Low justice was limited to jurisdiction over property, crimes, and petty offenses relating to real estate, which were punishable by fines. As for midlevel justice (which also included cases of low justice) courts attended to personal litigation relating to promises, debts, dowries, and other commitments, and to penalize criminals who had committed physical assault, adultery, theft, and minor offenses through banishment, forced pilgrimages of atonement, public ridicule, or relatively light corporal punishment.

Unless they were incorporated into a neighboring judicial system, certain territories prior to the Burgundian era were assured of their own special kind of justice and administration or were provided it within a geographic framework determined by inland water routes. Holland, Utrecht, Zeeland, Brabant, Flanders, and Friesland, where inhabitants struggled against the forces of water, established collective institutions necessary for specific solutions to problems pertaining to rivers and polders. These were the dike reeves, operating under the direction of the steward of dams, polders, or waterways, which possessed powers of low justice regarding issues involving the rivers. They acted as a local tribunal during their regular inspections. By necessity in extensive drainage constructions, several hamlets and justices were to collaborate in a new larger circumscription (*waterringen*) under a head polder board, a regional panel of aldermen governing waterways and dikes with powers of high justice. These officers became acquainted with river-related issues and judged fluvial delicts according to special customs or according to the ordinances of the prince. These proceedings were largely for correctional purposes. However, punishments for serious crimes related to the maintenance or any obligations concerning the waterways and dikes were severe and corporal, sentences passed only by the head aldermen of waters. Allegations of using subquality materials, or neglecting maintenance, or damaging dams or mills in order to manipulate the water supply illicitly were brought ex officio before the dam superintendent (*dijcgrave*). For many water boards, inspection was not the only occasion to exercise judgment. Several times a year, the panel of judges also sat on the bench for civil disputes and as a court of civil appeals.

Urban Communities

Based on traditional medieval privileges, municipalities had gained the right to dispense justice, with ultimate authority over criminal and civil law, within the territory of their communities. The quintessential competence of the municipal aldermanic bench was to dispense high justice, which necessarily incorporated low and midlevel justice. Customary judges passed sentences in a relatively discretionary manner according to local laws that were often irrational, incomplete, and valuable only in a limited jurisdiction. In the twelfth and thirteenth centuries, the civil and criminal judgments of urban aldermen were not subject to appeal at all. Any review of sentences handed down by aldermen before a superior court was incompatible with their legal sovereignty. The members of the urban benches normally rotated every one or two years. In some of the larger cities lawyers gradually attained the position of municipal magistrate in the sixteenth century, though in most municipalities the majority of political and judicial officeholders did not make a professional career out of these positions and did not have any university training. The modern concept and practice of sophisticated legal procedure was not very widespread in these areas. It was, nevertheless, the aldermen who in the vigorous pursuit of high justice judged civil disputes, infractions, and serious violations of the general public order "by sentence and by law."[5]

As for civil cases, private individuals solicited the city aldermen to adjudicate disputes on moveable and immoveable property, concerning easement rights, law of succession, contracts, and debts. In port towns, magistrates passed judgments in matters of maritime law. In addition to legal disputes, municipal aldermen became extremely busy with voluntary jurisdiction, rivaling that of the notaries; in fact, aldermen transacted many kinds of deeds *in forma iudicii*, including sales and other transfers of real property, establishment of annuities and hereditary interests, wills and legacies, trade contracts and marriage contracts, and reconciliations.

In criminal matters, a legal official close to the municipal tribunal could prosecute ex officio cases before the aldermen. Although responsible for the investigation and prosecution of offenders and delinquents and for the maintenance of public order, the officer of justice was nevertheless not obligated to prosecute. For a number of reasons, he could make a financial arrangement with the suspect or the accused, a practice known as *composition*. This arrangement bought off criminal legal proceedings after the defendant settled with the injured party in a satisfactory manner. It was the local officer of justice, a layman in legal matters, who determined whether the offender was capable of making a financial settlement, or, if the motives of the offending party justified it, an out-of-court settlement instead of legal prosecution. By virtue of his higher position, the officer of justice had the authority to set unilaterally the amount of the financial settlement, which could lead to blackmail and other abuses of power.[6]

On the other hand, in cases of refused or unsuccessful *composition* in the absence of a confession by the suspect, the officer of justice decided to prosecute and to undertake torture. It was a standard practice in interrogations before lay judges, since a confession was essential to a conviction. Customary judges were not likely to have taken into account what is considered in contemporary criminal law as reasons for justification or for immunity from culpability due to self-defense or another necessity. Moreover, these reasons were difficult to prove, especially when the accused was put in thumbscrews, and generally their influence on the sentence was minimal. As judges, aldermen enforced the customary principle of an eye for an eye, a tooth for a tooth. The fine line between homicide and murder remained unclear. According to customary norms, the confession of mortal violence and physical harm warranted *ipso iure* a death sentence by the aldermen; theft required the removal of one's hand, and so on. Criminal sentences in the sixteenth century still remained without the possibility of appeal because the accused had confessed.[7]

Because of its economic influence, the city was a powerful attraction for the surrounding countryside, particularly in the most urbanized areas. The city identified with the surrounding countryside, and vice versa. The municipal jurisdiction often succeeded in implementing high justice throughout the entire district. Many urban tribunals merged in one way or another with lower feudal courts and with regional courts that held authority to carry out high justice in the rural outskirts of the cities. Thus, in these areas the municipality also exercised authority in matters of appeal in civil cases. City jurisdiction in neighboring villages started to spread, especially in Brabant, Mechelen, and its dependencies (enclaves nestled in the interior of Brabant), Holland, Flanders, and Zeeland. The municipal judicial officer prosecuted cases of high justice in the surrounding district. Conversely, in some regions the rural bailiff or the dike reeve could function as officer of justice in the city.

New Princely Courts

Councils of Justice

After the incorporation of principalities, lordships, and manors into the Burgundian and Habsburg patrimonies, their traditional courts remained intact. In the course of the fifteenth century, however, they underwent an important transformation. First, learned jurists from the bourgeoisie or lesser nobility gradually replaced the feudal nobility (see below), and second, supraterritorial institutions emerged. Thus the courts became provincial councils, which were integrated into a hierarchy of judicial and administrative councils between the local, regional, and central level. Formally, they were the courts of appeal for judgments issued by subordinate tribunals.[8]

Above the provinces, a chancellor and a council of noble chamberlains close to the Burgundian dukes performed political functions in their service. In administrative and judicial matters, jurists served as assistants. From around 1440 this group of lawyers emerged as an entity within the central council and was sanctioned by law on December 8, 1473, as the Parliament of Mechelen. Originally a supplementary and extraordinary court, it became the superior court of appeals for civil judgments in the provinces under the jurisdiction of the Duke of Burgundy. It was the precursor to the Great Council in Mechelen that became permanently detached from the prince's Great Council by the beginning of the sixteenth century.

In 1512 the Privy Council, close to the monarch (or to its general governor) and one of the bodies that arose from the sovereign's Great Council, also started to administer justice. It served among other things as final court of revision for judgments made by the Great Council and for those of the Councils of Justice in Brabant and Hainaut, whose judgments had been declared sovereign. That is to say, the verdicts from these bodies could not be appealed. The submission of these court rulings to a final review within the Privy Council for procedural errors (*propositie van erreur*) was, then, the last legal means of redress. When in 1530 the county of Burgundy returned to the Netherlands under the reign of Charles V, the sentences of the Dole Parliament were, in principle, not subject to appeal before the Great Council in Mechelen. Only after the famous Burgundian ordinance in 1586 could parties in the county, henceforward, explicitly provide for a final revision before the Privy Council, which then could either deliver a final judgment or refer it to the Great Council in Mechelen.[9] After 1543, when the duchy of Gelre-Zutphen became incorporated into the Netherlands, its court was also authorized to function as a court of last resort, subject only to the Privy Council.

As courts of first instance, the princely central and provincial councils adjudicated cases relating to possession of property, both ecclesiastical and civil; disputes about the interpretation of ordinances promulgated by or in the name of the sovereign; ordinary competency conflicts between public institutions; and the most exclusive "reserved cases," such as *lese-majesty*, counterfeiting, and attacks on princely properties and prerogatives, as well as abuses of authority and offenses committed by monarchic officials. The notion of "reserved cases," however was not a limited one, for they were also submitted to the fiscal office and, if circumstances warranted, it could take over the court ex officio. A general prosecutor and a fiscal lawyer constituted each fiscal office. It was nevertheless the general prosecutor that controlled all lesser officers of justice and that prosecuted cases before the council of justice to which he was accredited. Further, he prosecuted offenses and infractions against the public order in rural areas of his jurisdiction that remained without prosecution or that slipped beyond the reach of regular judicial officials. Though matters related to rights to forests, hunting, private warfare, and so on that were traditionally under the competence of numerous special civil servants were, at the request of these officials, brought to trial by general prosecutors alongside the central and provincial councils of royal justice. By *ratione personae*, these councils considered themselves as ordinary judges in the initial proceedings of personal and real actions in which the princely household or all those who served the monarch in one capacity or another were involved.

Professionalization of the Councils of Justice

The enormous growth of territories and jurisdictions under the Burgundians and the growing realization of national sovereignty necessitated a professional body of modern civil servants that were familiar with Roman and canon law and that could treat highly complex issues. Their university legal education prepared them well for these tasks. For example, at the time of the incorporation of Holland into Burgundian rule, its court was not yet composed of a council of trained jurists; not even a fifth of counselors had a legal education. Twenty years later, the number of lawyers had grown to almost 40 percent, and in 1500 they comprised more than half of all counselors. Here, as in other provincial councils, counselors from the high nobility and the church, appointed because of their social status, finally disappeared before 1530. They were replaced by members from the urban bourgeoisie, officials who were interested in a professional career at a more national level, such as university professor in law. This new breed of counselors was considered, just as professional jurists, guarantors of good jurisdiction, as appropriate to modern law and justice.

Also, at the central level, the Duke of Burgundy increasingly diminished the power of the high nobility, conferring the key offices of chancellor, chief council, and chancellery offices to professional lawyers from the patrician class and urban bourgeoisie. Charles V and Philip II consistently attempted to rely upon salaried state employees, who were men of modest means but strong ambition aspiring to make a career in royal service. Around 1530 the Great Council of Mechelen, and from 1531 the Privy Council, was composed only of professional jurists. As with all royal officials, members of these councils were removable and could be transferred, being appointed by or in the name of the sovereign "as long as they pleased him." All counselors were individually responsible to him for the documents that they drafted.[10]

Appeals of Legal Subjects to the "Sovereign Judge"

The most common and most effective means that helped people and legal bodies solicit sovereign intervention in specific disputes or obtain his favor was the initiation of the humble request, prompted and written by a sworn solicitor accredited to a princely court. The solicitors were practitioners who by experience knew legal and administrative procedures and had access to the chancellery of the council. They could argue based on the name of the petitioner, his familial situation, his profession, his household, his personal and social quality, the facts with his personal circumstances, his complaints, and his demand for equity in suitable legal language. In the name of the applicant, solicitors had to submit evidence so that the request could be examined in the court.[11] In the councils the "masters of requests" owed their title to the reception of the requests and the study of the thousands of complaints by subjects. With this request, the private individual emerged out of anonymity with a definite identity and personal history. If necessary, the solicitors consulted with attorneys accredited to the court for referring to scholar law to treat the complicated legal questions of the concerned clients. However, one must look through the "subtly composed half-shades" in the legal language of the requests to penetrate the individual truths of the supplicants. Very often the requests outlined personal colorful situations that were both poignant and detailed.[12]

In Civil Justice

Finally, beginning in 1530, justice by the sovereign judge became the exclusive work of the jurist counselors. Under the influence of written procedural law applied by ecclesiastical judges and by the Parlement of Paris, the Burgundian dukes had promoted, from the beginning, the application of modern judicial techniques, at once more rational, refined, and uniform. For instance, when an individual person or legal body felt dissatisfied with an allegedly unjust sentence from a lower customary tribunal, the appeal procedure allowed him to proceed to a higher level against the "bad" judgment *and* against the relevant lower judge and to call for a new process at the core of the dispute. The appeal process also recalled the customary procedures of the medieval *hoofdvaarten* that permitted aldermen to consult more important cities for advice before passing judgment; the appeal procedure easily supplanted the procedure of the *hoofdvaart.*

Already since the first half of the fifteenth century, the implementation of the appeal process, at the initiation of subjects seeking justice, subjugated all subaltern magistrates of aldermen in Brabant, Mechelen, Holland, Dutch-speaking Flanders, and Zeeland to the direct control and test of royal law. Before 1500, regional tribunals also had been completely stripped of their previous authority as courts of *hoofdvaart* and as courts of appeal for judiciary issues in rural and urban tribunals and other lower courts. Because of the large number of appellants, the provincial councils and the Great Council of Mechelen had quickly succeeded in putting an end to the sovereignty of customary judgments in civil and feudal matters.[13]

Nevertheless, the courts of the sovereign judge not only were the jurisdiction for review in civil matters, but because of the demand by subjects, they also ruled conflicts of first instance at an increasing number and in ways that competed with proceedings normally under the jurisdiction of lower tribunals. By a procedure analogous to the French *prévention*, the court holding the first hearing for a plaintiff possessed the jurisdiction peculiar to an ordinary judge; originally the court handled the case only after denial of justice by local and regional tribunals. The typical legal route of the sovereign's *justice retenue*, however, was a process known as *evocation*. In *evocation*, knowledge of a lawsuit was evoked *lite pendente*, pending before an inferior level, to a superior court.[14] Legal jurisdictions were not very well defined among the different layers of princely justice, but what made them important to the *justiciables* was the intervention of royal authority. Defending the privileges of communal autonomy, the aldermen opposed it in vain.[15] Each dispute that slipped out of their hands and into the hands of a sovereign's council was, for them, a loss of authority and revenue.

The following graphs attempt to illustrate the judicial capacity of the Great Council in Mechelen and the Privy Council in Brussels, both supreme courts under Charles V, based on the number of their verdicts. At the beginning of the sixteenth century, until at least 1512, the Great Council was still the only supreme court, making an average of 40 judgments in contentious justice per year. Nearly a half century later, the judicial capacity of the central justice system had quadrupled: the Great Council and the Privy Council annually produced an average total of 170 final judgments. Comparisons always cloud matters, but even so, until 1966 the High Council of the present Netherlands produced 78 judgments per year[16] with a population that grew from 2 million to 12 million between 1830 and 1966. In the mid-sixteenth century, the seventeen provinces totaled only 3 million.

Since we do not know exactly the annual average of judgments passed by the royal courts on the provincial level, a complete and comprehensive study would very likely indicate that the more than ten thousand cases on which the two supreme courts pronounced sentence from 1460 to 1580 was only the tip of the iceberg with regard to princely judicial practice. An initial survey of the judgments by the provincial Council of Brabant seemed to confirm that in the mid-sixteenth century, the council rendered far more than one hundred final sentences in legal disputes per year.[17] It goes without saying that not only should the decisions handed down by the provincial councils of the sovereign be included but that also the judgments by the traditional tribunals should be studied in order to estimate the full capacity of the sovereign judge compared to customary justice. If possible, there is still much to be done in this area!

More than 80 percent of trials actually over civil disputes were submitted by individuals or groups of individuals. One can conclude then that the concerned *justiciables* demonstrated in this way their confidence in the sovereign judge to interpret customs and that they preferred monarchic justice to traditional local or regional justice. Even evocations of lawsuits were made at the request of individual parties, diverting a dispute from a customary aldermen's bench, and exceptionally at the instigation of superior court. (See figure 11.1.) Furthermore, numbers of requests appealed to the voluntary jurisdiction of the sovereign to sanction marriage conventions, wills and legacies, settlements of debt, and other contractual arrangements.[18]

For all types of conflicts, legal subjects preferred to go straight to the source of all law, the sovereign judge, hoping that professional judges would provide a better, speedier ruling. Around 1550 one notices, besides a growth in the number of proceedings in first and last hearings, a relative decline in appeals. It was especially through the procedure of *prévention* that the sovereign broadened his power. By quick and direct routes, parties looked for judgments close to royal justice in civil cases; often even they proved insignificant.[19] The

Annual average by province

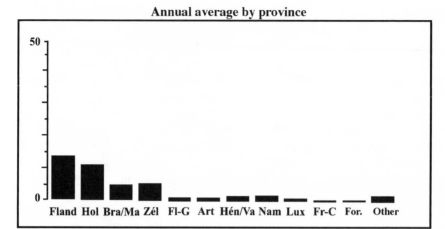

Figure 11.1a.   Judgments of the Supreme Justice, 1500–1504 (without provisional judgments). Average of all decisions: 40 per year

Annual average by province

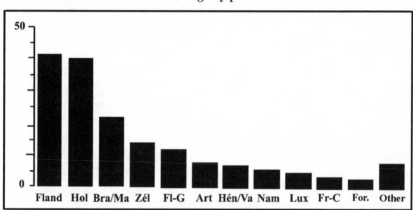

N.B. Only final judgments are taken into account (not including administrative decisions or provisional judgments).

Figure 11.1b.   Judgments of the Supreme Justice, 1546–1550 (without provisional judgments). Average of all decisions: 170 per year

social stratification of parties and the material stratification of litigation before the central courts were much more diversified than they had been originally. At first it was noble families in particular that brought proceedings before the princely courts for disputes over possession and inheritance. A half century later, lawsuits in contractual law dominated among the bourgeoisie. Other proceedings adjudicated an almost interminable range of litigation regarding personal, family, and real law, slander, ecclesiastical nominations and benefices, maritime and feudal matters, water and dike affairs, and conflicts about procedural defects or irregularities, and so on.

The legal parties did not concern themselves too much with the privileges *de non appellando et de non evocando* of their local or regional communities, nor did they worry very much about opposition from local or regional authorities in cases that came before the supreme courts. Even the towns and provincial states, although they were the traditional defenders of their privileges, introduced without hesitation demands for justice before the central councils against, for example, their debtors and recalcitrant taxpayers.[20] The Great Privilege of 1477 would have restored the Parliament of Mechelen to its original role as an exceptional court and as the superior court of appeals. Nevertheless, it was individual parties that requested parliament quickly resume holding first and final hearings and adjudicating cases that the lower common law courts were equally competent to judge.[21] The new framework of the professional councils was actually more transparent compared to the tangled state of the numerous older courts with territorial or personal jurisdiction (feudal, censorial, ecclesiastical, etc.) in which the parties found it difficult to distinguish competencies and jurisdictions. As for writing their judgments, the jurist-counselors probably made use of their knowledge of scholar law as explanatory and supplementary law to clarify or supplement issues. In cases of deficiencies, contradiction, or gaps, they completed customary law with the rules of learned law.[22]

The monarchic courts, as much at the central as at the provincial level, responded to the need for objectivity and judicial security and to the need for a larger legal validity in preindustrial, urbanized provinces. These needs did not incidentally stop growing as commercial relations expanded outside of the village, city, and province. The enforcement of princely sentences was assured in much larger areas than judgments of traditional tribunals did. The customary justice could not, indeed, offer the same guarantees, judicial subtleties, validity, and independence as professional judges in monarchic courts.

The extraordinary rise of princely justice in the Netherlands cannot be explained either by demographic change or by internal territorial expansion, for subjects from recently annexed territories were scarcely even represented. The figures demonstrate, in fact, that the reception of judicial centralization by wider strata of society appeared less often in rural, forested regions than in the urbanized, maritime provinces such as Brabant-Mechelen, Holland, Flanders, and Zeeland. The limited demographic importance and especially the different type of economy in the oriental periphery—from Friesland to Luxembourg—and in the Walloon periphery favored the autonomy of their respective communities and slowed down individual initiatives to judicial courts of the prince.[23] One must believe that at the beginning of the early modern era, the contentious and voluntary jurisdiction of the Burgundian-Habsburg ruler had little meaning in the peripheral provinces. It was only with great difficulty that the authority of the modern monarchy exerted an influence in these areas.[24] There, with the exception of Artois, traditional tribunals were always active and important. In spite of the existence of new princely councils, justice remained entirely within the hands of large property owners, abbeys, feudal lords, and other customary tribunals.[25] Doubtless, the judgments of these benches were, in principle, appealable to provincial legal councils or to central courts of the monarch, but appeals in these regions were rather rare, if not absent entirely.

Litterae Gratiae in Civil Disputes

Because the sovereign prince of the Netherlands was the supreme judge and the protector of law and order, he also wanted to be the sole authority to bestow several kinds of *litterae gratiae*. In administering justice, it was completely natural for him to oversee judicial actions on all levels and even to halt court procedures or enforcement of sentences, especially when subjects solicited his intervention. In this fashion, supplicants recognized his supremacy to grant derogations in the administration of justice. In a political system without separation of powers, the bench of the sovereign judge was the same as the one on which the princely legislator sat, so there was great opportunity for his intervention in trials. As with judicial procedures that went before his courts, the sovereign could easily regulate clemency procedures by legislation.[26] Following the example of the French kings, the Netherlandish prince's right of grace developed as a legal tool fully endowed with royal authority. This right, derived from his authority as "sovereign chief of justice," was the supreme expression of his *justice retenue*. In exercising his right of mercy, the monarch positioned himself to reinforce his monopoly over force in society at the expense of customary justice.

In that period, clemency was not associated solely with criminal cases. Since the monarch was considered the supreme judge, legal subjects also requested his clemency in private legal disputes. Through some princely letters of pardon, the beneficiary could abstain from a trial before a judge, have judicial action suspended, or have a sentence nullified. The great advantage was that the parties could enter quickly, either entirely or partially within their rights.

The supplicant party could not make claims in advance for princely intervention, neither could the supplicant assert his rights, since these infrajudiciary dispensations were bestowed "by the special favor" of the Privy Council on behalf of the sovereign. Nevertheless, in order to avoid any appearance of complete arbitrariness and in order to treat each person equally according to his individual merits, the law elaborated on the procedures involved in preparing the written mercy letters and controlling their enforcement. For the opposing party, who eventually could feel injured by such favor, the procedure provided for this an opposition procedure, which could lead to a complete or partial annihilation of the clemency letter. In this case nothing changed for the supplicant and he would have to avail himself of a competent court and to submit to the litigation in an initial hearing. Although all letters of clemency could still be formally canceled during the registration procedure, in practice it occurred very infrequently. In fact, the cooperation of the opposing party in the process of decision making and enforcement of a grace was necessary in every phase of it, because hostility could lead to an expensive and time-consuming civil trial.[27]

In the sector of civil law, the sovereign issued an array of clemency letters for most everything. The most common letter of pardon in civil matters was *l'estat et surceance* (defer payment). This action, undertaken at the request of an individual, summoned or not, suspended creditors' claims under sufficient bond until further notice.[28] Another frequently used means of mercy was the spread of payment. For one thing, it ordered creditors to accept spread debt payments under sufficient bond, handed over by the debtor and, meanwhile, suspended the judicial procedure or forbade bringing the debtor to trial. For another thing, this princely favor prevented the indebted supplicant from alienating his goods or from having his property mortgaged before the debt was paid. By presenting his request, the debtor needed to prove sufficiently in writing that he had incurred insolvency in good faith and not through his own fault.[29] The "transfer of goods" (*cession de biens*) was a favor awarded to a debtor threatened with being taken hostage or already detained at the demand of creditors, when he wanted to transfer goods in order to liquidate debts. In any case according to the law, the debtor could keep at least a bed and one piece of each type of furniture.[30] If the heirs feared that the debts of their inheritance surpassed its value, they could request a voluntary acceptance under condition of benefice of inventory. In the forty days after receipt of the *benefice*, the assets of the inheritance had to be declared and taxed by sworn experts.[31]

In view of the gaps within the archives of the Privy Council, certainly prior to 1580, it is difficult to specify the number of clemency letters issued. Research is needed in the archives of the provincial councils where those letters could be ratified. However, it is already clear that the responsibilities of the Privy Council included the daily examination of pardon requests and files in civil disputes, the consultation of opposing parties, and, finally, the granting of the letters. The beneficiaries of clemency letters in civil matters not only included businessmen, rural landowners, farmers, and so on, but also consisted of collective bodies such as municipalities, weighed down by financial burdens and hounded by creditors. In this way the monarch could consider on an extensive scale the specific wishes of those who submitted their litigations and other needs to him, which customary institutions usually could not and did not wish to satisfy, at least according to most subjects' expectations. It appears that within the realm of private law, most clemency letters granted in the name of the prince concerned debts. In granting these favors, he also encompassed the traditional domain of the aldermen, who, according to privileges, were the ordinary judges concerning contentious conflicts in their local communities.

Litterae Gratiae in Criminal Justice

The importance of clemency as a legal tool of power is even more spectacular in matters of criminal justice. For the vulnerable party, the condemned or the suspect in a customary tribunal, it was often a question of life or death. These individuals doubtless held the ultimate hope in the authority of the sovereign judge to procure reprieves and other favors in criminal matters. The authorities that held authority for clemency in these cases included the Audit Chambers in minor offenses and the Privy Council for homicides and other severe cases.[32]

In a certain way, the right of grace in penal cases was situated in the prolongation of the medieval *compositions*. In the Burgundian-Habsburg period, these financial transactions continued to be carried out by customary judicial officials. The possibility of a complete private agreement between the family of the criminal and that of the victim, however, had disappeared in the core provinces. For understandable reasons, the great majority of delinquents or supposed suspects did fear specific procedures and outcomes from traditional penal justice. Because of the lack of an efficient apparatus for criminal investigation and apprehension, suspected parties usually hid or fled. Before requesting princely clemency, the alleged offender had to reconcile with the victim or the victim's relatives and to provide them with financial reparation.[33] Once reconciliation and acceptable reparations were achieved, after a fixed period the supplicant could introduce his request to the competent central institution from the security of his hiding place and through the intervention of a solicitor in order to obtain a letter of mercy. In requests by guilty criminals, they confessed to the material acts of the violence, though they strongly emphasized the mitigating conditions (even family and social circumstances) for violating the social order and the law. The innocent suspect had to provide an alibi. Involuntary manslaughter, self-defense, mental insanity, accidental death, youth, drunkenness, or other factors of innocence or diminished capacity were admissible and taken into consideration. Among the petitioners for clemency in homicide cases one very often encounters common people.

The principal gesticulation of princely clemency in the sixteenth century was the letter of remission for manslaughter. With this motion, the sovereign declared his "preference for clemency rather than for rigor of justice," which rubbed out the charge of homicide and saved the suspect or the condemned from capital punishment. The reprieved individual could return to his native community. Eventually condemned offenders were getting reduced sanctions "according to their status and the circumstances of their crime." By the repeal of banishment, a refugee or an exile could safely return. Letters of *handlichting* (*mainlevee*) rescinded the confiscation of goods. Before ratifying them, the provincial council verified that all preliminary conditions for forgiveness had been met or, if not, obliged the pardoned to fulfill them immediately.[34]

Those suspected of homicide and other alleged criminals were not the only ones who applied for clemency, for there also were those suspected or accused of religious crimes who attempted to obtain specific letters of grace through the normal means of confession, penance and reconciliation. With regard to Protestants, the Privy Council of Charles V in Brussels responded in a rather liberal manner. Despite the famous "edict of blood" of 1550, penal accusations and sentences against allegedly guilty Protestants continued to be pardonable in matters of heresy.[35] For contrite heretics, the most usual form was the letter of *pardon*. This kind of mercy normally concerned delinquents who had committed a crime that did not result in death, such as violation of patrimonial rights, adultery, assault, vandalism, illegal hunting, defamation of a public official, and blasphemy, as well as complicity in major crimes such as kidnapping and counterfeiting.[36] The requirement that accused or suspected Protestants confess and show remorse, or cite mitigating circumstances, paralleled the conditions for reprieve in matters of criminal violence. Once reconciliation with the Catholic Church occurred, the supplicant could speak from prison (and before the sentence) with a legal solicitor who would help write and introduce the detailed and humble request to the Privy Council. These requests emphasized the good and moral life of the applicant, his family's position, and, above all, his reconciliation with the church.

Not only did mercy letters occur episodically at celebratory occasions, such as the ceremonial entry of Crown Prince Philip in 1549, but the intervention of the central authority also took place on a regular basis. Under Charles V and even under Philip II, the Privy Council frequently made use of the power of pardon. The council issued hundreds of letters of remission annually in cases of homicide, counterfeiting, and other severe criminal offenses. Thus, in the urbanized provinces of the Netherlands, the princely right of grace not only resolved many unsolved crimes, but also avoided cases of private justice, vengeance, and composition. The quantity of legal arrangements made by local and regional officials of justice obviously were decreasing.[37] As figure

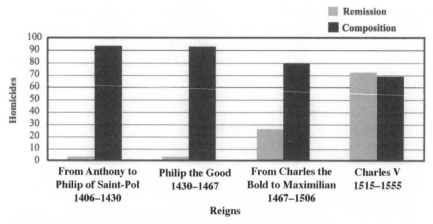

Figure 11.2.   Pardon for homicide in Walloon Brabat (1404–1555)

11.2 demonstrates, in the Walloon area of Brabant amiable agreements in homicide cases were declining, while monarchic remissions were rising.

We should not underestimate the socio-psychological influence of the right of mercy. It was a way of exercising authority that enlarged the imagination of a prince's subjects. For families and broad circles of friends and relatives of those pardoned, the clemency letters again and again created a feeling of warmth around the sovereign. He was conscious of his monopoly in matters of grace, treating each case in a similar and estimated just manner according to the individual merits of the case in mitigating "rigor of justice" and engaging appellants in a direct dialogue with him. He rightly intervened where feelings about equity among citizens came into question. Robert Muchembled calculated in his work on Artois, *La violence au village*, that each year two in one hundred families became directly involved in matters of reprieve for bloody crimes and that the total registration of remissions for homicides, including murders, reached 927 in this province during the first part of the sixteenth century and 536 later under Philip II.[38] In Flanders, the Provincial Council ratified an average of one hundred letters of remission per year, while the Council of Holland registered an annual average of forty. (See figure 11.3.) Flight or hiding followed by the introduction of a request for clemency was very likely, for common criminals as well as for innocent suspects, the most effective way of reintegrating into their community. The number of pardons for heresy was also greater than previously thought: 505 cases in Holland and Zeeland (among them the 430 Anabaptists arrested in 1534 while sailing on the Zuyderzee to Munster, the new Jerusalem), 6 in Flanders between 1531 and 1542, and under Philip of Spain between 1555 and 1566, 15 and 38 cases, respectively. In general, the rate of clemency letters appears lower under Philip

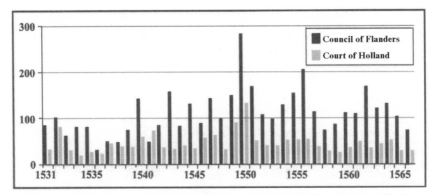

Figure 11.3.   Number of Letters of Remission per Year Ratified by the Councils of Flanders and Holland

II compared to the reign of Charles V. Philip II was personally convinced of the effectiveness of state repressive law, not only against heresy crimes in particular, but also against crimes of common law in general. Finally, we want to emphasize that remission only represents a part—albeit an important part—of the totality of mercy letters in criminal cases.

Because the sovereign by his frequent use of pardon violated the medieval privileges of the aldermen, one could expect lively opposition to this type of intervention at local levels. Recent studies have indicated a surprising collaboration in the urbanized provinces among customary jurisdictions during demand procedures of clemency for penal matters. Judicial officials and tribunals of aldermen seemed conscious of the fact that the customary principles of retaliation, which did not permit taking into account mitigating circumstances, no longer responded to human emotion in law or to new feeling of equity. Furthermore, the bestowal of mercy was a means to settle crimes that would otherwise remain unresolved as well as to restore order and peace to local communities. In Amsterdam, for example, between 1524 and 1552, a period of almost thirty years, in 219 capital crimes, only fifteen suspects (7 percent) fell into the hands of the local justice, a third of which were condemned to death and executed. Sixty persons (27 percent) of them who took flight had their requests of remission granted. The grand total, therefore, was, instead of a mere 7 percent resolution rate, a 34 percent rate of resolution.[39] Moreover, it is again striking that, except in Artois, Walloon Flanders, and Gelre,[40] in rural provinces traditional justice and traditional settlements solely permitted an insignificant place in the development of early modern grace by the sovereign judge. In most provinces on the periphery, only in very rare cases did individuals appear interested in princely clemency.[41] There the struggle against criminal activity continued in private agreements, reconciliation, and the satisfaction of the victim or the victim's parents by the offender; in amiable settlements between the local judicial official and the accused; and in customary repression of crime. Also, vengeance and other forms of taking the law into one's own hands still occurred.[42]

Conclusion

The transition from traditional civil and criminal justice to modern princely *justice retenue* in some form or other occurred in a completely different way in the preindustrial maritime provinces of the Netherlands and in the rural mainland provinces. As in France, in the urbanized provinces the increasing number of people coming into contact with the modern judicial system, put at their disposal by the Burgundian-Habsburg prince, preferred to pursue their rights in civil matters in his judicial system. In spite of local and provincial privileges and despite municipal resistance to common central authority, subjects presented appeals to the judicial councils of the sovereign against the judgments of aldermen or other customary tribunals. Moreover, skipping over their ordinary municipal courts, people increasingly made use of procedures in the first hearing in order to appeal to the sovereign power to claim their rights. A good number of legal subjects requested the evocation of their trials *lite pendente*, which was the typical judicial procedure in the system of the *justice retenue*. In order to avoid long and costly civil trials, individuals and legal bodies also resorted to the princely power of clemency, the supreme expression and derivation of his *justice retenue*.

The success and effectiveness of remission procedures by princely judges proved spectacular in the struggle against crime, exceeding the uncertainty and possible arbitrariness of customary arrangements and the repressive justice of customary tribunals that applied the principle of retaliation in criminal matters. Lacking a sufficient system of criminal investigation and apprehension and because of the impossibility of judicial appeal, the great majority of criminals or of suspected wrongdoers, often from the lower classes, succeeded in hiding or taking flight. Contrary to customary justice, the royal right of clemency responded to the increasing need for humaneness, judicial refinement, and diversified equity for individuals, who desired a more subtle resolution because of mitigating circumstances and exceptions of culpability. Flight or hiding followed by the request for pardon was, for hundreds of concerned persons, the safest procedure for achieving reintegration into their natural communities. Focusing on reconciliation and retribution for the victim (or those closest to the victim) and civil fines, the various clemency letters drew upon older forms of crime resolution.

Almost all of these interventions of *justice retenue* were not produced by the instigation of the sovereign or his officials, but on the initiative of ordinary people and legal bodies. Thus, individuals in urbanized regions greatly abetted the authority of the early modern monarch. The other side of the coin was that it worked to diminish or even put an end to judicial autonomy in lower communities in both civil and criminal cases. In the trade-oriented provinces, traditional sovereignty of subaltern judicial systems came to an end at the requests of subjects, who required modern, rational, refined, and uniform justice. The courts of the prince at the provincial and central level responded to them by bringing together professional jurists. In cases of deficiencies or contradictions within customary laws, the legal counselors could substitute their knowledge of learned law as explanatory or supplemental law. Their judgments and letters of mercy had stronger validity in a society with a foreign presence in the large towns and where human relations surpassed the local and provincial boundaries. The municipal jurisdictions no longer succeeded in escaping the judicial control of the princely judge; they had become a local cog in the administrative and judicial hierarchy of the early modern monarchy. The paradox is that the traditional defenders of the privileges and of provincial and local autonomy, the states and the municipalities, also appealed to the sovereign judge and submitted to him their disputes. These occurrences coincided with the more general transition from the oral tradition to a written culture, in keeping with the humanist spirit. The preference of so many *justiciables* for the princely *justice retenue* showed signs of the existence of a new idea of citizenship in a larger community of urbanized and maritime provinces, in which the individual citizen felt he belonged.

On the other hand, in the majority of rural regions, the inhabitants in general continued to have confidence in their lay judicial courts, who applied customary civil and criminal laws outside of written tradition. Here the will of subjects in order to use the judicial instruments of the *justice retenue* was missing, with the consequence being that sovereign power was weak. A profound study of these developments would provide a more balanced understanding of communal resistance to centralization and to the early modern state as the origins of the Dutch Revolt.

Notes

Except where otherwise noted, the first two sections of this chapter are taken from H. de Schepper and J. M. Cauchies, "Legal Tools of the Public Power in the Netherlands, 1200–1600," in *Legislation and Justice*, ed. A. Padoa Schioppa (Oxford: Oxford University Press, 1996), 235–58.

1. R. C. van Caenegem, *An Historical Introduction to Western Constitutional Law* (Cambridge: Cambridge University Press, 1995), 99.

2. P. L. Nève, *Het Rijkskamergerecht en de Nederlanden* (Assen: Van Gorcum, 1972), 518; A. G. Jongkees, *Burgundica et varia* (Hilversum: Verloren, 1990), 195.

3. H. de Schepper, "Iudicia in consilio principis, 1504–1702," in *Oberste Gerichtsbarkeit und zentrale Gewalt im Europa der frühen Neuzeit,* ed. B. Diestelkamp (Köln/Wien/Weimar: Böhlau, 1996), 177–79.

4. Which in fact meant all subjects.

5. H. de Ridder-Symoens, "De universitaire vorming van de Brabantse stadsmagistraat, 1430-1580," in *De Brabantse Stad* ('s Hertogenbosch: Provinciaal Genootschap van Kunsten en Wetenschappen in Noord-Brabant, 1978), 21–126; P. van Peteghem, "De Vier Ambachten en de receptie van het schriftelijk proces," in *'Over den Vier Ambachten',* ed. A. M. J. de Kraker et al. (Kloosterzande: Duerinck BV, 1992), 662–63.

6. D. A. Berents, *Misdaad in de Middeleeuwen. Een onderzoek naar de criminaliteit in het laat-middeleeuwse Utrecht* (Zutphen: Walberg Pers, 1976), 56–79.

7. R. van Caenegem, *Geschiedenis van het strafrecht in Vlaanderen van de XIe tot de XIVe eeuw* (Brussels: Palais der Academiën, 1954), 18–19, 311–19; X. Rousseaux, "Het ontstaan van het strafrecht in Brabant, 1400–1650," in *Uuytwysens d'Archiven,* ed. F. Stevens and D. van den Auweele (Louvain: Katholikeke Universiteit Leuven–Faculteit der Rechtsgeleerdheid, 1992), 210–11.

8. M. Ch. Le Bailly, *Recht voor de Raad. Rechtspraak voor het Hof van Holland, Zeeland en West-Friesland in het midden van de vijftiende eeuw* (Hilversum: Verloren, 2001), 56–87, 209–73.

9. Letter of "propositie van erreur," November 4, 1586, in Algemeen Rijksarchief Brussels [hereafter ARB], *Audiëntie,* nr. 193, f. 171–72; letter of the count of Champlite, governor of the Franche-Comté, to Archduke Albert, November 9, 1596, ARB, *Audiëntie,* nr. 1846/5, s.f.; sentences of the Great Council in Mechelen with revisions of trials on the Parliament of Dole, 1589–1610, in ARB, *Grote Raad der Nederlanden te Mechelen. Beroepen van diverse hoven, portefeuille* without pagination. See A. Wijffels and J. M. I. Koster-van Dijk, "Les procédures en révision au Grand Conseil de Malines, 1473–1580," *Publication du Centre Européen d'Études bourguignonnes, XIVe–XVIe s* 30 (1990): 67–97.

10. A. O. M. Damen, *De Staat van dienst. De gewestelijke ambtenaren van Holland en Zeeland in de Bourgondische periode 1425–1485* (Hilversum: Verloren, 2000), 61–105; H. Cools, *Mannen met macht. Edellieden en de Moderne Staat in de Bourgondisch-Habsburgse landen (1475–1530)* (Zutphen: Walberg Pers, 2001); J. Vanhoutte, "'Van robins tot très grands nobles'. Carrièreplanning en huwelijksstrategie 1540–1701," in *Adel en Macht. Politieke, cultuur, economie,* ed. G. Marnef and R. Vermeir (Maastricht: Shaker, 2004), 17–55.

11. J. Lameere and H. Simont, eds., *Recueil des ordonnances des Pays Bas,* vol. 4, *Contenant les ordonnances du 9 Janvier 1536 (1537, N. St.) au 24 Décembre 1543* (Brussels: Goemaere, 1907), 327; J. Lameere and H. Simont, eds., *Recueil des ordonnances des Pays Bas,* vol. 5, *Contenant les ordonnances du 1er janvier 1543(1544, N. St.) au 28 décembre 1549,* (Brussels: Koninklijke commissie voor de uitgave van oude wetten en verordeningen, 1910), 55, 332.

12. R. Muchembled, *La violence au village, XVe–XVIIe siècle* (Turnhout: Editions Brepols, 1989), 17–18; A. Wijffels, *Qui millies allegatur. Les allégations du droit savant dans les dossiers du Grand Conseil de Malines. Causes septentrionales ca. 1460–1580*, (Amsterdam: Ph. D. thesis, Universiteit van Amsterdam–Faculteit der Rechtsgeleerdheid, Amsterdam, and Universitaire Pers Leiden, 1985), passim.

13. D. P. Blok et al., eds., *Algemene Geschiedenis der Nederlanden*, 15 vols. (Haarlem: Fibula–Van Dishoeck, 1988), 4: 172–81; Ph. Godding, "De opkomst van de Raad van Brabant, 1427–1472," *Noordbrabants Historisch Jaarboek* 2 (1985): 7–8; J. Monballyu, "'Van Appellatiën ende Reformatiën,' ca. 1370–ca. 1550," *Tijdschrift voor rechtsgeschiedenis* 61 (1993): 237, 245–60.

14. J. van Rompaey, *De Grote Raad van de hertogen van Boergondië en het Parlement van Mechelen* (Brussels: Paleis der Academiën, 1973), 308–465; C. L. Verkerk, "Evocatie in de Landen van Herwaarts-over," in *Consilium Magnum 1473–1973* (Brussels: Algemeen Rijksarchief, 1977), 420–22, 436.

15. J. Th. de Smidt, "Op-treden van rechtspraak," in *Fabrica historiae forensis*, ed. J. M. J. Chorus and A. M. Elias (Leiden: Universiteit Leiden–Faculteit der Rechtsgeleerdhied,1989), 65–81.

16. J. Th. De Smidt and A. H. Huussen Jr., "De Grote Raad van Mechelen," *Holland* 2 (1970): 99.

17. ARB, *Raad van Brabant*, nrs. 592–96.

18. "Dicta" of the Privy Concil, 16th century, in ARB, *Geheime Raad. Registers* [hereafter *Geh.R.Reg.*], nrs. 670–74; J. Th. de Smidt et al., eds., *Chronologische lijsten van geëxtenteerde sententiën van de Grote Raad van Mechelen*, 6 vols. (Brussels: Koninklijke Commissie voor de Uitgave der Oude Wetten en Verordeningen van België, 1966–1988); C. H. van Rhee, *Litigation and Legislation. Civil Procedure at First Instance in the Great Council, 1522–1559* (Brussels: Archives générales du Royaume, 1997), 262.

19. For example, the judgment of the Privy Council, May 12, 1546, concerning "maintenance of some horses," ARB, *Geh.R.Reg.*, nr. 671, f.11v–12; February 1, 1547, concerning "demande destre receu . . . bouchier", ARB, *Geh.R.Reg.*, nr. 671, f.20.

20. J. W. Koopmans, *De Staten van Holland en de Opstand* ('s-Gravenhage: Hollandse Historische Reeks, 1990), 75–78; P. van Peteghem, *De Raad van Vlaanderen en Staatsvorming onder Karel V* (Nijmegen: Gerard Noodt Institut, 1990), 201–203, 421.

21. Blok et al., *Algemene Geschiedenis*, 5: 329–30. See nn 14 (above) and De Smidt et al., *Chronologische lijsten*, 1: 137–395.

22. J. Gilissen, "À propos de la réception du droit romain," *Revue du Nord* 157 (1958): 261–68.

23. J. Leerssen, "Macht, afstand en culturele diversiteit: bijvoorbeeld Overmaas," *Theoretische geschiedenis* 18 (1991): 428–30.

24. J. J. Woltjer, "Quelques remarques sur la législation et l'administration de la République des Provinces-Unies," in *Handelingen van de Nederlands-Spaanse historische colloquia*, ed. H. de Schepper and P. J. A. N. Rietbergen (Nijmegen/Madrid: Comité español de ciencias históricas, 1992), 119–20.

25. Among others, see instruction for the Council of Luxembourg, in Lameere, *Recueil*, 3: 305–11; J. M. Cauchies, "Centralisation et particularismes: Les procédures de recours en Hainaut," in *Hommages à la Wallonie*, ed. H. Hasquin (Brussels: Université

Libre de Bruxelles, 1981), 45–64; J. Kossmann-Putto, "Het Westfaalse veemgerecht, veertiende-vijftiende eeuw," *Bijdragen Mededelingen Geschiedenis der Nederlanden* 100 (1985), 205–24; J. Foucart, *Une institution baillivale française en Flandre. La gouvernance du souverain bailliage de Lille-Douai-Orchies* (Lille: Raoust, 1937). Also see n. 44.

26. H. de Schepper, "'Justitie door Gratie' krachtens vorstelijke wetgeving in de Nederlanden, 1400–1621," in *Interactie tussen wetgever en rechter vóór de Trias Política*, ed. E. J. M. F. C. Broers and B. C. M. Jacobs (Den Haag: Boom Juridische Uitgevers, 2003), 109–30.

27. H. de Schepper, "Het gratierecht in het Bourgondisch-Habsburgse Nederland, 1384–1633," in *Symposium over de Centrale Overheidsinstellingen van de Habsburgse Nederlanden. Tien bijdragen over de staat, de regering en de ambtenaren van de 16e tot de 18e eeuw*, ed. H. Coppens and K. van Honacker (Brussels: Standen en Landen–Bijzondere reeks nr. 2, 1995), 63–65. See B. Garnot, *L'infrajudiciaire du Moyen Age à l'Epoque contemporaine: actes du colloque de Dijon, 5–6 octobre 1995* (Dijon: Editions Universitaires de Dijon, 1996).

28. Requests and deferred payment, in ARB, *Geheime Raad. Spaanse Tijd* [hereafter *Sp.Geh.R.*], nrs. 783–98; appointments of the Privy Council concerning Brabant, 1527–1640, in Archivo General de Simancas, *Secretarías Provinciales-Flandes*, book 1420, passim.

29. Requests and spreads of payment, in ARB, *Sp.Geh.R.*, nrs. 709–25.

30. Lameere, *Recueil*, 3: 549–50; Lameere-Simont, *Recueil*, 4: 325, 328; requests and cessions of goods, in ARB, *Sp.Geh.R.*, nrs. 766–70.

31. ARB, *Sp.Geh.R.*, nrs. 1405–1407. See also Filips Wielant, *Practijke civile*, ed. E. I. Strubbe (Amsterdam: Graphic, 1968), 15–16.

32. M. Vrolijk, *Recht door Gratie. Gratie bij Doodslagen en andere Delicten, 1531–1567* (Hilversum: Verloren, 2004).

33. Lameere-Simont, *Recueil*, 4: 326–27, and 5: 54, 332.

34. Requests and repeals of banishment, in ARB, *Sp.Geh.R.*, nrs. 1090–97.

35. H. de Schepper, "Entre compromis et repressión: inquisition et clémence aux Pays-Bas sous Charles V," in *Charles Quint face aux Réformes*, ed. G. Le Thiec and A. Tallon (Paris/Genève: Centre d'histoire des Reformes et du Protestantisme; 2005), 93–95. Also see James D. Tracy, "Heresy Law and Centralisation under Mary of Hungary," *Archiv für Reformationsgeschichte* 73 (1982): 284–308.

36. Letters of pardon for illegal hunting, December 19, 1550, in ARB, *Geh.R.Reg.*, nr. 671, f. 84v–85r; requests and letters of pardon, in ARB, *Geh.R.Reg.*, nr. 896.

37. H. de Schepper and M. Vrolijk, "La grâce princière et la composition coutumière, 1384-1633," in *Anthropologies juridiques*, ed. J. Hoareau-Dodinau and P. Texier (Limoges: Presses Universitaires de Limoges,1998), 752–54; Vrolijk, *Recht door Gratie*, 43–46, 230–34.

38. Muchembled, *Violence*, 17–23.

39. Vrolijk, *Recht door Gratie*, 84–91, 299–300, 345–60, 393, 477–80.

40. M. Pineau, "Les lettres de rémission lilloises (fin du XVe, début du XVIe siècle)," *Revue du Nord* 55 (1973): 231–40; M. J. P. A. de Wilde, *Gratieverlening in Gelre ten tijde van de Republiek, 1581–1795* (Nijmegen: uned. Katholieke Universiteit Nijmegen–Nieuwe Geschiedenis, 1996); P. P. Beijers, *Gratieverlening in Gelre onder de Habsburg-*

ers, 1543–1581 (Nijmegen: uned. Katholieke Universiteit Nijmegen–Nieuwe Geschiedenis, Nijmegen, 2000).

41. De Schepper, "Het gratierecht," in *Symposium over de Centrale Overheidsinstellingen van de Habsburgse Nederlanden. Tien bijdragen over de staat, de regering en de ambtenaren van de 16e tot de 18e eeuw*, ed. H. Coppens and K. van Honacker (Brussels: Standen en Landen–Bijzondere reeks nr. 2, 1995), 51, 76–83.

42. See S. J. Fockema Andreae, *Hoofdstukken uit de geschiedenis van rechtsmacht en rechtsvorming*, vol. 4, *Bijdragen Nederlandsche Rechtsgeschiedenis* (Haarlem: Bohn, 1900), 242–54; F. Keverling Buisman, "Supplement op de Ordelen van den Etstoel van Drenthe, 1505–1579," in *Drentse Rechtsbronnen*, ed. J. Heringa et al. (Zutphen: Walburg, 1981), passim; A. Th. van Deursen, "De zestiende eeuw, 1522–1603," in *Geschiedenis van Drenthe*, ed. J. Heringa et al. (Meppel/Amsterdam: Boom, 1985), 242–81; M. S. Dupont-Bouchat and X. Rousseaux, "Le prix du sang: sang et justice du XIVe au XVIIIe siècle," in *Affaires de sang*, ed. A. Farge (Paris: Imago, 1988), 61.

12

"They Have Highly Offended the Community of God"

Rituals of Ecclesiastical Discipline and
Pastoral Membership in the Community in
Sixteenth- and Seventeenth-Century German Parishes

Susan C. Karant-Nunn

S EVERAL RENOWNED COLLEAGUES HAVE ASSERTED THAT collective values were crucial in launching the Reformation. Bernd Moeller has regarded the late medieval trend toward authoritarian, oligarchic governance in imperial cities, at the expense of collective decision making, to have produced a movement that was widely seen as a corrective.[1] Berndt Hamm has put forward the concept of *normative centering*, by which he means much of early sixteenth-century society's overthrow (*Sturz*) of a religious system that was "spiritually, socially, and economically burdensome" in favor of a legitimacy based on the Bible within society for laity and pastorate alike.[2] Peter Blickle has interpreted the Peasants' War as an effort, participated in by urban artisans and swaths of other ordinary citizens, to bring public life into accord with "godly law" as contained especially in the Gospels but also in the Bible as a whole.[3] None of these men has been so explicitly sanguine as to maintain that the people so motivated attained their goals for the longer term—although at least Moeller and Hamm are convinced that Lutheran society was better off than Catholic society, and Blickle has observed that after the bloodbath that brought the Peasants' War to an end, concessions were made in practice to survivors in some regions.[4]

A consensus concerning the need to introduce reforms moved some people, but by no means all people, of varying ranks within a hierarchically structured society to come together in support of change. They interpreted the Reformation as an expression and potentially the fulfillment of this impulse. What happened to this short-lived cohesion has not been sufficiently explored. The revolutionary force of the Bible, made available to Everyman through print and preaching, in part explains the credal diversity that ensued. But even overlooking, for the moment, the sectarianism to which *sola scriptura* contributed, we could well ask what the post-Reformation evangelical community was like. Was it cooperative and cohesive? Did the sacrament of Communion symbolize and reinforce solidarity among God's children? Were there values that most people continued to share and that bound them together? The ecclesiastical ordinances and visitation protocols of the sixteenth and seventeenth centuries maintained rhetorically that there were, employing the phrase "They have highly offended the community of God," or a variation of it, in denouncing transgressors. They said this often, if not quite as often, as they invoked "the common good."

These are large questions. In this chapter, I shall break off one piece and focus on the question: As the evangelical pastorate evolved during the second half of the sixteenth century, how did it fit into the local Christian community, especially the rural community? We regard clergymen as having been, in William Stafford's words, *domesticated* by the Reformation, that is, integrated into society.[5] Before the Reformation, they had made up quite a large caste outside lay polity and in some ways above it. What was the position of the smaller profession that remained in the post-Reformation era? In the *distant* post-Reformation period—that is, the late seventeenth and the whole eighteenth century—Luise Schorn-Schütte has told us, the pastorate was again a sociologically identifiable group, now linked to and intermarried with the urban and juridically trained bureaucracy.[6] How did the post-Reformation clergy once again become a class separate from the masses, but now in the villages even more than in the urban centers? Echoing and extending Andreas Bodenstein von Karlstadt's accusation of 1524 concerning the Lutheran mass, Steven Ozment has referred to the "new papists," not so much with reference to the clergy as a body as to those former "freedom fighters" who began increasingly to impose their theological will upon all; the theologians were nearly always, of course, high-ranking clergy.[7] Bob Scribner has coined the term *neoclericalism*, by which he means a recurrent elevation of the pastorate over the laity and the clergy's resumption of some of the powers that it had claimed before the Reformation.[8] How did this shift occur?

The answers are complex. For present purposes, I want to concentrate on the pastor's intensifying role in the punishment of sin as an aspect of reclericalization. The role quickly came to have three aspects: first, the general admonition of human failings from the pulpit, followed by private remonstration with the individuals whom he had in mind. The general admonition against sin was a perpetual homiletic message, one not new in this era. But added to it during the sixteenth century was the requirement that clergy formally, privately meet with the worst sinners and demand their reform. Second, with some territorial differences, the pastor could either himself decide to bar an unrepentant, unregenerate person from the Communion table and from serving as a godparent, and, if the guilty party died, from being buried in no longer consecrated but still sacred ground. He could, and was increasingly required to, turn the miscreant in to his superintendent, who in intractable cases proceeded further to the emerging consistories and synods. Sometimes he employed a rite of banning before the entire congregation. Third, the cleric oversaw and verified a sinner's repentance and at least occasionally presided over public rituals of reconciliation. In the first instance, the pastor himself approached the local secular authority, the *Amtmann* (an official with military functions too, often a knight, appointed by the prince) or *Richter* (the local judge, chosen traditionally by the peasant community), for enforcement. In the second alternative, the superintendent or the ruler himself instructed the officials to act in support of the pastor.

When sins such as adultery, premarital sex, blasphemy, frequent drunkenness, habitual "tyranny" by a husband toward his wife (by which is meant severe beating), assault upon other persons, murder, false belief, witchcraft and sorcery, and refusal to come to the sermon or to receive Communion came to the secular arm's attention, it was obliged to set its own procedures in motion.[9] My point is to note the ineluctable part of the pastor and/or the preacher-deacon in all these developments. The pastor was *required* to turn in people whose unacceptable behavior he became aware of. The consequences of crime and moral failing were set in motion by the pastor or one of his clerical assistants.

The tensions caused by this disciplinary assignment are evident from about midcentury on, when it began to be obligatory. Moritz of Saxony's decree of 1543 is a harbinger of patterns to come:

> You should diligently hold forth to the people, warning them to be penitent, and initially by means of Christian teaching and admonition punish their public vices. But if some should be contemptuous of this method, you should, with the foreknowledge of the authorities in each place, by means of the righteous Christian ban . . . separate and shut them out of the community. In that instance, the banned individuals may be admitted to no social gathering or position but until through proper penance they turn their lives around, they should be treated as separated and cast out. If they despise the ban, they should be brought to the attention of us or our *Amtleute*, and if even then they do not reform within a month, they will not be tolerated in our land.[10]

The three sons of Johann Friedrich the Magnanimous, Luther's ruler at the time the Reformer died, declared in instructions to parish visitors in 1554 that a pastor may move to another parish on account of the parishioners' disfavor.

"But should our visitors discover that the parishioners did not have a proper reason for their dislike, other than that as part of his office he rightly and in a Christian manner chastised them on account of their vices, . . . they, the visitors, should report the parishioners to the princes and not give the people room to exclude their pastors without [other] reason."[11] The Ernestine princes continued, in a style that will be typical through Protestant Germany in due course, that should a pastor, preacher, or deacon find out about particularly coarse vices that a sinner will not abandon despite private admonition and the preacher's public call to repent:

> they may inform us or the authorities of each place what the appearance, indication, and cause . . . is; we want properly to investigate them and will know how to show them that such public, raw vices should not be tolerated but will instead be seriously punished.[12]

After these dukes founded a consistory in Jena in 1561, the Thuringian rules became longer and more differentiated. After a pastor made the most concerted effort and failed to reconcile a sinner with Christian society, he was required to refer the guilty party further up the line. Increasingly, the decision whether formally to excommunicate lay with the consistory, not with either pastor or superintendent. When the consistory called, the miscreant, the pastor, and the superintendent were required to attend the hearing and the handing down of a verdict; they promised to sit (on the panel?) and to vote as well as to announce the outcome in the affected parish. The announcement was to be done from the pulpit and also in writing, by both media addressed to the congregation as a whole, which in the villages was ordinarily synonymous with the gathered residents. An unrepentant sinner—and this becomes the official standard throughout Protestant Germany—was denied the Sacrament and was forbidden to serve in any honorable capacity, such as godparent. He or she was forbidden to come to any social gathering. He was allowed, and indeed required, to come to church but was required to stand or sit in a particular place that the pastor indicated. A text was provided for a formal, public rite of excommunication.[13] Should a person under the ban die without readmission to the Christian community, she was buried away from others, outside the churchyard or cemetery, and completely without ceremony. Those who admitted their failings would, among regionally varied possibilities, kneel before the altar on three consecutive Sundays or, in Saxony, with the consistory's permission, pay a fine instead; in either case, the pastor was to add his public deprecation from the chancel.[14]

Further, pastors and preachers were instructed "in their Sunday sermons to admonish the people to hear the Word of God diligently and to receive the most worthy Sacrament more frequently, and with repeated and serious warning and threats [to say] that they [the clergymen] have the right to . . . and will use the above punishments against those who are contemptuous."[15]

The great 1580 church ordinance of Elector August of Saxony obliquely reveals that in their efforts to impose discipline, pastors did not always achieve the right balance between moderation and emphasis, nor between disinterest and personal bias. August declared that the pastors were not to display their private emotions or slander people in preaching against sins. Instead they were to employ Christian gentleness and modesty. However, this should not be interpreted to mean, the elector went on, that the servants of the church ought not to reprimand "with proper burning seriousness and Christian zeal" those parishioners who lead vicious and godless lives, or that they oughtn't to touch on the subject of these vices. On the contrary, God Almighty sincerely assigned them this duty and commanded them to carry it out. He was, when necessary, to inform the parish visitors of particular people's misdeeds.[16] The visitors, in turn, should proceed to the senior consistory, the *Oberkonsistorium*, in Dresden, "with, however, our advance knowledge and consent." A script for banning is provided, as are others for ritual reconciliation. The guilty party was presented before the congregation, the category of his or her sins announced. Although such a person was obliged to be in church and to sit in a designated place, when Holy Communion was about to begin, the verger must accompany him or her out of the sanctuary.[17]

Nevertheless, the banned, should they not be compelled to leave their home territory, were allowed, in late seventeenth-century electoral Brandenburg, to pursue their livelihood and be unforbidden "to work, to trade, and to enjoy the rights of citizens and neighbors, and [they are] obligated to fulfill [their] duties, obligations, and others."[18] The scripts for banning contained in the church ordinances are quite frequent and surprisingly long.[19] Yet I think it probable that rites of reconciliation were more often used. The most compelling reason for desisting from sin was physical arrest, and by modern standards the number of qualifying offenses was great. After an individual had been apprehended for a violation of civil law and had undergone trial and nonlethal punishment in that sphere, very likely he or she was thought unfit for Communion without being readmitted to Christian society.

Shortly after 1618, church inspectors in Wiesbaden asked specifically about public penance. They inquired whether those accused of significant moral offenses wore the stones of shame or held particular candles of humiliation.[20] In Zerbst in about the middle of the sixteenth century, the ceremony of penitence was to take place before the entire congregation after the sermon. The culprit was to kneel before the altar. Under the leadership of the cantor-schoolmaster, the sexton, and the pastor, all sang the hymn, "Have Mercy Upon Us, O Lord God!" based on Psalm 51, or "Out of the Depths I

Cry to Thee," Psalm 130. Then the minister or the district superintendent declared,

> Dear friends of Christ, you know that this person [name], through the sin he has committed [the sin is named], has deeply angered God, and has grieved and aggravated our Christian community. He has consequently rendered himself unworthy of the communion of saints and the people of God; he is unqualified to participate in the most worthy Sacrament [of Communion]; and he deserves the wrath of God and eternal damnation. Because of his act, he has been cut off from Christ and his holy body and has become a member of the devil, which is horrible to hear.
>
> But because [*sic*] God is the kind of God who does not desire a sinner's death, but rather desires that he turn himself around and live; and God Himself admonishes us to turn ourselves toward Him, and He will then turn toward us—that is, He will not count our sin and will show us grace and mercy.
>
> This person [name] here before us, in the presence of God and this Christian congregation, desires to turn back to God and by means of absolution and release from his sins to be reunited with the Christian community.
>
> So I ask you [name] now whether you committed such murder or adultery, etc., and if you did so, whether before God and this congregation you wish publicly to confess. . . . Say and confess whether you committed [the sin].
>
> Should he answer, "Yes, I did it," then the pastor should proceed. Are you sorry from your heart for this sin, by which you enraged God and grieved and upset the holy community [of God]? If he says, "Yes, I am heartily sorry," he [the officiant] should continue: Do you then desire from your heart pardon for this and all your other sins through Jesus Christ?
>
> If he should answer, "Yes, I desire this from my heart," then he [the pastor] should ask further: Do you intend then also to improve your life with God's help and to sin no more? Should he [the sinner] reply that with God's help he does wish to improve himself, the pastor should say [to the whole congregation]: Dear friends of Christ, you yourselves have now heard this person [name] publicly confess. But I want to admonish you not to regard this public penance and acknowledgment of sin as a spectacle, but to consider it a great and glorious work, one from which the Divine Majesty and the dear angels in heaven take hearty joy and pleasure. . . .

Bible readings and prayers follow. Thereupon, the pastor instructs the sinner to arise from her knees. The officiant declares, "Dear [name], now that you have publicly confessed your sin before this holy congregation, and beyond that have asked for absolution, so we heartily desire to communicate that to you. This your repentance causes the angels in heaven to rejoice."

> However, before you are released from this heavy sin of [the sin is again specified] and all other [sins], and so that your constancy in repentance becomes clear

and open, you should come here before the altar eight [varied opinion on the time] days [times] after the sermon. When you have done this, you will then be released from this sin and all other sins and receive absolution. You will then be rejoined to the body of Christ and admitted again to the enjoyment of the highly worthy Sacrament.[21]

With the passage of time, authorities dictated different responses to different categories of infraction.[22] The ecclesiastical ordinance for Hohenlohe of 1588 directs attention, for example, to youth who misbehave during the sermon, which includes sleeping. Those who were enrolled in school were to receive corporal punishment from the schoolmaster in the school. Those who were not were "to be flogged with switches (or rods; *mit Ruthen*) by their parents in the presence of the pastor, district official, or village mayor *(Schultheiß)* so that they are directed toward the fear of God, prayer, and good behavior. . . . Should the parents tolerate [their child's misbehavior] and therefore not wish to administer punishment, this should be reported to us." He will, the count says, penalize both young and old.[23] This is a combined secular and ecclesiastical penalty in view of the pastor's role in detection within a full sanctuary and his presence at its execution. A Hohenlohe ordinance of 1601 provides a script to be used in case a couple presented themselves to be wed and the bride was already pregnant. The presiding cleric was to say to the assembly,

Dear friends in Christ, the couple to be married here before us have been incited by the weakness of their sinful flesh and betrayed by the cunning of Satan. Before their Christian wedding, they have slept together, which is impermissible and prohibited. Pregnancy has resulted. This constitutes a dreadful encroachment upon the divine Majesty, His holy Commandments, and on outward Christian decency and honor. It has highly offended the community of God, and it well deserves the severe wrath of God and of the secular authority.

After much more, the clergyman was permitted to resort to the usual wedding ceremony.[24] Very likely, as was the case elsewhere, the bride could not wear the usual wreath nor the pair hold a large celebration. Once again, the pastor and his aides were those who took note of unmarried women's swelling abdomens, and they were to take action, whether in the church alone or by turning to the state as well. Such obligations had by no means been suspended by the second half of the seventeenth century. In 1664 the *Kirchenordnung* of four Ernestine brothers, dukes of Saxony, Jülich, Cleves, and Berg, "etc.," required the pastors to refer such couples to the consistory, where they had to undergo not only admonition but examination as to their eligibility to marry. Even if they might proceed to matrimony, several days had to elapse, and they had to perform ritual penance penance before the congregation, "unless there are substantial reasons why they should be spared this."[25] One may well imagine that those "substantial reasons" had to do with class and connection. In 1648, affected brides and grooms in Braunschweig argued in vain that the authorities should reckon pregnancies from the date of engagement and not the wedding itself.[26]

In Saxony, those who governed resorted to some creative ways of shaming. In 1583 the visitors ordered the village judge of Beyersdorff to put young men who sat in the balcony and misbehaved in neck irons. They were to remain confined and displayed not just for the remainder of that service but until the end of the afternoon or vesper service, without a single "*Bissen Brot*" to eat.[27] I have written separately about the use of a cross-shaped pillory in front of the church, into which transgressors were placed in the position of the crucified Christ.[28] The pastor himself decided who should be so displayed. One of the parish visitors to Battin (Saxony) in 1672 recorded that he himself had seen adults accused of indecency (*Unzucht*) standing in the church in a stock "during the sermon" three Sundays in succession.[29]

In territories that became Calvinist, stern discipline was imposed. In the Rhenish Palatinate (*Pfalz*), compelled to become Reformed rather than Lutheran from 1563, every person was required to attend church every week, on pain of a fine of half a Rhenish gulden, or, if impoverished, imprisonment. Clearly the pastor would play a part in detecting those who were absent without license. Pastors and deacons could remind the electors' secular officials of their own duties on this score in case they were negligent. If that should not be effective, the pastor was permitted to turn to the superintendent and further to the prince's own counselor (*Oberrath*). However, pastors should always make their reports with modesty and not behave as though they wanted to intrude in worldly governance. They should suppress their personal feeling.[30]

A legal dimension in the forging bond between territorial prince and pastorate may be seen in Elector Friedrich III's form for the appointment of clergymen throughout his domains, dated 1564:

> We have taken him, too, together with his wife and children and those pertaining to him, under our particular protection and shelter [*schutz unlit schirm*] and our promise. On that account, he should be faithful and obedient to us and seek to promote and maintain our honor and benefit, also to exert all diligence, insofar as he is able, so that the people are kept in good peace and unity under our governance, and not to consent to anything that is opposed to this, but [simply] to remain within his profession and service as described above, whether in peacetime, war, pestilence, or any other time.

The form ends with a statement that the candidate "has sworn fidelity to us with hand in hand and has taken a vow to God" on the many points listed before.[31]

Not later than during the second half of the sixteenth century, German pastors everywhere, and in Lutheran territories most certainly, had to take solemn oaths of increasing detail upon being ordained and/or upon induction into new posts. They did this in the presence of at least representatives of civil authority. Their oaths were increasingly long and specific.[32] This formula, however, is a feudally tinged loyalty oath. It goes farther than most in making each minister the "vassal" of his lord, holding clerical preferment as a kind *of beneficium.*

It is important to note that Calvinist lands all eventually instituted the office of presbyter or elder, which further complicated the disciplinary scene.[33] Raymond Mentzer has recently summarized the role that the presbyters in Reformed parishes in France played in barring transgressors from Communion.[34] Village residents may have found this supervisory and penalizing function of their own neighbors to be too much to bear. In a visitation of 1590 in the Calvinist county of Dietz, the parish inspectors reported that "the elders complain vehemently about the great thanklessness and abusive words that they have to endure in carry out their office."[35] Or, in other settings, the elders may have tended to be lackadaisical in view of the ostracism meted out to them by coresidents and family if they took their duty too seriously.[36]

But closer oversight sponsored by civil authorities was a feature of the day, not just among the descendants of John Calvin. Helga Schnabel-Schule is quite correct in observing that some Lutheran rulers, too, experimented with a lay board resembling elders who were to scrutinize everyone's morality and doctrine.[37] Paul Münch detects this development as early as the middle of the sixteenth century.[38] In one principality, these were called *Kirchen-Censores* and were appointed at some time long before 1693 but were reaffirmed in that year.

The primary instance in penalizing misbehavior was at the level of the parish clergy. Despite a tendency by the latter sixteenth century to remove from pastors' exclusive hands the decision to excommunicate or to impose rituals of banning without approval of higher church and secular officials, the role of the *curé* remained central in the initial phase of accusation. This was so despite the proliferation of bureaucratic offices, such that apart from local clergymen, there were now special superintendents, general superintendents, members of the consistory, members of the highest consistory (*Oberkonsistorium*), not to mention periodic synods—for all of whom work had to be found.[39] Nevertheless, in Lutheran lands, the pastor and his helpers scrutinized each parishioner, in part by means of obligatory auricular confession before receiving the Sacrament. Most likely, they also kept their ears to the ground and were hardly able to refrain, in a small-town setting, from using family and household members as sources of information. In Reformed territories, individual confession was abolished, but the scrutiny was at least as intense. The appointment of elders did not remove disciplinary participation from the ministry itself. Nonetheless, presbyters increased the numbers of those who pursued their neighbors' doctrinal and moral lapses.

Other kinds of strictures helped to detach the clergy from the larger community, more so in the countryside. Just as significant as the efforts from above to enforce disciplinary conformity upon the pastorate is the fact that, simultaneously, rulers forbade clerics to take part any longer in communal and familial festivities. They explicitly could not attend baptismal and wedding parties, but they were usually entitled to a meal from each, to be sent to them at the parsonage, or a money substitute. Nor should they darken the doorsteps of public houses. They were in no setting to drink with the laity, not even at the annual communal "beer." The result was that their social life was confined to interaction with other pastors, preachers, deacons, and schoolmasters. Further, they were not to leave town without compelling reason, which made it difficult for them to get together with neighboring colleagues. All of these men of God and their households were to form a small, distinctive cohort, but an internally striated one.

In sum, quite apart from other factors such as the pastors' increasing education and urban background, the duty of ecclesiastical discipline was imposed at a time when in other ways clergymen were drawing apart socially from the ordinary laity. They were even to dress distinctively, not like either peasants or common burghers, so that everyone could immediately recognize their status.

The question arises whether the pastors actually attempted to perform in accordance with the strict terms that were prescribed to them. In the main, the answers must for now remain anecdotal and theoretical. The pertinent anecdotes come from various ecclesiastical ordinances, visitation protocols, and *acta*, the recommendations for improvement that visitation committees submitted to pastors and local authorities after a visitation was complete. From these we gain an impression of pastors' frequently going so far as to let their voices rise in the pulpit in opposition to scandalous sin. But parishioners' offense at humiliation in public comes through. In 1580 the minister in Petersroda in Saxony reported that some people did not respect him as they ought: "Instead, when he admonishes them for their sins from the pulpit, they call out to him as he leaves the church, 'The godless, God-shaming *Pfaff* held us up by name'; they say that he and the sexton have betrayed them to the authorities." The authorities were clearly unhappy if pastors consequently did not react to infractions. Typical in this situation is their comment in the village of Brathe, near Wittenberg, in 1617:

The parents do not send their children diligently to the recitation of the Cate-chism, the menservants and maids do not want to learn it. The people willfully neglect the sermon, yet no one has been punished. Even swearing and working on Sundays are not penalized. The pastor reports that there is no household within which immorality does not occur, and still this is not punished. In danc-ing, they stay up until 10 o'clock at night and take off their caps and dance wan-tonly, but nobody says anything to them about it.[40]

At the other end of the spectrum, some ecclesiastical officers actually had to *moderate* the district pastors' disciplinary strictness. In the county of Nassau-Dillenburg, sinners who had repented were nevertheless not being allowed to receive Communion. The scribe remarks, "If one were to proceed like this with all infractions, there would be no Sunday when one did not have to pres-ent twenty [or] thirty [people]!"[41] In 1586 the visitors to a Württemberg vil-lage found that a man was completely barred from attending church. They in-sisted to the pastor that even great sinners had to be admitted to hear the Word of God.[42]

A considerable weight lay upon parish clergy as they considered how far to accommodate the wishes of their superiors. After all, they had to *live* within their communities, and this probably prevented them from alienating their charges unduly. They were doubtless increasingly segregated from their neigh-bors by not being allowed to mingle with them socially, by their own rising ed-ucational level, by their urban origins, by the increasing exaction of fees for ministerial services and the resentment that this aroused, and by their attitude toward themselves as better than the peasantry and most artisans. All of these contributed to the "new clericalism." But to betray their fellow citizens' every-day peccadilloes to the next level of authority without some convincing need to do so would have made their existence very uncomfortable, if not unten-able. One's neighbors had their ways of taking revenge. We may well suspect that acts of vandalism, such as cutting down fruit trees, chopping holes in water pipes, or of ritual humiliation such as nailing a dead dog to the preacher's front door, were the result of discipline-related conflicts.[43]

One of the guardians of the Ernestine duke in Coburg (who was a minor) noted in 1580 that "[t]hose individuals from the community [of Siebleben] who diligently keep themselves dead drunk subject the pastor to much mock-ery by tying verses to his door, throwing out [breaking?] his windows [*Außw-erfung der fenster*] and other improper, offensive shouting and similar gestures because he [the pastor] daily admonishes them for their godless and profligate existence." They had to be punished.[44]

What would have constituted "convincing need" for a pastor to take cor-rective action? If secular or ecclesiastical governors presented people to the pastor for correction, there was no evading this duty, but at least the public knew this background. Normally, however, the circumspect clergyman resorted to ecclesiastical discipline when some infraction clearly did violate communal values. An undated record of the mid-sixteenth century reveals the application of public penance to a couple, Caspar and Catherina Schilta, residents of Zerbst in the Merseburg chapter lands. The Schiltas had given a foster child—for keeping which, in German practice, they would have received a small fee for maintenance—inadequate food and had beaten it unduly, by both means causing its death.[45] In this instance, a script was used for the rite, which did not permit them immediately to resume taking Communion. They surely also underwent secular punishment. Pastors, I am arguing, could have reacted with impunity to instances like the Schiltas' child abuse because such behavior was a violation of every community's mores. Children ought to be adequately fed, and they should not be beaten to death. However, public humiliation for people who had merely sworn by God's wounds[46] or drank a good deal in a culture that sealed agreements with hearty tippling[47] would have been, by general consensus, inappropriate and would have produced unpleasant consequences for any clergyman. The social dynamics of each community included tacitly informing members how they were to act. Many of the faults now officially disapproved continued to lie at the heart of human relations and could not be dislodged, except, perhaps, in Geneva and other Reformed cities, as a result of unrelenting oversight and severe penalties. The intense resistance to becoming Reformed that Paul Münch has noted was doubtless a response to the tendency of that creed to interfere even more drastically than Lutheranism with traditional culture.[48] German rulers of every persuasion sought such oversight as well, but could simply not achieve it to the same degree of thoroughness in every setting. Country people's "bad behavior" persisted partly because local clergy, in order not to be harassed and hounded by their parishioners, did not make a wholehearted effort to eradicate it. Probably also in the service of peace, rural officials were less than meticulous in their enforcement. They also resented the fact that the pastor presumed to correct *their* deportment and the way in which they executed their offices. The scribe records in Bethau in 1602, "The old and new judges are both blasphemers and maintain no [standard of] decency. They reproach the pastor as a betrayer. The other peasants too hold him in contempt and refuse to remove their hats in his presence."[49]

The post-Reformation community as a whole was probably as cohesive as earlier, taking into account its hierarchical makeup then as later. The integration of the clergy, however, was a brief interlude marking the transition from late medieval Catholicism to Protestantism. However ubiquitous ministers and preachers were as players on the local scene, they were increasingly removed from the social life of the laity and identified with those upper eche-lons that were determined to modify the long-term patterns of human inter-action that they judged to be unchristian. This is by no means to say that many parishioners did not bear their pastors and deacons with gratitude, even af-fection, for their spiritual services. This was an individual matter. From a so-ciological point of view, however, the clergy became separate.

Apropos of the settled urban Reformation, Scribner outlined in 1977 four means of social control that those in power sought to maintain: (1) compul-sion through physical force and laws, (2) political regulations that were short of outright law, (3) the legitimation of the existing order such that efforts to de-part from it were *illegitimate,* and (4) the invocation of ideology based on shared values.[50] We need in the future to move beyond our concentration pri-marily upon urban centers in studying the outcomes of the Reformation. As in the earliest stage of the evangelical movement, when preachers in key market towns first aroused people to adopt the Gospel as their exclusive religious touchstone, the cities were merely the beginning points. The four means that Scribner puts forward are equally applicable to the village setting. A general as-pect of early modern Germany is the efforts of towns to expand their domina-tion of their hinterlands, just as, at the same time, princes attempted to inte-grate the towns within their borders into the lands over which they directly ruled, either in person or through their growing, more specialized, increasingly rationalized bureaucracies. The Reformation, whether Lutheran or Reformed, unsettled existing relationships sufficiently to promote fresh configurations among existing strands of authority. Some strands gained in prominence, while others lost. Even within the cities, the outcomes of reconfiguration sel-dom fulfilled the ideals of many of the ordinary people who had expressed their hopes, sometimes with their actions, during its incipient phases. Yet within the urban context there were numbers of educated and idealistic people whom higher principle could sustain, and/or who were beneficiaries of shifts in the locus of power. For these groups, the Reformation as it evolved held re-wards that compensated them for the sacrifice of old-fashioned social and cul-tural habits. Their members were generally agreeable to compromising with church and state on moral discipline. In exchange, they were probably spared the more rigorous, public consequences of their indiscretions and were fined rather than displayed before their congregations. The *städtische* pastorate from the second or third generation forward derived from and identified with these groups. Indeed, these provided the town-based clergy with a circle of laypeo-ple with whom it could interact socially, sparing ministers, preachers, and schoolmasters the isolation of the village parishes. One can speak, then, of urban clerics as members of a community, even as the disciplinary role of men of the cloth expanded. Nonetheless, we have taken insufficient cognizance of the less educated artisan and laborer segment of the citizenry within the walls—those whose interest in the Reformation was initially aroused but whose fantasies of its mature shape may well have been disappointed. At least by the mid-sixteenth century, congregations can hardly be said to have manifested the communal principles and other values that Moeller and Hamm assert were initially motivating.

In the countryside, full peasants, *Gärtner, Häusler,* laborers, and all their families were inscribed in the contumely of their urban neighbors, and most particularly in the contumely of that very class from which pastors increasingly derived. Not just Martin Luther's *Table Talk* but also visitation protocols across Germany express dislike of the peasant way of existing. The peasants were by nature, they repeatedly alleged and implied, slovenly, inclined to drunkenness, aggressively blasphemous, sexually overactive and quite indiscriminate, and given to spontaneous violence toward one another. They were seen to be governed by their emotions. The burgher-critics, one suspects, would hardly have recognized in the rustics they knew Blickle's champions of the godly law. Instead, residents of the villages needed to be *made* godly. The clergymen who were posted to the hamlets, parish visitors, city councilors, and princes saw it as their bounden duty to make them so—for God would not abide serious transgressions without exacting His revenge on all of society. The very task of moral reform contained within itself the righteous disruption of traditional patterns of interaction. The reform-bent outsiders implicitly regarded only one kind of *communal spirit* to be worthy of pursuit: one that humbly, submissively focused upon Christ's unblemished Lordship as manifested in the Word of God and symbolized in the sacraments of baptism and the eucharist. In the service of this ideal, pastors not only were, but had to be socially and ethically apart from those to whom they ministered.[51]

The need of pastors to live satisfactorily among their rural charges led them to moderate whatever moral determination they felt. If they did not yield to pragmatic flexibility, they could hardly have borne their appointments. Furthermore, it is highly likely—as visitors sometimes lamented—that at least some clerics came to appreciate the established modes of country interaction. While disciplinary processes for moral and doctrinal offenses categorically required the participation of the parish ministry, many, as indicated, at least *seemed* to comply but probably just as often "looked through their fingers," a popular German metaphor of the day. Rituals of penance encapsulate the princes' and urban magistrates' expectations of the clergy as well as the upright Christian behavior demanded of all residents. Despite the articulation of "communal" values and the survival of some sense of cohesion among village dwellers, and despite villagers' appreciation of clerical aid, the pastors and their assistants became part of the growing personnel commanded to curb and report on their more obvious sins. They were not part of the rural community but, like the *Amtleute*, people who lived among them but were not social and psychological insiders.

In the late Middle Ages, village priests lived among and virtually on the same level as their human flocks. Their ability to effect transubstantiation may have set them apart in theory, but in practice they were hardly distinct from their fellows. In the post-Reformation era, those wielding power deliberately disrupted this commonality. To do so, they thought, was essential to carrying out the divine will. Despite all disciplinary efforts, rural communities sought to retain the ways that were entrenched in their lifestyles, and particularly those ways that lay at the heart of their social relations. Very likely their common need to negotiate the rocky path between command from above with its threat of unpleasant enforcing measures, and necessary transactions with one another thickened the glue that bound them together. One ingredient of that glue was a revived anticlericalism. Scribner saw that anticlericalism did not end with the Reformation and that the reelevation of the clergy (*neoclericalism*) injected the earlier sentiment with fresh energy.[52]

Notes

1. Bernd Moeller, *Reichsstadt und Reformation* (Gütersloh: Gütersloher Verlagshaus Gerd Mohn, 1962), passim, but effectively summarized on 33.

2. See Berndt Hamm, "Reformation als normative Zentrierung von Religion und Gesellschaft," *Jahrbuch für biblische Theologie* 79 (1992): 241–79; "Von der spätmittelalterliche *reformatio* zur Reformation: Der Prozeß normativer Zentrierung von Religion und Gesellschaft in Deutschland," *Archiv für Reformationsgeschichte* 84 (1993), 7–82; "Einheit und Vielfalt der Reformation—oder: was die Reformation zu Reformation machte," in Berndt Hamm, Bernd Moeller, and Dorothea Wendebourg, *Reformations-theorien: Ein kirchenhistorischer Disput über Einheit und Vielfalt der Reformation* (Göttingen: Vandenhoeck & Ruprecht, 1995), 57–127. From a historiographical point of view, Hamm's concept of *Verdichtung* more urgently demands discussion, and he put this forward simultaneously with *normative centering*, intending it as a near synonym: "Das Gewicht von Religion, Glaube, Frömmigkeit und Theologie innerhalb der Verdichtungsvorgänge des ausgehenden Mittelalters und der frühen Neuzeit," in *Krisenbewußtsein und Krisenbewältigung in der Frühen Neuzeit—Crisis in Early Modern Europe: Festschrift für Hans-Christoph Rublack*, ed. Monika Hagenmaier and Sabine Holtz (Frankfurt/Main and Berlin: Peter Lang, 1992), 163–96.

3. See Pieter Blickle, *Gemeindereformation: Die Menschen des 16. Jahrhunderts auf dem Weg zum Heil* (Munich: Oldenbourg, 1985). For a historiographical treatment, see Hans-Christoph Rublack, "Forschungsbericht Stadt und Reformation," in *Stadt und Kirche im 16. Jahrhundert*. Schriften des Vereins für Reformationsgeschichte 190, ed. Bernd Moeller (Gütersloh: Gütersloher Verlagshaus Gerd Mohn, 1978), 9–26. One

of the earliest scholars to observe the withdrawal of the pastorate from the community was Alfred Schultze, *Stadt und Reformation: Ein Antrittsvorlesung in erweiterter Fassung*, Recht und Staat in Geschichte und Gegenwart 11 (Tübingen: J. C. B. Mohr [Paul Siebeck], 1918), especially 49–50.

4. *The Revolution of 1525: The German Peasants' War from a New Perspective*, trans. Thomas A. Brady Jr. and H. C. Erik Midelfort (Baltimore: Johns Hopkins University Press, 1981), part 3, "The Consequences of the Revolution: Restoration and Cooperation," 163–93.

5. William S. Stafford, *Domesticating the Clergy: The Inception of the Reformation in Strasbourg 1522–1524*, Dissertation Series 17 (Missoula, MN: Scholars Press, 1976).

6. Schorn-Schütte, *Evangelische Geistlichkeit in der Frühneuzeit: Deren Anteil an der Entfa/tung frühmoderner Staatlichkeit und Gesellschaft* (Gütersloh: Gütersloher Verlagshaus, 1996), especially chap. 2, "Soziale Herkunft und Verflechtung," 84–151. Of interest is the way in which pastors' wives served as a conduit into higher rank.

7. Karlstadt, *Wjder die alte vnd newe Papistische Messen* (1524), a pamphlet of four leaves; Steven Ozment, *The Reformation in the Cities: The Appeal of Protestantism to Sixteenth-Century Germany and Switzerland* (New Haven, CT: Yale University Press, 1975), 164–66.

8. R. W. Scribner, "Anticlericalism and the Reformation in Germany," in *Popular Culture and Popular Movements in Reformation Germany* (London: Hambledon Press, 1987), 243–56, especially 255–56.

9. See Heinz Schilling, "'History of Crime' or 'History of Sin'?—Some Reflections on the Social History of Early Modern Church Discipline," in *Politics and Society in Reformation Europe: Essays for Sir Geoffrey Elton on His Sixty-Fifth Birthday*, ed. E. I. Kouri and Tom Scott (London: St. Martin's, 1987), 239–310.

10. Emil Sehling, *Die evangelischen Kirchenordnungen des XVI. Jahrhunderts*, approximately 16 vols. (various cities, various publishers, 1902–77, and now being brought to completion under the Akademie der Wissenschaften in Heidelberg), here (Leipzig: O. R. Reisland, 1902), 1: 223; hereafter *KOO*.

11. Sehling, *KOO*, 1: 223.

12. Sehling, *KOO*, 1: 225.

13. Sehling, *KOO*, 1: 240–41.

14. Karl Pallas, *Die Registraturen der Kirchenvisitationen im ehemals sächsischen Kurkreise*, 7 vols. (Halle: O. Hendel, 1906–18), 4: 540, parish of Beyern.

15. Sehling, *KOO*, 1: 244.

16. Sehling, *KOO*, 1: 421–22, also 432–33.

17. Medieval *curés* had the right to do this in theory, but they seldom, if ever, did so.

18. *Chur Fürstliche Brandenburgische Im Hertzogthum Magdeburg Publicirte Kirchen Ordnung* (Halle/Saxony: Christoph Salfelden, 1685), 131.

19. Another fine example, from the seventeenth century, is *Herrn Johann Ernsts, Herrn Adolph Wilhelms, Herrn Johann Georgens und Herrn Bernhards Gebrüderer, Herzogen zu Sachsen, Jülich, Cleve und Bergen, Land-Grafen in Thüringen, Marck-Grafen zu Meissen . . . Verbesserte Kirchen-Ordnung . . .* (Weimar: Eylikers Witben, 1664), 502–22, entitled "'Formul del Kirchen-busse, wegen offenbarer Gottlosigkeit, Lästerung und Sacraments-Verachtung." Additional rituals are provided for particular

categories of sin, 522–52, such as "Formul der Abbitte wegen verübtes Todschlages," "Formul, wegen Wuchers und Betrugs," and "Formul der Abkündigung," for a couple who had sex before their wedding ceremony.

20. Hessisches Hauptstaatsarchiv Wiesbaden, Abt. 131, Nr. Xa, 1, 52. *Lastersteine* were carved or painted stones mounted on a metal neck-ring that in many parts of Germany specifically women donned and displayed as they walked around the marketplace as a penalty for fighting among themselves or being persistent "scolds." It is likely that this prescription is made for female transgressors only.

21. Sehling, *KOO*, vol. 2 (Leipzig: O. R. Reisland, 1904), 38–40.

22. See n. 19.

23. Sehling, *KOO*, vol. 15 (Tübingen: J. C. B. Mohr [Paul Siebeck], 1977), 574.

24. Sehling, *KOO*, 15: 666–67. On the County of Hohenlohe and the religious and disciplinary quest there, see Thomas Robisheaux, *Rural Society and the Search for Order in Early Modern Germany* (New York: Cambridge University Press, 1989).

25. *Herrn Johann Ernsts . . .*, 165–66. See n. 19 above.

26. Landeskirchenarchiv Braunschweig, V1937, "Berichte über Pfarrer and Kirchengemeinden auf die Umfragen von 1638 and 1648," fol. 3r. See Terence McIntosh, "Confessionalization and the Campaign against Prenuptial Coitus in Sixteenth-Century Germany," in *Confessionalization in Europe, 1555–1700: Essays in Honor and Memory of Bodo Nischan*, ed. John M. Headley, Hans J. Hillerbrand, and Anthony J. Papalas (Aldershot, UK: Ashgate, 2004), 155–74.

27. Pallas, *Registraturen,* 3: 351.

28. Susan C. Karant-Nunn, "Neoclericalism and Anticlericalism in Saxony, 1555–1675," *Journal of Interdisciplinary History* 24 (1994): 615–35, especially 624.

29. Pallas, *Registraturen,* 4: 102.

30. Sehling, *KOO*, 15: 421–24.

31. Sehling, *KOO*, vol. 14 (Tübingen: J. C. B. Mohr [Paul Siebeck], 1969), 426.

32. See, for example, *Gebete und andere Kirchen-Dienste, für die Pfarrer des Fürstenthumbs Anhalt, Cöthenischen Theils: Aus ihrer üblichen gemeinen Kirchen-Ordnung ausgezogen, und auf sie insonderheit gerichtet* (Cöthen: n.p., 1699), 155–67, an oath of fifteen points for every new clergyman to take. The oath begins, "Ich Endesbenanter, als nunmehr ein ordentlich beruffener Diener der Kirchen GOttes [*sic*] in diesem Fürstenthume Anhalt, etc. Gelobe an, und Verspreche mit Handgegebener Treue, an eines geschworenen leiblichen Eydes statt nachfolgende Puncte, die ich mit gutemm bedachte gelesen und erwogen, auch freywillig mil eigenen Händen unterschrieben habe, stet und fest zu halten."

33. See Volker Press, *Calvinismus und Territorialstaat: Regierung und Zentra/behörden der Kurpfa/z 1559–1619,* Kieler historische Studien 7 (Stuttgart: Ernst Klett Verlag, 1970), esp. 245–54; Paul Münch, "Kirchenzucht und Nachbarschaft: Zur sozialen Problematik des calvinistischen Seniorats um 1600," in *Kirche und Visitation: Beiträge zur Erforschung des frühneuzeitlichen Visitationwesens in Europe,* ed. Ernst Walter Zeeden and Peter Thaddäus Lang (Stuttgart: Klett-Cotta, 1984), 216–48; and Heinz Schilling, "Sündenzucht und Frühneuzeitliche Sozialdisziplinierung: Die calvinistische presbyteriale Kirchenzucht in Emden vom 16. bis 18. Jahrhundert," in *Stände und Gesellschaft im Alten Reich,* ed. Georg Schmidt (Stuttgart: Franz Steiner Verlag Wiesbaden, 1989), 265–302.

34. Raymond A. Mentzer, "Masculinity and the Reformation in France" (paper presented at the meetings of the Sixteenth Century Studies Conference and the Society for Reformation Research, Pittsburgh, October 2003).

35. Hessisches Hauptstaatsarchiv Wiesbaden, Abt. 171, Nr. D245, 140, village of Nieder Hadamer.

36. Münch, "Kirchenzucht und Nachbarschaft," especially 217–22, 242–44, 247. At 222, n. 24, Münch argues against Heinz Schilling's critique. Cf. Heinz Schilling and H. Sydow, "Calvinistische Presbyterien in Städten der Frühneuzeit: Eine kirchliche Alternativform zur bürgerlichen Repräsentation?" in *Städtische Führungsgruppen und Gemeinde in der werdenden Neuzeit*, ed. Wilfried Ehbrecht (Vienna: Böhlau, 1980), 385–444, especially 422, n. 149. See also by Münch, "Volkskultur in Calvinismus: Zu Theorie und Praxis der 'reformatio vitae' während der 'Zweiten Reformation,'" in *Die reformierte Konfessionalisierung in Deutschland: Das Problem der "Zweiten Reformation,"* ed. Heinz Schilling (Gütersloh: Mohn, 1986), 291–307.

37. "Der große Unterschied und seine Folgen: Zum Problem der Kirchenzucht als Unterscheidungskriterium zwischen lutherischer und reformierter Konfession," in *Krisenbewußtsein und Krisenbewältigung in der Frühen Neuzeit—Crisis in Early Modern Europe: Festschrift für Hans-Christoph Rublack*, ed. Monika Hagenmaier and Sabine Holtz (Frankfurt/Main and Berlin: Peter Lang, 1992), 197–214. Schnabel-Schule concludes that the sphere of practice differed notably from that of theology and other theory, which up till the present has informed our views of the distinctions between confessional disciplinary practices (214).

38. Paul Münch, *Zucht und Ordnung: Reformierte Kirchenverfassungen im 16. und 17. Jahrhundert* (Stuttgart: Klett-Cotta, 1978), 54, 69–71. Münch suspects that some of the structural similarities to Calvinism within Lutheran church polity at midcentury facilitated the transition to the Reformed confession.

39. For a very detailed study of the relations between state and local government and their evolution, see André Holenstein, *"Gute Policey" und Lokale Gesellschaft im Staat des Ancien Régime: Das Fallbeispiel der Markgrafschaft Baden(-Durlach)*, 2 vols., Frühneuzeit-Forschungen 9 (n.p.: Bibliotheca Academica Verlag, 2003), which concentrates, however, on the eighteenth century.

40. Pallas, *Registraturen*, 2: 153.

41. Hessisches Hauptstaatsarchiv Wiesbaden, Abt. 171, Nr. Z1975, 29.

42. Evangelisches Landeskirchliches Archiv Stuttgart, A 1, Nr. 1, 1586, 47.

43. Pallas, *Registraturen*, 5: xi, for a brief list of such acts.

44. "Visitation und geistliche Sachen Vom 23. Augusti des 1580tn jahrs, biß uff den 30. July des 1584. Jahrs," Thüringisches Staatsarchiv Gotha, Oberkonsistorium Generalia, Loc. 19, Nr. 6.

45. Sehling, "Ordnung der öffentlichen Busse," in *KOO*, 2: 38.

46. Gerd Schwerhoff, "Starke Worte: Blasphemie als theatralische Inszenierung von Männlichkeit an der Wende vom Mittelalter zur Frühen Neuzeit," in *Hausväter, Priester, Kastraten: Zur Konstruktion von Männlichkeit in Spätmittelalter und Früher Neuzeit*, ed. Martin Dinges (Göttingen: Vandenhoeck & Ruprecht, 1998), 237–63.

47. B. Ann Tlusty, *Bacchus and Civic Order: The Culture of Drink in Early Modern Germany* (Charlottesville: University of Virginia Press, 2001).

48. Münch, *Zucht und Ordnung*, 114. Cf. Gerhard Menk, "Die Konfessionspolitik des Landgrafen Moritz," in *Landgraf Moritz der Gelehrte: Ein Kalvinist zwischen Politik und Wissenschaft*, Beiträge zur hessischen Geschichte 15, ed. Gerhard Menk (Marburg an der Lahn: Trautvetter und Fischer Nachfolger, 2000), 95–138, on this point 114.

49. Pallas, *Registraturen*, 4: 118.

50. Scribner, "Sozialkontrolle und die Möglichkeit einer städtischen Reformation," in *Stadt und Kirche im 16. Jahrhundert*. Schriften des Vereins für Reformationsgeschichte 190, ed. Bernd Moeller (Gütersloh: Gütersloher Verlagshaus Gerd Mohn, 1978), 58–59. See n. 3.

51. Please note that I am confining this chapter to religious and social mentalities.

52. Scribner, "Anticlericalism and the Reformation," 256, where he lays out three successive phases of anticlericalism covering most of the sixteenth century: 1480–1520, 1520–1550, and 1550–1580, the last "accompanied by the rise of a neo-clericalism and a corresponding anticlericalism." Cf. Leonhard von Muralt, "Stadtgemeinde und Reformation in der Schweiz," *Zeitschrift für schweizerische Geschichte* 10 (1930), 350–51, 354; Wilhelm Maurer, "Die Entstehung des Landeskirchentums in der Reformation," in *Staat und Kirche im Wandel der Jahrhunderte*, ed. Walther Peter Fuchs (Stuttgart: Kohlhammer, 1966), 69–78. Heinrich Richard Schmidt, *Dorf und Religion: Reformierte Sittenzucht in Berner Landgemeinden der Frühen Neuzeit* (Stuttgart: Gustav Fischer Verlag, 1995), deals mainly with the eighteenth century and, owing to a lack of records, not at all with the period before 1570. A brief section, "Die Rolle der Pfarrer" (149–56), does not take up the place of clergymen within the community.

13

Embodying the Middle Ages, Advancing Modernity

Religious Women in Sixteenth- and
Seventeenth-Century Europe and Beyond

Ulrike Strasser

IN THE GRAND RECITS THAT NARRATE THE TRANSITION from the early modern to the modern period, religious women have been marginal characters at best. Privileging the emergence of secular institutions and the experience of men, these paradigmatic narratives left little room for women dedicated to communal religious life and thus relegated them to the medieval past that modernizing societies had to leave behind. For example, Jacob Burckhardt's tale of the rise of the modern individual was set against the foil of a medieval world of communal commitments and religious belief of which the monastic life seemed a prime example. It took as its red thread the vision of the well-educated male citizen. A religious woman was doubly excluded in this scheme, on account of gender as well as vocation. Though scholars have considerably refined Burckhardt's account in recent decades, their reformulations have not led them to integrate systematically the history of Catholic women religious and the newer history of the self.[1]

Literature on the state has proven equally inhospitable to religious women. In its most Rankean variants, this literature started with modern understandings of what constituted a political institution and worked its way backward in search of premodern precursors. Given the profoundly secular and male-dominated nature of modern institutions, this analytical move diverted scholarly attention away from religious institutions and women's political participation. Yet women's "legitimate exercise of rule," including that of abbesses, was well known and widely respected throughout the ancien régime, part and parcel of a world with multiple sites of public power and decentralized, interlocking networks of political rule. Women were merely excluded from the evolving bureaucratic forms of government associated with territorial centralization.[2]

More recent political histories have taken a broader view and pointed to alternate political traditions. Anthony Black famously recovered the foundational importance of political models generated within guild associations for the political history of the West; these corporate political templates thrived alongside and in competition with those of civil society.[3] Others have revisited the scholarly terrain of the Protestant Reformation to consider political paths not taken, such as alternate communal and republican visions, including those most revolutionary views of the "common man."[4]

Yet although Black's approach extended the analysis of political modernization to associational structures beyond the state's bureaucratic apparatus, he focused on an association that linked masculinity and political participation to the detriment of women.[5] Similarly, Reformation scholarship, as it concerned itself with the "common man" and his small-scale communities as political laboratories, remained tethered to a vision of the political as a male domain without problematizing its constitutive partiality.[6] In addition, the Protestant orientation of this literature has not lent itself to making Catholic religious women and their political roles visible other than as obstructionist to Protestant political visions.

This points to the abiding presence of Protestant-centered or Weberian categories even in more recent scholarship. Max Weber's thesis linking Protestantism with rationalization and modernization in the West has cast a long shadow indeed. In the Weberian view, Protestantism propelled the inhabitants of the medieval world of magic and ritual into the modern universe of reason, hard work, and voluntary surrender to state bureaucracies. Somewhat ironically, Protestantism here has its greatest impact in its least religious guise—as a system of belief that advances secularization or, differently put, the overcoming of religion itself. Catholicism, by contrast, epitomizes the backwardness of religious belief, with monastic rituals and religious virgins embodying Catholicism's seemingly most outdated features.[7]

In the last decades, critical reappraisal of the Weber thesis among historians has made much headway. Documenting the parallel nature of sociopolitical change in territories of all confessional stripes, Heinz Schilling and Wolfgang Reinhard have made the case that each religious confession contained the same transformative force, encapsulated in its respective creed and unleashed through collision with the centralizing state. During a first phase of "sacralization," religion is harnessed to politics. During a second phase of "secularization," religion is marginalized by a state gaining in strength and sovereignty.[8]

Although confessionalization theory grants Catholics their own modernization narrative, Catholic religious women have made no more than occasional cameo appearances. A conceptual obstacle obstructs their permanent presence. While the confessionialization paradigm successfully corrects the confessional biases of older Weberian accounts, its proponents retain the residual Weberian framework of progressive rationalization and secularization in which religion operates as a tool of governmental expansion. This framework implicitly hinges on a Protestant definition of religion as based on the primacy of belief. As such, it poses a serious definitional impediment to recognizing the role of religious women—whose lives pivoted on the performance of rituals—in the making of modern rule and modern subjects.

This chapter works toward such recognition. Drawing on select recent literature that documents the presence of female religious communities in key areas of the modernization process, it first locates women religious in the story of the state for three related phenomena: the attempted dissolution of female convents in Protestant areas, the Catholic drive toward enclosure and the emergence of new religious orders following the Council of Trent, and women's involvement in the burgeoning new orders whose evangelization efforts extended to the New World. Even if we judge their activities by traditional parameters, we find that religious women were active participants in processes of political centralization in Europe and beyond. A brief concluding section of the chapter attempts to situate women religious in histories of the self. Rather than assume that religious women epitomize the premodern collective from which the modern individual had to wrest *himself* away, it considers the subjectivity of religious women as an alternative formation of the modern self that emerged alongside the humanist-liberal individual.

It is important to note that the evidence and arguments presented in this chapter are intended less to contradict than complement and complicate the extensive feminist literature on modernization's patriarchal structures and their undeniably disadvantageous effects on women's lives. Above all, this scholarship has highlighted the progressive control of women's sexuality and reproductive capacity within publicly controlled patriarchal marriages.[9] While this is surely one of modernization's most prominent features, the scholarly focus on this aspect runs the risk of obscuring further the experience of single women and religious virgins as well as the importance of the all-female institution of the convent to the modernization project. This chapter calls attention to this other history of women and modernization.

Holy Households and Protestant Nunneries: Religious Women and Political Centralization under Protestantism

As monastic establishments and female institutions, women's convents were inevitably swept up in the process of political centralization in Protestant lands. Their communities instantaneously were rendered spiritually obsolete once reforming authorities shifted the social site of sacrality away from continent clerics to the procreative patriarchal family, severing traditional ties between sacredness, sexuality, and the body social. Protestant reformers sought to abolish the dual structure of ecclesiastical and temporal authority and rebuild public order on one secular yet sacralized system of patriarchal households. As female-headed households whose inhabitants were allied with one another in a spiritual kinship that placed them beyond the control of their biological male kin, convents seemingly flouted the Protestant blueprint for a new society.[10]

All of this would suggest that the political role of convents in Protestant polities consisted of giving way to other, "more modern" political formations. But while convents did suffer dissolution in many places and their inhabitants and assets were inserted into the Protestant sociopolitical grid, a different history of convents in Protestant lands has begun to surface. Most notably, a number of German-speaking areas witnessed the Protestant reform rather than abolition of convents and even the foundation of new female religious communities, leaving us with the historical oxymoron of a "Protestant nunnery." The existence of these houses sheds light on the continuing sociopolitical importance of religious women's communities in modernizing Protestant polities.

Convents offered an institutional solution to a host of social problems that remained acute in Protestant polities. While Protestant critics negated the spiritual value of convents, they could ill afford to ignore altogether their social purposes, such as offering an honorable setting for unmarried women and enabling patrimonial strategizing. This became immediately apparent when Protestants attempted to close these houses and confronted the problem of accommodating ex-nuns. Unlike ex-monks, who could find professional niches as scholars, teachers, or even Protestant pastors, ex-nuns had limited options: marriage and motherhood. Not only did these prospects hold little appeal for many women religious, the chances of actualizing them were in fact limited for older nuns or those living in areas with unfavorable demographics.[11]

From the very beginning, as Amy Leonard has shown, Protestant pamphleteers went to great lengths to debate the utility of convents, with some advocating reform instead of dissolution. Although all convent critics were in agreement that women's religious houses were useless from a spiritual point of view, many critics advocated maintaining convents in modified form and redirecting their work toward socially useful goals.[12] Martin Luther and Philip Melanchthon both argued that convents, prior to appropriation by papists, had been schools and therefore should be returned to their original purpose.[13]

Reform, for example, prevailed over dissolution in the case of Strasbourg's Dominican nuns. Although one of the three convents was shut down eventually in 1592 as the result of a scandal, the other two survived long enough for Catholic France to take over the city in 1681 and remained intact until 1789. Aside from the nuns' determined resistance and skillful maneuvering of local and even imperial power politics, the key to the convents' success lay in a willingness to perform services in support of the new public order, which earned the approval of magistrates and the local elite, including avowed Protestant families. Although pursuing a not-so-hidden Catholic agenda, the sisters made themselves useful to the Protestant civic community by teaching Christian virtues and domestic skills, simultaneously guarding women's honor and preparing them for marriage. The convents' tangible social contributions kept overriding doctrinal concerns harbored by the city fathers, who again and again accommodated the nuns while Lutheran clergy repeatedly kept pushing for the abolition of these female houses.[14]

Social usefulness also accounts for the survival of female religious communities in the territory of Nassau. Technically *Damenstifte* rather than convents, these religious houses did not require permanent vows, renunciation of property, or a lifelong commitment. However, they imposed the same spiritual labors upon their members as those performed by nuns and contemporaries often referred to them as *cloisters*. During the sixteenth and seventeenth centuries, Nassau's Lutheran and Calvinist princes passed a series of "cloister ordinances" that capitalized on these communities' potential to meet sociopolitical needs while reshaping their spirituality along Protestant lines.[15] They turned some *Damenstifte* into hospitals for the sick, old, or otherwise needy. Other communities became schools that prepared young women for their roles as bona fide Protestant wives and mothers.[16]

Tellingly, what had been a central social function of the convents under Catholicism, to provide a safe haven for unmarried daughters and help consolidate familial property, was taken up under Protestantism but reworked to fit a new social context that privileged matrimony. The reformed communities served as affordable and honorable way stations for women while their parents looked for a proper match. Should the parents succeed, the woman left the house, received back significant parts of her entry fee, and lay claim to her share of the parental inheritance. Alternatively, if no adequate spouse was found, she stayed in the convent until her death, upon which the community was entitled to collect a share of her inheritance.[17] Reformed institutions thus aided parents in multiple fashion: shaping daughters into desirable marriage partners, allowing for flexible patrimonial strategizing, and guarding the virginity of female offspring in the meantime.

The reformed *Damenstift* was so successful that it actually became a Protestant institutional prototype. While some female inmates probably viewed these institutions as a vehicle for living a Catholic life of the cloister in a

Protestant context, governing authorities soon looked upon these houses as essentially Protestant institutions and began establishing new *Damenstifte* in places that did not have Catholic convents to reform, such as Franken or Kraichgau.[18]

This emerging history of convents simultaneously challenges and supports the premises of the confessionalization paradigm. It provides additional fuel to the ongoing debate over the effectiveness of the alliance between church and state in imposing religious orthodoxy, and the extent to which pressure from below shaped the course of confessionalization in different regions of the highly particularized Empire.[19] To be sure, the story of Protestant convents suggests that the hardening of creeds and the alliances of religious leaders and centralizing authorities did not inevitably result in the emergence of distinct and intolerant confessional cultures. Strasbourg's Lutheran magistrate quite readily adapted or neglected evangelical doctrine when it came to finding a place for the city's Catholic nuns in a reconfigured Christian commonwealth, and tacitly tolerated vestiges of Catholic practice in the convents, while the convents accepted their new status as civic institutions and cooperated with the Protestant council.[20] Confessional hybridity also characterized female convents that survived under Protestantism elsewhere. Catholic, Lutheran, and Calvinist women, for example, lived under one roof in the *Damenstifte* in Herdecke, Neuenheerse, and Schildesche.[21]

The abiding importance of convents in Protestant lands indicates that it is too simple to view women's religious houses as mere obstacles to Protestant political modernization. Strasbourg's Lutheran magistrate, albeit somewhat flexible with regard to religious practices inside the convents, actively directed the sisters' external mission toward desirable social and political goals. In so doing, the city fathers "made the convents 'useful' in the full Weberian sense by binding them to the citizens and controlling them."[22] Far from being a relic of a moribund medieval past, the communities moved to the center of early modern Protestant polity building.

Along analogous lines, *Damenstifte* advanced to the forefront of political centralization in Protestant Nassau. While they had been subject to an ecclesiastical superior prior to the Reformation and closely allied with the lower nobility whose daughters staffed the convents, the *Stifte* became integrated into the territory's increasingly centralized institutional structure and directly subordinated to the *Landesherren* (rulers of the land). Nassau's princes pushed out the lower nobility and broadened the communities' constituency to Protestant *Landeskinder* (children of the land). Where purity of blood had been a prerequisite for acceptance, purity of faith and loyalty toward state authorities determined admission after the Reformation.[23] Moreover, reformed female religious houses aided in the formation of a Protestant subject population in Nassau. A primary purpose was to inculcate Protestant values into young women and help produce a reliable female elite for the territory. Convent curricula emphasized not just religious doctrine but also the skills of a Protestant *Hausmutter* (mother of the household) and obedience toward parents, preachers, and state authorities.[24]

Convents, in other words, could be virtual instruments of Protestant confessionalization and modernization. This was especially true of the imperial abbeys and canoness houses that turned Protestant in the Holy Roman Empire, such as Gernrode or Quedlinburg, whose fascinating story Merry Wiesner has unearthed. Their abbesses' unique position as religious leaders–cum–territorial lords allowed them to propagate Protestantism most effectively in their lands.[25] Beyond their spiritual and administrative authority inside the convent, imperial abbesses had the power to appoint clergy and oversee the cure of the souls in parishes, and they also enjoyed feudal and judicial authority in the villages on the abbey lands.[26]

In sum, convents played a crucial role in the restructuring of political life during the Reformation in many areas of the particularized German Empire; further research is needed to assess the exact extent of this phenomenon. Although in their Catholic incarnation these religious houses conflicted with the Protestant vision of a godly society in crucial respects, their abolition was not always easy to effect, nor was it always desirable to Protestant authorities. Convents had traditionally fulfilled a multiplicity of roles as places of spiritual devotion, centers of cultures, and sites of patrimonial as well as political strategizing. While Protestants negated the spiritual value of these Catholic institutions, they could not gainsay the convents' importance in solving sociopolitical problems that also beset their own polities. As a result, models of transforming female convents into Protestant institutions developed quickly in various parts of the empire. These reformed institutions, far from being merely a transitory phenomenon of the Reformation period and extraneous to the new Protestant sociopolitical order, helped form the institutional infrastructure on which this order could flourish in the centuries to come.

Serving God and Government:
Religious Virgins, State Formation, and Tridentine Reform

In facing the Protestant challenge, Catholics defended the superiority of virginity to marriage and asserted the legitimacy and importance of monastic institutions. They outlined reforms at the Council of Trent that aimed at reinvigorating and strengthening the spiritual role of monastic houses at the expense of their social purposes. The council decreed more regulations for nuns than monks, though, and put a premium on reining in the conduct of women religious. Tridentine reforms for female convents stood on two main pillars: first, intensified male supervision, and second, the requirement of strict enclosure.[27]

It is tempting to see this gender-specific program of mandatory supervision and sequestration as evidence of a conservative, patriarchal backlash that moved along a temporal axis that stretched backward into the Middle Ages. Indeed an argument can be made that these ecclesiastical policies were at least somewhat reactive to the quest for greater independence that many women religious had undertaken so successfully in the late Middle Ages.[28] Yet a growing body of literature places women religious squarely at the center of early modern *political* rather than religious history and indicates that female convents were also present in key areas of Weberian-style modernization in Catholic polities.

Gabriella Zarri, for example, has made the case that Tridentine monastic reforms belong within a context of European-wide rationalization. Like the reform measures that contemporary secular governments pursued on all sociopolitical levels, ecclesiastical reforms were predicated on attempts to impose a single institutional norm on diverse institutions and thereby improve governmental efficiency. As nuns implemented Trent's institutional reforms in their communities, Zarri's work suggests, religious women were invariably also advancing this large-scale project of centralization. The monastic reforms resulted in a reduction of the influence that kin and patronage networks exercised on female religious communities and, correspondingly, a heightened dependence of nuns on clerics and ecclesiastical structures.[29] Although these prospects prompted resistance to Tridentine reforms among many nuns, it inspired others to embrace them, most famously Teresa of Avila, who sought enclosure for its promise of freedom from patronage networks.[30] Even if the supporters of convent reform had spiritual goals, the reforms had political effects and furthered the institutional homogenization under way in society at large.

These ecclesiastical reform efforts, like their secular counterparts, furthermore reflect the constitutive function of gender in reorganizing politics along more modern lines. One encounters the same attempt in early modern church and society to use the male-headed household as the smallest building block of centralized government. Because governing authorities still lacked the power to exert effective social control on the lowest social level, they passed legal measures to strengthen the position of male heads of household vis-à-vis women, children, and servants, and hold men publicly accountable for their household community. In this manner, the regulatory powers of household governance could be harnessed to the goals of a central administration.[31]

Tridentine monastic reforms, with their gender-specific biases and particular stipulations, mirrored secular reform measures. Elizabeth Rapley has noted that the Council of Trent pushed radically different institutional models for male and female monastic reform. Whereas the formation of congregations and centralization drove male monastic reform, female religious communities were forbidden to form congregational affiliations and were forced into subordination to male superiors.[32] Tridentine monastic reforms, in other words, tried to re-create nunneries in the image of male-headed households, with the added component of confinement. Just as secular heads of households disciplined and represented their wives and daughters, male ecclesiastics would be held accountable for their female charges' behavior. In advancing a uniform yet gender-specific institutional norm for monastic houses, the ecclesiastical reforms paralleled and reinforced institutional developments in early modern society at large.[33]

Jutta Sperling's study of late Renaissance Venice further illuminates the connection between convent reform and governmental evolution. She traces how the enclosure of women facilitated the Venetian state's gaining governmental autonomy from other social groups and political rivals. Starting in 1450 an increasing number of Venetian patricians compelled their daughters to take the veil. By the seventeenth century a patrician woman was more likely to become a bride of Christ than marry a man of her social class. These forced monachizations enabled Venice's ruling class to maintain "purity of blood" and monopoly on the republic's institutions.[34]

During the sixteenth century Venice's patriciate refashioned itself from a mercantile class into an endogamous caste of landowning nobles, who literally embodied the republic's government. This process was predicated on the competitive exchange of women. Venetian patricians embraced agnatic inheritance rules, granting daughters only dowries while excluding them from the patrimony. Whereas sons were allowed to marry downward (if the dowry warranted it), daughters could not pass titles on to commoners and had to marry upward. Should a daughter's dowry prove either too high or too low to find a proper match, patrician patriarchs preferred to withdraw her from the exchange through monachization. Forced vocations, Sperling concludes, resulted from a systemic problem: agnatic inheritance rules coupled with class endogamy and mandatory upward female social mobility produced a steady surplus of daughters. Women who could not be offered as brides best aided social reproduction by forgoing sexual reproduction altogether.

Sperling reads the coerced enclosure of virginal women as a form of conspicuous destruction of resources that could not be exchanged. Because brides of Christ both symbolized and embodied the intact body politic, their physical integrity had to be protected with the strongest means. Strict cloister bolstered this agenda by equipping upper-class virgins with an "additional hymen." By imposing enclosure on female convents, the Venetian state could be sure of its offspring's purity and the women's status as perfect objects of spectacular sacrificial waste.[35]

This type of analysis foregrounds the familiar and political pressures that pushed women toward life in a convent. But an emphasis on structural constraints should not let us ignore the complex motivations that made the convent a desirable place, including pious impulses that drove women to obey their parents or to seek out the religious life of their own accord. Only if we bury these religious motivations and experiences within analytical frameworks that view religion as epiphenomenal and equate agency with autonomy do early modern Venetian nuns seem to mere victims of a secular logic of family and state rather than religious agents in their own right.[36]

Venice's cloistered nuns also found other ways to be actively involved in public life. Mary Laven has found that many an office appointment in the Venetian Republic was first decided in the convent parlor, among the female members of the ruling class. Venice's nuns were effective lobbyists and influential political pundits who could be more accessible than their uncloistered male counterparts. In this light, Laven has proposed to consider convent parlors as part of a public sphere that exceeds Habermasian boundaries.[37]

A tight nexus between state formation and female religious communities also existed in Bavaria, the first absolutist state in the German Empire. Maximilian I turned the enclosure of women's convents into an occasion for bringing ecclesiastical geography in line with more recent political geographies, a typical feature of state building all over Europe.[38] He invited a particularly ascetic group of Franciscans from Italy to implement Tridentine reforms and authorized them to dislodge their less collaborative predecessors and found a new Franciscan province in Bavaria. The geographical boundaries of this new institutional entity, in revealing contrast to those of the former province, were the exact same as Bavaria's political boundaries.[39]

If political considerations led Bavaria's rulers to place some religious women under lock and key, *raison d'état* also motivated their recruitment of the unenclosed English Ladies under the leadership of Mary Ward. Ward's Institute is a prime example of the new orders that emerged after Trent. As women heeded the Tridentine call for Catholic renewal, they attempted to forge an active female apostolate of teaching and social service. It has been noted that these new orders most directly met the social needs of the time.[40] Here we might add that that they also met the interest of the modernizing state, in this instance the development of state-sponsored education. Just as Bavaria's state authorities relied upon the Jesuits to educate boys in Catholic citizenship, they resorted to Ward's "Jesuitesses" to train girls as good Catholic citizens, wives, or nuns.

This explains why the Bavarian state supported Ward's educational enterprise even after the papacy outlawed the "Jesuitesses" in 1631 because of their persistent refusal of Tridentine enclosure. Maximilian I procured an exemption from the papacy for the community of English Ladies in his capital. The only community to survive dissolution, the Munich house soon turned into the hub of a new and expanding Institute of English Ladies, launching schools in Bavaria and other European cities and gaining papal recognition as a pious institute in the early eighteenth century.[41]

A parallel story can be told about the Daughters of Charity in France and their relationship to the center of power. In this instance, as Susan Dinan has shown, the work of religious women appealed to a state bent on disciplining the poor and lazy. Like the English Ladies, the French Daughters of Charity strove to bypass Trent's enclosure requirement for all women religious, but they chose care of the sick and poor as their primary mission. Well aware that this project would attract ecclesiastical criticism, the founding team of Louise de Marillac and Vincent de Paul worked to portray the community as a secular confraternity that did not aspire to the status of a religious order. More important, the two founders lobbied for and obtained financial and political support from the French court of Louis XIII.[42]

The alliance between the Daughters of Charity and the French court was equally beneficial from the central authority's point of view. Socioeconomic and environmental crises of the sixteenth and seventeenth centuries had driven up the numbers of the vagabond poor, to the dismay of state authorities in France and elsewhere. The French state tried to control the swelling ranks of the poor through a discriminatory form of relief that rewarded only the "deserving poor" while putting the "undeserving" to work. The state welcomed the help of private institutions like the Daughters of Charity in regulating the poor and administering insane asylums and orphanages.[43] Their work and its political uses mirrored that of other active congregations expanding in France at the time, the teachers, nurses, and social workers, whose fortunes Rapley has traced.[44]

More recently, Rapley has shown that cloistered religious women contributed to the French state's political projects. Enclosed teaching nuns helped acculturate and alphabetize girls in the most remote regions of France. Denouncing local customs and local dialects, nuns were forceful evangelizers of bourgeois culture and the French language. They instructed young women in the idiom of the state.[45] Furthermore, by their very nature, cloistered communities provided authorities with secure sites of detainment. French kings increasingly used women's cloisters to imprison obstreperous Protestants, parents boarded willful offspring, and husbands used them to discipline unruly wives. The "age of confinement" in no small part depended upon the availability of enclosed female convents.[46]

In sum, virginal religious women, embodiments of Catholicism's most outdated and otherworldly features from a Weberian viewpoint, clearly advanced the western European modernizing project of political centralization. Convents, some more voluntarily than others, let themselves be drawn into the processes of institutional streamlining that accompanied the formation of modern government. Their inmates served the reproduction of the political elite by forgoing sexual reproduction and endowing state power with the aura of the sacred. Religious virgins schooled young women in the type of citizenship political authorities found desirable, offered much-needed social services to the sick and poor, and helped inculcate an ethics of work and discipline among populations viewed as problematic by the state.

Catholicism Goes Abroad:
Religious Virgins and Colonial Empire Building

While many religious virgins actively aided political centralization in Europe, others joined the great missionary adventures of their time and relocated to the Americas to spread the faith. Whatever their individual motivations might have been, women religious played an undeniably political role abroad, where they advanced European expansion and acted as virtual cocreators of colonial rule.

In *Colonial Habits*, Kathryn Burns gives a fascinating account of how Cuzco's convents served Spanish empire building in Peru. Shortly after military conquest, these institutions helped solidify Spanish hegemony by raising *mestizas*. The women were destined to become either missionaries for the evangelization of the Andes or culturally Spanish women who accepted Spanish patriarchal rule and made suitable wives for the conquerors. Tellingly, the Spanish did not place the same value on acculturation of *mestizos*, since they, as men with indigenous ties, were likely to lay rival claims to the colonial patrimony and challenge Spanish hegemony.[47]

With the evolution of colonial society and the growth of a *criolla* population, this function of the convents gradually receded, but religious communities soon contributed to the stability of colonial rule in another and more long-term manner: They supplied much-needed credit for the local economy. Loans and credit were of paramount importance to the development of regional economies and to the organization of social relations in the chronically cash-stripped Spanish American Empire.

The nuns of Cuzco utilized the influx of dowry payments such as cash, liens, or real estate to generate income by means of the so-called *censo al quittar*. This contractual agreement circumvented the ecclesiastical prohibition against usury, as it authorized the nuns to "purchase" annual pensions or interest rates from another party with a much larger amount of money, in effect masking the act of lending as an act of acquisition. The loans of Cuzco's cloistered virgins supported key sectors of the colonial economy, helped make the fortunes of elite families, and cemented their political dominance in the colonies. As a result, families had a vested interest in placing their daughters into Cuzco's convents and having a say over the apportioning of loans to the local community. The power of *criollos* in local government grew parallel to the power of *criolla* nuns inside Cuzco's convents; daughters of the Andean elite in turn were barred from the highest convent offices. By the seventeenth century, the nuns of Cuzco were the primary ecclesiastical lender for the propertied elite, in particular its white members.[48]

A similar picture presents itself in colonial Mexico, where convents as lending agencies also played a central role for the functioning of the economy.[49] More generally speaking, female religious communities were founded in New Spain for the same purposes for which they were founded in Europe, but also for reasons unique to the colonial context. Leaving aside the undeniably strong religious motivations behind these foundations, these institutions, like their Old World counterparts, addressed pressing economic and social needs. Some housed the unmarriageable daughters of the emerging colonial elite or otherwise needy female members of the founding families. Other convents accommodated poor orphans, women without sufficient dowry money, or women simply deemed in danger of falling into ill repute. Yet another group served a broader public through educating girls and young women.[50]

Convents in New Spain, however, also represented an institutional response to the distinct social and racial issues that haunted their colonial sponsors. Who could be the wives of the European conquistadores? Was it possible to transform indigenous women into sexually and spiritually pure Christians? And what would happen to the growing numbers of illegitimate offspring and abandoned orphans from unions of Spanish men and indigenous women? Convents turned into invaluable tools in drawing racial boundaries and maintaining distinctions between colonizer and colonized as the points of intimate contact between the Spanish conquerors and the indigenous populations multiplied rapidly.

Not surprisingly, New Spain's convents, in taking on these Herculean tasks, mirrored the contradictions of colonial society. They were set up as monuments to the spiritual purity, whiteness, and superiority of the Spanish; the female descendants of ruling families that had colonial holdings and connections

to Spain ran these institutions. Yet the daily operations of these houses were entirely dependent on indigenous servants. The presence of Indian women, *mestizas*, and mulattas in "white" convents thus undercut the claims to racial purity and natural dominance. La Encarnacian in Mexico City housed only one
hundred nuns at the end of the seventeenth century, but as many as three hundred servants.[51] How could one sustain a socially and racially distinct ruling
class when extensive quotidian contact with the conquered and very real dependencies on their labor blurred those distinctions and pushed colonial society toward hybridity?

Over time, New Spain saw the establishment of convents for indigenous
women of the upper classes. Such foundations sparked heated debate over the
spiritual capacities of natives, as Allan Greer has shown for the convent of
Corpus Christi in Mexico City. Supporters of the community even initiated
the Spanish translation of a French hagiography of Catherine Tekakwitha, the
Iroquois virgin converted by the Jesuits, to prove that indigenous women
could reach spiritual perfection. These convent foundations hence implied
negotiating much larger questions of assimilation and colonization. How to
balance Catholicism's potential for integrating diverse populations into a
Christian commonwealth with the exclusionary mechanisms of a colonial
regime that derived its legitimacy from Catholicism?[52]

Like the religious women of colonial Peru and colonial Mexico, sisters in
New France supported colonial endeavors yet their support took slightly different and more overtly practical forms. Even the most confined sisters in New
France were on the forefront of active evangelizing, as Natalie Davis has documented for Marie L'Incarnation, who directed the wilderness mission of the
Ursulines in Quebec. Marie's convent parlor, Dominique Deslandres recently
pointed out, was an obligatory stopover for everyone arriving in New France
and learning about local customs and native languages.[53]

Other religious women embarked upon a more active path from the start.
Inspired by the same post-Trent quest as the English Ladies or Daughters of
Charity, they came to New France to pursue an active ministry of teaching, social service, and hospital work. Marguerite Bourgeoys of Notre-Dame de
Montreal deliberately modeled her female community after European examples. When her initial plan to teach the catechism to indigenous girls was obstructed by a change in political fortunes, she redirected the apostolic activity
of her community toward acculturating French women—and some men—
into their roles as colonists and inhabitants of New France. Bourgeoys's sisters
taught girls born in New France as well as female newcomers to the colony,
such as the *filles de roi*, whom the French government sent as spouses for the
colonists. A powerful institutional vehicle for forging the first generation of
women in New France, Bourgeoys's community was constitutive of the French

colonial project. In 1701 Bourgeoys's initial plan came to fruition and the sisters received permission to bring the faith to indigenous girls in return for accepting a stricter rule. Thus they extended their acculturation mission to the indigenous populations.[54]

Sisters in New France moreover assisted in developing the infrastructure of social welfare, as settlers requested that they set up hospitals or teaching convents in their communities. Jeanne Mance, who established the Hôtel-Dieu in Ville-Marie, the future Montreal, was revered as one of the city's founding mothers. The sisters at the Hôtel-Dieu, like the Hospitalières in Quebec, tended to indigenous peoples and colonists. The Jesuit Paul Le Jeune predicted the efficacy of the women's approach in 1636 when he speculated that "the charity [of hospital nuns] would do more for the conversion of the Savages than all our expeditions and words."[55]

These examples indicate that religious virgins also proved themselves indispensable to the establishment of European hegemony in the colonial setting. They were certainly as important as the European women sent to the colonies to marry and bear children. In some respects the work of religious women, albeit grounded in faith, had even greater political ramifications. Putting the institutional mechanisms and economic resources of their convent communities at the disposal of the emerging colonial elite, nuns aided in the formation of colonial economies and the production of novel hierarchies based on class, race, and gender. They also attenuated the frictions of colonial society by providing a reliable network of social and religious support.

Final Reflections: Religious Women and the
Making of the State Subject

This chapter has mined new scholarship in order to locate religious women at the heart of political modernization and colonialism and write them back into the story of the state. This speculative conclusion asks how we could write religious women back into the history of the self. It suggests one way to approach this task, namely, to consider the subjectivity of monastics as a template for the obedient state subject that came into being in the early modern period alongside the Burckhardtian individual.

In theorizing the modern self, Judith Butler's work *Psychic Life of Power* describes the process of becoming a subject as inextricably tied to becoming subjugated and desiring subjugation. To simplify a complex argument, Butler contends that only through submission to an outside power can a subject become intelligible to him- or herself. Power, however, can never shape the subject in a teleological manner, so the conditions of the subject's subjugation do not hamper the subject's agency. Quite the opposite: they form the very conditions of the capacity to act.[56]

Arguably, it is possible to characterize the institutional goal of early modern monastic houses as putting this kind of theory about subject formation into lived practice and developing mechanisms of self-regulation that later became harnessed to modern and largely secular forms of disciplinary practice. Only by subjugating themselves entirely to a monastic rule—a code of conformity, imitation, and saintly sameness—did inmates come into being as "individual" nuns or monks. The overarching objective was not the disciplining of behavior but rather the development of distinct emotional dispositions. Obedience was the mainstay of this program. The habituated attachment to obedience, the drive to exercise this virtue before all others and to berate oneself whenever one failed to do so—those features distinguished the Christian monastic subject. The monastic person was not just a person who obeys but a person who has *learned* to deeply desire to obey. For this reason, monastic discipline has much to reveal about the kinds of "conditions within which obedient wills are created."[57]

Monastic dictates of obedience and sameness, however, did not necessarily streamline the desires and wills of inmates and deprive them of possibilities for individual expression. Rather, obedience and sameness formed a strong basis for agency as well as individuality. The monastic setting therefore also has much to reveal about the exercise of agency and individuality under inner and outer constraints.

We find examples of this in the historical contexts discussed in this chapter. When faced with Protestant Reformers, Catholic nuns confidently invoked obedience to a higher authority, be it the abbess or God, to insist on their own way of being in the world. The battles of the dissolution of convents gave rise to a whole genre of resistance literature, most famously Caritas Pirckheimer's *Denkwuerdigkeiten*.[58] As Charlotte Woodford has shown, this literature at once stood in a tradition of convent historiography while it also made room for the personality of individual nuns to emerge. Remembrance of the community went hand in hand with remembrance of the author.[59]

Similarly, Catholic nuns, in confronting Tridentine enclosure, produced chronicles and eyewitness accounts of collective remembrance and individual articulation. Not only did these texts seek to strengthen commitment to a religious tradition perceived to be under attack, they also accorded their authors an opportunity to reveal something about themselves and explore the emotional impact of events on their individual lives. Differently put, a form of self-fashioning does occur in and through these religious texts.[60]

Religious women as self-fashioning subjects of history also appear in the colonial setting. Life stories of individual women, cloistered educators, providers of social services, or recluses offering spiritual advice proliferated in print. Authors and their audiences imagined the female subjects of these hagiographic and biographical accounts as protagonists of a sacred history whose most recent theater was New France. They were exemplary individuals deserving of collective commemoration and they frequently inspired other women to join the evangelizing adventure abroad.[61]

Submission to a religious order did not preclude the formation of an agentic self while it simultaneously facilitated the formation of a self that accepts collective rule.[62] In this light, it seems no accident that monastic ideals of self-regulation and techniques of discipline influenced how some of the most skilled architects of European absolutism organized their courts. Rejecting the indulgence of the Renaissance court in favor of austere self-discipline, a new generation of rulers embraced the very concept of the palace as a monastery and used convent discipline as a model for social and political discipline, which originated at the court but then radiated outward.[63]

We have yet to examine how monastic discipline intersected with and supported large efforts of social disciplining and shaping a population of reliable state subjects. The monastic sphere held many resources for the formation of self-regulating individuals, including rituals and patterns of organizing space, movement, and psychic dispositions. The effect of these multiple "techniques of the self" far exceeded that of even the most forceful indoctrination with the right creed, which has stood in the limelight in Weberian histories of the state. Experts of ritual and religious discipline, nuns (and monks) undoubtedly had much to teach about creating the conditions in which a self-ruled subject accepting of state power could begin to flourish. Looking at how the monastic setting's history intersected with larger histories of the state and the subject in modernizing Europe and its colonies will allow us to approach older questions about "community and individual" from yet another direction.[64]

Notes

1. In general see Natalie Zemon Davis, "Boundaries and the Sense of Self in Sixteenth-Century France," in *Reconstructing Individualism: Autonomy, Individuality, and the Self in Western Thought,* ed. Thomas C. Heller et al. (Stanford: Stanford University Press, 1986), 53–63; David Sabean, "The Production of the Self during the Age of Confessionalism," *Central European History* 29 (1996): 1–18. For good examples of contributions by literary scholars see Stephen Greenblatt, *Renaissance Self-Fashioning: From More to Shakespeare* (Chicago: University of Chicago Press, 1980); David Aers, "A Whisper in the Ear of the Early Modernists: or, Reflections on Literary Critics Writing the 'History of the Subject,'" in *Culture and History 1350–1600: Essays on English Communities, Identities and Writing,* ed. David Aers (New York: Harvester Wheatsheaf, 1992), 177–202.

2. Heide Wunder, "Herrschaft und öffentliches Handeln von Frauen in der Gesellschaft der Frühen Neuzeit," in *Frauen in der Geschichte des Rechts: Von der Frühen Neuzeit bis zur Gegenwart*, ed. Ute Gerhard (München: C. H. Beck, 1997), 27–54.

3. Anthony Black, *Guilds and Civil Society in European Political Thought from the Twelfth Century to the Present* (London: Methuen, 1984).

4. Among others, Thomas A. Brady, *Turning Swiss: Cities and Empire, 1450–1550* (Cambridge: Cambridge University Press, 1985); Bernd Moeller, "Imperial Cities and the Reformation," in *Imperial Cities and the Reformation. Three Essays*, ed. and trans. H. C. Erik Midelfort and Mark U. Edwards (Philadelphia: Fortress, 1972), 41–115; Peter Blickle, *The Revolution of 1525 from a New Perspective*, trans. Thomas A. Brady and H. C. Erik Midelfort (Baltimore: Johns Hopkins University Press, 1981).

5. Merry E. Wiesner, "Guilds, Male Bonding and Women's Work in Early Modern Germany," *Gender and History* 1 (1989), 125–37; and "*Wandervögel* and Women: Journeymen's Concepts of Masculinity in Early Modern Germany," *Journal of Social History* 24 (1991): 767–82.

6. Lyndal Roper, "'The Common Man,' 'The Common Good,' 'Common Women': Reflections on Gender and Meaning in the Reformation German Commune," *Social History* 12 (1987): 1–21.

7. Because of the great complexity of Weber's work, a summary statement of this kind of inevitably appears somewhat reductionist. Yet this interpretation responds to the prevalent theoretical strand in Weber's own reflections on the topic and those of his many commentators, who were often more Weberian than Weber himself. See Ulrike Strasser, *State of Virginity: Gender, Religion, and Politics in an Early Modern Catholic State* (Ann Arbor: University of Michigan Press, 2004).

8 Early examples of this literature include Wolfgang Reinhard, "Zwang zur Konfessionalisierung? Prolegomena zu einer Theorie des konfessionellen Zeitalters," *Zeitschrift für Historische Forschung* 10 (1983): 257–77; and Heinz Schilling, "Die Konfessionalisierung im Reich," *Historische Zeitschrift* 246 (1988): 1–45.

9. For an excellent example see Isabel Hull, *Sexuality, State, and Civil Society in Germany, 1700–1815* (Ithaca, NY: Cornell University Press, 1996).

10. Lyndal Roper, *The Holy Household: Women and Morals in Reformation Ausgburg* (Oxford: Clarendon, 1989).

11. Merry Wiesner, "Ideology Meets the Empire: Reformed Convents and the Reformation," in *Germania Illustrata: Essays on Early Modern Germany Presented to Gerald Strauss*, ed. Andrew C. Fix and Susan Karant-Nunn (Kirksville, MO: Sixteenth Century Journal Publisher, 1992), 181–96.

12. Amy Leonard, *Nails in the Wall: Catholic Nuns in Reformation Germany* (Chicago and London: University of Chicago Press, 2005), 38–58.

13. Lucia Koch, "Eingezogenes stilles Wesen? Protestantische Damenstifte an der Wende zum 17. Jahrhundert," in *In Christo ist weder man noch weyb: Frauen in der Zeit der Reformation und der katholischen Reform*, ed. Anne Conrad (Münster: Aschendorffsche Verlagsbuchhandlung GmbH & Co, 1999), 208–10. This line of argument appears frequently among pamphlet writers. Leonard, *Nails in the Wall*, 54–57.

14. Leonard, *Nails in the Wall*.

15. Koch, "Damenstifte," 200–202, 224.

16. Koch, "Damenstifte," 215–18.

17. Koch, "Damenstifte," 213.

18. Koch, "Damenstifte," 214.

19. Examples include Heinz Schilling, "Disziplinierung oder 'Selbstregulierung der Untertanen'?—Ein Plädoyer für die Doppelperspektive von Makro- und Mikrohistorie bei der Erforschung der frühmodernen Kirchenzucht," *Historische Zeitschrift* 264 (1997): 675–92; Heinrich Richard Schmidt, "Sozialdisziplinierung? Ein Plädoyer für das Ende des Etatismus in der Konfessionalisierungsforschung," *Historische Zeitschrift* 265 (1997): 639–82; Marc Forster, *The Counter-Reformation in the Villages* (Ithaca, NY: Cornell University Press, 1992); *Catholic Revival in the Age of the Baroque: Religious Identity in Southwest Germany* (Cambridge: Cambridge University Press, 2001).

20. Leonard, *Nails in the Wall*, especially 85–106.

21. Wunder, "Herrschaft" 40–41, n. 56.

22. Leonard, *Nails in the Wall*, 150.

23. Koch, "Damenstifte," 220–21.

24. Koch, "Damenstifte," 211–12, 217–19, 227–28.

25. Merry Wiesner, "Ideology," 186.

26. Wunder, "Herrschaft," 38–45.

27. Wilhelm Smets, ed., *Des hochheiligen, ökumenischen und allgemeinen Concils von Trient Canones und Beschlüsse* (Bielefeld: Velhagen & Klasing 1869); reprint, ed. Christine Maria Esser (Sinzing: Fotomechanischer Nachdruck, erschienen im Sankt Meinrad Verlag für Theologie, 1989), 167–79. Ruth P. Liebowitz, "Virgins in the Service of Christ: The Dispute over an Active Apostolate for Women during the Counter-Reformation," in *Women of Spirit: Female Leadership in the Jewish and Christian Tradition*, ed. Rosemary Ruether and Eleanor McLauglin (New York: Simon & Schuster, 1979), 150 n. 27.

28. See, for example, Caroline Walker Bynum, *Holy Feast and Holy Fast: The Religious Significance of Food to Medieval Women*. (Berkeley and Los Angeles: University of California Press, 1987).

29. Gabriella Zarri, "Gender, Religious Institutions and Social Discipline: The Reform of the Regulars," in *Gender and Society in Renaissance Italy*, ed. Judith Brown and Robert C. Davis (London and New York: Longman, 1998), 193–212.

30. On Saint Teresa see especially Jodi Bilinkoff, *The Avila of Saint Teresa* (Ithaca, NY: Cornell University Press, 1989). See Craig Harline, "Actives and Contemplatives: The Female Religious of the Low Countries before and after Trent," *Catholic Historical Review* 89 (1995): 541–67. Still, some communities resisted enclosure. Craig Monson has shown how sequestered nuns used music making to have a voice in public. Craig Monson, *Disembodied Voices: Music and Culture in an Early Modern Italian Convent* (Berkeley and Los Angeles: University of California Press, 1995). Munich's cloistered female tertiary communities found in the exhibition of decorated relics a means to counter their exclusion from the larger public. See Ulrike Strasser, "Bones of Contention: Cloistered Nuns, Decorated Relics, and the Contest Over Women's Place in the Public Sphere of Counterreformation Munich," *Archive for Reformation History* 90 (1999): 255–88.

31. See, among others, Sarah Hanley, "Engendering the State: Family Formation and State Building in Early Modern Europe," *French Historical Review* 16 (1989): 4–27; Hermann Rebel, *Peasant Classes: The Bureaucratization of Property and Family Relations under Early Habsburg Absolutism, 1511–1636* (Princeton, NJ: Princeton University Press, 1983).

32. Elizabeth Rapley, *The Dévotes: Women and Church in Seventeenth-Century France* (Montreal and Kingston: McGill-Queen's University Press, 1990), 28.

33. Strasser, *State of Virginity*, especially 57–85.

34. Jutta Sperling, *Covenants and the Body Politic in Late Renaissance Venice* (Chicago: University of Chicago Press, 1999).

35. This strategy ultimately failed. Faced with biologically extinction due to cloistering of its women, the patriciate had to sell offices to outsiders, quote from 134.

36. See the thought-provoking reflections of Phyllis Mack, "Religion, Feminism, and the Problem of Agency: Reflections on Eighteenth-Century Quakerism," *Journal of Women in Culture and Society* 29 (2003): 149–77.

37. Mary Laven, *Virgins of Venice: Broken Vows and Cloistered Lives in the Renaissance Convent* (New York: Viking, 2002), especially chap. 3, "Blood of the Republic," 45–67; "The Venetian Nuns Revisited" (paper presented at conference on Female Monasticism in Early Modern Europe, Cambridge University, July 2003).

38. Wolfgang Reinhard, *Geschichte der Staatsgewalt: Eine vergleichende Verfassungsgeschichte Europas von den Anfängen bis zur Gegenwart* (Munich: C. H. Beck,) 264–65.

39. Strasser, *State of Virginity*, 121–23.

40. See, for example, Anne Conrad, *Zwischen Kloster und Welt: Ursulinen und Jesuitinnen in der katholschen Reformbewegung des 16./17. Jahrhunderts* (Mainz: Verlag Philipp von Zabern, 1991).

41. Strasser, *State of Virginity*, 149–71.

42. See Susan E. Dinan, "Spheres of Female Religious Expression in Early Modern France," in *Women and Religion in Old and New Worlds*, ed. Susan E. Dinan and Debra Meyers (London and New York: Routledge, 2001), 71–92, especially 78–85.

43. Dinan, "Sphere," 79, 85. On French confraternities and their political uses, see Colin Jones, *The Charitable Imperative: Hospitals and Nursing in Ancien Régime and Revolutionary France* (New York: Routledge, 1989).

44. Rapley, *The Dévotes*.

45. Elizabeth Rapley, *A Social History of the Cloister: Daily Life in the Teaching Monasteries of the Old Regime* (Montreal and Kingston: McGill-Queen's University Press, 2001), especially 83 and 93.

46. Rapley, *Social History*, 250–55.

47. Kathryn Burns, *Colonial Habits: Convents and the Spiritual Economy of Cuzco, Peru* (Durham, NC: Duke University Press, 1999), especially chap. 1.

48. Burns, *Colonial Habits*, especially chap. 5. See also Kathryn Burns, "Nuns, Kurakas, and Credit," in *Women and Religion in Old and New Worlds*, 43–67.

49. Asuncion Lavrin, "Ecclesiastical Reform of Nunneries in New Spain in the Eighteenth Century," *The Americas* 22 (1965): 182–203; and "The Role of Nunneries in the Economy of New Spain in the Eighteenth Century," *Hispanic American Historical Review* 46 (1966), 371–93. Also Ann Miriam Gallagher, "The Family Background of the

Nuns of Two *Monasterios* in Colonial Mexico: Santa Clara, Queretaro; and Corpus Christi, Mexico City (1724–1822)" (Ph.D. thesis, Catholic University of America, 1972).

50. See Gallagher, "Family Background," 213–21.

51. Gallagher, "Family Background," 53–54, 62.

52. Allan Greer, "Iroquois Virgin: The Story of Catherine Tekakwitha in New France and New Spain," in *Colonial Saints. Discovering the Holy in the Americas, 1500–1800*, ed. Allan Greer and Jodi Bilinkoff (New York and London: Routledge, 2003), 235–50.

53. Natalie Zemon Davis, "New Worlds: Marie de l'Incarnation," in *Women on the Margins: Three Seventeenth Century Lives* (Cambridge, MA: Harvard University Press, 1995), 63–140; Dominique Deslandres, "In the Shadow of the Cloister: Representations of Female Holiness in New France," in *Colonial Saints*, 142.

54. William Henry Foster, "Women at the Centers, Men at the Margins: The Wilderness Mission of the Secular Sisters of Early Montreal Reconsidered," in *Women and Religion in Old and New Worlds*, ed. Susan E. Dinan and Debra Meyers (London and New York: Routledge, 2001), 93.

55. Deslandres, "Shadow of Cloister," 129–52; quote from 136.

56. Judith Butler, *The Psychic Life of Power* (Stanford: Stanford University Press, 1997).

57. Talal Asad, *Genealogies of Religion: Discipline and Reason of Power in Christianity and Islam* (Baltimore: Johns Hopkins University Press, 1993), 125.

58. Frumentius Renner, ed., *Die Denkwürdigkeiten der Äbtissin Caritas Pirckheimer* (St. Ottilien: EOS, 1982).

59. Charlotte Woodford, *Nuns as Historians in Early Modern Germany* (Oxford: Oxford University Press, 2002).

60. Woodford, *Nuns as Historians*, 50ff. For an example of an eyewitness account of Tridentine enclosure, see Ulrike Strasser, "Cloistering Women's Past. Conflicting Accounts of Tridentine Enclosure in a Seventeenth-Century Munich Nunnery," in *Gender in Early Modern German History*, ed. Ulinka Rublack (Cambridge: Cambridge University Press, 2002), 221–46. On religious women's written articulations of a "self," see the introduction by Daniele Hacke, "Selbstzeugnisse von Frauen in der Frühen Neuzeit: Eine Einführung," in *Frauen in der Stadt. Selbstzeugnisse des 16.–18. Jahrhunderts*, ed. Daniela Hacke (Ostfildern: Thorbecke Verlag, 2004).

61. Deslandres, "Shadow of Cloister," 147.

62. See also Mack, "Religion, Feminism, and the Problem of Agency."

63. Maximilian I of Bavaria successfully combined political centralization with a quasi-monastic social discipline. Andreas Kraus, *Maximilian I: Bayerns großer Kurfürst* (Graz: Verlag Styria, 1990).

64. Wolfgang Reinhard registers the regulatory potential of monastic discipline for the modernizing state in passing. Wolfgang Reinhard, *Gebhardt: Handbuch der deutschen Geschichte. Band 9—Probleme deutscher Geschichte: 1495–1806* and *Reichsreform und Reformation: 1495–1555* (Stuttgart: Klett-Cotta, 2001), 106. Weber invokes this potential too, but then focuses on the supposedly greater disciplinary effects of Protestantism. See *The Protestant Ethic and the Spirit of Capitalism*, trans. Talcott Parsons (London: G. Allen & Unwin; reprint, New York: Routledge, 2001), 72–75, 105, 118.

14

The Transitional Role of Jacques Coeur in the Fifteenth Century

Kathryn L. Reyerson

THE LATER FIFTEENTH CENTURY HAS LEFT US ASSESSMENTS of Jacques Coeur (ca. 1395–1456). His near contemporaries called him, "the" *argentier,* or *argentier du roi* or *commissaire du roi* (king's commissioner), but fifteenth-century texts also spoke of him as a merchant. The Burgundian chronicler Georges Chastellain (1415–1475), in his *Recollection des merveilles advenues en nostre temps,* mixed the official, mercantile, and financial roles for Coeur:

> Then an *argentier* was seen to rise
> By mystery, the highest in the land,
> Merchant and financier,
> Who, by fate, went to die in exile
> After his many good deeds done
> For the king.[1]

The cumulation of functions by Coeur was unique in his era; yet it set a precedent for the future.[2]

The level of Coeur's wealth puts us in mind of the Fuggers or the Rothschilds. His focus on state-sponsored trade with a particular monopoly on the spice trade foreshadows the mercantilist policies of the seventeenth-century finance minister, Jean Baptiste Colbert. His promotion to noble rank from urban beginnings reflects a career trajectory for commoners entering the *noblesse de robe.* Although Coeur's economic engagements spanned tax farming, mining, minting, and royal finance, this chapter will focus on Coeur's innovation in French royal trade and shipping in the Mediterranean, on his management and organizational techniques, and finally on the portability of his role beyond France in order to highlight the transitional aspects of Coeur's career in the fifteenth century.[3] Coeur established a French fleet, coordinated a system of supply, transport, and distribution through his own agencies, staffed by his personnel, with goods carried in the ships he built and transported overland in his carts, by his transporters, to the *Argenterie* and other markets.[4] In exile at the end of his life, Coeur from his base in Rome began to reconstitute his fortune and briefly performed the same functions for the pope that he had earlier for the king of France. The success of this individual merchant in mercantile and maritime activities had an impact on French trading practices in the early modern period.

The Mediterranean commerce and economic activities of Jacques Coeur provide historians with methods foreshadowing mercantilist enterprise of the sixteenth and seventeenth centuries.[5] Before Coeur's time Frenchmen of the center and north of France had rarely been present, except as crusaders, in the Mediterranean. In contrast, southern French merchants had been active traders in the Mediterranean world from at least the eleventh century, following the lead of Italians. After the Albigensian crusade and the introduction of French rule in Lower Languedoc, Louis IX (1226–1270) acquired land from the abbey of Psalmody in the 1240s to create the first French Mediterranean port at Aigues-Mortes, from which his crusading forces sailed for the Levant in August 1248.[6] In 1278 Philip III (1270–1285) attempted to impose control over Mediterranean trade, forcing Italian merchants to import goods through Aigues-Mortes and establish themselves at Nîmes, both sites of French royal rule.[7] However, the Mediterranean entrepôt of Montpellier, an Aragonese and, from 1276, Majorcan enclave in the south, escaped the introduction of French regulation until the 1293 purchase of the episcopal quarter of the town by Philip IV (1285–1314). In 1339 Philip VI of Valois (1328–1350) tried to control trade through the south of France, making an offer of monopoly over the transport of goods from this area to the Genoese admirals/pirates Antonio Doria and Carlo Grimaldi. Protests from the consuls of Montpellier caused the king to revoke his offer in 1340.[8] Philip VI finally purchased the remaining seigneurial quarter of Montpellier in 1349, but southern French and Italian merchants continued to dominate Mediterranean trade, along with Catalans of the kingdom of Aragon, who also laid claim to commercial and maritime dominance, particularly in the western Mediterranean. Merchants from the French royal sphere of northern and central France were simply not participants in Mediterranean commerce.

By the time of Jacques Coeur, the Mediterranean trade in the south of France had declined considerably from the late thirteenth century. The Angevin conquest of Marseille and Provence in the 1260s redirected the remarkable trading network of the Massilian port to the furtherance of Angevin political aims in the Mediterranean.[9] Rival and then heir to the position of commercial prominence of Marseille on the Mediterranean coast of France, Languedocian Montpellier suffered setbacks with the fall of the last crusader stronghold on the Syrian coast—Saint-Jean d'Acre—and although Montpellier merchants rebounded in the first half of the fourteenth century, they were buffeted by the vicissitudes of fourteenth-century crises: agricultural difficulties, shifting trade patterns, plague, demographic disasters, and the Hundred Years' War. However, at the end of the fourteenth century and in the early fifteenth century, southern French towns continued to send merchants to trade in the Levant.[10] With royal financing Jacques Coeur established a northern French presence in Mediterranean trade in the 1440s, underpinned by the creation of a French fleet. Though he dealt in many products, his particular specialty in the Mediterranean was the trade in spices. Louis XI (1461–1483) continued what Coeur had begun in his patronage of galleys trading under the French flag in the Mediterranean. He took into his service former close associates of Coeur's. In 1481 at the death of a nephew of King René of Anjou, Louis XI acquired Provence and even envisioned developing the port of Marseille.[11] A Mediterranean focus persisted under François I (1515–1547), who promoted French Mediterranean trade and made alliances with the Turks from 1525 that resulted in the creation of a Franco-Turkish fleet.[12] Coeur's actions on behalf of the royal economy, traced below, provided a precedent for early modern mercantilism that would ultimately lead France to commercial adventures in North America and Asia.

Coeur assumed the office of *argentier* in 1439, acting as a bursar or supply agent for the king, having already been employed in the royal mints and as financial adviser. The *Argenterie* was a kind of company store or commissary, furnishing goods to the royal court, to the nobility, and to some important royal officials and bourgeois. Coeur became a royal commissioner in Languedoc and Auvergne in 1440, with a particular focus on the *Gabelle*, or salt tax, for which he was a tax inspector. He and his family were ennobled in 1441, and he was elevated to the royal council in 1442. Having traveled in 1432 to the Levant, making some contacts in the south of France, particularly in Montpellier at that time, Coeur took it upon himself in the early 1440s to organize French trade in the Mediterranean. The *Argenterie* was in need of products of the Mediterranean world until then delivered through the hands of intermediaries to French markets, particularly Italians and, to a lesser extent, southern French merchants and Catalans.[13] While harboring no design for participation in world exploration, Coeur desired direct access to goods from the eastern Mediterranean, south Asia, and the Orient in their Levantine markets.[14]

To further this end, Coeur built a fleet of at least seven ships, four of them galleys, in the 1440s and early 1450s: the *Saint-Denis*, the *Saint-Jacques*, the *Saint-Michel*, and the *Madeleine*.[15] Charles VII had the *Saint-Denis* commissioned in Genoa in 1443. Coeur was ordered to arm and equip it in 1444. In service by 1445, this galley put in at Marseille and took on board merchants in search of spices. In 1446 in Marseille Coeur purchased the *Madeleine*, previously a galley of the Hospitallers of Rhodes. By 1447 or 1448 Coeur had acquired the *Saint-Jacques* and the *Saint-Michel*. His captains skippered these galleys. Two other names of the seven ships, the *Santa-Maria–Sant-Jacme*, and the *Rose*, have survived. The former, apparently destined for Atlantic trade, was constructed as a joint venture with Catalan and Roussillonnais merchants at Collioure in the territory of the king of Aragon.[16] Historian Michel Mollat has suggested that Coeur may have had even more than seven vessels in his fleet.[17]

Some trace of the financing of ship purchase and construction has also survived. Just before his arrest in July 1451, Coeur acknowledged his receipt of 3, 591 *l. t.* from Charles VII, along with reference to other sums for galley construction and ship maintenance.[18] In all Charles VII seems to have contributed on the order of 15, 600 *l. t.* in royal taxation for the construction of the fleet.[19] Coeur flew the colors of France on these ships, even though this gesture angered the Catalans who had collaborated in the construction of the *Santa-Maria–Sant-Jacme*, leading to their seizure of this ship, which was later recovered.[20]

To support the operation of his fleet, from 1444 Coeur improved port facilities in Aigues-Mortes as his base. He convinced municipal authorities in Montpellier to construct a merchant exchange (*loge*) to facilitate his southern French operations.[21] By 1445, thanks to the king of France, he enjoyed the right to conscript oarsmen for his galleys.[22] In 1445 he arranged a treaty between the sultan of Egypt and the knights of Rhodes that served both French and papal purposes and made it easier for Westerners to trade in the Levant. In 1446 he obtained permission from the pope to trade for five years with the infidel. Coeur had targeted Alexandria as the principal port of his Levant trade, and since it was in Muslim hands, he needed papal dispensation to trade there. In 1447 Coeur's assistant, Jean de Village, negotiated an alliance on behalf of the king of France with the sultan of Egypt. In 1448 Charles VII sent an embassy to Rome to celebrate the accession of Pope Nicholas V. Coeur was present in the delegation and organized an impressive parade of three hundred French horses. During his stay in Rome, the pope granted Coeur the lifetime privilege to trade with the infidel and also accorded him the right to transport pilgrims and Muslims throughout the Mediterranean world. Finally, Coeur obtained safe-conducts for his galleys to trade in the western

Mediterranean from Mediterranean powers such as the city of Genoa and King Alfonso the Magnificent of Aragon.[23]

Fiscally, Coeur solidified his hold on the spice trade for French markets. By 1445 he had an exclusive tax advantage on spice imports through Aigues-Mortes. His goods were duty free there, though a tax of 10 percent was imposed at every other port. This tax privilege riled the competition. The city council of Barcelona stated on August 11, 1449, that Coeur's trade had caused considerable hardship for the Catalan spice trade.[24] Coeur also undertook leadership roles in the administration of law of marque disputes, that is, reprisals for loss due to piracy and privateering, securing influence in yet another dimension of Mediterranean trade in this era.[25] Coeur was exceedingly thorough in assuring that his trade in spices would succeed. His monopoly of spice imports in France and his control over the transport of French merchandise laid the groundwork for a new prominence for French Mediterranean trade.[26]

Coeur's management techniques and administration also speak to a new level of coordination that could be put at the service of the state. Coeur devised an integrated system of factors and agencies throughout France and Europe in order to supply the *Argenterie* and to trade in the Mediterranean. The fifteenth-century chroniclers Mathieu d'Escouchy (1420–1482) and Georges Chastellain were sufficiently impressed to state that Coeur had three hundred factors (commercial agents) on land and on sea.[27] One of Coeur's highly placed friends, Jean II Juvénal des Ursins (1388–1473), bishop of Laon (later bishop of Beauvais and then archbishop of Reims), wrote about Coeur in a letter to one of his brothers: "He has all the merchandise of the realm in his hand and everywhere has his factors."[28] It would seem that Coeur possessed personal charisma, demonstrated in the loyalty of his friends and associates after his arrest.[29] He also had a talent for managing men. Coeur relied on men of his homeland of Berry first and foremost in his management structure. His right-hand man was Guillaume de Varye from Bourges, a boyhood friend. Varye, who joined Coeur in exile in Rome, was a talented associate in whom Coeur would place all his trust. A very successful businessman in his own right, Varye would later be employed by Louis XI. Antoine Noir of Valence and his brothers operated on Coeur's behalf in business taking them from Montpellier to Marseille, Avignon, Lyon, and Geneva, and beyond to Barcelona, Rome, and Naples. Coeur also had the company of the Noir brothers in exile in Rome. Among the galley skippers, Coeur placed close associates such as Guillaume Gimart and Jean de Village, his nephew by marriage. Later it would be Jean who managed Coeur's affairs in the south of France, first in Montpellier and then in Angevin Marseille, where he continued to handle Coeur's affairs while the latter was in prison. Village and Varye were Coeur's closest business confidants.

Coeur's business network was staffed by his associates and major factors at the apex but included many other employees under each of the top personnel, creating a management hierarchy. Lesser employees included a host of clerks, servants, brokers, secretaries, and subagents. There was the characteristic mixing of domestic service with business functions such as packing, handling, and storing of goods. Coeur's representatives saw to his orders throughout Europe. This was a remarkable structure, much more tightly controlled than those of the large Italian business firms.[30] Coeur supervised this network by traveling throughout France and constructing homes at key commercial sites such as Lyon, Montpellier, Marseille, and, of course, at his hometown of Bourges. The commercial success Coeur generated from this remarkable organization served both the king and his own fortune. It was crucial for the support of the French war effort. Not only did Coeur satisfy his powerful clients, he also turned a formidable profit in his business that, when combined with his contributions in monetary policy, minting, and taxation, permitted him to generate the necessary funds to assist Charles VII in his victory in the Hundred Years' War.

The legal ties between Coeur and his associates are difficult to reconstruct. Coeur formed one commercial partnership (a 1430 *societas*) early on with associates at the mint of Bourges.[31] There also survives a procuration between Coeur and his closest associates, Village, Gimart, and Noir. Procuration was a common business technique of medieval merchants, involving the delegation of authority with a broad or narrow mandate. Such an institution permitted representation at a distance. On December 1, 1450, Coeur appointed his collaborators as procurators with a broad mandate to represent his interests and work on his behalf. With procuration, and perhaps other partnerships such as the early one that lasted until 1439, with obligatory notes, mandates of payment, and credit lines, all micromanaged by Coeur himself, he was able to provide extraordinary service to Charles VII, assisting the king by financing victory in the Hundred Years' War (in the Normandy campaign 200,000 *écus*)—his public role—and in his private role, to achieve extraordinary financial success.[32] Jacques du Clercq (1420–1501), one of the chroniclers of the duke of Burgundy and a Flemish lawyer, thought Coeur to be worth 1,000,000 in gold *écus*.[33] Though Coeur denied an ability to pay the 400,000 *écus* in fines and debts owed to the king in his condemnation of 1453, he was clearly a very wealthy man.[34]

Coeur was a new man in the fifteenth century, a business success, ennobled by the French king Charles VII, a royal official, and member of the king's council.[35] His rapid ascension to power was not well viewed in all circles. Many in the nobility were in debt financially to him. Adverse opinion at the court of Charles VII culminated in 1451 when Coeur was imprisoned. He was condemned by the king in 1453, only to escape and go into exile in Rome. The chronicler, Martial d'Auvergne (1430/35–1508), wrote in 1477–1483 of the reign of Charles VII in a poem, *Vigiles de Charles VII*, in which there were multiple lessons, including the "Quatrième leçon chantée par Marchandise" that spoke of the experiences of Coeur:

> And if certain of them [the merchants] . . .
> Were enriched, does this nevertheless mean
> That one should take them,
> Whether right or wrong,
> Pillage or sell their goods,
> Confiscate them and give them away without misjudging? . . .
> Alas, what danger from false accusers,
> Bad boys and drastic reducers,
> Who tell lies to lords
> To undo many good merchants,
> To take their money
> Without hearing them in justice
> Or doing right or reason.
> And then be their adversary
> In a trial,
> And taking judges of their bent and access,
> O what abuse and what horrible excess.[36]

Coeur, the merchant whose goods were confiscated, was falsely accused. D'Auvergne recognized the vulnerability of merchants in his day. They could be pillaged of their resources and brought down by false accusation and questionable legal proceedings, with the judges aligned against them.[37] Men of merchant origin who rose to high position in fifteenth-century France were open to criticism and attacks stemming from envy of their status and wealth. For d'Auvergne such treatment was a matter of abuse and excess. As a *procureur* (prosecutor) at the Parlement of Paris, he was well placed to observe such miscarriages of justice firsthand. Coeur's remarkable combination of talents only served to exacerbate his situation.

That Coeur, the exile, landed on his feet in Rome in papal employ at the end of his life is quite extraordinary after his judicial experiences in France, but his ability to adapt his talents to new circumstances speaks to his role as a transitional figure in the fifteenth century. Coeur was in self-imposed exile outside France from 1455 to his death in 1456. Though his wife, Macée, had died at the end of 1452 and his children were grown, Coeur was separated from his homeland and his native culture. However, exile in Rome provided Coeur with a new life of privilege at the papal court. He reestablished himself financially through trade, and he made himself useful to the pope in a fashion that resembled his official role in France.

Pope Nicholas V, though near death at Coeur's arrival, welcomed him in
Rome. On March 16, 1455, Nicholas V addressed the cardinals regarding
Coeur, noting that he had performed many favors for the papacy. Nicholas alleged that Coeur was innocent of the charges against him and that he should
be assisted in efforts to clear his name in France.[38] The pope also noted that
Coeur had been criticized for his activities on behalf of the papacy, utilizing as
much as 100,000 ducats in papal funds to obtain what the pope needed. Coeur
and Nicholas knew each other from the earlier diplomatic dealings surrounding the French embassy to Rome in 1448, mentioned above, during which
time Coeur had fallen ill and been nursed to health by the papal physician.
Participants in the embassy had stayed only a month, but Coeur stayed longer
and became well acquainted with the pope during his recuperation. Nicholas
had reason to be grateful to Coeur, who in 1449 was influential in obtaining
the resignation of the antipope Felix V, the former Amadeus of Savoy, whose
election in 1439 had come about at the Council of Basil in a move to reject Eugenius IV, Nicholas's predecessor. In turn, Nicholas V intervened with the king
of France for leniency after Coeur's arrest in 1451. At the time of Coeur's sentencing in 1453, it was again Nicholas who was instrumental in getting the
death sentence commuted to banishment.[39] The rehabilitation proceedings
instituted by Coeur's sons after his death in 1456 revealed the close relations
between Coeur and Nicholas V.[40]

Calixtus III, Nicholas V's successor as pope, continued to patronize Coeur
and would soon employ him in his crusade planning. Varye, the Noir brothers, and Gimart joined Coeur in exile in Rome. Calixtus III authorized Coeur
to have a small armed guard around him in Rome for protection against attack
by henchmen of his enemies who had engineered his arrest and condemnation. Financially, Coeur was said to have over 60,000 *écus* to maintain himself
in Rome. He had benefited from the likely spiriting out of France of funds by
his closest associates at the time of his arrest. Moreover, Village continued to
manage his business operations in Angevin Marseille. Foreign trade remained
the source of Coeur's fortune. His galleys sailed with the safe-conducts of the
king of Aragon, Alfonso V, after his condemnation, though they were ultimately seized by Jean Dauvet, *procureur* of the Parlement of Paris, charged
with the confiscation of Coeur's fortune for reuse and sale.[41] Coeur continued
to enjoy the friendship of King René of Anjou, the ruler of Provence, for whom
Coeur's establishment of the center of his affairs in Marseille must have been
a boon. He had been of service to both of these rulers, as he had been to the
king of France. Coeur now had the opportunity to offer his services once again
to the pope.

Pope Calixtus held dear the idea of a crusade against Turkish expansion in
the Levant.[42] To this end he approached Coeur to enlist his assistance in or-

ganizing the crusade against Rhodes. The situation in the Mediterranean was of increasing concern to Westerners because of the Turkish conquest of Constantinople on May 29, 1453.[43] The pope's request for help seems to have resonated with Coeur. On a certain level he considered himself a man with a mission.[44] Coeur had a desire to reestablish a trading enterprise under his leadership in the Mediterranean. The privilege of trading with the infidel in the Mediterranean had been granted to him for life by Pope Eugenius IV, as noted earlier. Coeur enjoyed the continued support of his close colleagues in Marseille and in Rome. Though Dauvet ultimately got his hands on Coeur's French galleys, Coeur could acquire other ships. He may even have envisioned recovering his position in France with the benefit of a royal pardon. Royal letters of remission frequently excused misdeeds, and Coeur himself had been the beneficiary of remission early on in his career in regard to monetary fraud.[45] He may have believed he could clear his name once again. There is, furthermore, no evidence that Coeur was embittered as a result of his betrayal by Charles VII. Whatever his mix of motives, Coeur could easily have been drawn to crusade by the contemporary crisis. Turkish expansion under Mehmed II threatened Coeur's commercial prospects with a huge army, cannon, and many galleys.[46] Mehmed's ambitions knew no bounds. Coeur brought his customary energy and skill to the assignment of organizing the crusade. The early modern era would see numerous crusades to preserve Mediterranean trade interests.

Pope Calixtus III, at age seventy-seven, took over the crusade preparations begun by Nicholas V. He published a crusading bull on May 15, 1455. Crusade preaching commenced in Italy, at Venice, Milan, and Bologna, and then was extended to all of Western Christendom. On September 8 Calixtus appointed cardinals Alain de Coëtivy (a Frenchman) and John of Carvajal (a Spaniard) to preach the crusade and Petro d'Urrea to organize a fleet at Ostia. The papacy was in desperate need of funds for the crusade effort. The pope called upon Coeur, with his skills in finance and in public relations, to assist. There is some dispute about the capacity in which he was invited to serve. After Coeur's death his children wanted to have his responsibilities construed as those of leadership for the crusade. In this vein, the obituary book of the Bourges cathedral noted that he was the "general captain" of the crusade. Records of the papal chancellery simply called him "expert for preparing the crusade," a less ambitious title.[47] It was ultimately Cardinal Aloiso Trevisano, patriarch of Aquileia in southern Italy, who took charge of the crusade fleet as "general governor and captain."[48]

Some of Coeur's movements following his enlistment in the crusade planning can be tracked. On September 17, 1455, Coeur was present in Provence and assigned two of his ships to the purposes of the crusade.[49] Coëtivy and

Coeur were charged with recruiting the religious orders to preach the enterprise; they were also to engage in efforts to publicize the crusade in France, England, Savoy, the Dauphiné, and Flanders. To assist Calixtus in crusade financing, Coeur and Coëtivy also had the responsibility of collecting taxes in the form of tithes. Coeur had the further charge of attracting maritime personnel for the crusade ships mustering in Provence. Coeur was a clear choice for the pope in these matters, given his previous business connections and the continued presence of Village as manager of his affairs in Marseille. The combination of responsibilities placed on Coeur played to his public relations skills and his managerial and entrepreneurial talents, the very talents that he had earlier put at the disposal of the French king. Coeur was able to shift masters from king to pope and re-create himself as a bursar and commission agent. Coeur as a capitalist/mercantilist official was truly a new breed of individual with a future in a royal politics.

The first squadron of ships departed on crusade from Ostia on September 23, 1455. Two galleys of Coeur's were listed as part of this fleet. Coeur does not seem to have been on board. It is believed that the two galleys left the crusade in Syracuse for unknown reasons. It is likely that Coeur and Gimart, his former galley skipper and close associate, departed on crusade in the spring of 1456 with a second fleet of ships. Further additions to the papal fleet were made at a slightly later date. The fleet sailed first to Rhodes and then around the Aegean, from Chios to other islands. The crusaders put up a front against the Turks, but little was accomplished. Coeur was wounded in the fall of 1456, and his comrade Gimart was killed. Coeur died on November 25, 1456, on the island of Chios, where the fleet was to winter.[50]

Coeur's involvement in the crusade enterprise at the end of his life is consistent with his career-long focus on the Mediterranean world. In this regard a possible venue for his entrepreneurial/commission agent skills presented itself early in Coeur's career. From the mid-1430s, the Mediterranean became a focus for Burgundian crusading ambitions. Coeur went to the Levant in 1432 on a voyage that is difficult to interpret and for which there is little remaining evidence. The Burgundian squire Bertrandon de La Broquière recorded the trip years after it took place. He stated that he had encountered a Frenchmen (Coeur) at Damascus, "who since then has played an important role in France as *argentier* of the king."[51] Coeur told La Broquière that he was to meet four Burgundian nobles in Beirut. Jacques Heers has done the most to problematize this trip, speculating that Coeur was perhaps on a mission of diplomacy.[52] Indeed, there are elements such as the lack of evidence for any commercial activity on Coeur's part during this trip and Coeur's connection with Burgundian nobles in the Levant that leave open the possibility of his association with the Duke of Burgundy on a prospecting venture for the planning of a future crusade.[53] One can ask, in fact, whether he was toying with a role of service to the Burgundian duke early in his career, in light of this intriguing voyage to the Levant in 1432; the same might be said later in regard to the services he rendered over many years to the Aragonese king Alfonso the Magnificent and the Angevin king René. The portability of Coeur's skills reinforces his transitional role, making him, on a certain level, a man for hire, willing to perform for more than one master and able to make himself indispensable. Indeed in Rome, he transferred the expertise gained in service to the king of France to serve the needs of the pope, as just noted. Coeur had a unique set of talents: vision and foresight combined with charisma and a salesman's charm. He was also a genius in public relations and networking. He paved the way for the capitalism and mercantilism of later ages.

As *argentier du roi* Coeur proved himself remarkably successful at organizing a commercial system to supply the needs of royalty and nobility, catering to diverse tastes. The level of his financial success was certainly on par with the wealthiest merchants of his day; he was a forerunner in fortune to the Fuggers and the Rothschilds. Coeur crafted an elaborate network of associates, assistants, and agents to oversee the acquisition of goods in markets of the Levant and their transport in French ships to French destinations. This organization easily rivaled and arguably surpassed the network of agencies of the most significant Italian company. Though Coeur's position in France offered an unusual mix of personal and official activities, one finds parallels for this mingling of roles among the merchants of northern Italian cities such as Venice, Genoa, and Florence. These merchants, who set the standard by which mercantile activities have been judged in the Middle Ages, served in city government and acted as ambassadors of their communities. However, there was no king in northern Italy at this time, though the south of the peninsula had long been incorporated into a Mediterranean kingdom; rather, there were city-states and city republics. The home cities of these merchants were independent of any outside political authority. There are significant similarities between Coeur and the Italian merchants of his day, but Coeur could claim identity as both merchant and royal official, and in his case the royal dimension is the precedent that foreshadowed actions of later French officials.[54]

In the end, with a far more subtle agenda than that of the Burgundians, Coeur made the Mediterranean a focus for French trade by venturing east. He sought to create a direct route of supply of spices for French markets from the Near East. In the process Coeur was willing to negotiate with Muslims. At the end of his life he was prepared to crusade against Turkish expansion. His actions are not dissimilar to European responses in regard to the Muslims in the later fifteenth century and beyond. The Ottoman advance in the Near East threatened trade and heightened the issue of crusade in the Mediterranean in the late Middle Ages. Coeur's focus on the Mediterranean, his creation of a galley fleet for France, and his negotiation of trade advantages for the French set the tone for the reigns of Louis XI and François I.

From the institution of the French galley fleet to the mining operations Coeur patronized in the Lyonnais, Coeur's legacy bore fruit.[55] In the 1460s Louis XI supported "galleys of France" in the Mediterranean spice trade via the intermediary of French ports. Coeur's cross-cultural initiatives to negotiate favorable trading conditions in Muslim ports anticipated future French actions. François I continued the tradition of a French Mediterranean fleet and at times collaborated with the Ottomans. Coeur's formula of state-funded trade blossomed in the form of mercantilism in the early modern period. Coeur's entrepreneurial efforts deserve comparison with the later activities of Jean-Baptiste Colbert (1619–1683), Louis XIV's great minister, perhaps nowhere more clearly than in regard to the spice trade monopoly.

The French were late in positioning themselves for global trade in the era of European expansion. The English in 1600 and the Dutch in 1602 had founded companies to trade in Asia. It was Colbert, propelled by mercantilism, who entered the arena of fierce economic competition for the riches of the East in his foundation in 1664 of the French East India Company. Bolstered by a monopoly of trade in the region of the Orient for which it had a charter, Colbert championed the trade of company merchants.[56] In the mid-fifteenth century Coeur had pioneered such a role for merchants in royal commercial enterprise, acting with the support of the French monarchy. But in his day, his protomercantilist and protocapitalist instincts were not the norm.

Nonetheless, Coeur's tremendous success in business and his rapid rise to power in royal circles were acknowledged by contemporaries. François Villon (1431–1463), the great French lyricist of the mid-fifteenth century, evoked Coeur in his *Testament*:

> Lamenting my poverty
> Often my heart tells me
> Man do not be so sad
> Nor dwell in such despair,
> If you have not as much as Jacques Coeur.
> Better to live without great offices,
> Poor, than to have been a lord
> And rot under rich tombs.
>
> To have been a lord! What do you say?
> Lord, alas, is he not more?
> As the famous say,
> His place will never be known.

As for the surplus, I detach myself,
It will never belong to me, sinner,
To the theologians the tears
Because it is the function of a preacher.[57]

The model set by Coeur's mixed service in official and mercantile activities would have a brilliant future. Indeed, he is perhaps the first to present with such a wide set of talents in the service of the king of France. This study has argued that he was indeed "more," in the words of Villon.

Notes

It is a pleasure to contribute to a volume in honor of my esteemed colleague, James Tracy, a friend of over thirty years. I would like to thank Marguerite Ragnow for her comments on this chapter. The translations in this chapter are my own.

1. Georges Chastellain, "Puy ay veu par mistère, Monter un argentier, Le plus hault de la terre, Marchand et financier, Que depuis par fortune, Veis mourir en exil, Après bonté mainte une, Faite au Ry par icil," in *Oeuvres*, 8 vols. (Brussels: F. Heussner, 1863-1866), 7: 190–91. See Pierre Clément, *Jacques Coeur et Charles VII*, 2 vols. (Paris: Librairie de Guillaumin et Cie, 1853), for many comments by fifteenth-century authors about Jacques Coeur.

2. Among the most recent studies of Jacques Coeur are Michel Mollat, *Jacques Coeur ou l'esprit d'entreprise* (Paris: Aubier, 1988); and Jacques Heers, *Jacques Coeur* (Paris: Perrin, 1997).

3. My recent book, *Jacques Coeur: Entrepreneur and King's Bursar* (New York: Pearson Longman, 2004), examines both the traditional and the transitional roles of Jacques Coeur.

4. Mollat, *Jacques Coeur*, 103, terms this *intégration verticale*. For a general treatment of Coeur, see my article, "Jacques Coeur: French Trade in the Mediterranean World in the Mid-Fifteenth Century," *Proceedings of the Western Society for French History* 28 (2002): 99–112.

5. For the traditional dimensions of Coeur's trade, see my *Entrepreneur and King's Bursar*, especially 88–92. Robert Guillot, in *Le Procès de Jacques Coeur (1451–1457)* (Bourges: Imprimerie Dusser, 1974), 20, stated, "Enfin, quand il obtient pour ses galées le monopole d'importation des épices et de transport des marchandises françaises dans les ports musulmans, Jacques Coeur contribue à orienter la politique commerciale de la couronne vers des solutions dirigistes qui, du règne de Louis XI à la Révolution française, seront souvent imposées au monde des affaires." On the economic policies of Louis XI, see René Gandilhon, *Politique économique de Louis XI* (Paris: Presses universitaires de France, 1941). It should be noted that Coeur has also had his discounters who downplay the innovations in his Mediterranean strategy (Jean Favier) or attribute it (Heers) to his official functions. Jean Favier, in *De l'or et*

des épices. Naissance de l'homme d'affaires au Moyen Age (Paris: Fayard, 1987), 67, says Coeur was "three generations behind in his approach to the economic map." I dispute this assessment in *Entrepreneur and King's Bursar*, and in my article "Jacques Coeur: French Trade in the Mediterranean World."

6. An excellent treatment of the crusade remains W. L. Wakefield, *Heresy, Crusade and Inquisition in Southern France 1100–1250* (London: George Allen & Unwin, 1974). On Aigues Mortes, see Georges Jehel, *Aigues Mortes. Un port pour un roi. Les Capétiens et la Méditerranée* (Roanne/Le Coteau: Editions Horvath, 1985).

7. See my article "Montpellier and Genoa: The Dilemma of Dominance," *Journal of Medieval History* 20 (1994): 367.

8. Reyerson, "Montpellier and Genoa," 370–71.

9. Edouard Baratier and Félix Reynaud, *De 1291 à 1480*, vol. 2 of *Histoire du commerce de Marseille*, Chambre de Commerce de Marseille, ed. Gaston Rambert (Paris: Plon, 1951).

10. Jean Combes, in "Un groupe d'hommes d'affaires montpelliérains à la fin du XIVe siècle et au commencement du XVe," *Montpellier et le Languedoc au Moyen-Age. Mémoires de la Société Archéologique de Montpellier* 20 (1990): 85–120, argued that southern French towns sent only one or two ships per year to the Levant. However, Bernard Doumerc gave a somewhat more nuanced evaluation of the level of trade in "Les marchands du Midi à Alexandrie au XVe siècle," *Annales du Midi* 97 (1985): 269–84; "Documents commerciaux rédigés en langue d'oc enregistrés à Alexandrie par les notaires vénitiens," *Annales du Midi* 99 (1987): 227–44; and "La lente agonie des ports du Midi (fin XVe–début XVIe)," *Annales du Midi* 207 (1994): 316–31.

11. Paul Murray Kendall, *Louis XI, The Universal Spider* (New York: Norton, 1971), 116, 348.

12. James D. Tracy, *Emperor Charles V, Impresario of War* (Cambridge: Cambridge University Press, 2002), 307, on the Franco-Ottoman fleet.

13. Mollat, in *Jacques Coeur*, chap. 1, treats the *Argenterie* in detail. See also my discussion in chap. 3 of *Entrepreneur and King's Bursar*.

14. I discuss this issue of Coeur's lack of involvement in fifteenth-century exploration in *Entrepreneur and King's Bursar*, 90–92.

15. See Jean Combes, "Un groupe d'hommes d'affaires montpelliérains à la fin du XIVe siècle et au commencement du XVe," 101, n104. Louise Guiraud, *Recherches et conclusions nouvelles sur le prétendu rôle de Jacques Coeur* (Paris: Picard, 1900), Pièces justificatives, 144, published the names of the four galleys. See also Mollat, *Jacques Coeur*, 118; and Guillot, *Le procès de Jacques Coeur*, 80.

16. See Guy Romestan, "Quelques relations d'affaires de Jacques Coeur à Perpignan," *Annales du Midi* 79 (1967): 19–28.

17. For a detailed discussion of Coeur's ships, see Mollat, *Jacques Coeur*, chap. 6. See also Herrs, *Jacques Coeur*, chap. 3.

18. Mollat, *Jacques Coeur*, annexes 3.X, 388.

19. For a slightly different accounting, see Heers, *Jacques Coeur*, 102.

20. See my discussion in "Commercial Law and Merchant Disputes: Jacques Coeur and the Law of Marque," *Medieval Encounters* 9 (2003): 244–55.

21. On the *loge* in Montpellier, see Guiraud, *Le prétendu rôle de Jacques Coeur, passim*. See also Christian de Mérindol, "L'Emblématique des demeures et chapelles de Jacques Coeur. Une nouvelle lecture. La Grande Loge de Montpellier et les monuments de Bourges," *Actes du 110e Congrès national des Sociétés savantes, II: Recherches sur l'histoire de Montpellier et du Languedoc* (Paris: Ministère de l'éducation nationale, comité des travaux historiques et scientifiques, 1986), 153–78.

22. Mollat, *Jacques Coeur*, 128–30.

23. See the discussion by Heers, *Jacques Coeur*, 120–26; and Mollat, *Jacques Coeur*, 145–50.

24. Constantin Marinesco, "Nouveaux renseignements sur Jacques Coeur," *Eventail de l'histoire vivante. Hommage à Lucien Febvre*, 2 vols. (Paris: Armand Colin, 1953), II: 168–69: "It was exposed in the present Council that the *argentier* of the king of France had two galleys at sea and that, in order to prohibit other persons from bringing spices to France, and in order to reserve the profits to his galleys, he provoked the imposition by the king of France of a tax of ten percent on all the spices that would be imported, unless through the port of Aigues-Mortes which is reserved for the *argentier*, in such a way that France (which used to get its provisions in spices in this principality [Catalonia] and especially in the this city [Barcelona], now receives neither large nor small quantities."

25. See Reyerson, "Commercial Law and Merchant Disputes."

26. Guillot, *Le procès*, 20, n. 19, refers to Gandilhon's discovery of a document from the Archives Communales de Lyon (AA 149) that mentioned this monopoly. Guillot also cites the confirming evidence for this monopoly in the Barcelona archives found by Marinesco, "Nouveaux renseignements sur Jacques Coeur," 163–74.

27. Mollat, *Jacques Coeur*, 54 and 402 n. 2. See also Michel Mollat, "Une équipe: les commis de Jacques Coeur," *Eventail de l'histoire vivante. Hommage à Lucien Febvre*, II (Paris: Armand Colin, 1953), 175–85.

28. Mollat, *Jacques Coeur*, 53: "Il a empoigné toute la marchandise et partout a ses facteurs." (B. N. ms. fr. 2701, f. 53v.)

29. See my treatment of Coeur's interpersonal relations in *Entrepreneur and King's Bursar*, 67–73.

30. See Reyerson, *Entrepreneur and King's Bursar*, 89–90, for comparisons between Italian companies and Coeur.

31. Mollat, *Jacques Coeur*, 18; and Guillot, *Le procès*, 71.

32. Chastellain, in *Oeuvres*, 8: 92, discusses Coeur's loans to Charles VII.

33. Jacques du Clercq, *Mémoires de Jacques Du Clercq, escuier, sieur de Beauvoir en Ternois, commençant en 1448, et finissant en 1467* (Paris: 1836–1839), 618; Clément, *Jacques Coeur and Charles VII*, 1: xx.

34. For a discussion of his condemnation and trial, see my forthcoming article, "Le Procès de Jacques Coeur," in *Les procès politiques*, to be published by the École française de Rome.

35. See Reyerson, *Entrepreneur and King's Bursar*, introduction and passim.

36. "Et s'aucuns d'eux [les marchands] . . . Sont enrichez, est-ce pourtant à dire, Qu'on les doit prendre, Soit tort or droit, leurs biens piller ou vendre, Les confisquer

et donner sans mesprendre? . . . , Las! quels dangier de faulx accusateurs, Meschans garçons et mauvais emputeurs, Qui vont dire mensonges aux seigneurs, Pour deffaire, Mainz bons Marchans, et leur argent substraire, Sans les oyr en justice, ne faire, Droit ou raison, et puis leur adversaire, Estre ou [au] procès, Et prenant Juges de leur bende et acès. O! quel abus et quel horrible excez, . . ." Martial d'Auvergne, *Les vigiles de la mort du roy Charles VII* (also *Les poësies de Martial de Paris, dit d'Auvergne*), 8 vols. (Paris: A. U. Coustelier, 1724), 4:18–19.

37. Notably in Coeur's case, the accusation of poisoning the king's mistress, Agnes Morel, was false. For a discussion of the legal proceedings against Coeur, see Robert Guillot, *Le procès*. See also my forthcoming article "Le Procès de Jacques Coeur." One of the most valuable remaining documentary sources for a study of Jacques Coeur is the journal of the royal *procureur* Jean Dauvet, charged with the confiscation of Coeur's fortune after his condemnation, ms. KK328 of the *fonds français* of the Archives Nationales, called "Compte de la vente des biens de Jacques Coeur." Michel Mollat and his team edited this as *Journal du Procureur Dauvet*, 2 vols. (Paris: Librairie Armand Colin, 1952–53).

38. Albert Boardman Kerr, *Jacques Coeur. Merchant Prince of the Middle Ages* (London and New York: Charles Scribner's Sons, 1927; reprint, 1971), 264–65, has published a translation of this Consistory decree. He also included a photograph of the original document. Pope Nicholas said, "And we charge you to favor and justify his cause before the King and all other persons whatsoever."

39. A Venetian ducat, a gold coin minted since 1284, was worth 28 *s.* 9 *d. tournois* in 1470 and thus was almost on a par with the *écu* at 30 *s. t.* in 1450.

40. Mollat, *Jacques Coeur*, 315. The testimony of Guillaume d'Estouteville, archbishop of Rouen and cardinal of Ostia, recalled the relations between Nicholas V and Coeur; d'Estouteville stated that the pope had been very fond of the *argentier* ("*multum eumdem Argentarium diligebat*").

41. Heers, *Jacques Coeur*, 246–47, traces the end of the galleys. As early as May 1446, Alfonso had written to Coeur, "You will have occasion to realize that we will always accord a particular attention to you and your affairs, and that, when the captains of your galleys wish for safe-conducts, we will accord them with the greatest benevolence, out of esteem for you."(Mollat, *Jacques Coeur*, 148.) At one point Coeur had lent funds to Alfonso's son, a gesture that may have encouraged Alfonso's favorable disposition toward him.

42. See my discussion of Coeur and the crusade in *Entrepreneur and King's Bursar*, chap. 8.

43. This is the date, as well, of Coeur's condemnation by the king.

44. Mollat, *Jacques Coeur*, annexes 3.II: 377–78. Coeur had earlier, in a letter of 1447 to royal ambassadors about affairs in Genoa, spoken of himself as indispensable to the conquest of the Holy Grail. This comment may reflect a spiritual commitment, simple self-aggrandizement, or realistic pragmatism tied to Genoese politics and French ambitions of the moment.

45. On letters of remission, see Claude Gauvard, *"De grace especial." Crime, état et société à la fin du Moyen Age*, 2 vols. (Paris: Publications de la Sorbonne, 1991). On Coeur's pardons, see Reyerson, *Entrepreneur and King's Bursar*, chap. 3.

46. See Norman Housley, *The Later Crusades* (Oxford: Oxford University Press, 1992).

47. Heers, *Jacques Coeur*, 216.

48. Heers, *Jacques Coeur*, 217.

49. Heers, *Jacques Coeur*, 215–16.

50. Kerr, *Jacques Coeur*, 276; and Heers, *Jacques Coeur*, 217.

51. Mollat, *Jacques Coeur*, 21; and Heers, *Jacques Coeur*, 32.

52. Heers, *Jacques Coeur*, 32.

53. Coeur was, in fact, shipwrecked near Corsica on his way home and seized along with his companions by pirates from the island, who took the victims' goods. In later law of marque proceedings, Coeur's share of remuneration was very modest, suggesting either that his merchandise was lost and undocumentable or that he really had not traded much in the Levant. See my article "Commercial Law and Merchant Disputes."

54. See my discussion in *Entrepreneur and King's Bursar*, 162–69.

55. On Coeur's mining operations see Reyerson, *Entrepreneur and King's Bursar*, 97.

56. See Glenn J. Ames, *Colbert, Mercantilism, and the French Quest for Asian Trade* (DeKalb: Northern Illinois University Press, 1996).

57. "De pauvreté me guermentant, Souventes fois me dit le coeur: Homme ne te doulouse tant, Et ne demaine tel douleur, Se tu n'as tant que Jacques Cueur. Myeux vault vivre soubs gros bureaux, Pauvre, qu'avoir esté seigneur, Et pourrir, soubs riches tombeux. Q'avoir esté seigneur! Que dys? Seigneur, hélas, ne l'est-il mais? Selon les autenctiques dict, Son lieu ne congnaistra jamais. Quant au surplus, je m'en desmets, Il n'appartient à moi pescheur, Auz théologiens lermetes: Car c'est office de prescheur." François Villon, *Le testament*, ed. Jérome Vérain (Paris: Mille et une nuits, 2000), 18–19.

15

The Individual Merchant and the Trading Nation in Sixteenth-Century Antwerp

Donald J. Harreld

A NTWERP'S GOLDEN AGE CAME INTO FULL FLOWER as a result of a unique convergence between the city's marketplaces of merchants from various parts of Europe and the goods they brought to trade from all over the world. In Antwerp a truly international market was established where goods were imported into the city less for local consumption than for reexport to other areas of Europe.[1] By the opening years of the sixteenth century Antwerp saw its markets teeming with goods in demand all over the continent.

The variety of factors that contributed to Antwerp's commercial success can be summed up as "advantages of agglomeration."[2] It was the totality of the products, financial services, and institutions that developed over time that attracted merchants to Antwerp and made it a European *métropole*. At the heart of this agglomeration were the foreign merchant nations, institutions with deep roots in medieval urban society that offered a structure for individual merchants to negotiate the commercial life of the city. In essence, the foreign merchant nations were associations of merchants from various foreign cities or regions, which interacted with the city as a corporate body. Nations enjoyed various commercial privileges in the city that gave them particular advantages compared to unaffiliated merchants. However, merchant nations struggled to hold their place in early modern cities as new institutions developed that allowed merchants to function as individuals rather than as members of a corporate entity.

The relationship between individual merchants and the institution of the merchant nation is at once obvious and confused. Certainly associations based on occupation could not exist without their many individual members; the members *are* the association. But in early modern Europe not all members of an organization had equal standing, nor did they necessarily have a voice in the organization's governance. However, some merchants enjoyed the benefits that the merchant nations brought without being members or otherwise participating in the association. These "free riders" probably made up the majority of Antwerp's merchant population in the sixteenth century.

The Corporation and the Individual

The quintessential medieval urban institution was the corporate body, a sworn association of its members. The medieval town itself was a sworn association, a brotherhood of citizens bound together in defense of civic liberty.[3] In turn, the town was home to various corporate bodies, each dedicated to its own advancement and collectively to the success of the town as a whole. Membership in a corporation, often a merchant or craft guild, conferred upon the citizen standing in the community. Rulers, however, conferred liberties and privileges on the corporate body, not on individuals. Thus individual freedom must be understood not in the modern sense, but as freedom bestowed upon the individual through the mechanism of the association and dependent on membership in the association.

Guildsmen also commonly participated in a variety of other associations, religious and secular, as well as the guild.[4] The individual operated within a structure of competing loyalties and associations, so the complex of a person's associations together contributed to identity formation.[5] In the case of foreign merchant guilds, called foreign merchant nations in Antwerp, the individual foreign merchant's participation in guild activities varied depending on whether or not the towns within his area of operation recognized foreign merchant nations. Overall, the individual merchant "operated freely within this framework" of foreign merchant nations as he traveled from one market town to the next.[6]

Scholars have probably given more attention to the economic function of the guild, usually identified as a creation of monopolies—monopoly of labor, monopoly of production, monopoly of trade, and so on—than the guild's societal functions as a corporate body. Michael Postan has suggested that the guild was "the instrument of the monopoly" and that it was "the town government's commercial guise."[7] Others have countered that the monopolistic function of the guild was really chimerical. According to this view the guild formed as a way for the underdeveloped medieval urban government to exact defense taxes from its citizenry.[8]

Examining the role of transaction costs in commercial relations offers scholars a better way to understand the economic function of the merchant nations. Foreign merchant associations developed during the Middle Ages as a way to enforce property rights in the absence of strong political institutions. Bound together as a corporate body and presenting to the city a unified front, merchants were able to minimize the impact of some fees and taxes on trade. Merchant associations enhanced commerce through their ability to decrease transaction costs and also strengthened socially the foreign merchant community. Social benefits for foreign merchants included both the creation of enclaves of foreigners within a city and the development of a sense of loyalty to the foreign community.

Émile Durkheim conceptualized medieval and early modern occupational associations, such as guilds, as "conscience collectives."[9] According to his model, the guild formed in response to governmental structures that repressed the individual. Individuals within the guild structure, however, were bound together by their shared value system, and each member joined in the collective voice that the association projected in the community. Yet according to Durkheim, even within the corporation the individual interests of a powerful few eventually dictated the direction the corporation would take. The tenacious desire for the maintenance of privilege and status came to be more important than solidarity of the membership.[10]

At first glance, Durkheim's ideas about occupational associations during the Middle Ages as institutions responding to the repression of the individual seem somewhat in line with the old notion put forward by Jacob Burckhardt in which Renaissance Europe saw the triumph of the individual over the corporation. For Burckhardt, medieval man "was conscious of himself only as a member of a race, people, party, family, or corporation."[11] The "common veil" that covered medieval man was only lifted with the Renaissance; modern man was to become an individual. But Durkheim suggested that this modern man had a continuing need for occupational associations like the guild.

Anthony Black has suggested that the communal mentality of the corporate body was not the only social ideal known to medieval town dwellers. What Black calls *civil society*, or liberal ideals, which stressed the liberty of the individual even outside of his status in the corporation, was very much a part of medieval society.[12] Certainly, as Black points out, the corporate structure of the guild and the ideals of civil society centered on the individual coexisted and even complemented each other well into the early modern period. But competing loyalties to communal solidarity produced tensions that ultimately led to the demise of the corporate body and to an emphasis on the idealization of individualism.

These tensions emerged, in part, as the nature of town governance shifted to the will of the ruler as the tendency toward state centralization began to emerge in the sixteenth century.[13] Once the town ceased to be a corporate body autonomous from the central state, the focus on collective action gave way to a focus on individual action. But just as state centralization was not a revolutionary action, the gradual development of institutions that decreased the individual's dependence on the corporate body also had a role to play in this process. In Antwerp some of these institutions, like the exchange and the various specialty markets (or *panden*), developed because of the efforts of the foreign merchant nations, but by the sixteenth century individual merchants distinct from the nation benefited from these innovations as well.[14]

Burckhardt's distinct break between medieval and early modern man and the suggestion that corporate action was old-fashioned by the sixteenth century obscures rather than clarifies early modern social organization. The development of institutions catering to the needs of individuals would have set the occupational association, the corporate body, adrift from its moorings. Nevertheless, because they served a purpose, older forms of association like the guild persisted during the early modern period despite the development of institutions more suited to individual than corporate action. The economic function of the merchant guild may have seen better days by the middle of the sixteenth century, but the social functions of corporate bodies that contributed to group loyalty and identity formation persisted, even though these kinds of activities were often most visible outside of the usual commercial venues.

Antwerp's Trading Nations

In a town like Antwerp in the sixteenth century, where citizens equated the economic success of foreign merchants with the town's prosperity, the foreign merchant nations were the most important corporate bodies. A foreign merchant nation was essentially a merchant guild; barriers to entry in a foreign merchant guild usually had to do with the merchant's place of origin. Merchant guilds differed from craft guilds due to their focus on long-distance trade and because of the capital required to conduct business.

Members of guilds ordinarily appointed, with many limitations, the individuals who would serve as officials of the guild to establish and enforce guild regulations, and who would represent the guild in the public life of the town.[15] Guilds, however, were not democratic institutions; the masters of the guilds certainly dominated them.[16] Organizational structure and the privileges of the foreign merchant nations varied from group to group. Some nations imposed fairly strict regulations on their members, while others were rather fluid organizations with few or no formal strictures.

Antwerp's High German nation placed no real restrictions on its merchants, but they enjoyed none of the privileges usually associated with late medieval merchant nations. The governing structure, if any even existed, had little interaction with the town magistracy. More than anything else the High German nation concerned itself with social events and participation in public spectacle. Loyalty to the High German nation was slight; loyalty was given more out of convenience than necessity.

The German Hanse and the English merchant nation heavily regulated their merchants and jealously guarded their privileges. The English merchants in particular had fairly strict regulations. The English nation determined the days and times its merchants could display their goods and offer them for sale. English merchants tended to sequester themselves within the confines of the English house and conduct their commercial operations out of the English *pand* (or market) attached to the English establishment in Antwerp.

The several Italian merchant nations based their position in Antwerp on a succession of privileges they had obtained from the rulers of the Low Countries. Patterned on the privileges granted to the Genoese community in Bruges by the Count of Flanders in 1315, Antwerp's Italian merchants also received privileges from the ruler that were regularly reconfirmed. In the Genoese privileges reconfirmed in Antwerp in 1532, Charles V included a stipulation that the Genoese would be required to contribute to the cost of the joyous entries of princes and princesses, and to the cost of great festivals.[17] But while the Genoese and other Italian nations in Antwerp had privileges that specified their rights within the commercial life of the town as well as the concessions they were required to make in order to exact these privileges, they were not usually restricted in their activities. Indeed, relatively few Genoese could actually become official members of the nation—only members of the twenty-eight noble merchant families of Genoa.[18] So while many Genoese merchants enjoyed the privileges the nation had obtained, barriers to formal entry into the nation allowed them to operate rather freely in Antwerp without the potentially coercive restrictions and financial burdens that could have been imposed by membership in the nation.

Only large-scale merchants, those most likely to be residents of the city for long periods of time, seem to have been closely associated with Antwerp's foreign merchant nations. Other merchants operated as free riders within the orbit of the merchant nations enjoying the advantages the nations had secured for foreigners, but without the kind of burdens that came with formal membership.

Merchant Types in Antwerp

When telling Antwerp's sixteenth-century success story, scholars have tended to highlight the highest value goods and the merchants and merchant firms that operated on the highest levels of European international commerce, who were most apt to be associated formally with the foreign merchant nations.[19] The thousands of merchants doing business in Antwerp around the middle of the sixteenth century when the city's economy reached its zenith exhibited extreme differences in wealth, degree of market participation, types of goods, destinations, and so on. Because scholars have usually focused on just one group of merchants (the large-scale merchants), the way the merchant experience has been characterized in the literature probably tells the story of only a minority of merchants, resulting in an overemphasis on the role of the formal activities of the merchant nations. Merchants associated with the great firms dominated merchant nations, while small-scale merchants played a relatively minor role in these organizations. Between these two groups were hundreds of merchants of significant means, some of whose experience approximated the great merchant firms of Europe, while others were much more like small-scale merchants.

One way to approach the relationship between the individual merchant and the merchant nation is to identify the variety of merchant types by looking at their experiences and how likely merchants of various types were to participate in the structure of the nation. Creating typologies, however, is a risky business, as they often have little to do with historical reality. But despite the fact that they are artificial constructs, typologies can be useful aids in forming an understanding of historical processes. Studying merchants with certain observed similarities as a group (regardless of the artificiality of the grouping) and their relationships with commercial and social institutions makes it possible to draw conclusions and estimate the experience of all merchants associated with a given group. Based on value of exports, it is possible to distinguish between at least four different types of foreign merchants in sixteenth-century Antwerp: large-scale merchants, middle-range merchants, small-scale merchants, and peddlers.

Antwerp's merchant elite, the large-scale merchants, operated at the highest levels of commerce. The merchant elite was the group most well known to scholars, and it comprised those most closely associated with the merchant nations. While the activities of this group certainly constituted the highest valued and most profitable transactions at the Antwerp markets, there were many more merchants whose commerce was also important for the economy of Antwerp and the southern Netherlands. For example, about twenty-one hundred merchants or factors listed in the registers of Charles

V's Hundredth Penny tax engaged in the export trade between Antwerp and Germany. Ninety-five merchants (most representing the great German firms) controlled 80 percent of Antwerp's export trade with Germany during the period from 1543 to 1545.[20] The case of Antwerp's overland trade with Italy is much the same as that for Germany. Seventy-seven merchants controlled almost 90 percent of the export trade with Italy during the same period.[21] This select group of large-scale merchants included those who represented the nation in dealings with the city. A toll dispute between German merchants and the city resulted in the agents of the Fuggers and Welsers appealing to Antwerp's treasurer for redress in 1550, and the prominent members of the Genoese nation joined with the High Germans in petitioning for a freight terminal in 1560.[22]

It is true that the great merchant houses of Europe drove much of Antwerp's commercial expansion. In the case of Antwerp's trade with the German lands, the great German firms and their agents controlled commerce. All the major German firms were active in Antwerp during the city's golden age. The Fugger firm opened a permanent branch office in Antwerp as early as 1508 even though the firm had been operating in the city before that. The Welsers and the Hochstetters were both active in Antwerp from an early date and had permanent offices there by the 1530s. An army of factors of the large German firms and their commission agents took up residence in the city. These functionaries usually remained in Antwerp for years before returning to their city of origin, and many Germans also migrated to Antwerp throughout the sixteenth century in search of work or fortune.

Since Antwerp's success in world trade in the sixteenth century was based on the tripartite commerce in English cloth, Portuguese spices, and German metals, the fact that the largest firms dominated trade should come as no surprise. Already in the sixteenth century, economies of scale were important in business. Usually only the largest firms had the capital available to transport large volumes of goods over great distances, and even then they tended to be those goods with the highest profit margins.[23]

Despite the commercial dominance enjoyed by the large-scale merchants in Antwerp's overland trade and their control of merchant nations, medium- and small-scale merchants had a significant role to play in the commercial vitality of the city even though they rarely associated formally with the nations. Indeed, most of the small-scale merchants were engaged in the same commercial activities that merchants had been pursuing for generations before Antwerp became a world entrepôt. In one respect, the small-scale merchants could be seen as a force for commercial stability in an economy that otherwise depended on transshipping imported merchandise by merchants who dominated the foreign merchant nations.

While the great merchant firms were in control of the bulk of the Antwerp-German trade, merchants operating on a much smaller scale comprised the vast majority of those engaged in trade with German cities, even though they did not account for the greatest value of the goods exported out of Antwerp. The roughly two thousand merchants engaged in trade with Germany who had exports valued at less than 1000 £ Flemish *groot* during the period between 1543 and 1545 accounted for 20 percent of Antwerp's overland export trade with German cities. Far fewer merchants were involved in the overland trade with Italy (only about 300), but the majority of them (about 223) had exports less than 1000 £ Flemish *groot*. The 223 merchants with goods bound for Italy accounted for only just over 10 percent of the total value of all goods sent to Italy during the same period. The focus as well as the scale of their efforts was necessarily quite different from the great merchant firms, but even within this group of small-scale merchants there was an amazing amount of differentiation.

Several characteristics served to differentiate the various merchant types in sixteenth-century Antwerp. The first and most obvious characteristic concerned the value of the merchants' shipments. Export values were considerably less for small-scale merchants than they were for those merchants in control of the most valuable sectors of trade. The median total value of the merchants' exports to Germany during the period of the Hundredth Penny tax amounted to just 25 £ Flemish *groot*, almost twice the annual wage of a master mason in Antwerp. Merchants with trade valued at this level were more than mere peddlers even if they were not in the same league as the great merchants. Small-scale merchants could be defined as those with exports between the annual wage of a master mason (or about 15 £ Flemish *groot*) and an amount ten times the annual wage of a master mason. This group constitutes about 1000 of the merchants (roughly half) engaged in trade with Germany around midcentury. Almost two-thirds, or about 193 merchants, engaged in overland trade with Italy had total exports less than 500 £ Flemish *groot* during the period between 1543 and 1545. Probably because of the great distances involved, the median total value of goods merchants shipped to Italian destinations were higher than that of those sent to Germany. In any event, the names of small-scale foreign merchants never appear in the records of Antwerp's foreign merchant nations.

Comparing the exports of the great merchant firms with those of small-scale merchants suggests a second characteristic: Small-scale merchants were more likely to trade in the products of the southern Netherlands than their large-scale competitors. There are some obvious reasons for this. Because of the costs involved, small-scale merchants were only rarely involved in the spice trade. A pack of pepper usually had a value of about 70 £ Flemish *groot* in the early 1540s, about 4.5 times the annual wage of a master mason of Antwerp for the same period,[24] and almost three times the median value of merchants total exports to German cities. Few small-scale merchants could have afforded this product.

Likewise, success in the English cloth trade required a considerable infrastructure that most merchants could not afford, and contacts that resulted from association with the foreign merchant nations. English ships carrying cloth arrived in Antwerp on a regular, but not frequent, schedule. This required merchants to warehouse these goods. Most of the English cloth shipped out of Antwerp was finished and otherwise handled before shipment, adding to its cost. Large-scale merchants also controlled the export of the more popular cloths from other southern Netherlands cities like Lier, Leuven, and Mechelen. But Antwerp's small-scale merchants were able to capitalize on trafficking in the more traditional textile products of Flanders that the great firms ignored. For instance, small-scale merchants exported more than 40 percent of the traditional Flemish cloth from Antwerp to Germany. Thirty percent of the exports of the cloth of Bruges were sent to Germany by small-scale merchants.

Besides the most heavily traded items such as English cloth, Portuguese pepper, and other spices, what other merchandise was left? The kinds of goods small-scale merchants traded in were very different from the goods the great merchant firms were interested in. Small-scale merchant exports included the agricultural products of the Low Countries such as butter and cheese, and, from Flanders and Holland, dried fish and other foodstuffs, including imported wine. Small-scale merchants sent virtually all of the Flemish cheese exports to Germany, with the exception of cheese exports to Aachen.[25] Dairy products sent from Antwerp to Germany were normally in the hands of small-scale merchants bound for Cologne, Julich, and Aachen. Things like dyestuffs and fixatives such as alum, madder and brazilwood, "dry goods" (which could mean almost anything), skins and leather, and items produced in Antwerp such as books and paintings were also in the hands of small-scale merchants.

Third, small-scale merchants usually engaged in trade with one city, or with cities that most merchants associated with the great firms were less interested in. The great German merchant firms directed virtually all of their exports to five German cities: Augsburg, Nuremberg, Leipzig, Frankfurt, and Cologne. Cologne had been one of Antwerp's most important trading partners for generations, so many small-scale merchants were involved in the Cologne trade, but they also traded with Cleves, Münster, Julich, Trier, and other cities that the large-scale merchants ignored. While some of the small-scale merchants engaged in trade with these cities were north Germans, many more were from Antwerp.

Finally, Antwerp's small-scale merchants were much less active in the trading nations of the city. They played an important but subordinate role to the great merchants in both the commercial life and in the social life of the city. They were only loosely affiliated with the structure of Antwerp's merchant nations, if at all. This brings into question the whole structure of corporate versus individual action. It might seem that small-scale merchants would have the most to benefit from membership in a merchant association, yet in sixteenth-century Antwerp it was the large-scale merchants who controlled the nations and seem to have been its principal members. In order for small-scale merchants to compete at the Antwerp market, they must have employed commercial techniques that decreased transaction costs. The foreign merchant nations retained their power in the city, but not to the exclusion of medium- and small-scale merchants.

Commercial Institutions and Individual Action

From a fairly early date, the English used the leverage they had thanks to their wool and woolens trade to exact concessions from the city. The merchants of the English nation left Antwerp in 1457, vowing not to return. They moved to Bruges and stayed there for about a year, shrugging off Antwerp's attempts to entice them back. It all began when the weigh master at the Antwerp beam insulted an English merchant by calling him a liar. The weigh master not only called him a liar, but also said that he "lied like an Englishman." The English merchants in Antwerp considered the insult an offense against the entire English nation.[26]

The long-held power of the foreign merchant nations was probably at its peak at the turn of the sixteenth century, but even in an era when their importance was decreasing, the influence of the merchant nations had a long reach. In 1552, about one hundred years after the English threw their weight around, an individual member of a merchant nation again caused a row when he requested the arrest of a merchant in Ghent. Diego de Pardo, a member of the Spanish nation in Bruges, had a certain Jan de Looper, an Antwerp merchant, arrested. This set off a chain reaction resulting in the arrest of several merchants of Ghent in retaliation when they were visiting one of Antwerp's fairs.[27]

But as practices developed in Antwerp that facilitated individual action, dependence on the privileges and power of the merchant nations became less common. The privileges foreign merchant communities had been able to negotiate in the fourteenth century were becoming a much less important part of their overall commercial strategies by the sixteenth century. The same was true of local Antwerp merchants. Not only were most of the small-scale merchants exporting goods to German cities from the area around Antwerp, many of the largest merchants involved in shipping goods to Germany and Italy were local, too. Since they were local merchants, membership in the foreign trading nations was obviously not open to them, but Antwerp merchants had been trying to obtain privileges from the city that would put them on an even playing field with the foreigners since the late fifteenth century. They do not seem to have had much success.[28] Not even the High German nation enjoyed any privileges in Antwerp. While other foreign merchant groups had been able to obtain privileges from the ruler, by the sixteenth century they were becoming less important as institutions developed in Antwerp that facilitated trade without recourse to privilege.

The ability of merchants to negotiate a market town the size of Antwerp (and in particular the small-scale merchants) without privileges may be due to the innovations developed to suit the needs of the large-scale foreign merchant firms and the foreign merchant nations. Commercial techniques that obviated the need for merchants to band together developed throughout the sixteenth century. The transformation of the fair cycle, for example, from a time to buy and sell goods to a time frame for accounts to come due and interest to be paid, benefited not only members of the merchant nations, but the small operator as well. Payment of accounts was almost always a concern between individual merchants, but the merchant nation might become involved if one of its members was not paid.

The development of the concept of commission agents allowed the small-scale merchant to expand his area of operation. In this kind of relationship a merchant resident in one city contracted with a merchant in a different city to buy and sell goods on a commission basis. This allowed merchants to be commercially active in more than one city without the infrastructure and employees that the large-scale firms needed and that often the foreign nation might provide.

Several well-known merchants, including a number of Germans and Italians, petitioned the city for a freight terminal where they could have their goods loaded and unloaded and as a place where they could hire transporters.[29] The construction of a freight terminal, the *Hessenhuis*, in Antwerp facilitated overland shipment for the small-scale merchant as well as the largest merchant concerns. The rules of the *Hessenhuis* outlining fees, handling of bills of lading, and so on worked to the advantage of merchants of all sizes.

Perhaps the most important commercial technique in Antwerp was the ability to use witnesses in a variety of ways before the city magistrates. The use of merchant witness to increase information available about new merchants in the city allowed merchants outside of the nation to participate in commerce without unnecessary risk. The usual form these attestations took was for a merchant who was not known in the city to be "introduced" by a merchant who was either of high status, perhaps the chief of a merchant nation, or had long operated in Antwerp to vouch for the good name of the newcomer.[30]

Even though merchants were employing techniques that decreased the economic importance of the merchant nation, the nations' social functions may have increased during the sixteenth century as the ranks of prosperous merchants grew. Even so, relatively few foreign merchants shared the spotlight in public events. Only fifty merchants represented the High German merchant nation in the Antwerp *Joyeux Entrée* of the future Philip II in 1549. About the same number of merchants from the German Hanse participated. In total, the foreign merchant community in Antwerp fielded about two or three hundred merchants for this event.[31] This represents only a small portion of the nearly four thousand people in Antwerp (citizens included) who made their livelihood in trade, and illustrates the gap in wealth among Antwerp's merchants. Only wealthy merchants would have had the discretionary wealth necessary to outfit themselves for events like the *Joyeuse Entrées*.

As their privileges decreased in importance, the value of the foreign merchant nation became more social than commercial, but the merchant nation continued to be an important part of Antwerp's commercial structure. Large-scale merchants and the factors of Europe's great merchant firms were most actively involved in the nations, while merchants of more limited means had little to do with them. Small-scale merchants acted individually rather than in groups.

Burckhardt's idea of a clean break in mentality between the corporate forms of thinking during the Middle Ages to the individualism of the Renaissance certainly never played out among the foreign merchant nations of sixteenth-century Antwerp. The evidence suggests that both corporate and individual action coexisted during the sixteenth century. As economic reasons for the development of merchant associations decreased, their social functions remained important to identity formation and group loyalty. For the most part only the richest merchants participated in these associations. The small-scale merchant in Antwerp had little to do with the trading nations and other merchant associations, but certainly exploited the commercial institutions that were developing in sixteenth-century Antwerp in response to the needs of the foreign merchant nations.

Notes

1. Jan van Houtte, "Bruges et Anvers, marchés 'nationaux' ou 'internationaux' du XIVe au XVIe siècles," *Revue du Nord* 34 (1952): 89–108.

2. Michael Limberger, "No Town in the World Provides More Advantages: Economies of Agglomeration and the Golden Age of Antwerp" in *Urban Achievement in Early Modern Europe: Golden Ages in Antwerp, Amsterdam and London*, ed. Patrick O'Brien et al. (Cambridge: Cambridge University Press, 2001), 39–62; see particularly 50 and 53.

3. This concept is nicely summarized in the short monograph by Richard Mackenney, *The City-State, 1500–1700: Republican Liberty in an Age of Princely Power* (Atlantic Heights, NJ: Humanities, 1989), 2–3.

4. Francis Aidan Hibbert, *The Influence and Development of English Gilds* (Cambridge: Cambridge University Press, 1891; reprint, A. M. Kelley, 1970), 8–9.

5. Joseph P. Ward, *Metropolitan Communities: Trade Guilds, Identity, and Change in Early Modern London* (Stanford: Stanford University Press, 1997), 3.

6. J. N. Ball, *Merchants and Merchandise: The Expansion of Trade in Europe, 1500–1630* (London: Croom Helm, 1977), 34.

7. M. M. Postan, *The Medieval Economy and Society: An Economic History of Britain in the Middle Ages* (London: Weidenfeld and Nicolson, 1972), 214.

8. Charles R. Hickson and Earl A. Thompson, "A New Theory of Guilds and European Economic Development," *Explorations in Economic History* 28 (1991): 127–68.

9. M. J. Hawkins, "Durkheim on Occupational Corporations: An Exegesis and Interpretation," *Journal of the History of Ideas* 55 (1994): 464.

10. Émile Durkheim, *The Division of Labor in Society*, trans. George Simpson (Glencoe, IL: Free Press, 1933), 9–10. The citation refers to Durkheim's preface to the second edition of *De la division du travail social*.

11. Jacob Burckhardt, *The Civilization of Renaissance Italy*, trans. S. G. C. Middlemore (New York: Mentor, 1960), 121.

12. Anthony Black, *Guilds and Civil Society in European Political Thought from the Twelfth Century to the Present* (London: Methuen, 1984), 32–34.

13. Donald J. Harreld, "Urban Particularism and State Centralization in the Revolt of Ghent, 1538–40," *Proteus: a Journal of Ideas* 20 (2003): 39–44.

14. Donald J. Harreld, "Trading Places: the Public and Private Spaces of Merchants in Sixteenth-Century Antwerp," *Journal of Urban History* 29 (2003): 657–69.

15. Fr. Olivier-Martin, *L'organisation corporative de la France d'ancien régime* (Paris: Library du Recueil Sirey, 1938), 93.

16. Steven A. Epstein, *Wage Labor and Guilds in Medieval Europe* (Chapel Hill: University of North Carolina Press, 1991), 135.

17. Stadsarchief Antwerpen (SAA), Privilegiekamer 1075, *Natie van Genua*, Privilege of 13 March 1532.

18. Colette Beck, "Éléments sociaux et économiques de la vie des marchands génois à Anvers entre 1528 et 1555," *Revue de Nord* 64 (1982): 763.

19. For some examples see Hans Pohl, *Die Portugiesen in Antwerpen: (1567–1648): Zur Geschichte E. Minderheit*, 1. Aufl., *Vierteljahrschrift Für Sozial- Und Wirtschaftsgeschichte* Beihefte Nr. 63 (Wiesbaden: Steiner, 1977); G. D. Ramsay, *The Queen's Merchants and the Revolt of the Netherlands* (Manchester: Manchester University Press, 1986); Oskar de Smedt, *De Engelse Natie Te Antwerpen in De 16e Eeuw (1496–1582)* (Antwerp: De Sikkel, 1950).

20. For a fuller discussion of these large-scale merchants see Donald J. Harreld, "German Merchants and their Trade in Sixteenth-Century Antwerp," in *International Trade in the Low Countries (14th–16th Centuries): Merchants, Organization, Infrastructure,* ed. Peter Stabel, Bruno Blondé, and Anke Greve (Leuven: Garant, 2000), 175–79.

21. Wilfred Brulez, "L'exportation des Pays-Bas vers l'Italie par voie de terre au milieu du XVIᵉ siècle," *Annales: Économies, Sociétés, Civilisations* 14 (1959): 471.

22. Donald J. Harreld, *High Germans in the Low Countries: German Merchants and Commerce in Golden Age Antwerp* (Leiden: Brill, 2004), 108, 125.

23. See Meir Kohn's, "Organized Markets in Pre-Industrial Europe," a draft chapter from his manuscript, *The Origins of Western Economic Success,* Dartmouth College Economics Department Working Paper 03-12.

24. For wage estimates, see appendices 27/2 and 27/4 in Herman van der Wee, *The Growth of the Antwerp Market and the European Economy (fourteenth–sixteenth centuries),* vol. 1, *Statistics* (The Hague: Martinus Nijhoff, 1963).

25. A large-scale Aachener merchant, Jan Stempel, controlled most of the trade with Aachen.

26. Floris Prims, "Hoe de Engelschen ons Verlieten in 1457," *Antwerpensia,* 27 vols. (Antwerp: De Vlijt, 1928–1954), 10: 112.

27. SAA, Tresorij 1112, Jaarmarkten, March 18, 1569.

28. SAA, *Privilegiekamer* 1012, Raeckt den Handel, 1464–1610, document dated May 5, 1485.

29. SAA, *Privilegiekamer* 2208, Hessenhuis, about 1562, f⁰ 1.

30. For just one example, see SAA, *Certificatieboek* 5, 28 August 1542, f⁰ 19.

31. See the description in Cornelius Grapheus, *Les très admirable, très magnificque, et triumphate entrée, du trèsahault et très puissant Prince Philipes, Prince d'Espaignes, filz de l'Empereur Charles V ensemble la vraye description des Spectacles, Theatres, archz triumphaulx, etc. Lesquelz ont este faictz et bastis a sa très desiree reception en la très renommee florissante ville d'Anvers. Anno 1549* (Antwerp, 1550).

16

Between Profit and Power

The Dutch East India Company and
Institutional Early Modernities in the
"Age of Mercantilism"

Markus P. M. Vink

HISTORIANS HAVE IDENTIFIED THE DUTCH REPUBLIC as the "first modern state," the "first modern economy," and the "first true world entrepôt," while the Dutch East India Company (VOC) has, deservedly or not, received the designation of being the "world's first multinational" or "first modern corporation," "Europe's first effective joint-stock company," and the "Dutch Republic's most original commercial institution."[1] This chapter argues against these overly facile "ideal type" interpretations and instead demonstrates that the VOC (1602–1799) existed neither as a "redistributive enterprise" nor as an "institutional innovation," but rather as a typical early modern transitional institution, straddling the divide between the collective and the individual, the affective and the impersonal, the traditional and the innovative; in brief, an institution that bridged the medieval and the modern worlds, combining profit and power, and "a perfect example of what we today understand as the spirit of mercantilism."[2]

In similar fashion, the Dutch Republic has been identified as an intermediate stage between the medieval commune (with a restricted form of citizenship) and the nineteenth-century nation-state (when the concept became more inclusive, covering all inhabitants). The United Provinces was dominated by merchant-regent families, deriving their wealth from the perquisites and opportunities of civic and provincial office and accumulations of investments both of the traditional type, in provincial bonds, and in the new large-scale capital ventures—drainage projects, urban development, and, from the late 1590s, the colonial companies.[3]

Interestingly enough, the factory system, the semipublic establishment of separate premises for foreign merchants or factors, which had first evolved in medieval Flanders, began to disappear within Europe in the sixteenth century, just as it began to reappear as a common way of dealing with long-distance trade with Africa, the Americas, and Asia. Whereas between the sixteenth and eighteenth centuries in Europe trade came to depend much more on local commission agents, rather than having each merchant house maintain agents of its own nation in a foreign city. Africa, the Americas, and Asia saw the rise of European trading-post empires. These "militarized trade diasporas" were finally superseded by the Industrial Revolution, true territorial empires, multinational corporations, and the spread of a common culture of commerce between 1740 and 1860.[4]

Inspired by the two volumes, *The Rise of Merchant Empires* (1990) and *The Political Economy of Merchant Empires* (1991), edited by James D. Tracy,[5] this chapter addresses the historiographical debate among scholars of Portuguese and Dutch overseas expansion, area studies specialists, and world historians on institutional early modernities, more specifically on the character of the early Asian trade, the Portuguese Estado da India, and the Dutch East India Company. Their widely differing assessments do not simply reflect existing divisions in the historical profession, but they are also illustrative of the ambiguity and transitional character of the period between the Middle Ages and the modern era that perhaps can be best subsumed under the phrase "unity in diversity." As a chartered company with delegated government rights, the VOC or "merchant-warrior" was a politico-economic organization founded on the twin mercantilist pillars of profit and power (and the related principles of rational bureaucracy and corporate patrimonialism).[6]

Van Leur, Meilink-Roelofsz, Steensgaard, and the "New Institutional Historians"

The parameters of the post–World War II debate on the nature of early modern Asian trade and the instruments of European expansion have been defined by the seminal studies of J. C. van Leur, M. A. P. Meilink-Roelofsz, and Niels Steensgaard. As Tracy has argued, these works combined have provided "the scaffolding on which scholars writing in the last quarter century have begun to build a more nuanced picture of Southeast Asian trade in the early modern era."[7]

Inspired by the writings and methodology of B. J. O. Schrieke, W. H. Moreland, and Max Weber, the Dutch "colonial ethnologist"–civil servant van Leur argued in his *Indonesian Trade and Society* (1955) that modern capitalism took shape only after 1820, suggesting an equality or near equality between Asian and European commercial organization in the sixteenth and seventeenth centuries.[8] A corollary of this view was his negative assessment of the Portuguese achievement in Southeast Asia, his refusal to accord them technical or organizational superiority except in a limited military sense, his insistence upon the small and unimportant Portuguese share of intra-Asian trade, and his denunciation of the Portuguese as little better than a band of *condottieri* who lacked an effective central administration.

Against his few Portuguese *condottieri*, van Leur set a multitude of Asian traders. The trade of Indonesia as he envisaged it was essentially an exchange of limited quantities of highly valuable wares. The organization and financing of this "peddling trade," however, sprang from forms as well developed as those prevailing in contemporary Europe. Asian capital holdings were as extensive; the ships involved were as large, if not larger, than their European counterparts; and the Indonesian princes, nobles, state officials, and "merchant gentlemen" were the equivalents of European banking families such as the Fuggers and Welsers of Augsburg.[9] Despite his contention that the Javanese elite engaged in overseas trade, van Leur adhered to his conception of Southeast Asian commerce as "peddling" and recognized only the rice trade as involving the purchase and shipment of vast quantities.[10] Similarly, although van Leur accorded to the Dutch East India Company the complete technological superiority over its rivals that he denied to the Portuguese, he claimed that the Dutch did not enjoy a political preponderance in the archipelago by 1650 and that even the coveted spice trade was not entirely in their hands by that time.[11]

Whereas the prewar Eurocentric narrative had focused largely on external processes in the Indian Ocean region and the extent to which they shaped, or were shaped by, local cultures, the new Indocentric discourse, inspired by van Leur, was concerned with the notion of the autonomy of Asian history. Van Leur himself argued that European influence had been overemphasized by earlier historians and made almost no difference at least until the late eighteenth century. In his classical formulation, van Leur argued that with the arrival of European ships in the Indian Ocean, once again "the view . . . turned a hundred eighty degrees and from then on the Indies are observed from the deck of the ship, the ramparts of the fortress, the high gallery of the trading-house."[12]

The Dutch East India Company was not unlike a merchant-prince financing successive voyages, and its employees in the Indies were performing functions similar to those of the peddlers. To that extent it fitted into the existing patterns of trade of the archipelago. Even as its power expanded and it was able to impose its own monopoly over the area, and acquired territorial footholds, it was still far short of being a sovereign ruler. Its relations with indigenous authorities, van Leur argued, were more like international relations than relations between ruler and subjects. At the very most it might be regarded as a paramount power, stronger than other individual polities but not entirely different from them in kind.

Influenced by the ideas of K. Polanyi, T. P. van der Kooy, P. W. Klein, F. C. Lane, J. Hurstfield, J. van Klaveren, and, last but not least, J. C. van Leur, the Danish historian Niels Steensgaard, in *The Asian Trade Revolution of the Seventeenth Century* (1973), contrasted the "early Asian trade" and the Portuguese Estado da India as dominated by peddlers, political merchants, intransparent markets, and protection costs, portraying the Dutch East India Company instead as an institutional innovation by its internalization of protection costs and control of the market. The corporate joint-stock companies represented a metamorphosis distinct from medieval guilds, rudimentary joint-stock associations, and regulated companies, blending the concept of partnership aimed at the aggregation of capital with incorporation and its perpetual succession and clear legal personality.[13]

By internalizing protection costs, the Dutch East India Company could obtain its protection at cost price and was able to foresee its protection costs. In addition, the Company's quasimonopolistic or oligopolistic regulation of supplies and prices served to reduce the number of unknowns in its calculations by raising or lowering orders, accumulation of stocks, price fixation, dumping, and changing the preferred methods of sale. Steensgaard, however, acknowledged that the Dutch East India Company was not a pure type, containing features in its constitution, its structure, and its policy more reminiscent of a redistributive enterprise than of a business, representing the compromise struck between economic and political considerations in the founding charter. Yet contrary to the Estado, "the Dutch never forgot to take their economic pulse, no matter how high feelings might run." Though not achieving centralized bookkeeping, the company accounts were more than adequate, providing crucial insights in the gross profit on every single commodity and the profitability of every single factory: "The important thing here is the innovation as compared with older entrepreneurial forms, not their clumsiness as compared with the corporations of the 19th and 20th centuries."[14]

Interestingly, the later Steensgaard subsequently recognized, though the companies constituted a more effective form of organization, the internalization of protection costs and greater control of the market were not of decisive importance on every route or every market in the intra-Asian trade. The peddling trade was able to survive due to the high overhead costs of the company and the greater shrewdness and superior knowledge of craftsmanship and consumers' tastes of the peddlers when dealing with nonstandardized commodities such as cotton textiles.[15] Europeans were not able to take over or direct Indian Ocean trade, but they were certainly very often in a position to interfere with its regular mechanism. The arrival of the northwest Europeans, for instance, seriously weakened the position of Goa, strengthened the Gujarat trade, while access to southeast Asian commodities became largely controlled by the Dutch East India Company. By creating a "false" or "excentric centre" at Batavia, the VOC controlled a strong, multilateral trade network in the Indian Ocean, cutting some lines of communication and redirecting some activities according to interests external to the Indian Ocean.[16]

In *Asian Trade and European Influence* (1962), the Dutch scholar-archivist M. A. P. Meilink-Roelofsz severely criticized van Leur's views, among others, for falling victim to the Weberian "ideal type" approach, in particular his overemphasis on the peddling character of Asian shipping trade, the underestimation of the status of merchants, the resulting internal contradiction with his thesis of equality between Asian and European trade, the exclusion of the trade in bulk commodities, the exaggeration of the degree of isolation and nontransparency of Asian markets, the failure to recognize the political, military, technical, and economic superiority of the Europeans and the influence of European trade in especially Indonesia.[17]

As far as the Dutch East India Company was concerned, Meilink-Roelofsz asserted that van Leur had underestimated the modern elements in the organization of the VOC, "the structure of which may be considered as a more highly organized form of trade than the partnership still generally current at that time in Asia and Europe in general." Economically, the company represented a power factor in the Indonesian Archipelago, which seriously disturbed or even utterly destroyed various aspects of the native economy. Apart from improved maritime techniques and naval and military strength, the Dutch East India Company, despite its still somewhat primitive system of bookkeeping, "represented a far more efficient and, above all, much more business-like system than the government undertaking of the Portuguese." Unlike the Estado da India, the VOC kept the sales of products it imported into Europe and the inter-Asian trade in its own hands. Servants of the VOC received fixed wages paid at regular intervals, and vigorous action was taken against private trading when discovered. The Dutch did even more than the Portuguese to bring the various parts of Asia into contact with one another, establishing direct lines of communication between areas that had hitherto been separated. Whereas for the Portuguese the propagation of Christianity was more important, trade was the primary concern of the Dutch. With their larger capital resources, the Dutch, by concentrating on the Indonesian archipelago at first, acquired a good strategic position from which they could operate at all times of the year.[18] The rigorous monopoly achieved in the Spice Islands, however, could not be enforced elsewhere as far as either European competitors or Asian traders were concerned. Moreover, the Dutch were confronted with the heavy costs of military actions, punitive expeditions against the natives, and the upkeep of forts, ships, and garrisons.[19]

Influenced by the views of Kristof Glamann, W. M. F. Mansvelt, G. C. Klerk de Reus, and J. P. de Korte, Meilink-Roelofsz's subsequent review article of Steensgaard in *Mare Luso-Indicum* (1980) was a highly "critical appraisal" of his "structural method" and "preconceived theoretical and mental constructs," simultaneously reevaluating some of her earlier comparative assessments of Portuguese and Dutch overseas expansion in island Southeast Asia.[20] According to Meilink-Roelofsz, Steensgaard's analysis was geographically, analytically, and conceptually limited with its focus on the Persian Gulf, its overemphasis on social and economic aspects to the detriment of technical military and naval factors, and its exclusionary portrayal of the three structures: the peddling caravan trade, the redistributive Portuguese Estado, and the purely commercial companies. The VOC showed marked redistributive characteristics, imposing customs duties, compelling Asian traders to obtain safe conducts, seizing ships and confiscating cargoes, farming out taxes, and introducing a system of forced deliveries in Java.[21]

According to Meilink-Roelofsz, Steensgaard had also greatly exaggerated the extent to which the VOC dominated the market, enjoying a monopoly neither in Europe nor in Asia. The capitalistic inter-Asiatic trade of the company was centralized, rationalized, and aimed at the market, but the company's inter-Asiatic trade merely extended a network of trade routes already established by the Portuguese. In fact, because of the internalization of protection costs the company found itself unable to compete on equal terms with peddlers, with their lesser overhead costs and greater market knowledge.[22]

Moreover, in calculating protection costs there were inevitable unknown and uncertain factors, while the apparatus required hindered the flexibility of company decisions, as witnessed by the maintenance of unprofitable establishments, the delay in reducing the defense system, or the need to carry Asian goods in *commenda* because of the dependence on local rulers. The company's behavior in Asia was determined, therefore, more by political than economic factors and "consideration of the market took second place."[23] In this respect, Meilink-Roelofsz also pointed to several other atavistic features: widespread corruption, private trade, hierarchic conventions of courtesies and display of pomp and circumstance, conspicuous consumption, and investment of profits into land ownership and foreign national loans.[24]

The VOC failed to increase its initial basic capital, preferring first to arrange long-term loans and subsequently short-term loans to finance its business.

One of the weakest features of the management of the VOC was its unreliable estimates of costs and an increasing failure to oversee the profit and loss accounts of its empire due to "the Company's antiquated structure" and decentralized bookkeeping system, compounded by the existence of similar coins with different values in the Netherlands and in Asia, leading to "irreparable confusion."[25]

Meilink-Roelofsz finally dismissed the company's alleged greater internal solidarity and the "community of interests" between the VOC and the States General. The company was an institution rife with discord between the various chambers, the directors in the Netherlands and the High Government in Batavia, and shareholders and management: "All these internal conflicts certainly did not encourage modern tendencies in the Company."[26] Recognizing Steensgaard's contribution as an "important work" (perhaps the most deadly "compliment" that can be made by one's professional colleagues), Meilink-Roelofsz wryly concluded, "One may doubt whether such theoretical models will sharpen 'the analytical tools' required in the science of history."[27]

The initial polemical rhetoric employed in the institutional debate on precolonial European overseas expansion has become somewhat muted and arguments more nuanced. First, in the wake of Meilink-Roelofsz and other critics, recent scholarship on Portuguese overseas expansion has reevaluated the economic significance of both official and private Portuguese trade activities, stressing "renascence," "survival," "second wind," or "reorientations" rather than the alleged *decadência* of the latter half of the sixteenth and seventeenth centuries found in traditional narratives.[28] On the other hand, company historians (though, perhaps somewhat surprisingly, revisionist to a lesser extent than their Portuguese counterparts and less willing to abandon Steensgaard) have recognized certain less than modern, redistributive aspects in Dutch East India Company policies, yet still emphasizing, paraphrasing Steensgaard, the ultimate commercial nature and superiority of the chartered companies. At the same time, they have also stressed the need for sensitivity toward internal divisions within the company, and the differing chronological and spatial patterns of Dutch Asia.[29]

Second, "new institutional historians" have come to realize that both the Estado and the VOC were anything but value monoliths or homogeneous organizations. Rather, they were institutions rife with factionalism, personal animosities, and people with differing principles and private agendas. Third, both groups have displayed greater sensitivity toward temporal and regional variations in policies and impact of European activities interacting with an ever-changing Asian political, economic, social, and cultural environment. Fourth, scholars of Portuguese and Dutch overseas expansion have widened their horizon to assume a more comparative "globocentric" perspective, recognizing the mixed outcome of the worldwide Luso-Dutch conflict, mediated by contingencies and military force rather than dictated by unidirectional institutional determinism—victory for the Dutch in Asia, a draw in West Africa, and victory for the Portuguese in Brazil.[30]

In *Bewind en Beleid bij de VOC* (1989), F. S. Gaastra dismisses Meilink-Roelofsz's criticism pace Mansvelt and de Korte against the company's monopoly policy, inadequate financing and bookkeeping methods, the company directors' lack of commercial insight, and irresponsible dividend disbursements as unfounded. The VOC displayed flexibility in issuing safe-conducts to Asian shipping, resorted to diverse marketing policies in Europe based on the individual commodity involved, while the directors in fact had much more understanding of the company than is sometimes assumed and were able to set the costs and benefits of a particular factory against each other, and to calculate net profit on a specific product. Gaastra's conclusion arguably best represents the existing *communis opinio* among company historians: VOC management was characterized by "a solid financial policy, a cautious dividend policy, and a first-rate commercial policy, based on a wide knowledge of the European market of Asian goods."

In the standard business history of the company, *The Dutch East India Company: Expansion and Decline* (2003), Gaastra underwrites Steensgaard's position, describing the Dutch East India Company and its Atlantic counterpart, the West India Company (founded 1621), as "institutional innovations of great significance and, to a certain degree, the precursors of the modern corporation."[31] Similar to Steensgaard, Gaastra views the transition from the precompanies to the VOC as a metamorphosis in view of the latter's more broadly defined objectives, including use of the military option, and more permanent character backed by the States General. Although the VOC did display some redistributive features, military action remained always subservient to the acquisition of markets, its expenses were considered running costs, and in the end were to be paid for by a profitable commerce. Though it did create some new direct linkages and markets, for the largest part the company fit into previously existing commodity exchanges in the Indian Ocean. It did, however, possess an important advantage: None of its competitors was able to compare the price of silver in Japan, Persia, and Amsterdam with market conditions in Surat, China, and the archipelago. The VOC could choose to purchase silk in Persia, China, or Bengal, and opt to sell it in Japan or Europe. Except for the monopolistic commodities, there was no question of market control, whereas the system of communications operated far from smoothly. However, the existence of alternative commercial opportunities and mercantile relations extending across half the globe must have influenced market conditions in Asia for a number of commodities, such as pepper, textiles, and precious metals.[32]

The "Merchant-Warrior" Revisited:
The Early Modern Redistributive Innovation

Rather than absolute truths, history is a science of relative certainties. Whereas the Estado da India was a mixture of the medieval and the modern (in that order), the VOC was a mixture of the modern and the medieval typical of the "age of mercantilism" reflecting both continuity and change. The company was both an "institutional innovation" and a "redistributive enterprise" with profit and power complimentary in theory, though at times diametrically opposed in practice based on geopolitical realities and chronological contingencies. As Jan de Vries and Ad van der Woude described the perennial mercantilist conundrum of the VOC: "In this statelike firm seeking monopoly power in a competitive environment, the correct mix of the political and the commercial, of centralization and flexibility, was never obvious."[33] From the point of view of its overall position in the economic and political system of the Dutch Republic, however, the directors (intimately linked to the political establishment) never overlooked the commercial foundations on which its existence and activities depended.

Regarding profit, the company directors did have internal documents at their disposal and possessed an intuitive *Fingerspitzengefühl* acquired by intimate knowledge of all aspects of this many-sided business, that more than made up for the relative intransparency of the VOC's accounting practices. Any cursory investigation in the massive paper trail of the company archives suffices to demonstrate the unparalleled quantity of statistical materials and "data collection mania" of VOC officials, such as the Amsterdam burgomaster-director Johannes Hudde (1628–1704) and Governor General Gustaaf Willem, Baron van Imhoff (1705–1750), especially during periods of reform efforts (1680–1700; 1740–1760)—profit margins of specific commodities (*rendementen*), expenses and revenues of individual settlements, shipping movements and cargo lists, and so forth.

Apart from bringing in the Americas and Europe via importing vast quantities of bullion and growing demand for Asiatica, the Dutch did even more than the Portuguese (and the English and French for that matter as well) to bring the various parts of the Indian Ocean into contact with one another, establishing direct lines of communication between areas that had hitherto been separated. Batavia became the center of an extensive intra-Asiatic network stretching from Canton to the Cape of Good Hope. One notable example was the (until 1685) highly profitable Bengal-Japan trade in raw silk for precious metals—gold *kobans*, silver *kinjos* or *schuitzilver*, and bar copper.[34] At the same time, they were still subject to the same structural constraints as their Asian and European counterparts, including largely immobile natural and human "geohistorical" features and realities—monsoons and trade winds, ocean currents, tides, and waves, and so forth. These Braudelian *structures* hindered the regular supply of information, the proper functioning of transparent markets, cost predictability, and the effective monitoring of company servants scattered across the Indian Ocean Basin.

Metropolitan mercantile concerns, moreover, were often countermanded by more "frontier" or "subimperialist" perceptions and apprehensions of the High Government at Batavia and "subordinate" company officials elsewhere in Asia about the reputation of the "Honorable" *(Edele)* company among the local societies and cultures. Having been reprimanded by the directors, for instance, Governor General Cornelis van der Lijn (1645-1650) and the Council of the Indies in 1649 intimated to their superiors: "When we believe that the interest of the Company requires otherwise and time and occasion do not permit to wait for further advice from Your Honors, we need to deviate [from your instructions] and do what we consider best for the interest and well-being of the Company, which Your Honors should commend completely to us in view of various considerations rather than treat us here like small children." This (semi)independent mindset, given latitude by the realities of distance and the extreme difficulties of effective centralized control, is reminiscent of the maxims of Spanish colonial officials (and arguably most European "servants" overseas in general): "God is in Heaven, the King is far, and I give the orders here" or "I obey but do not comply." Imperialist-minded governors general, such as Jan Pieterszoon Coen (1619–1623; 1627–1629), Rijckloff van Goens Sr. (1678–1681), and Cornelis Speelman (1681–1684) were perfectly prepared to present the directors in patria with a fait accompli. As Coen wrote to the directors in 1614: "By experience [you] should be well aware that in the Indies trade has to be pursued and maintained under the protection and favor of one's own arms and that the weapons must be financed through the profits so earned by trade. In short, trade without war or war without trade cannot be maintained."[35]

As far as power is concerned, the company, when deemed possible and necessary, routinely employed violence in the establishment and enforcement of monopolies and exclusive agreements, especially in maritime Asia. One part of the Portuguese model duplicated wholesale by the Dutch East India Company was the redistributive *cartaz*-armada-and-*cafila* system. In the position of their Portuguese rivals, the Dutch not only showed themselves the successors of the Lusitanian physical heritage in the way that they took over many of their strongholds, but they also appointed themselves the heirs of their mental legacy in the introduction of the *pascedul* and *protectierechten*, or passes and protection rights system. Reflecting the ever-latent tension between the polarities of national interests and international principles in history, the

Dutch opportunistically switched from idealistic champions of freedom of the seas (*mare liberum*) against their Portuguese-Spanish opponents to pragmatic defenders of the closed seas (*mare clausum*) once they had replaced their rivals as the dominant European power in the Indian Ocean.[36]

The principles of forced trade, combined with the passes and protection rights system, were applied most systematically in the Spice Islands of eastern Indonesia and the Javanese north coast, and more intermittently in Malacca and the Malaysian "tin districts," the Malabar coast, extreme southern India and Ceylon littoral, and elsewhere.[37] Following the capture of Portuguese Malacca (1641), "the second foundation for the domination of the South," company vessels routinely cruised the Straits of Malacca between Cabo Rochado (Tanjung Tuan) and the coast of Sumatra and (occasionally) the Straits of Singapore— five or six yachts, *tingangs*, and *chaloups* with 160 crew during the southeastern monsoon (May–October), and three or four yachts with 120 crew during the northwestern monsoon (November–April). In addition, one or two vessels were regularly dispatched to the tin districts of Perak, Kedah, Bangeri, and Ujung Salang (Phuket) in order to levy the Malacca tolls and the Dutch share of the tin from foreign traders in accordance with treaties forced on local rulers. Between 1641 and 1662, toll incomes averaged between 12 percent (1643–1644) and 28.8 percent (1661–1662) of total revenues in the government of Malacca.[38] Relatively effective in parts of the archipelago, the system foundered elsewhere on a combination of European diplomacy and Asian economics. As the company concluded in 1680: "The rightful force (*regte stem*) of the passes is dead, which will most likely not improve with time."[39]

The VOC recognized these politico-economic limitations. In the "General Instruction" for the Governor General and Council of the Indies in April 1650, the company directors divided its activities in Asia in three categories: areas where the company exercised its own jurisdiction "by right of conquest"; regions where the company had concluded exclusive agreements with indigenous rulers; and areas where the company merely resided on "sufferance," holding no privileged position whatsoever.[40]

The core region of the Dutch militarized trade diaspora was formed to a great extent by either spice producing areas or spice emporia. This improved and corrected version of *Asia portuguesa* limited itself not merely to former Lusitanian strongholds, but also covered jurisdiction of relatively large territorial possessions in eastern Indonesia, Java, the Coromandel Coast, Ceylon, and South Africa. All these possessions were designated as *gouvernementen*, and administered by company officials with the title of governor.

Next to the areas where the company exercised its own jurisdiction came the countries and places where the company had succeeded in making exclusive agreements with indigenous rulers. These areas occupied a semiperipheral status in Dutch Asia. It included monopolistic treaties made with the rulers of the tin districts on the Malaysian Peninsula, and the pepper-producing regions of the Malabar Coast, along with the east and west coasts of Sumatra. These settlements were usually designated as *commandementen*, and administered by company officials with the title of commander.

The third category consisted of those areas where the Dutch resided "by virtue of an agreement, to be allowed (by indigenous rulers) to trade in their countries as free merchants just like all other nations." In these regions, the company resided merely on "sufferance," holding no privileged position whatsoever, and was unable and/or unwilling to enforce its politico-commercial agenda. This was because either these early modern "gunpowder empires" were too powerful to be fooled around with, such as Safavid Persia, Mughal India, Ming and Qing China, and Tokugawa Japan, or these regions formed only a peripheral part of the Dutch trading world, and therefore were considered not worth the trouble (and expense)—including Siam, the Solor and Timor islands, Arakan, Pegu, and Cochin-China. Economically significant settlements, such as Mocha (Persia), Surat, and Bengal, were designated as *directies*, administered by company officials with the title of director. The VOC factory at Deshima (Japan) was an exception to the rule, being headed by a chief. Peripheral settlements were presided over by low-ranking company residents and chiefs.

In addition to geographical variations, there were important temporal variations. The balance between commercial and political activities shifted significantly after 1680 due to declining trade revenues and growing territorialization on the islands of Java and Ceylon. Company history can be conveniently divided into three distinct periods: rapid growth during a monopolistic golden age based on monopsonistic positions in the production areas of fine spices and markets of precious metals of eastern Indonesia, Ceylon, and Japan with high gross margins (1600–1680); profitless growth during a competitive phase based on the textiles, tea, and coffee markets of India, China, and Arabia with deteriorating gross margins (1680–1740); and stagnation and "squeezed profits" due to structural commercial changes and the growing burden of territorial possessions (1740–1799). To illustrate the shifting balance between profit and power: the share of trade revenues in the total income of Dutch Asia declined from 90 to 95 percent until the 1680s and 73 percent in the 1740s to 55 percent in the 1780s (see table 16.1).

Based on the annual financial balances of the bookkeeper general in Batavia, the 0.2 million guilders in "direct" redistributive income (tolls, anchorage dues, pass moneys, and others) made up approximately 4.6 percent of the total revenues of Dutch Asia in the financial year 1701–1702. Half a century later, in 1751–1752, it had risen more than fivefold to 1.12 million

Table 16.1
Financial Results of the Dutch East India Company in Asia, 1650–1790 (annual averages, in thousands of guilders)

Period	Total Revenue	Trade Revenue	Trade as % of Total Revenue	Total Expenses	Asian Surplus
1650–1660	4,068	3,716	91.3	3,838	230
1660–1670	5,780	5,483	94.9	4,187	1,593
1670–1680	5,897	5,403	91.6	5,608	289
1680–1690	4,834	4,381	90.6	4,462	372
1690–1700	5,870	4,505	76.7	6,905	−1,035
1700–1710	4,428	3,354	75.7	5,584	−1,156
1710–1720	5,411	3,948	73.0	6,338	−927
1720–1730	4,119	2,823	68.5	5,346	−1,127
1730–1740	4,532	3,020	66.6	6,621	−1,729
1740–1750	6,561	4,787	73.0	7,623	−1,062
1750–1760	7,260	5,239	72.2	8,047	−787
1760–1768	5,972	3,692	61.8	8,142	−2,170
1768–1780	4,870	2,577	52.9	7,375	−2,505
1780–1790	4,998	2,768	55.4	10,036	5,038

Sources: Gaastra, *Bewind en Beleid*, appendix 2b; J. P. de Korte, *De Jaarlijkse Financiële Verantwoording in de Verenigde Oostindische Compagnie* (Leiden: M. Nijhoff, 1984), appendices 8 and 11; De Vries and Van der Woude, *The First Modern Economy*, 429–64.

guilders or 10.8 percent of total revenues in Asia—the joint outcome of the ongoing process of territorialization, especially on the islands of Java (Batavia, Cheribon, and Samarang) and Ceylon, and the decline of the Company's intra-Asiatic network in the eighteenth century.

The unraveling of the VOC's carefully balanced trading system in Asia after 1680 was the result of increasing restrictions imposed by the Tokugawa authorities on the Japan trade, the loss of alternative sources of precious metals in Asia, diminishing sales of Indian textiles to impoverished consumers in the archipelago, political instability associated with the breakdown of the three Muslim empires (Mughal, Safavid, and Ottoman), and growing competition from English "country traders." After 1692 the annual balances of Dutch Asia showed permanent deficits. In a "caesura" in the financial relationship, the VOC chambers in the Dutch Republic now had to sustain the "Indian capital" by ever-increasing shipments of precious metals from patria (see table 16.2).[41]

Company policies at home and overseas were influenced by principles of modern rational bureaucracy and individual merit, on the one hand, and traditional emotive bonds of corporate patrimonialism and rival party factions

Table 16.2
Dutch East India Company Redistributive Income Derived from Tolls, Anchorage Dues, Pass Moneys, etc., 1701–1702 and 1751–1752 (in guilders)

	1701–1702	*1751–1752*
Ambon	1,292	13,968
Banda	527	6,765
Banjarmasin	—	712
Banten	538	46
Batavia	94,564	357,137
Bengal	—	1,914
Ceylon	48,812	164,648
Cheribon	188	48,600
Coromandel	13,148	13,469
Japara	1,662	—
Makassar	—	25,095
Malabar	8,179	29,103
Malacca	25,047	53,887
Padang	—	6,285
Samarang	—	379,391
Ternate	847	10,277
Timor	—	12,156
"Direct" redistributive revenue	201,051	1,123,452
Total revenue (%)	5,681,961 (4.6%)	10,339,466 (10.8%)

Sources: Nationaal Archief, Archief van de Boekhouder-Generaal 10752, Financiële balans van de Aziatische comptoiren, 1701–1702; 10766, Financiële balans van de Aziatische comptoiren, 1751–1752; Vink, "Passes and Protection Rights," 83.

or family networks, on the other. Whereas the Dutch Republic has been characterized as a "familial state," the principles of "family government" reigned supreme in Batavia and the subordinate company settlements in Asia.[42] Party factions represented both informal groups with conflicting political ideologies and theological viewpoints and rival patron-client systems and family networks competing for office, influence, and material benefits. Despite some spectacular examples of self-made men, such as governors general van Goens and Speelman, the road to social advancement and upward mobility was more usually paved by nepotism and patronage. While men of ability were not necessarily kept out of office by this patriarchal patrimonial system, the fact remained that a candidate's primary qualification was apt to be not so much his character as his family connections. Even the "self-made" men were not descended from the common people, but came from respectable middle-class families. They would certainly have had letters of recommendation with them and in a number of cases were helped by family members already in Asia. Kinship and connections played an important part in appointments and promotions. Every year at the autumn meeting of the Gentlemen Seventeen, the representatives of the chambers brought along lists of favorites who the chamber concerned wished to see promoted in Asia.[43]

Much of the history of the Dutch Republic was dominated by the conflict between republican (States)–moderate Calvinist (Remonstrant) and dynastic (Orangist)–orthodox Calvinist (Counter Remonstrant) party factions over the religious and political positions on the Dutch Reformed faith and constitution of the United Provinces. These ideological conflicts blended into more mundane rivalries among elite families over key positions or lucrative posts, including the colonial companies.[44] The ruling city burgomasters' party factions of Amsterdam, Middelburg (Zeeland), Delft, Enkhuisen, Hoorn, and Rotterdam, for instance, quickly assumed control of the appointment of local directors in each of the six VOC chambers.

In the presiding chamber of Amsterdam, the influence of the Orangist, Counter Remonstrant party faction headed by Burgomaster Reynier Pauw (1564–1636) peaked in the immediate aftermath of the Calvinist Revolution (1618–1619). Following the election of Andries Bicker (1586–1652) as burgomaster in 1627, the States, Remonstrant party faction led by the Bicker–De Graeff faction was dominant until the end of the First Stadholderless Period (1650–1672). Patronage and strategic marriage alliances also brought in other influential merchant-regent networks, such as the Witsen, Reynst, and van Beuningen families. The "First Family of Amsterdam" even extended its family tentacles far beyond the city, including the Grand Pensionary of Holland, Johan de Witt, who along with Amsterdam regents, directed Dutch commercial and colonial policy during the era of "True Freedom."

In the Year of Disaster (1672), however, the Bicker League was supplanted by the party faction under Burgomaster Gillis Valckenier (1623–1680), who decided to jump on the Orangist bandwagon of Stadholder William III. Relations among the Amsterdam merchant-regents became less contentious after 1677 with appeasement between Valckenier and the local leader of the States, Remonstrant party faction, Hendrik Hooft (1617–1678). The "order for electing burgomasters" achieved at a grand gathering of the Amsterdam regent patriciate foreshadowed the "contracts of correspondence" of the eighteenth century made between members of a town council to take turns in appointing their relatives and friends to office or public employment. It is important to remember, however, that despite all factionalism and personal preferences, the Amsterdam burgomasters, at least in the seventeenth century, also continued to take account of a proper representation of the merchant element in the company directorate. Events in the other presiding chamber of Zeeland and the smaller VOC chambers roughly resembled those in Amsterdam.[45]

Factionalism and infighting, nepotism and patronage networks both in the republic and in Asia, corruption (to use an anachronistic term) and illegal private trade, hierarchic conventions of courtesies and display of pomp and circumstance, and conspicuous consumption may be less than modern features deeply engrained in company *mentalités*.[46] One has to keep in mind, though, that rational choice, transparent markets guided by the invisible hand, predictable overhead and transaction costs, and similar concepts are merely theoretical constructs, not to be confused with everyday reality encountered and observed by contemporary modern corporations—witness the spectacular implosion of Enron in December 2001.

In view of the previous observations, it is hardly surprising that historians have described the Dutch East India Company in various dualistic terms— *merchant-warrior*, a *hybrid political-economic organization*, or two-faced *Janus, merchant prince* founded on a varying mixture of profit and power (and the related principles of rational bureaucracy and family patronage networks or party factions).[47] We are left, then, with K. N. Chaudhuri's observation regarding European overseas expansion in the "age of mercantilism": "The phenomenon that is in need of explanation is not the system of peaceful but of armed trading."[48] As Tracy wonders:

> How does one account for the combination, characteristically if not uniquely European, of state power and trading interest, whether in the form of an arm of state that conducts trade, or a trading company that behaves like a state? Does this peculiar combination explain the eventual success of the Europeans on their commercial struggles with formidable indigenous rivals, especially in Asia? Or might the policy of armed trading have served rather to offset the benefits of dynamic innovations (such as the full-rigged ship or new forms of commercial

credit), which thus bore fruit only in the eighteenth century, as Europe's warring nations gradually came to recognize the freedom of the seas?[49]

Afterthoughts

Rather than ending with a (rather unsatisfactory) open-ended question, I would suggest that the ambiguous assessment of the relative modernity of the VOC is not simply reflective of existing divisions in the historical profession, but also illustrative of the transitional character of the period between the Middle Ages and the modern era itself. This ambiguity is evinced not only in the dual nature of the Dutch East India Company but also in the simultaneous existence of a wide range of modes of cross-cultural interaction between the VOC and Indian Ocean societies and cultures, and the recognition of "multiple modernities" across early modern Afro-Eurasia.

Historians have assessed cross-cultural encounters in the early modern Indian Ocean in various ways. If European-Asian relations are mapped along a continuum, one can distinguish two extreme traditional models and one revisionist *via medium*, each emphasizing different components of the encounter. On the one end of the spectrum is the so-called Vasco da Gama epoch with its emphasis on the military-nautical context and disequilibria and conflict.[50] At the other end is the "Age of Partnership," largely coterminous with the "Age of Commerce," "Reciprocity," or "Convivência," emphasizing the commercial (and cultural) along with equality and respect.[51] More recently, a revisionist golden mean has become the *communis opinio* with regard to the bulk of the Indian subcontinent (Malabar excepted), expressed in analogous epitaphs such as the "Balance of Blackmail," the "Age of Contained Conflict," "Perceived Mutual Advantage," "Conflict-Ridden Symbiosis," "Co-operation or Acquiescence" and "Accommodations," and "Two-Way Dependency."[52] The new paradigm emphasizes political economy (combining the military and the commercial) and some mixture of conflict and cooperation with greater sensitivity for temporal and spatial variations.[53]

Most company historians differentiate between an aggressive, expansionist, monopolistic phase (ca. 1600–1680); a more competitive mercantile period (ca. 1680–1740); and a period of disengagement and decline (1740–1800). In addition, they distinguish maritime Asia from the rest of the Indian Ocean world. In the archipelago, production center of the coveted spices, the numerous smaller states were dependent on overseas trade and hence extremely vulnerable to the maritime and commercial power of the VOC. Elsewhere the company was permitted to trade, but its influence remained limited because of the strength of indigenous polities and more limited objectives.[54] This sensitivity to geopolitical and chronological variations by modern historians was,

as we have seen, reflected in contemporary VOC documents and official terminology.

Europeanists, Southeast Asianists, south Asianists, and other area specialists
have dealt with the issue of early modernity in extenso.[55] Though there is considerable disagreement on the particular political, economic, social, and cultural
features that were shared across Eurasia, there remains a certain consensus that
the period stretching roughly between 1350/1500 and 1750/1800 is somehow
marked off from the centuries before and after. The early modern period was a
time of both continuity and change, characterized by a series of parallel political, social and economic, and cultural developments across Afro-Eurasia. Historians have identified military and financial revolutions in politics; agricultural,
demographic, urban, industrious, and commercial revolutions in society and
economics; and religious, linguistic, and consumer revolutions in culture.[56] If
properly detached from its European moorings, most historians would agree on
the manifestation of localized "translations" of modernity's (admittedly embry-
onic) universalism in the early modern era. This paradox has led to the recognition of "unity in diversity" defined by "multiple modernities," the "principle of
divergence," "parallel developments" or "evolutions," and "synchronisms."[57]

To be sure, the historians' verdict on the validity of the concept of early modern, or, rather, early modernities, is far from unanimous. However, whereas
most revisionist scholarship has embraced with some reservations early
modernity, world historians, most notably Jack Goldstone and the Sinocentric
"California school" (including Ken Pomeranz, Ray Bin Wong, and Richard Von
Glahn), have even denied the existence of any modernity or Great Divergence
at all prior to 1800, in turn calling it "a wholly meaningless term."[58] To dismiss,
however, the concept of early modernity as a "wholly meaningless term" as part
of an emergent global orthodoxy would be a wholly meaningless action, ig-
noring the unique institutional, cross-cultural, and Eurasian features of the period between the Middle Ages and modernity. The dual nature of European
overseas expansion in the "age of mercantilism," the simultaneous existence of
various modes of cross-cultural interaction throughout the Indian Ocean
Basin, and the recognition of "parallel developments" and "synchronisms"
across Eurasia vitiate any such rash dismissal. In short, this chapter is a strong
plea for the continued validity of the concept of the early modern.

Notes

1. N. Davies, *Europe: A History* (New York: Harper Collins, 1998), 539; J. de Vries
and A. van der Woude, *The First Modern Economy: Success, Failure, and Perseverance of
the Dutch Economy, 1500–1815* (New York: Cambridge University Press, 1997), 4, 385;
J. I. Israel, *Dutch Primacy in World Trade, 1585–1740* (Oxford: Clarendon, 1989), 7, 69;

L. Blussé and J. de Moor, *Nederlanders Overzee: De Eerste Vijftig Jaar, 1600–1650* (Franeker: Uitgeverij T. Wever, 1983), 42.

2. K. N. Chaudhuri, *The Trading World of Asia and the English East India Company, 1660–1760* (Cambridge: Cambridge University Press, 1978), 20. Particularly insightful is the section on "the influence of the medieval legacy" in De Vries and Van der Woude, *The First Modern Economy*, 159–65.

3. J. I. Israel, *The Dutch Republic: Its Rise, Greatness, and Fall, 1477–1806* (Oxford: Clarendon, 1995), 341–48; J. Adams, *The Familial State: Ruling Families and Merchant Capitalism in Early Modern Europe* (Ithaca, NY: Cornell University Press, 2005); J. L van Zanden and M. Prak, "Towards an Economic Interpretation of Citizenship: The Dutch Republic Between Medieval Communes and Modern Nation States," a working paper available at www.lowcountries.nl/workingpapers.html.

4. P. D. Curtin, *Cross-Cultural Trade in World History* (New York: Cambridge University Press, 1984), 3–5, and 230–31.

5. J. D. Tracy, introduction to *The Political Economy of Merchant Empires: State Power and World Trade, 1350–1750*, ed. J. D. Tracy (New York: Cambridge University Press, 1991), especially 19–20; introduction to *The Rise of Merchant Empires: Long-Distance Trade in the Early Modern World, 1350–1750*, ed. J. D. Tracy (New York: Cambridge University Press, 1990), especially 6, 11.

6. D. Ormrod, *The Rise of Commercial Empires: England and the Netherlands in the Age of Mercantilism, 1650–1770* (New York: Cambridge University Press, 2003).

7. Tracy, introduction to *Political Economy*, 14.

8. J. C. van Leur, *Indonesian Trade and Society: Essays in Asian Social and Economic History* (The Hague: W. van Hoeve, 1955), 117–18, and 188–89.

9. Van Leur, *Indonesian Trade*, 117–18, 130–34.

10. Van Leur, *Indonesian Trade*, 129.

11. Van Leur, *Indonesian Trade*, 188.

12. Van Leur, *Indonesian Trade*, 261.

13. N. Steensgaard, *The Asian Trade Revolution of the Seventeenth Century: The East India Companies and the Decline of the Caravan Trade* (Chicago: University of Chicago Press, 1973), 22–59.

14. Steensgaard, *Asian Trade Revolution*, 114–53, especially 137, 146. Steensgaard rejected the findings of Van Leur pace W. M. F. Mansvelt, underwriting instead the conclusions of K. Glamann.

15. Steensgaard, *Asian Trade Revolution*, 410–11; "The Indian Ocean Network and the Emerging World-Economy, c. 1500–1750," in *The Indian Ocean: Explorations in History, Commerce and Politics*, ed. S. Chandra (London: Sage, 1987), 139–43.

16. Steensgaard, "Indian Ocean Network," 144–49.

17. M. A. P. Meilink-Roelofsz, *Asian Trade and European Influence in the Indonesian Archipelago between 1500 and 1630* (The Hague: M. Nijhoff, 1962), 10–11.

18. Meilink-Roelofsz, *Asian Trade*, 175–91.

19. Meilink-Roelofsz, *Asian Trade*, 203, 206.

20. M. A. P. Meilink-Roelofsz, "The Structures of Trade in Asia in the Sixteenth and Seventeenth Centuries, Niels Steensgaard's 'Carracks, Caravans and Companies.' The Asian Trade Revolutions. A Critical Appraisal," *Mare Luso-Indicum* 4 (1980): 1, 43.

21. Meilink-Roelofsz, "Structures of Trade," 6, 17, 27, and 42.

22. Meilink-Roelofsz, "Structures of Trade," 11, 22–23, 24, 38–40.

23. Meilink-Roelofsz, "Structures of Trade," 17; see also 12, 23, 37.

24. Meilink-Roelofsz, "Structures of Trade," 12, 13, 16.

25. Meilink-Roelofsz, "Structures of Trade," 12, 21–22.

26. Meilink-Roelofsz, "Structures of Trade," 18–21.

27. Meilink-Roelofsz, "Structures of Trade," 43.

28. See the works by G. J. Ames, J. C. Boyajian, G. B. Souza, and S. Subrahmanyam, *The Portuguese Empire in Asia, 1500–1700: A Political and Economic History* (New York: Longman, 1993), 107–108, 142–44.

29. C. R. Boxer already identified certain less than modern characteristics of the VOC in *The Dutch Seaborne Empire 1600–1800* (London: Hutchinson, 1965), 26–27, 34–35, 37–38, 41–49, 53.

30. For similar points: C. R. Boxer, *The Portuguese Seaborne Empire 1415–1825* (London: Hutchinson, 1969), 112, 150.

31. F. S. Gaastra and P. C. Emmer, "De Vaart Buiten Europa," in *Maritieme Geschiedenis der Nederlanden*, 4 vols., ed. L. M. Akveld, S. Hart, and W. J. van Hoboken (Bussum: De Boer Maritiem, 1977), 2: 242.

32. F. S. Gaastra, *De Geschiedenis van de VOC*, 2nd ed. (Zutphen: Walburg Pers, 1991), 23, 108–109, 111; *Bewind en Beleid bij de VOC: De Financiële en Commerciële Politiek van de Bewindhebbers, 1672–1702* (Zutphen: Walburg Pers, 1989), 15–21, 240–54.

33. De Vries and Van der Woude, *First Modern Economy*, 431–33.

34. O. Prakash, *The Dutch East India Company and the Economy of Bengal, 1630–1720* (Princeton: Princeton University Press, 1985), 118–41.

35. Gaastra, *Geschiedenis van de VOC*, 67–68; Boxer, *Dutch Seaborne Empire*, 106–109, 212; Subrahmanyam, *Portuguese Empire in Asia*, 109; G. D. Winius and M. P. M. Vink, *The Merchant-Warrior Pacified: The VOC (The Dutch East India Co.) and its Changing Political Economy in India* (Delhi: Oxford University Press, 1991), 30–31.

36. M. P. M. Vink, "Passes and Protection Rights: The Dutch East India Company as a Redistributive Enterprise in Malacca, 1641–1662," *Moyen Orient & Océan Indien* 7 (1990): 80–84; "Mare Liberum and Dominium Maris: Legal Arguments and Implications of the Luso-Dutch struggle for Control over Asian Waters, ca. 1600–1663," in *Studies in Maritime History*, ed. K. S. Mathew (Pondicherry, India: Mission, 1990), 38–68; "The Entente Cordiale: The Dutch East India Company and Portuguese Shipping Through the Straits of Malacca, 1641–1663," *Revista da Cultura* 13/14 (1991): 288–309.

37. For the company efforts to tax and monitor the Indo-Ceylon trade (1670–1697): S. Arasaratnam, "Mare Clausum, the Dutch and Regional Trade in the Indian Ocean, 1650–1740," *Journal of Indian History* 61 (1983):117–28; "Dutch Commercial Policy in Ceylon and Its Effects on the Indo-Ceylon Trade (1690–1750)," *Indian Economic and Social History Review* 4, no. 2 (1967): 109–30.

38. Nationaal Archief, Archief VOC 1141, OBP 1643, fl. 245r, 15.12.1642; VOC 1151, OBP 1645, fl. 531v, 11.11.1644; VOC 1157, OBP 1646, fl. 530v, 1.12.1644; VOC 1240, OBP 1663, fl. 1443r, 1.11.1662.

39. VOC 1353, OBP 1681, fls. 662r–662v [1680].

40. J. A. van der Chijs ed., *Nederlandsch-Indisch Plakaatboek, 1602–1811*, 17 vols. (The Hague: Landsdrukkerij, 1885–1900), 2: 138ff.

41. The most comprehensive account is: E. M. Jacobs, *Koopman in Azië: De Handel van de Verenigde Oost-Indische Compagnie Tijdens de 18de Eeuw* (Zutphen: Walburg Pers, 2000); Gaastra, *Bewind en Beleid*, 203–13, 240–41, 253.

42. Adams, *Familial State*; J. K. J de Jonge, *De Opkomst van het Nederlandsch Gezag in Oost-Indië: Verzameling van Onuitgegeven Stukken uit het Oud-Koloniaal Archief*, 18 vols. (The Hague: M. Nijhoff, 1862–1909), 8: 117.

43. Gaastra, *Dutch East India Company*, 94–95.

44. The classic studies are S. Groenveld, *Evidente Factiën in den Staet: Sociaal-Politieke Verhoudingen in de 17e-Eeuwse Republiek der Verenigde Nederlanden* (Hilversum:Verloren, 1990); D. Roorda, *Partij en Factie: De Oproeren van 1672 in de Steden van Holland en Zeeland, Een Krachtmeting tussen Partijen en Facties* (Groningen: Wolters-Noordhoff, 1978).

45. Adams, *Familial State*, 59–63, 98–103; J. E. Elias, *De Vroedschap van Amsterdam 1578–1795*. 2 vols. (Amsterdam: N. Israel, 1963); Gaastra, *Bewind en Beleid*, 33–47, 255–77; Israel, *Dutch Republic*, passim.

46. Gaastra, *Dutch East India Company*, 94–104.

47. C. R. Boxer, *Jan Compagnie in Oorlog en Vrede: Beknopte Geschiedenis van de VOC* (Bussum: De Boer Maritiem, 1977), 7; R. Vos, *Gentle Janus, Merchant Prince: The VOC and the Tightrope of Diplomacy in the Malay World, 1740–1800* (Leiden: KITLV Press, 1993), 1–2; J. van Goor, "De Verenigde Oost-Indische Compagnie in de Historiografie," in *De Verenigde Oostindische Compagnie tussen Oorlog en Diplomatie*, ed. G. Knaap and G. Teitler (Leiden: KITLV Uitgeverij, 2001), 27.

48. Chaudhuri, *Trade and Civilization*, 14.

49. Tracy, introduction to *Political Economy*, 19–20. Even the contributions in the two-volume series reflect the widely differing opinions among contemporary historians.

50. K. M. Panikkar, *Asia and Western Dominance: A Survey of the Vasco da Gama Epoch of Asian History, 1498–1945*, 2nd ed. (London: Allen & Unwin, 1959), 13–15.

51. H. Furber, *Rival Empires of Trade in the Orient, 1600–1800* (Minneapolis: University of Minnesota Press, 1976); A. Reid, *Southeast Asia in the Age of Commerce, 1450–1680*, 2 vols. (New Haven, CT, and London: Yale University Press, 1988–95); M. N. Pearson, *The Portuguese in India* (New York: Cambridge University Press, 1987), 2, 61, 81, 103–106, 115; A. J. R. Russell-Wood, *The Portuguese Empire, 1415–1808: A World on the Move* (Baltimore: Johns Hopkins University Press, 1998), xxi, 21, 220.

52. A. Das Gupta, "Europeans in India Before the Empire," in *The World of the Indian Merchant: Collected Essays of Ashin Das Gupta*, ed. U. Das Gupta (New York: Oxford University Press, 2001), 229–30; S. Subrahmanyam, *The Political Economy of Commerce: Southern India, 1500–1650* (New York: Cambridge University Press, 1990), 254; O. Prakash, *European Commercial Enterprise in Pre-Colonial India* (New York: Cambridge University Press, 1998), 337–43. See also the contributions of the "Cambridge school" of Indian colonial historians, such as C. A. Bayly, P. J. Marshall, and D. Ludden.

53. H. W. van Santen, *VOC-Dienaar in India: Geleynssen de Jongh in het Land van de Groot-Mogol* (Franeker: Van Wijnen, 2001), 38–42, and 162–68.

54. See Winius and Vink, *Merchant-Warrior Pacified*; Gaastra, *Geschiedenis van de VOC*, 37-38; Prakash, *European Commercial Enterprise*, chaps. 5, 6, 7; Boxer, *Dutch Seaborne Empire*, 217–20.

55. Most notably, Victor Lieberman, Anthony Reid, Denys Lombard, Leonard Andaya, and Barbara Watson Andaya for Southeast Asia; and John Richards, Sanjay Subrahmanyam, Irfan Habib, and Burton Stein for south Asia.

56. M. P. M. Vink, "From Port-City to World-System: Spatial Constructs in Dutch Indian Ocean Studies, 1500–1800," *Itinerario* 28 (2004): 45–116; "The Afro-Eurasian Web, 1500–1700" in *Spinning Planet: A Short History of Humankind*, ed. R. Dunn, E. Cobbs Hoffman, and M. P. M. Vink (New York: McGraw-Hill, forthcoming).

57. S. N. Eisenstadt and W. Schluchter, "Introduction: Paths to Early Modernity—A Comparative View," *Daedalus* 127 (1998): 1–18; J. Fletcher, "Integrative History: Parallels and Interconnections in the Early Modern Period, 1500–1800," *Studies on Chinese and Islamic Culture* (Aldershot: Ashgate, 1995), x, 1–33; B. Watson Andaya, "Historicising 'Modernity' in Southeast Asia," *Journal of the Economic and Social History of the Orient* 40 (1997): 392 and 406; D. Lombard, "Network and Synchronisms in Southeast Asian History," *Journal of Southeast Asian History* 26 (1995): 10–16; V. Lieberman, *Integration of the Mainland Southeast Asia in Global Context, c. 800–1830*, vol. 1, *Strange Parallels* (New York: Cambridge University Press, 2003), 1–80.

58. J. A. Goldstone, "The Problem of the 'Early Modern' World," *Journal of the Economic and Social History of the Orient* 41 (1998): 261; "Efflorescences and Economic Growth in World History: Rethinking the 'Rise of the West' and the Industrial Revolution," *Journal of World History* 13 (2002): 375–76.

Index

About the Contributors

Jerry H. Bentley is professor of history at the University of Hawaii and editor of the *Journal of World History*. Concentrating more recently on the history of cross-cultural interactions, his publications include *Old World Encounters: Cross-Cultural Contacts and Exchanges in Pre-Modern Times* (1993), *Shapes of World History in Twentieth-Century Scholarship* (1996), and (with Herbert Ziegler) *Traditions and Encounters: A Global Perspective on the Past* (2000, 2003).

Thomas A. Brady Jr. is Peder Sather Professor of History in the University of California, Berkeley. His publications include *Ruling Class, Regime, and Reformation at Strasbourg, 1520–1555* (1978), *Turning Swiss* (1985), *Protestant Politics* (1995), and *Communities, Politics, and Reformation in Early Modern Europe* (1998).

Douglas Catterall is an assistant professor of history at Cameron University of Oklahoma. He has published on migration history, emphasizing the Scots diaspora in Atlantic and comparative perspective, and also has interests in identity, social memory, women's history, religious history, and the role of outsider groups in the North Sea zone.

Donald J. Harreld is an assistant professor of early modern history at Brigham Young University. He received his Ph.D. from the University of Minnesota in 2000. Harreld is the author of *High Germans in the Low Countries: German Merchants and Commerce in Golden Age Antwerp* (2004).

Susan C. Karant-Nunn is director of the Division for Late Medieval and Reformation Studies and professor of history at the University of Arizona. Her recent books include *The Reformation of Ritual* (1997), and (coedited with Merry E. Wiesner-Hanks), *Luther on Women* (2003). She is North American managing coeditor of the *Archive for Reformation History*.

Marie Seong-Hak Kim is professor of history at St. Cloud State University and attorney at law. She is the author of *Michel de L'Hôpital: The Vision of a Reformist Chancellor during the French Religious Wars* (1997). Her research interests include early modern France, comparative law, and Korean legal history.

Henk van Nierop is professor of early modern history at the University of Amsterdam and academic director of the Amsterdam Centre for the Study of the Golden Age. He has published widely on the social, political, and religious history of the Revolt of the Netherlands and the Dutch golden age.

Charles H. Parker is an associate professor of history at Saint Louis University. He has published on the religious and cultural history of the Netherlands in the sixteenth and seventeenth centuries. His publications include *The Reformation of Community: Social Welfare and Calvinist Charity in Holland, 1572–1620* (1998).

Michael N. Pearson is an adjunct professor at the University of Technology, Sydney, where he is part of the project "Culture and Commerce in the Indian Ocean," www.indianoceanproject.net/pages/1/index.htm. Among his recent publications are *The Indian Ocean* (2003), and *The World of the Indian Ocean, 1500–1800* (2005).

Carla Rahn Phillips is Union Pacific Professor in Comparative Early Modern History at the University of Minnesota, specializing in Spain and the Hispanic world. Her publications include *Six Galleons for the King of Spain* (1986) and (with William Phillips) *The Worlds of Christopher Columbus* (1992) and *Spain's Golden Fleece* (1997).

William D. Phillips Jr. is professor of history and director of the Center for Early Modern History at the University of Minnesota, with interests in medieval and early modern Spain and European interactions with the wider world. He has published two books on slavery as well as (with Carla Rahn Phillips) *The Worlds of Christopher Columbus* (1992) and *Spain's Golden Fleece* (1997).

Elizabeth Bradbury Pollnow, B.A. Denison University, M.A. University of San Diego, is currently a doctoral candidate in medieval and early modern European history at Saint Louis University. Her areas of specialization include the intellectual history of France.

Kathryn L. Reyerson, professor of history at the University of Minnesota and founding director of the Center for Medieval Studies, has published widely, including *The Art of the Deal: Intermediaries of Trade in Medieval Montpellier* (2002) and *Jacques Coeur: Entrepreneur and King's Bursar* (2004).

Hugo de Schepper, emeritus professor of history at the University of Nijmegan, has published extensively on the Low Countries' legal and political history. He served as an editor and author for the *Algemene Geschiedenis der Nederlanden* (1977–1984) and participated in the "Origins of the Modern State" European Science Foundation program.

Ulrike Strasser is associate professor of history and affiliate faculty in women's studies and religious studies at the University of California at Irvine. Her monograph *State of Virginity* won the Society for the Study of Early Modern Women's Award for the best book published in 2004.

Sanjay Subrahmanyam is professor and Doshi Chair of History at UCLA. Earlier he taught in Delhi, Paris, and Oxford. His newest work in two volumes is *Explorations in Connected History* (2005). In addition, he has authored or jointly authored eight other books on early modern history.

Markus P. M. Vink, an associate professor at SUNY Fredonia and book review editor of *Itinerario,* has published on numerous topics related to cross-cultural encounters in the early modern Indian Ocean, including slavery, religion, political economy, international law, representation, and agency. He is coauthor of *The Merchant-Warrior Pacified* (1991, 1994).